McCALL'S BIG Book

of

KNIT AND CROCHET
for HOME AND FAMILY

D0924498

BIG Book

McCALL'S

of

KNIT AND CROCHET
for HOME AND FAMILY

The Editors of
McCall's Needlework & Crafts Magazine

CHILTON BOOK COMPANY
Radnor, Pennsylvania

Copyright © 1982 by ABC Needlework and Crafts Magazines, Inc.
All International Rights Reserved
Published in Radnor, Pennsylvania 19089, by Chilton Book Company
and simultaneously in Canada by VNR Publishers,
1410 Birchmount Road, Scarborough, Ontario M1P 2E7

Manufactured in the United States of America

Library of Congress Cataloging in Publication Data
Main entry under title:

McCall's big book of knit and crochet for
home and family.

(The Chilton needlework series)
Includes index.
1. Knitting. 2. Crocheting. I. McCall's
needlework & crafts. II. Title: Big book of
knit and crochet for home and family.
III. Series.
TT820.M484 1982   746.43′041   82-70538
ISBN 0-8019-7253-1   AACR2

1 2 3 4 5 6 7 8 9 0   1 0 9 8 7 6 5 4 3 2

CONTENTS

Part 1 KNITTING

General Instructions: Needles and Accessories, 9; Knitting Lesson for Beginners, 10; Abbreviations, 23; Knitting Left-Handed, 25; Interchanging Yarns, 25; Continental Knitting 26; Finishing Stitches, 27; Beginners' Projects, 28; Pattern Stitches, 47; Knitting with Two Colors, 74; Knitting with Four Needles, 80

Projects: Garter Stitch Puppy, 28; Pussy Cat, 29; Basket Weave Pot Holder, 30; Box-Stitch Pot Holder, 30; Garter Stitch Afghan, 31; Lounge Slippers, 32; Child's Reindeer Set, 33; Tyrolean Sweaters, 34; Zipped Jacket, 35; Puff Pattern Pullover, 35; Flower-Spray Cardigan, 36; Lace Pattern Baby Set, 37; Woven Plaid Afghan, 38; Pinwheel Afghan, 39; Double Knit Pillows, 40; Rainbow Pillow, 41; Layette Sweater, 42; Turtleneck Dickey, 43; Owl Pillow, 44; Girls' Snow Set, 45; Raised Diamond Pullover, 46; Socks with French Heels, 85; Argyle Socks, 87; Reversible Double-Thick Mittens, 88; Snowflake Pattern Gloves, 89; Tubular Knit Rug, 91; Aster Doily, 93; Chrysanthemum Mat, 94; Cornflower Doily, 96; Gothic Cobweb Doily, 98; Knitted Placemat, 100; Reverse Stripe Pillow, 104; Diagonal Stripe Pillow, 104; Norse Sweater Dress, 105; Mosaic Pullover, 106; Fair Isle Set, 107; Aran Baby Set, 108; Honeycomb Blocks, 109; Popcorn Pillows, 110; Rose Afghan Set, 111; Lily Pond, 112

Part II CROCHET

Part III TATTING

Finishing, Laundering, and Blocking Instructions

PART 1
KNITTING

The origin of knitting, the art of pulling up loops of yarn from one needle to another, is lost in antiquity. Shepherds who tended their flocks in ancient times were probably the first knitters. Many centuries ago, Arab traders knit as they rode with their camel caravans east to India and west to Egypt. In Europe, knitting was unknown before the 14th century. The invention of the process is generally attributed to the Spaniards though the Scots claim it and perhaps devised it independently.

Hand knitting was man's work in the days of the guilds. Women were expected to know how to knit and knitted at home and in the convents. The invention of a commercial knitting machine in England in 1589 made it impractical for men to knit by hand. Women then became the hand knitters. Today, women in many countries knit for a livelihood, each area producing designs and patterns which are distinctive. In America, women for the most part knit for themselves and their families for the sheer joy of knitting, for the sense of accomplishment that all creative work provides.

KNITTING NEEDLES AND ACCESSORIES

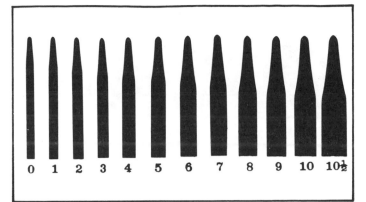

STANDARD U.S. SIZES

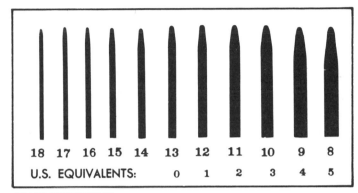

ENGLISH SIZES

Single-pointed needles of aluminum, plastic or wood are used in pairs to knit back and forth in rows. For ease in working, choose a color to contrast with the yarn. Colored aluminum and plastic needles come in 7″, 10″, and 14″ lengths in sizes varying from 1 to 5 in the shorter lengths, and 1 to 10½, 11, 13 and 15 in the longer lengths. Colored aluminum needles also come in size 0. Wood needles, 14″ long, come in sizes 11 to 15. Even larger sizes for jiffy knitting–17, 18, 19, 35 and 50 are available in hollow plastic. Flexible "jumper" needles of nylon or nylon and aluminum are available in 18″ lengths in sizes 1 to 15.

Double-pointed (dp) needles are used in sets of four for tubular knitting for such items as socks, mittens, gloves and sleeves worked without seams. Of plastic or aluminum, they come in 5″, 7″ and 10″ lengths. Plastic double-pointed needles come in sizes 1 to 15, aluminum in 0 to 8.

Circular knitting needles of nylon come in 16″ to 29″ lengths in sizes 0 to 10½; the 29″ length is also made in sizes 11, 13 and 15; a 36″ length is made in sizes 5 to 15. Circular needles are used for knitting skirts without seams, circular yokes and other tubular pieces, but may be used for knitting back and forth in flat knitting, too. They are especially useful for afghans and other large pieces that require a great many stitches.

Many accessories are available to the knitter: stitch holders to keep one section of knitting from ravelling while another section is being worked; counters to keep track of increases, decreases, stitches and rows; needle point guards to keep knitting on needles when not in use; bobbins or snap yarn holders to use when knitting in small areas of color; little ring markers; needle gauges to determine correct sizes of needles.

KNITTING NEEDLES															
U. S.	0	1	2	3	4	5	6	7	8	9	10	10½	11	13	15
English	13	12	11	10	9	8	7	6	5	4	3	2	1	00	000
Continental — mm.	2¼	2½	3	3¼	3½	4	4½	5	5½	6	6½	7		7½	8½	9

KNITTING LESSON FOR BEGINNERS

Knitting is based on two stitches, KNIT STITCH and PURL STITCH. Many knitted articles can be made with these two stitches alone. Before starting any knitted piece, it is necessary to CAST ON a certain number of stitches; that is, to place a series of loops on one needle so that you can work your first row of knitting. After you have finished your piece of knitting, it is necessary to BIND OFF your stitches so that they will not ravel out. On the following pages, in step-by-step illustrations and directions, you will be shown how to cast on, knit, purl and bind off.

TO CAST ON WITH ONE NEEDLE
1. For your practice piece, use a ball of knitting worsted and a pair of knitting needles No. 8.

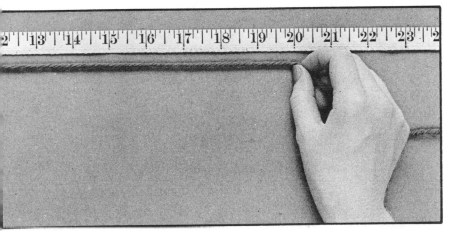

2. With a tape measure or yardstick, measure off about 20 inches from end of yarn to cast on 20 stitches.

3. At this point, bring yarn end from ball over left index finger. Bring yarn end under and over thumb.

KNITTING LESSON FOR BEGINNERS

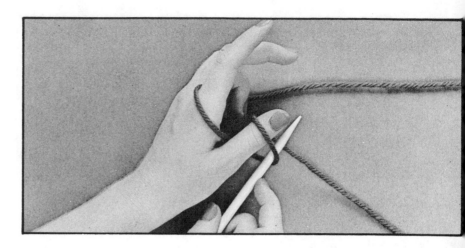

4. Hold one needle in right hand. Insert point of needle from left to right through the loop on thumb.

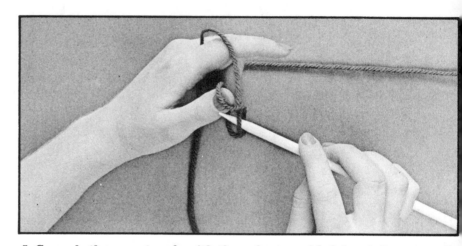

5. Grasp both yarn strands with three fingers of left hand. Insert needle under strand on index finger.

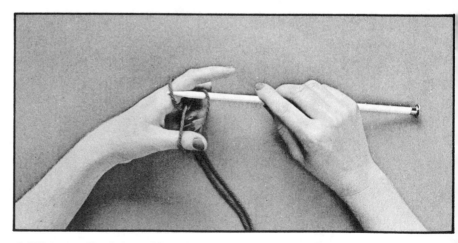

6. With needle, bring this strand toward you and through loop on thumb. Remove thumb from loop.

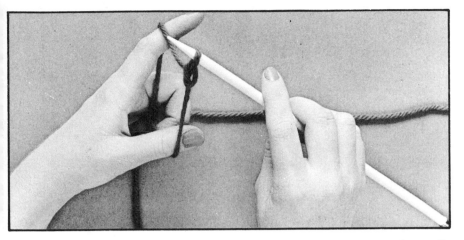

7. Place thumb under strand which is nearest to you. Pull gently until slipknot is close to needle.

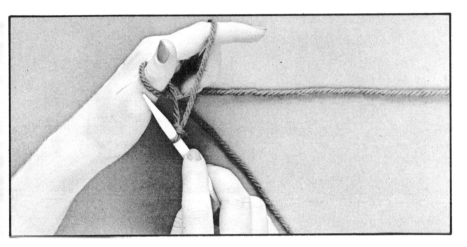

8. With thumb back, bring needle in front of thumb and to left of the strand, forming a loop on thumb.

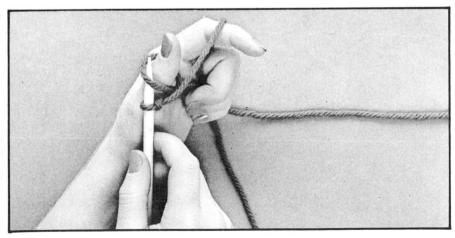

9. Still grasping both strands of the yarn, insert needle from left to right up through loop on thumb.

KNITTING LESSON FOR BEGINNERS

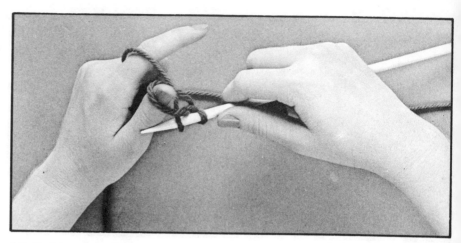

10. Pick up strand on index finger, bring it through loop on thumb, removing thumb at the same time.

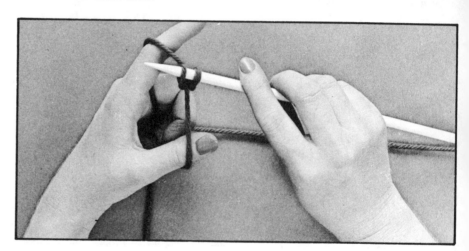

11. Place thumb under front strand as before and tighten second stitch close to first stitch on needle.

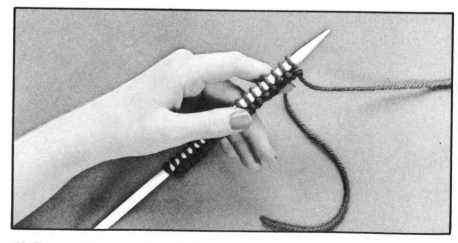

12. Repeat this procedure until you have cast on 20 stitches. Place the casting-on needle in left hand.

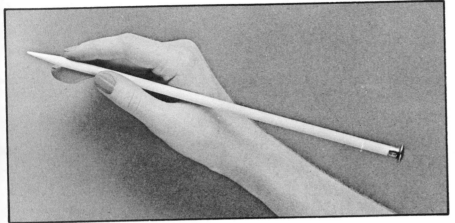

TO KNIT
13. The needle with which you will knit the stitches should be held in the right hand like a pencil.

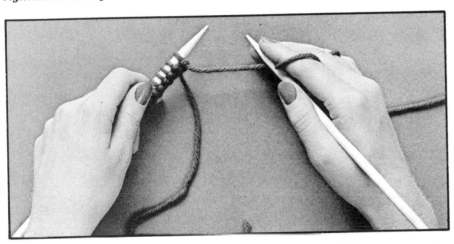

14. Weave yarn over index finger of right hand, under middle finger, over third, under little finger.

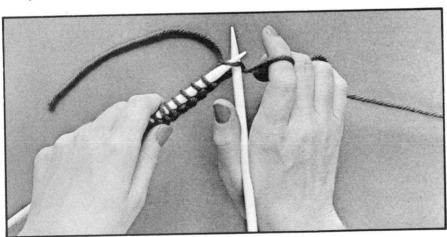

15. To knit the first stitch, insert right needle into front of stitch on left needle from left to right.

KNITTING LESSON FOR BEGINNERS

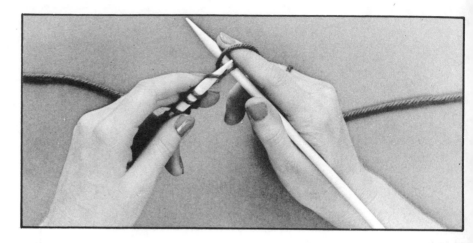

16. Point of right needle is now behind left point. Bring yarn under and over point of right needle.

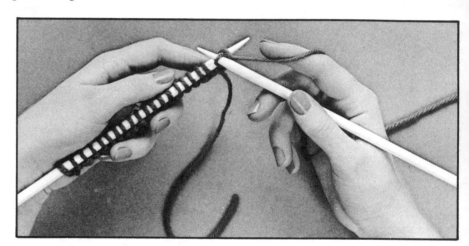

17. Bring point of right needle down and under left needle to front, thus drawing yarn through stitch.

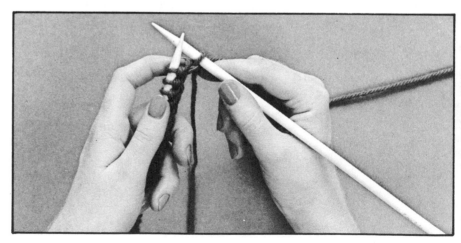

18. Slip the loop through which you drew yarn off left needle. One knit stitch is now on right needle.

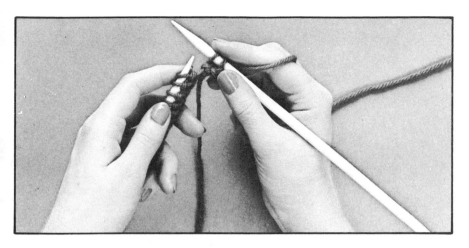

19. Insert right needle into the next stitch and knit another stitch. Knit all 20 stitches in same way.

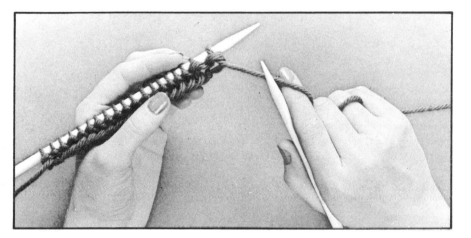

20. When row is finished, turn work around and place it in left hand. Work another row of knit stitch.

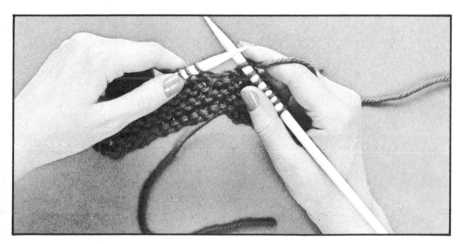

21. Continue to knit rows of stitches. Plain knitting is called garter stitch and has a ridged effect.

KNITTING LESSON FOR BEGINNERS

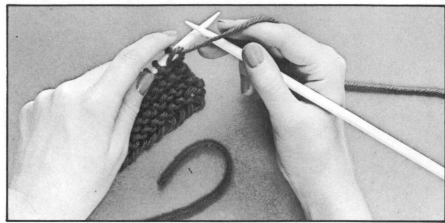

TO PURL
22. To make a purl stitch, bring yarn which comes from first stitch to the front of your right needle.

23. Insert point of right needle from right to left through the front of first stitch on left needle.

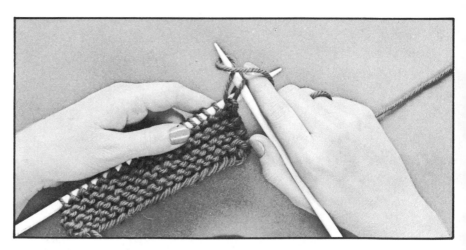

24. Bring yarn back between points of needles, then bring it down under point of right needle to front.

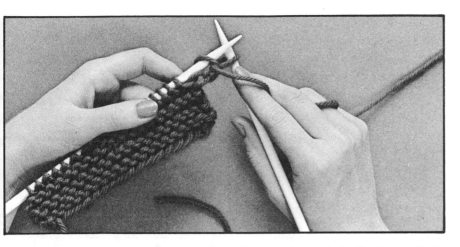

25. Bring point of right needle back through the first stitch. Right needle is now behind left needle.

26. Slip the loop through which you drew yarn off left needle. One purl stitch is on right needle.

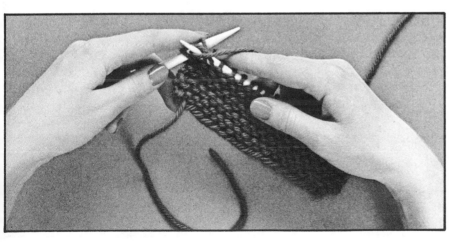

27. Continue across row until you have purled all 20 stitches. Work the following row in knit stitch.

KNITTING LESSON FOR BEGINNERS

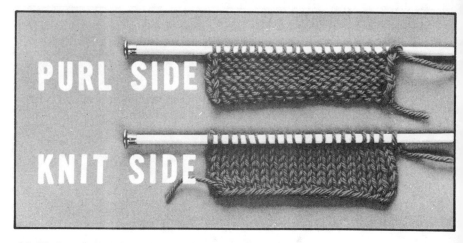

28. Make a practice piece of stockinette stitch, alternating one row of knitting, one row of purling.

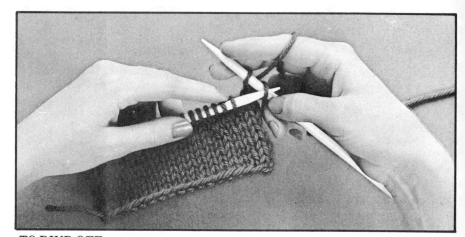

TO BIND OFF

29. Knit the first two stitches. Insert left needle from left to right through front of first stitch.

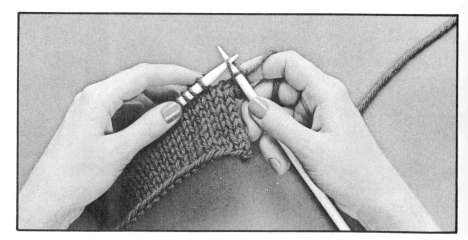

30. Lift the first stitch over the second stitch and over tip of needle. One stitch has been bound off.

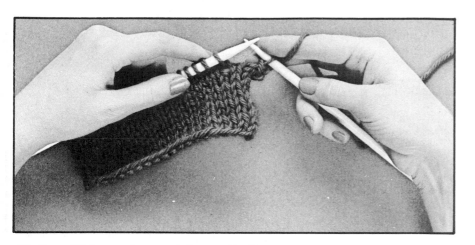

31. One stitch remains on right needle. To bind off this stitch, knit another stitch onto right needle.

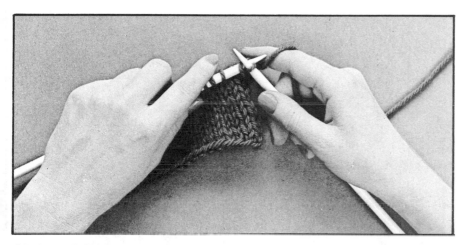

32. Again lift first stitch over second stitch and off right needle. Two stitches have been bound off.

33. Continue across until all stitches are bound off. One loop remains. Cut yarn, pull end through loop.

OTHER METHODS OF CASTING ON STITCHES: There are several ways to cast on in addition to the method given in the Knitting Lesson for Beginners.

The simplest one-needle method is shown in

Figures 1-5. Make a slip loop on needle; Fig. 1. Loop yarn around left thumb; Fig. 2. Insert needle in loop; Fig. 3. Remove thumb; Fig. 4. Pull yarn to tighten stitch; Fig. 5. This method is suitable if the cast-on edge will not show or receive wear.

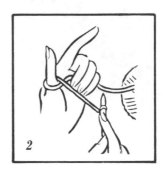

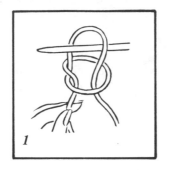

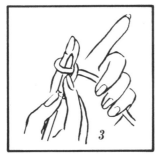

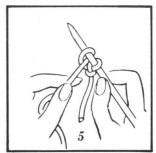

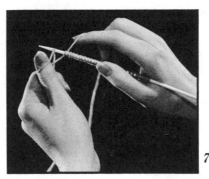

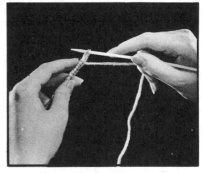

Another one-needle method is shown in Figures 6 and 7. Start with a slip loop the same number of inches from end of yarn as number of stitches to be cast on; e.g. 30 stitches, 30″ from end of yarn. Hold needle with slip loop in right hand. * With short end of yarn make a loop on left thumb by bringing yarn up around thumb from left to right; Fig. 6. Insert needle in this loop from left to right; Fig. 7. Bring yarn from ball under and over needle, draw through loop on thumb, tighten short end with left hand. Repeat from * for required number of stitches. This method gives the same sturdy edge as method shown in Knitting for Beginners.

The two-needle method for casting on makes a firm knitted edge. First make a slip loop over left needle. * Pass right needle through loop from left to right, yarn under and over right needle. Draw yarn through loop and transfer loop on right needle to left needle by inserting left needle in loop from right to left; Fig. 8. Repeat from * for desired number of stitches. This method is used

when stitches must be added to the side of your knitting as, for example, when sleeves are knitted with the body of the garment. In this case, the first added stitch is made in the end stitch of your knitting.

TO CAST ON STITCHES LOOSELY: For most garments, it is best to cast on stitches loosely. If you tend to cast on tightly, use a larger needle for casting on than for knitting the garment.

TO BIND OFF STITCHES: Binding off is usually done in the pattern stitch of the garment; that is, each stitch to be bound off is worked in the way it would be if you were not binding off. Unless the directions read "bind off tightly," or "bind off loosely," the bound-off edge should be the same tension as the knitting. If you tend to bind off too tightly, use a larger needle for binding off than for knitting the garment. On a high ribbed neckline, it is absolutely essential to bind off loosely.

TO INCREASE ONE STITCH: Method 1: Knit 1 stitch in the usual way but do not slip it off left needle. Bring right needle behind left needle, insert it from right to left in same stitch (called "the back of the stitch") and make another knit stitch. Slip stitch off left needle. To increase 1 stitch on the purl side, purl 1 stitch in the usual way but do not slip if off left needle. Bring yarn between needles to back, knit 1 stitch in back of same stitch.

Method 2: Pick up horizontal strand between stitch just knitted and next stitch, place it on left needle. Knit 1 stitch in back of this strand, thus twisting it.

Method 3: Place right needle behind left needle. Insert right needle in stitch *below* next stitch, knit this stitch; then knit stitch above it in the usual way.

YARN OVER: This is an increase stitch. It is used primarily in lace patterns or for the open-work increases on raglan sleeve shapings.

To Make a Yarn Over When Knitting: Bring yarn under right needle to front, then over needle to back, ready to knit next stitch.

To Make a Yarn Over When Purling: Bring yarn up over right needle to back, then under needle to front, ready to purl next stitch.

TO SLIP A STITCH: Insert needle in stitch as if to knit stitch (unless directions read "as if to purl") and slip stitch from left needle to right needle without knitting or purling it.

TO DECREASE ONE STITCH: On the right side of work, knit 2 stitches together either through the front of the stitches (the decrease slants to the right) or through the back of the stitches (the decrease slants to the left). On the purl side, purl 2 stitches together.

PSSO (pass slip stitch over) is a decrease stitch. When directions say "sl 1, k 1, psso," slip first stitch, knit next stitch, bring slip stitch over knit stitch as in binding off.

ABBREVIATIONS USED IN KNITTING DIRECTIONS

k—knit	psso—pass slip stitch over
p—purl	inc—increase
st—stitch	dec—decrease
sts—stitches	beg—beginning
yo—yarn over	pat—pattern
sl—slip	lp—loop
sk—skip	MC—main color
tog—together	CC—contrasting color
rnd—round	dp—double-pointed

THE USE OF ASTERISKS IN DIRECTIONS: The asterisk (*) is used in directions to mark the beginning and end of any part of the directions that is to be repeated one or more times. For example, "* k 9, p 3, repeat from * 4 times" means to work directions after first * until second * is reached, then go back to first * 4 times more. Work 5 times in all.

THE USE OF PARENTHESES IN DIRECTIONS: When parentheses ( ) are used to show repetition, work directions in parentheses as many times as specified. For example, "(k 9, p 3) 4 times" means to do what is in ( ) 4 times altogether.

TO TIE IN A NEW STRAND OF YARN: Join a new ball of yarn at beginning of a row by making a slipknot with new strand around working strand; see illustration. Move slipknot up to edge of work and continue with new ball. If yarn cannot be joined at beginning of row, splice yarn by threading new yarn into a tapestry needle and weaving it into the end of the old yarn for about 3", leaving short end on wrong side to be cut off after a few rows have been knitted. If the yarn cannot be spliced (e.g. nubby yarn), leave a 4" end of yarn, work next stitch with new yarn leaving a 4" end. Work a few rows, tie ends together and weave them into work.

MULTIPLE: In pattern stitches, multiple means the number of stitches required for one pattern. The number of stitches on needle should be evenly divisible by the multiple. If pattern is a multiple of 6 stitches, number of stitches to be worked might be 180, 186, 192, etc. If directions say "multiple of 6 sts plus 2," 2 extra stitches are required: 182, 188, 194, etc.

TYING IN A NEW STRAND

GAUGE: All knitting directions for garments include a stitch gauge. The stitch gauge gives the number of stitches to the inch with the yarn and needles recommended in the pattern stitch of the garment. The directions for each size are based on the given gauge. The gauge (or tension) at which you work controls the size of each finished piece. It is therefore essential to work to the gauge given for each garment if you want the garment to fit. To test your gauge, cast on 20 or 30 stitches, using the needles specified. Work in the *pattern stitch* for 3″. Smooth out your swatch and pin it down. Measure across 2″ and place pins 2″ apart as shown. Count number of stitches between pins. If you have *more* stitches to the inch than directions specify, you are knitting too tightly; use larger needles. If you have *fewer* stitches to the inch, you are knitting too loosely; use smaller needles.

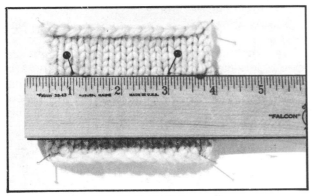

MEASURING YOUR GAUGE

TO PICK UP DROPPED STITCH: Use a crochet hook. In stockinette stitch, from knit side of work, insert hook through loop of dropped stitch from front to back of work, hook facing upward. * Pull horizontal thread of row above stitch through loop on hook; repeat from * to top.

Most patterns give a row gauge too. Although the proper length of a finished garment does not usually depend upon the row gauge (directions usually give lengths in inches rather than rows), in some patterns it is important to have the proper row gauge too.

TO RAVEL OUT KNITTING: When it is necessary to ravel work and then pick up stitches again, remove needles from work. Rip down to row of error. Rip this row stitch by stitch, placing each stitch (as if to purl) on a fine needle. Then knit these stitches onto correct size needle.

TO PICK UP AND KNIT STITCHES ALONG EDGE: From right side of work, insert needle into edge of work, put yarn around needle, finish as a knit stitch. When picking up on bound-off or cast-on edge, pick up and knit 1 stitch in each stitch (going through 2 loops at top of each bound-off stitch). On front or side edges, pick up and knit 1 stitch in each knot formed on edge of each row.

TO COUNT STITCHES WHEN BINDING OFF: At the beginning of a row, when directions read "bind off 7 sts," knit 2 stitches; * insert left needle under first stitch on right needle and lift it over the second stitch. This is 1 stitch bound off. Knit 1 more stitch and repeat from * 6 times—7 stitches bound off (8 stitches have been knitted to bind off 7 stitches but 1 stitch, already knitted, is on right needle).

When binding off within a row (as for buttonholes), knit the required number of stitches to point of binding off, then knit next 2 stitches to bind off first stitch. Bind off required number of stitches (1 stitch is already knitted after bound-off stitches). When directions read "knit until 7 sts after bound-off stitches," this means to knit 6 more stitches or until there are 7 stitches after bound-off stitches.

TO INSERT MARKERS: When directions read "sl a marker on needle," put a small safety pin, paper clip, or commercial ring marker on needle. In working, always slip marker from one needle to another. To mark a row or stitch, tie contrasting thread around end of row or stitch.

TO MEASURE WORK: Spread piece on flat surface to required width, measure length at center.

WORK EVEN: This term means to work in same stitch without increasing or decreasing.

TO CHANGE FROM ONE COLOR TO ANOTHER: When changing from one color to another, whether working on right or wrong side, pick up the new strand from underneath dropped strand. This prevents a hole in your work. Carry the unused color loosely across back of work. Illustration shows wrong side of work with light strand being picked up under dropped strand in position to be purled.

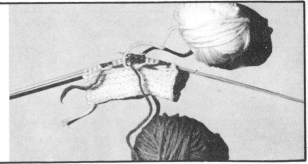

CHANGING COLORS

KNITTING LEFT-HANDED

HINTS FOR THE LEFT-HANDED: There is no simple answer to the question asked by left-handed people, "How can I learn to knit?" Here are some suggestions:

If you are not strongly left-handed and can do some things with your right hand, you should first try to knit in the way shown in "Knitting Lesson for Beginners." Since knitting is basically a two-handed process, you may be able to master knitting by the conventional method. The awkwardness you experience may well be simply that of a beginner, rather than caused by your left-handedness. If you can learn to knit by this method, you will be spared some difficulties in reading directions.

If this method does not work for you, you might try the so-called "German" method. This is right-handed knitting too, in the sense that the needle in the right hand knits the stitches from the needle in the left hand. The difference is that the *yarn* is held by the left hand. The yarn is not thrown around the needle as it is in the "Knitting Lesson for Beginners," but is pulled through the stitch by the right needle. To hold the yarn in your left hand, weave it through your fingers as follows: under the little finger, over the ring finger, under the middle finger, over the index finger and once more around the index finger. Grasp both needles the same, with your hands over the needles. To make a knit stitch, insert right needle in stitch from left to right as shown in "Knitting Lesson for Beginners," put needle over strand which comes from left index finger and pull loop through stitch. To make a purl stitch, insert right needle in stitch from right to left as shown in "Knitting Lesson for Beginners," bring strand over and under point of right needle to front, place right thumb on strand to keep it from sliding off needle and push right needle under left needle to back. Many right-handed knitters use this method. It is faster than the method usually taught today because there is less motion of the hands involved. The disadvantages are: the tension is not as easy to control; flat ribbon knitting cannot be done by this method.

If you find the "German" method too awkward for you, you can learn to knit left-handed by placing a mirror to each step given in the "Knitting Lesson for Beginners" and substituting the word "left" for "right" and "right" for "left" in every case.

Some left-handed knitters have learned to knit by sitting opposite a right-handed knitter and copying all motions with the hand directly opposite.

In reading directions, the following problems will arise: Whenever the word "left" is used, substitute the word "right" and vice versa; when a garment has two fronts, therefore, and directions are given for the left front, you will be working on the right front. In a misses' cardigan or coat, where there are buttonholes on the right front, you will either have to figure out from the right front directions how to make the buttonholes, or have them made after the garment is finished.

In men's cardigans, directions for the right front are usually given first. You will be working on the left front, on which the buttonholes should be made.

If the sleeves of a garment are shaped differently (if the back of the sleeve is different from the front), when directions are given for the right sleeve, you will be working on the left sleeve.

If a pattern stitch forms a diagonal pattern, your diagonal lines will run counter to the stitch pictured.

INTERCHANGING YARNS

TO SUBSTITUTE ONE YARN FOR ANOTHER: When a knitted garment is designed, the yarn in which it is made is an integral part of the design. The thickness of the yarn in relation to the pattern stitch is important; the same pattern stitch would not be used for a bulky jacket and a lightweight cardigan. The texture of the yarn in relation to the pattern stitch is also important; pattern stitches for hairy, looped, slubbed, or tweed yarns tend to be simpler than pattern stitches for the smooth yarns. In general, therefore, it is advisable to use the yarn called for in the directions.

If you wish to substitute a yarn, choose one as similar as possible to the specified yarn. Be sure you can work to the proper gauge in the substitute yarn. If your gauge is not correct, the garment will be too big or too small. Be sure you like the texture of the pattern stitch in the new yarn. It may be too limp or too stiff even though the gauge is correct.

Yarns have different degrees of elasticity, depending upon the fiber content. Care should be taken in substituting cotton or linen for wool as these fibers have less elasticity and additional stitches are needed.

Generally, the thicker a yarn is the less yardage it has per ounce and the more ounces it takes to cover the same area. That is why more ounces of bulky yarn are required to make sweater than ounces of finer yarn. If you wish to substitute a thicker yarn than the pattern calls for, even though you can work to the stitch gauge, you will need more ounces of yarn. Yarns of the same type, thickness and fiber content have approximately the same yardage per ounce. In interchanging these yarns, the same number of ounces is usually required.

If you wish to make a garment in an entirely different weight of yarn, this is, in effect, a new design. The design should be re-planned and the directions rewritten to the new stitch gauge.

CONTINENTAL KNITTING

In this country, knitting books, teachers of knitting and instructresses show the English style of knitting almost exclusively. Many knitters, however, taught to knit by relatives and friends, use the continental or "German" style, illustrated below. Some consider knitting with this method quicker than knitting in the English or American style shown in "Knitting Lesson for Beginners." With the continental style, there is less motion of the hands. The yarn is not thrown around the right-hand needle by the right hand. It is simply caught by the point of the right-hand needle as it comes from the left index finger and is pulled through the stitch. There are two disadvantages of the continental method: the tension is not as easy to control; flat ribbon knitting cannot be done by this method.

Ideally, a knitter should learn to knit by both methods. Two-color pattern knitting can be done with ease by anyone who can hold the yarn in either hand. When each hand holds one color, the yarns do not have to be dropped and picked up at each color change.

To learn the continental style of knitting, first cast on stitches as shown in "Knitting Lesson for Beginners," or use any convenient method of casting on. Wind yarn through your left hand: under the little finger, over the ring finger, under the middle finger, over and around the index finger twice.

Grasp both needles in the same way, with thumbs in front of needles and other fingers going over needles to back. Bend little fingers so needles rest on them. You are now ready to knit.

KNIT STITCH

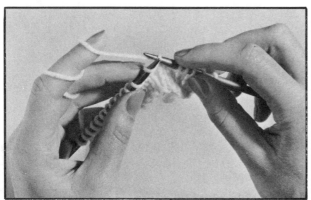

1. Insert the point of right needle into front of stitch on left needle from left to right. Move the point of the right needle to the right of yarn coming from the left index finger, then toward the back and behind yarn.

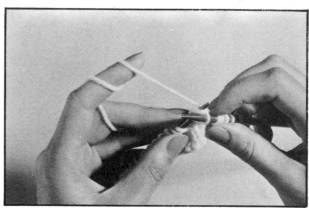

2. Move the left index finger back so that yarn lies taut over needle. Move the right needle point forward and through loop on left needle, pull yarn through loop. Slip loop off left needle—one knit stitch.

PURL STITCH

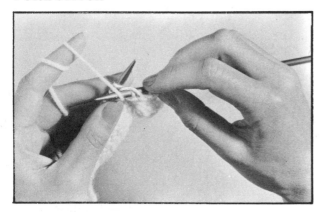

1. With the yarn in front of work, place the point of right needle behind the yarn, insert it from right to left through the front of stitch. Bring point up in front of yarn, down from right to left behind yarn.

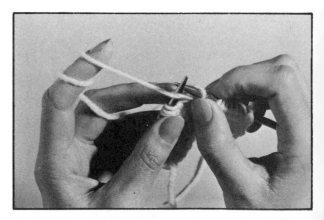

2. Holding strand of yarn on the needle with right thumb, push right needle point back through the loop on left needle, going under left needle point. Slip loop off left needle—one purl stitch made.

FINISHING STITCHES

TO SEW SEAMS WITH BACKSTITCH: Most seams should be sewn with backstitch. Pin right sides of pieces together, keeping edges even and matching rows or patterns. Thread matching yarn in tapestry needle. Run end of yarn through several stitches along edge to secure; backstitch pieces together close to edge. Do not draw yarn too tight. See illustration.

TO SEW IN SLEEVES: Place sleeve seam at center underarm and center of sleeve cap at shoulder seam. Ease in any extra fulness evenly. Backstitch seam.

TO WEAVE SEAMS TOGETHER: Straight vertical edges, such as those at the back seam of a sock, can be woven together invisibly from the right side. Thread matching yarn in tapestry needle. Hold edges together, right side up. Bring needle up through first stitch on left edge. Insert needle down through center of first stitch on right edge, pass under 2 rows, draw yarn through to right side. Insert needle in center of stitch on corresponding row of left edge, pass under 2 rows as before, draw yarn through to right side. Continue working from side to side, matching rows. Keep seam flat and elastic.

TO WEAVE TOP EDGES OF STOCKINETTE STITCH: Two equal top edges of stockinette stitch can be joined by an invisible seam. In this case, the stitches are not bound off, but are kept on the needles or stitch holders until they are ready to be woven. Thread yarn in tapestry needle. Lay the two pieces together so that the edge stitches match. Draw up yarn in first stitch of upper piece, inserting needle from wrong side; insert needle from right side in first stitch on lower piece, bring up through next stitch on lower piece, from wrong side. Draw up yarn, * insert needle from right side in same stitch as before on upper piece, bring up through next stitch on upper piece from wrong side. Draw up yarn, insert needle in same stitch as before on lower piece. Repeat from * until all stitches are joined.

TO CROCHET EDGE ON KNITTING: From right side, unless otherwise specified, work 1 sc (1 single crochet) in each stitch on bound-off or cast-on edges; work 1 sc in each knot formed on edge of each row on front or side edges; work 2 or 3 sc at corners to keep work flat. To make a single crochet, start with a loop on hook, insert hook under 2 loops of stitch on edge, draw yarn through, yarn over hook and through both loops on hook. To end off, make a sl st (slip stitch): Insert hook under both loops of stitch. Catch yarn with hook and draw through stitch and loop on hook.

BACKSTITCHING SEAMS

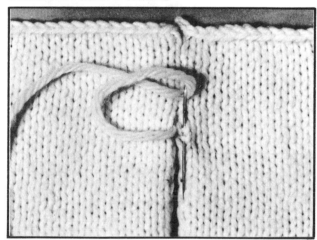

WEAVING VERTICAL SEAMS

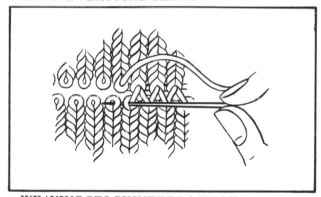

WEAVING STOCKINETTE STITCH

SINGLE CROCHET EDGE

BEGINNERS' PROJECTS

GARTER STITCH PUPPY

SIZE: 11″ high.

MATERIALS: Knitting worsted, 3 ozs. pink. Knitting needles No. 5. ¾ yard green satin ribbon. Scraps of blue, black and red felt. Cotton batting.

GAUGE: 9 sts = 2″; 10 rows (5 ridges) = 1″.

Note: Work in garter st (k every row).

HEAD: Beg at neck edge, cast on 10 sts. K each row, inc 1 st each side every other row until there are 22 sts. Work even until piece is 3½″ long. Dec 1 st each side every other row until 14 sts remain. Bind off.

Front: Work as for back. Sew pieces tog at top and sides. Stuff firmly.

BODY: Back: Beg at lower edge, cast on 20 sts. Work even for 5″. Dec 1 st each side every other row until 10 sts remain. Bind off.

Front: Work as for back. Sew pieces tog at bottom and sides. Stuff. Sew head to body.

LOWER LEG (make 2): Cast on 15 sts. Work even for 40 rows (20 ridges). Bind off. Sew cast-on and bound-off edges tog. Tie a strand of yarn

tightly around one end, ½″ from edge, for foot. Stuff. Sew open end to lower front of body.

UPPER LEG (make 2): Cast on 9 sts. Work even for 36 rows (18 ridges). Bind off. Complete as for lower leg. Sew in place to upper front of body below shaped top.

EAR (make 2): Beg at upper edge, cast on 10 sts. Work even for 4½″. Bind off. Gather bound-off edge slightly, sew to side of head.

TAIL: Cast on 8 sts. Work even for 16 rows. Bind off. Sew cast-on and bound-off edges tog. Gather one end to close. Stuff. Sew in place.

FINISHING: Make 6 pompons: wind yarn 36 times around 2 fingers; slip strands from fingers, tie tog at one end, cut through strands at other end. Sew a pompon to side of each foot, to tail and over right ear.

From felt, cut 2 blue ovals 1″ x ¾″, 2 black circles ½″ in diameter. Sew in place for eyes. Cut red triangle for nose, red oval for tongue, black crescent for mouth. Sew in place. Cut 16″ length of ribbon; tie around neck in a bow. Make bow from remaining ribbon; sew to head.

Floppy puppy is pink, wears two green ribbons. Knit him all in garter stitch of orlon yarn or knitting worsted; stuff with cotton; sew on pompons, a felt face.

Bewhiskered kitten in garter stitch is a perfect project for beginners. Pussy, 12" high, has cotton stuffing, features and soles of felt, a neck bow.

PUSSY CAT

MATERIALS: Knitting worsted, 1 4-oz. skein. Knitting needles No. 6. Tapestry needle. Cotton batting for stuffing. Six-strand embroidery floss, 1 skein each of red and black. Scraps of pink, white, black and red felt. Sewing thread to match felt. Red grosgrain ribbon, ¾ yard.

GAUGE: 5 sts = 1"; 10 rows (5 ridges) = 1".

PUSSY CAT: HEAD: Beg at neck, cast on 9 sts.

Row 1: Knit.

Row 2: Inc 1 st (k and p in same st) in each st across–18 sts.

Row 3: Inc 1 st in each of first 2 sts, k to last 3 sts, inc 1 st in each of last 3 sts–23 sts. Work even in garter st (k each row) for 38 rows (19 ridges). Dec 1 st each side of next row–21 sts.

Shape Ears: K 7, join another ball of yarn and bind off next 7 sts, finish row. Work on both sides at once for 8 rows. Dec 1 st each side of each ear every other row twice. K 3 tog on each ear. End off. Make another piece in same way. Leaving neck edge open, sew both pieces tog; stuff head, sew neck edges tog.

BODY: Side Section: Beg at top of neck, cast on 12 sts. Work in garter st for 12 rows (6 ridges). Cast on 4 sts at beg of next row for back. Cast on 4 sts at beg of rows at back edge 3 times–28 sts. Work even for 32 rows (16 ridges) above last cast-on sts.

Shape Legs: Work first 9 sts, join another ball of yarn and bind off center 10 sts, finish row. Work even on both sides at once for 12 rows.

Dec Row: Dec 1 st at beg of row on first leg (outside edge); dec 1 st at end of row on 2nd leg (outside edge). Work even on 8 sts of each leg for 6 rows. Repeat dec row once more. Work even on 7 sts of each leg for 8 rows. Bind off. Make another side section in same way. Sew sides of neck and top of back tog.

INNER FORELEG SECTION: Beg at lower edge, cast on 10 sts. Work in garter st, inc 1 st at beg of every 8th row (outside edge) twice. Work even on 12 sts for 16 rows, ending at even edge (inside edge).

Shape Top: Dec 1 st at beg of next row (inside edge), then dec 1 st at same edge every other row until 3 sts remain. Bind off. Make another piece in same way. Sew tog top dec edges of inner forelegs. Sew inner legs to forelegs, easing in extra rows of inner legs, with top point ending 9 ridge rows above legs at front edge of body. Sew front seam of body tog above forelegs. Stuff forelegs; leave lower edges of legs open.

INNER HIND LEG SECTION: Work as for inner foreleg section to top shaping.

Shape Top: Bind off 2 sts at beg of each row at inside edge 6 times. Make another piece in same way. Sew tog top bound-off edges of inner hind legs. Sew inner legs to hind legs, easing in extra rows of inner legs, with top point ending 5 ridge rows above legs on back edge of body. Sew back seam of body tog above hind legs. Sew hind legs and body, sew center under body seam between legs.

Insert head into neck with center back of neck covering 4 ridge rows of head; sew in place.

TAIL: Beg at larger end, cast on 11 sts. Work in garter st, dec 1 at each side every 1½" twice–7 sts. Work even until piece measures 7" from start. Bind off (tip). Fold tail over a tapered roll of stuffing and sew long edges of tail tog. Sew larger end of tail to body.

Cut four pink felt circles the size of a quarter; with matching sewing thread, sew to bottom of feet for soles. Cut and sew pink felt triangles to front of ears as pictured. Cut two white felt ovals for eyes, black felt triangles for pupils of eyes and nose and red tongue. With matching sewing thread, sew eyes, nose and tongue to head.

With embroidery floss, embroider red mouth. Tack four 1½" pieces of black embroidery floss each side of nose for whiskers. Tie on bow.

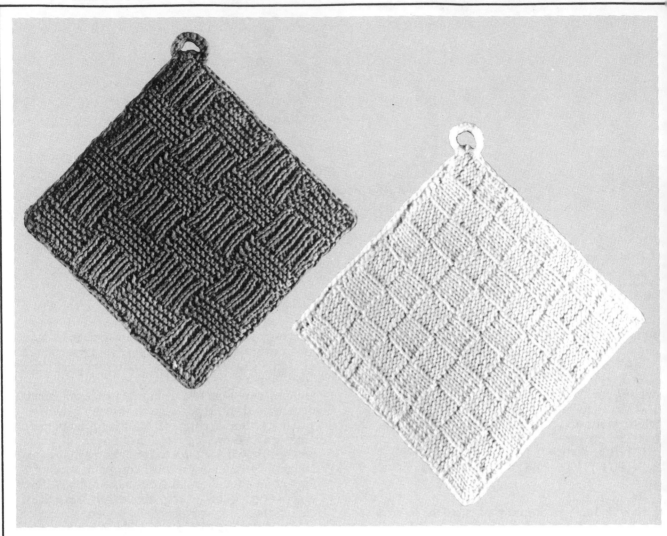

King-size pot holders in easy pattern stitches: garter stitch and ribbing alternate for basket weave; blocks of stockinette and reverse stockinette make box stitch. Both are knit of cotton yarn in two pieces and crocheted together.

BASKET WEAVE POT HOLDER

SIZE: About 7½″ square.

MATERIALS: Lily Cotton Yarn (Sugar-'n-Cream Yarn), 1 ball. Knitting needles No. 3. Steel crochet hook No. 0.

GAUGE: 5 sts = 1″; 10 rows = 1″ (garter st). 7 rows = 1″ (ribbing).

POT HOLDER: Cast on 40 sts loosely.

Rows 1, 3, 5, 7, 9: * K 10, (k 1, p 1) 5 times, repeat from * once.

Rows 2, 4, 6, 8, 10: * (K 1, p 1) 5 times, k 10, repeat from * once.

Rows 11, 13, 15, 17, 19: Same as row 2.

Rows 12, 14, 16, 18, 20: Same as row 1.

Repeat these 20 rows twice. Bind off loosely. Make another piece the same.

FINISHING: Crochet pieces together and make loop for hanging same as for Box-Stitch Pot Holder.

BOX-STITCH POT HOLDER

SIZE: About 8″ square.

MATERIALS: Lily Cotton Yarn (Sugar-'n-Cream Yarn), 1 ball. Knitting needles No. 3. Steel crochet hook No. 0.

GAUGE: 5 sts = 1″; 7 rows = 1″.

POT HOLDER: Cast on 40 sts loosely.

Rows 1-8: * K 5, p 5, repeat from * 3 times.

Rows 9-16: * P 5, k 5, repeat from * 3 times. Repeat rows 1-16 twice, then rows 1-8 once. Bind off loosely. Make another piece the same.

FINISHING: Single crochet the two pieces together on all sides, working 3 single crochet in each corner.

Loop: At one corner, join yarn in first of 3 single crochet, chain 10, skip 1 single crochet, slip stitch in next single crochet, turn. Work 12 single crochet in loop, join and fasten off.

Soft blues and greens color this easy-to-make afghan, knit of bulky yarn in five panels of garter stitch.

GARTER STITCH AFGHAN

SIZE: About 74″ x 50″.

MATERIALS: Bulky knitting yarn, 22 ozs. each aqua and green; 20 ozs. blue. Knitting needles No.10·

GAUGE: 3 sts = 1″; 6 rows = 1″.

PANEL A (make 3): With green, cast on 30 sts. Work in garter st (knit every row), 20 rows green, 20 rows blue, and 20 rows aqua. Repeat these 60 rows 6 times more, then work 20 rows green. Bind off.

PANEL B (make 2): With aqua, cast on 30 sts. Work in garter st, 20 rows aqua, 20 rows green, and 20 rows blue. Repeat these 60 rows 6 times more, then work 20 rows aqua. Bind off.

FINISHING: Alternating Panels A and B, sew panels together.

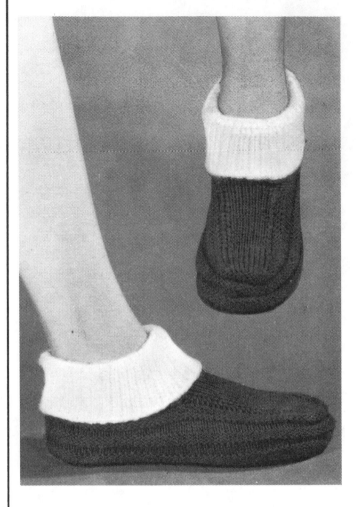

"Booties" for grown-up ladies are knit with a combination of four stitches. Double strand of knitting worsted makes the garter stitch soles extra sturdy; feet are in quaker pattern, with stockinette insteps; the white cuffs are ribbed.

LOUNGE SLIPPERS

SIZES: Directions are for small size (4-5½). Changes for medium (6-7½) and large (8-8½) are in parentheses.

MATERIALS: Knitting worsted, 2 2-oz. skeins main color (MC); 1 skein contrasting color (CC). Knitting needles No. 2. Large-eyed sewing needle.

GAUGE: 5 sts = 1″ (garter st, double strand); 6 sts = 1″ (quaker pat, single strand).

QUAKER PATTERN: Row 1 (right side): Purl.
Row 2: Knit.
Row 3: Purl.
Rows 4 and 5: Knit (reversing pat).
Row 6: Purl.
Row 7: Knit.
Row 8: Purl. Repeat these 8 rows for pat (1 p rib, 1 k rib).

SOLE: Beg at heel with double strand of MC, cast on 5 (6-8) sts. Work in garter st (k every row), inc 1 st at beg of next 6 rows. Work even on 11 (12-14) sts until piece measures 5″ (5¼″-5¼″) from start. Inc 1 st at beg of next 4 (6-6) rows. Work even on 15 (18-20) sts until piece measures 8½″ (9½″-10½″) from start. Dec 1 st at beg of next 6 (6-8) rows. Bind off remaining 9 (12-12) sts (toe).

FOOT: Beg at lower edge with single strand of MC, cast on 111 (123-135) sts. Work in quaker pat until there are on right side 3 p ribs and 2 k ribs, end row 4 of pat.

Shape Instep: Row 1: K first 59 (65-71) sts, k 2 tog, turn.

Row 2 (wrong side): Sl first st, p 7, p 2 tog (9 instep sts), turn.

Row 3: Sl first st, k 7, k 2 tog, turn. Repeat rows 2 and 3 until there are 28 (32-34) sts left each side of 9 instep sts, end wrong side, turn. Sl 1, k across to end of needle, turn. P across to within 2 sts of end of needle, p 2 tog—64 (72-76) sts. Break off MC.

LEG: With CC, work in ribbing of k 1, p 1 on all sts for 2″.

CUFF: Row 1: K across, inc 10 (8-8) sts evenly spaced across row—74 (80-84) sts. **Row 2:** Knit (turning ridge).

Work in ribbing of k 1, p 1 for 2″. Bind off loosely in ribbing.

FINISHING: Sew back seam. Sew foot to sole with seam at center back of heel. Turn down cuff.

Child's two-piece play suit with its own matching cap is worked around and around in knit stitch without purling. Reindeer, snowflakes and border patterns are knitted in. See Child's Reindeer Set, sizes 3–8, page 80. One kitten who found his mittens is knitted of mohair and fingering yarn; page 82.

White cardigan and black pull-over are versions of the same idea: "mistake stitch" ribbing hugs the waist, rises to V-shaped yoke that is crisscrossed with popcorns and decked with flower embroidery. In sizes 8 to 14. Tyrolean Sweaters, page 59.

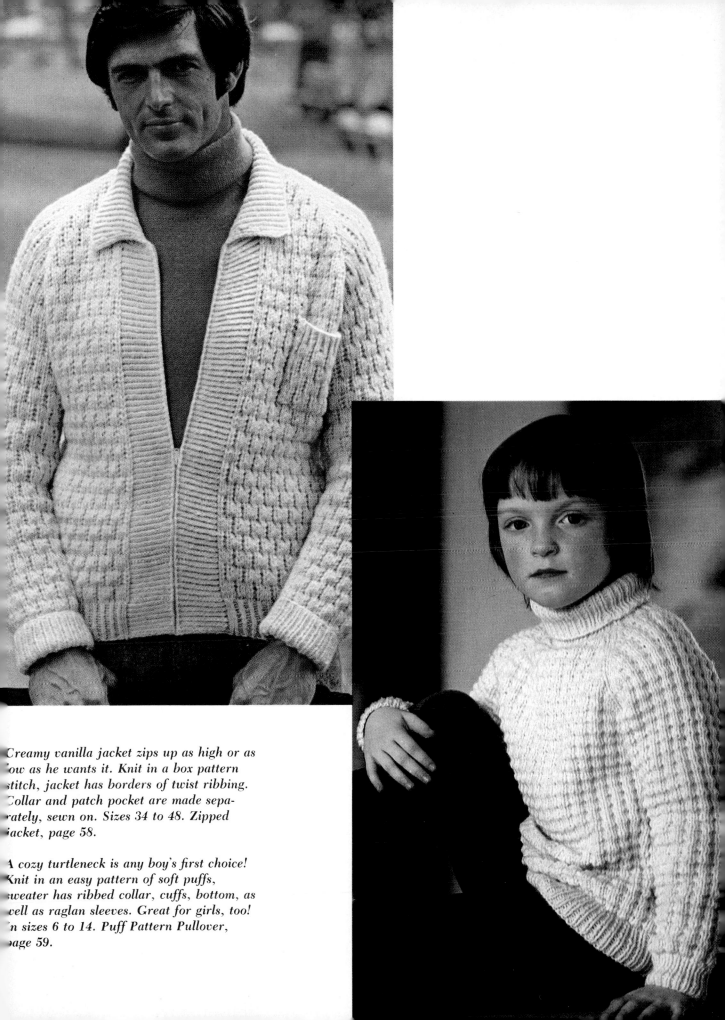

Creamy vanilla jacket zips up as high or as low as he wants it. Knit in a box pattern stitch, jacket has borders of twist ribbing. Collar and patch pocket are made separately, sewn on. Sizes 34 to 48. Zipped Jacket, page 58.

A cozy turtleneck is any boy's first choice! Knit in an easy pattern of soft puffs, sweater has ribbed collar, cuffs, bottom, as well as raglan sleeves. Great for girls, too! In sizes 6 to 14. Puff Pattern Pullover, page 59.

Mother and daughter cardigans
are irresistibly pretty in alternating panels of lace and plain
stockinette stitch. The solid
panels are sprigged with flowers
in pastel colors, embroidered in
lazy daisy stitch and straight
stitches. Mother's cardigan is in
sizes 10–16; daughter's is in
sizes 4–8. Directions for these
Flower-Spray Cardigans are on
page 63.

Lacy arrows combine with simple ribbing to pattern a delicate mint green sacque and bonnet set. Add pink rosebuds embroidered with bullion stitch or French knots and little lazy-daisy stitch leaves. See Lace Pattern Baby Set, page 64.

Red, emerald green and white plaid a light navy afghan, knit in one piece. Horizontal stripes are knitted in, vertical stripes are crocheted in along the spaces made by dropping a stitch at regular intervals. Afghan has a jaunty fringe on all sides. Woven Plain Afghan, p. 70.

Triangles of four clear colors are joined in pinwheel fashion to black triangles to create an easy-to-knit and extra-warm afghan in garter stitch. Twelve pinwheels form the afghan. Directions, p. 71.

*Two-pattern pillows are double knit in a pattern that produces
a textured honeycomb design on one side, a dotted design on
the other. Work both the same, then select the side to show.
Borders are stockinette. 16″ square. See page 92.*

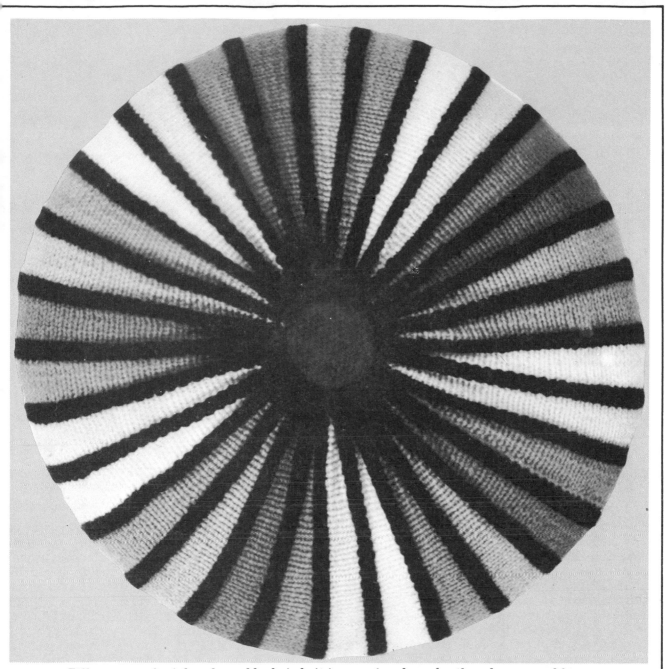

Pillow cover of rainbow hues, black, is knit in a rectangle, and gathered over round form.

RAINBOW PILLOW

SIZE: 18″ in diameter.

MATERIALS: Knitting worsted, 2 2-oz. skeins black; 1 skein each of contrasting colors red (R), orange (O), yellow (Y), kelly green (G), medium blue (B) and purple (P). Knitting needles No. 8. Foam rubber pillow, 18″ in diameter. Two 2″ cardboard circles for button molds. Large-eyed tapestry needle.

GAUGE: 4 sts = 1″; 7 rows = 1″ (stockinette st).

COVER: With R, cast on 60 sts.

First Contrasting (CC) Stripe: With R, work in stockinette st (k 1 row, p 1 row) for 8 rows. Break off R.

Black Stripe: With B, k 2 rows, p 1 row, k 1 row. Break off B.

Following Stripes: Alternating colors, work CC stripes in O, Y, G, B, P and R with a black stripe between each CC stripe until there are 5 CC stripes of each of the 6 CC colors, end with black stripe–30 CC stripes and 30 black stripes in all. Bind off.

FINISHING: With black and tapestry needle, gather rows tog at one edge so that only black stripes show at edge, leaving a small opening. Fasten securely on wrong side. Bring all yarn ends to wrong side. Insert pillow, gather rows tog in same way at other edge.

BUTTONS (make 2): With black, cast on 9 sts. Work in stockinette st, inc 1 st at beg of next 9 rows–18 sts. Dec 1 st at beg of next 9 rows–9 sts. Bind off.

On p side of piece, with black and tapestry needle, gather sts tog around entire edge, insert cardboard circle and fasten securely. Sew a button on each side, covering center openings.

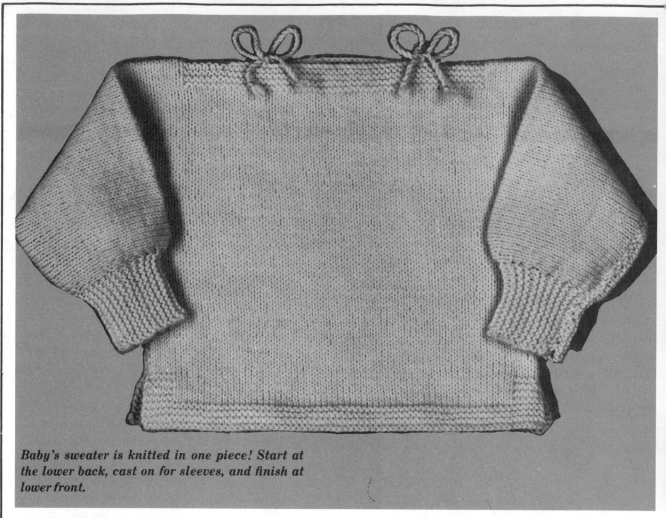

Baby's sweater is knitted in one piece! Start at the lower back, cast on for sleeves, and finish at lower front.

LAYETTE SWEATER

SIZE: Infants'.

Fits Chest: Up to 19″.

MATERIALS: Baby yarn, 3 ply, 3 1-oz. skeins. Knitting needles No. 3.

GAUGE: 15 sts = 2″; 11″ rows = 1″.

SWEATER: BACK: Beg at lower edge, cast on 72 sts. Work in garter st (knit every row) for 8 rows (4 ridges). Keeping 6 sts at each side edge in garter st, work in stockinette st (k 1 row, p 1 row) for 8 rows. Discontinue garter st borders, work in stockinette st on all sts for 36 rows, ending p row. Piece measures 4½″ from start.

Shape Sleeves: Next Row: Cast on 50 sts at beg of row, k to end of row, cast on 50 sts at end of row–172 sts. Work as follows:

Rows 1 and 3 (wrong side): K 14 (cuff), p across to last 14 sts, k 14 (cuff).

Rows 2 and 4 (right side): Knit.

Row 5: Repeat row 1.

Short Rows: * K across to last 14 sts, turn; sl 1, p across to last 14 sts, turn; sl 1, k to end of row, turn; k 14 cuff sts, p to last 14 sts, k 14 cuff sts. Repeat from * 6 times more.

Back Neckband: ** K across to last 14 sts, turn; sl 1; p 45, k 52 for neckband, p 46, turn; sl 1, k to end of row, turn; k 14 cuff sts, p 46, k 52 neckband sts, p 46, k 14 cuff sts. Repeat from ** once more.

Shape Neck and Front Neckband: K across to last 14 sts, turn; sl 1, p 45, k 6, bind off in k next 40 sts for back of neck, k until 6 sts from bound-off sts, p 46, turn; sl 1, k 51, cast on 40 sts for front of neck, k to end of row, turn; k 14 cuff sts, p 46, k 52 neckband sts, p 46, k 14 cuff sts. Work from first ** to 2nd ** of Back Neckband twice.

FRONT: Work from first * to 2nd * of Short Rows as for back 7 times in all. Work as follows:

Rows 1 and 3 (right side): Knit all sts.

Rows 2 and 4: K 14 cuff sts, p across to last 14 sts, k 14 cuff sts.

Next Row: Bind off in k 50 sts, k to end of row.

Next Row: Bind off in p next 50 sts, p to end of row. Continue in stockinette st (k 1 row, p 1 row) for 36 rows. Work as follows:

Rows 1, 3, 5, 7 (right side): Knit.

Rows 2, 4, 6, 8: K 6, p across to last 6 sts, k 6. Then work in garter st on all sts for 8 rows. Bind off.

CORD (make two): Cut two pieces of yarn 25″ long. Twist strands tog tightly. Fold in half and twist in opposite direction. Tie a knot about ½″ from each end of cord; form tassels.

FINISHING: Sew sleeve and side seams, leaving garter st borders at lower edge of sides open for side slits. Steam-press lightly. Draw cords through top row at neck edges of front and back about 1″ (or as desired) from each neck opening, tie cords.

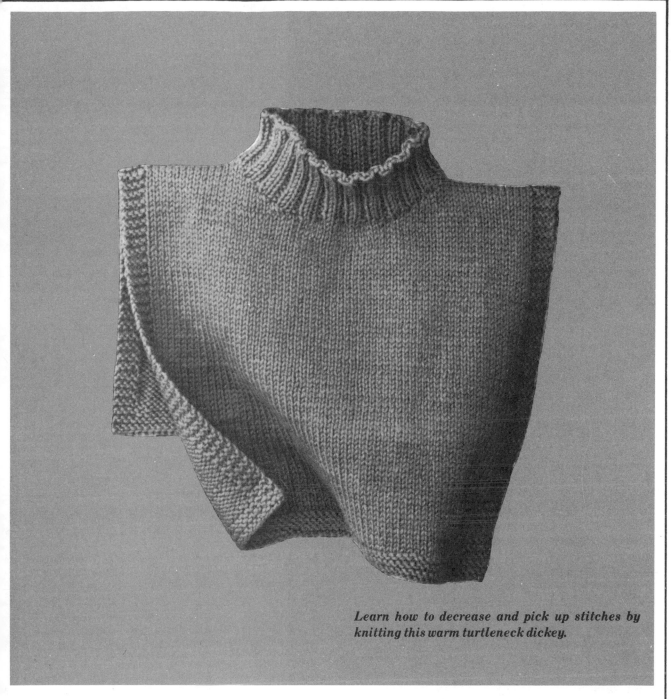

Learn how to decrease and pick up stitches by knitting this warm turtleneck dickey.

TURTLENECK DICKEY

MATERIALS: Knitting worsted 5 ozs. Knitting needles No. 8. One stitch holder.

GAUGE: 9 sts = 2"; 6 rows = 1".

DICKEY: Beg at lower front edge, cast on 68 sts. Knit 6 rows. Work as follows:

Row 1: Knit across.

Row 2: K 4 (border), p to within last 4 sts, k 4. Repeat last 2 rows until total length is 12", ending with row 2.

Shape Neck: Left Front Shoulder: K across the first 27 sts, turn. Maintaining border, work 9 rows on these 27 sts, decreasing 1 st at neck edge each row. Work 2 rows even on remaining 18 sts. Bind off. Slip next 14 sts on a stitch holder for front neck. Attach yarn at right neck edge and work right front shoulder to correspond to left front shoulder, ending at neck edge. **Do not bind off.** On same needle cast on 50 sts for back of neck and back left shoulder.

BACK: Continue as before over these 68 sts until length from back of neck is 7½", ending with a k row. K next 5 rows. Bind off.

NECKBAND: With right side facing, starting at left shoulder, pick up and k 19 sts evenly along side neck edge to front stitch holder, k the 14 sts on holder, pick up and k 19 sts along side neck edge to back of neck; leaving last 18 sts free for left shoulder, pick up and k 32 sts along back of neck–84 sts. Work in k 2, p 2 ribbing for 2¼". Bind off very loosely in ribbing to allow for head.

FINISHING: Sew left shoulder and neckband. Steam-press.

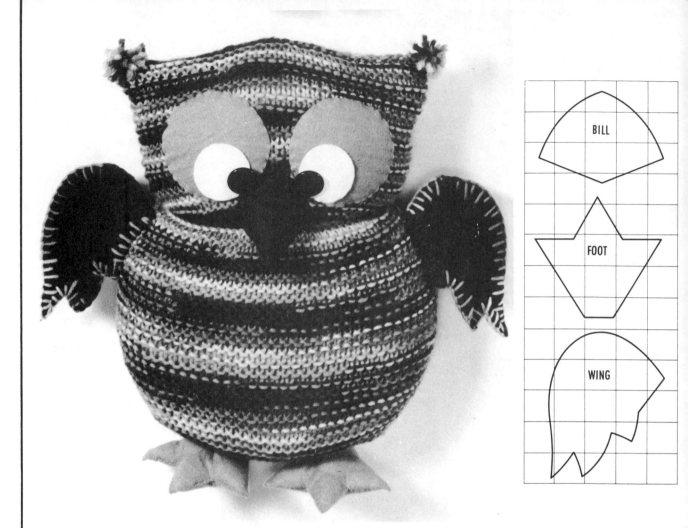

Multicolored owl pillow is easy to knit of one skein of variegated knitting worsted (pink, rose, brown, green). Make flat piece in garter stitch, fit it over 12" round pillow; tie at neck. Add felt wings, feet, bill, and eyes.

OWL PILLOW

SIZE: 12" high.

MATERIALS: Knitting worsted, 1 3½-oz. skein variegated yarn. Knitting needles No. 10. Crochet hook size F. One 12" round foam rubber pillow. Small amount of tan and brown felt. Scrap of white felt. Two dark 1" shank buttons. Sewing thread to match felt. Absorbent cotton for stuffing. Paper for patterns. Ruler. Pencil. Compass. Sharp yarn needle.

KNITTED COVER: Cast on 70 sts. Work in garter st (k each row) for 82 rows (41 ridges). Bind off.

FINISHING: Sew side edges together. With seam at one side of pillow, slip pillow into cover. Close top opening, stuffing corners for ears while sewing. Make two small tassels and sew to points of ears. (To make tassel, wind yarn 12 times around 3 fingers; slip windings off fingers. Tie loops together at one end; cut through; cut through loops at opposite end. Wind a strand of yarn tightly around all strands near tied end; fasten.) With yarn and crochet hook, ch 40. Sc in 2nd ch from hook and in each ch across. End off. Tie chain tightly around pillow 5½" from top to form neck. Secure ends.

Felt Pieces: Rule paper for patterns in 1" squares. Enlarge patterns to actual size by copying patterns on ruled paper. Cut out patterns. From felt, using compass, cut two tan circles 3½" diameter, and two white circles 1⅝" diameter for eyes. Sew white circles to tan circles, sew to head. Sew on buttons for eyes. Using patterns, cut one brown bill, four brown wing pieces and four tan foot pieces. Join straight edges of bill; stuff bill; sew to face, joined edge at bottom. Stitch two pieces for each foot together, leaving opening for stuffing. Stuff; close opening. Sew feet to body. Place two pieces for each wing together. With strand of yarn in sharp needle, work blanket stitch around edges, alternating long and short stitches (see detail, page 282). Sew wings to side of owl's body as shown.

*Round-yoked pullover
and cap, knitted in
plain blue stripes on
red, has raised designs
of white and red em-
broidered in a double
duplicate stitch. Sizes
4–8. Directions for
Girl's Snow Set, page 61.*

An allover raised motif and doubled V neckline vary this classic pullover. To knit in sizes 8–14 of knitting worsted. For Raised Diamond Pullover, see page 57.

PATTERN STITCHES

RIBBING: Most knitted sweaters use ribbing around cuffs, lower edge and neckline. Ribbing holds in these edges to fit more snugly than the rest of the sweater. Ribbing combines knitting and purling in the same row. For example, cast on a multiple of 4 sts. * K 2, p 2, repeat from * across row. Repeat this row. Various multiples of knit and purl stitches may be used to form different rib patterns.

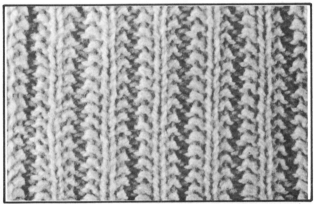

RIBBING VARIATION

1. RIBBING VARIATION (Mutliple of 2 sts):
Row 1: * Yo, sl 1 as if to p, k 1, repeat from * across.
Row 2: * Yo, sl 1 as if to p, k 2 tog (sl-st and yo-st of last row), repeat from * across. Repeat row 2 for pattern.
To Bind Off: Omit yo, p 1, k 2 tog as you bind off.

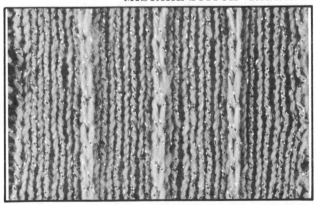

"MISTAKE STITCH" RIBBING

2. "MISTAKE STITCH" RIBBING (Multiple of 4 sts plus 3).
Row 1: * K 2, p 2, repeat from * across, end k 2, p 1. Repeat this row for pattern. Bind off in pattern.

SLIPPED STITCH RIDGES

3. SLIPPED STITCH RIDGES (Multiple of 6 sts plus 5):
Row 1: (right side): K 5, * yarn in back, sl 1 as if to p, k 5, repeat from * across.
Row 2: P 5, * yarn in front, sl 1 as if to p, p 5, repeat from * across.
Row 3: Repeat row 1.
Row 4: Purl. Repeat these 4 rows for pattern. Bind off on last row of pattern.

SEED STITCH or MOSS STITCH is worked on an uneven number of stitches. On the first row, * k 1, p 1, repeat from * across, end k 1. Repeat this row.

4. DOUBLE SEED STITCH (Multiple of 4 sts):
Rows 1 and 2: * K 2, p 2, repeat from * across.
Rows 3 and 4: * P 2, k 2, repeat from * across. Repeat these 4 rows for pattern. Bind off in pattern.

DOUBLE SEED STITCH

5. SEED AND STOCKINETTE STITCH RIBS (Multiple of 5 sts):

Row 1 (right side): Knit.

Row 2: * K 2, p 3, repeat from * across. Repeat these 2 rows for pattern. Bind off in pattern.

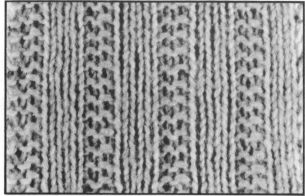

SEED AND STOCKINETTE STITCH RIBS

6. GULL STITCH (Multiple of 7 sts plus 1):

Row 1 (right side): P 1, * k 6, p 1, repeat from * across.

Row 2 (wrong side): K 1, * p 6, k 1, repeat from * across.

Row 3: P 1, * k 2, yarn in back, sl next 2 sts as if to p, k 2, p 1, repeat from * across.

Row 4: K 1, * p 2, yarn in front, sl next 2 sts as if to p, p 2, k 1, repeat from * across.

Row 5: P 1, * sl as if to p next 2 sts to dp needle, hold in back, k next sl-st, then k sts from dp needle (right cross st made), sl next sl-st to dp needle, hold in front, k next 2 sts, then k st from dp needle (left cross st made), p 1, repeat from * across. Repeat rows 2-5 for pattern.

To Bind Off: Omit pat, k the k sts, p the p sts.

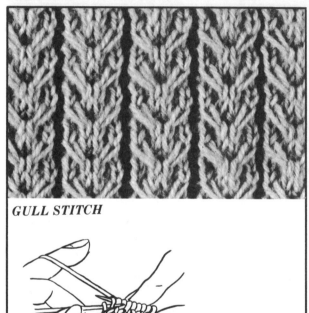

GULL STITCH

7. BASIC CABLE STITCH (Multiple of 11 sts plus 5):

Row 1 (right side): P 5, * k 6, p 5, repeat from * across.

Row 2: K 5, * p 6, k 5, repeat from * across.

Rows 3-10: Repeat rows 1 and 2.

Row 11 (cable row): P 5, * sl next 3 sts on a dp needle, hold dp needle in back of work, k next 3 sts; k the 3 sts from the dp needle without twisting sts (see detail drawing), p 5, repeat from * across. Repeat rows 2-11 for pattern. Repeat rows 2-10 after last cable row. Bind off on next row, knitting the k sts and purling the p sts.

BASIC CABLE STITCH

SIMPLE CABLES AND RIBBING

PLAIT STITCH

DOUBLE CABLES

MOCK CABLE PATTERN

8. SIMPLE CABLES AND RIBBING (Multiple of 12 sts plus 2):

Rows 1, 3, 5 (right side): * K 2, p 2, k 6, p 2, repeat from * across, end k 2.

Rows 2, 4, 6: * P 2, k 2, p 6, k 2, repeat from * across, end p 2.

Row 7: * K 2, p 2, sl next 3 sts as if to p on a dp needle, hold in front, k next 3 sts, then k sts from dp needle (cable made), p 2, repeat from * across, end k 2. Repeat rows 2-7 for pattern. Bind off in pattern.

9. PLAIT STITCH (Multiple of 12 sts plus 3):

Row 1 (right side): * P 3, k 9, repeat from * across row, end p 3.

Row 2: * K 3, p 9, repeat from * across, end k 3.

Row 3: * P 3, sl 3 sts on dp needle, hold in back of work, k next 3 sts, then k 3 sts from dp needle, k 3, repeat from * across row, end p 3.

Row 4: Repeat row 2.

Row 5: Repeat row 1.

Row 6: Repeat row 2.

Row 7: * P 3, k 3, sl 3 sts on dp needle, hold in front of work, k 3 sts, then k 3 sts from dp needle, repeat from * across row, p 3.

Row 8: Repeat row 2.

Row 9: Repeat row 1.

Row 10: Repeat row 2. Repeat rows 3-10 for pattern. Bind off in pattern.

10. DOUBLE CABLES (Multiple of 12 sts plus 4):

Rows 1, 3, 5, 7 (right side): * P 4, k 8, repeat from * across, end p 4.

Rows 2, 4, 6, 8: * K 4, p 8, repeat from * across, end k 4.

Row 9: * P 4, sl next 2 sts as if to p on a dp needle, hold in back, k next 2 sts, then k sts from dp needle, sl next 2 sts on a dp needle, hold in front, k next 2 sts, then k sts from dp needle, repeat from * across, end p 4. Repeat rows 2-9 for pattern. Bind off in pattern.

11. MOCK CABLE PATTERN (Multiple of 8 sts plus 3):

Rows 1 and 3 (right side): P 3, * k 2, p 1, k 2, p 3, repeat from * across.

Rows 2 and 4: K 3, * p 2, k 1, p 2, k 3, repeat from * across.

Row 5: P 3, * sk 1 st, k in front lp of next st, k in front lp of skipped st (cable), sl both sts off needle, p 1, cable on next 2 sts, p 3, repeat from * across. Repeat rows 2-5 for pattern. Bind off in pattern.

12. BASKET WEAVE STITCH (Multiple of 10 sts plus 3):

Row 1 (right side): * K 3, p 7, repeat from * across row, end k 3.

Row 2: * P 3, k 7, repeat from * across row, end p 3.

Row 3: Repeat row 1.

Row 4: P across row.

Row 5: P 5, * k 3, p 7, repeat from * across to last 8 sts, k 3, p 5.

Row 6: K 5, * p 3, k 7, repeat from * across row to last 8 sts, p 3, k 5.

Row 7: Repeat row 5.

Row 8: P across row. Repeat rows 1-8 for pattern. Bind off in pattern.

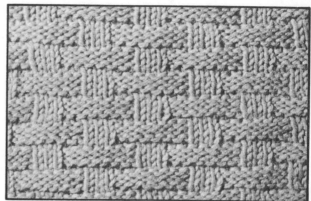

BASKET WEAVE STITCH

13. HERRINGBONE STITCH (Multiple of 7 sts plus 1):

Row 1 (wrong side): P across row.

Row 2: * K 2 tog, k 2, inc 1 st in next st (to inc, place point of right needle behind left needle, insert point of right needle from top down through st below next st, k this st, then k st above it), k 2, repeat from * across, end k 3.

Row 3: P across row.

Row 4: K 3, * inc 1 st in next st as in row 2, k 2, k 2 tog, k 2, repeat from * across, end k 2 tog. Repeat these 4 rows for pattern.

HERRINGBONE STITCH

14. POPCORNS ON STOCKINETTE STITCH (Multiple of 4 sts plus 3):

Row 1 (right side): Knit.

Row 2: Purl.

Row 3: Knit.

Row 4 (wrong side): P 3, * in next st (k 1, p 1, k 1, p 1) loosely, p 3, repeat from * across.

Row 5: K 3, * sl next 3 sts as if to p, k next st, pass separately 3rd, 2nd and first of the sl sts over last k st, k 3, repeat from * across.

Rows 6 and 7: Repeat rows 2 and 3.

Row 8: P 1, * in next st (k 1, p 1, k 1, p 1) loosely, p 3, repeat from * across, end last repeat p 1.

Row 9: K 1, * sl next 3 sts as if to p, k next st, pass the sl sts over k st (as in row 5), k 3, repeat from * across, end last repeat k 1. Repeat rows 2-9 for pattern. Bind off on k or p row.

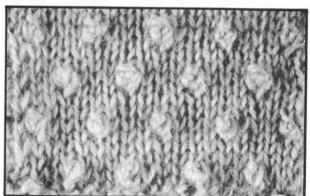

POPCORNS ON STOCKINETTE STITCH

15. TRINITY STITCH (Multiple of 4 sts):

Row 1 (right side): Purl.

Row 2: * (K 1, p 1, k 1) all in one st, p next 3 sts tog, repeat from * across.

Row 3: Purl.

Row 4: * P 3 sts tog, (k 1, p 1, k 1) in next st, repeat from * across. Repeat these 4 rows for pattern. Bind off on the right side.

TRINITY STITCH

HONEYCOMB STITCH

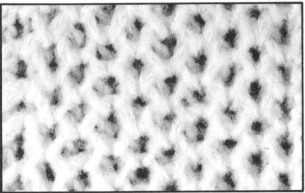

THREE-DIMENSIONAL HONEYCOMB

QUAKER STITCH OR RIDGING

GARTER STITCH AND LACE RIBS

16. HONEYCOMB STITCH (Multiple of 2 sts):
Row 1 (right side): Purl.
Row 2: Purl.
Row 3: * Yo, sl 1, k 1, psso, repeat from * across.
Row 4: Purl. Repeat these 4 rows for pattern. Bind off on a purl row.

17. THREE-DIMENSIONAL HONEYCOMB (Multiple of 2 sts): When slipping sts, hold yarn in back, sl all sts as if to p.
Row 1 (wrong side): * K 1, yo, sl 1, repeat from * across. Yo and sl st count as 1 st.
Row 2: K 1, * sl yo st, k 2, repeat from * across, end sl yo st, k 1.
Row 3: * Yo, sl 1, k tog the yo and next k st of last row as 1 st, repeat from * across.
Row 4 (right side): * K 2, sl yo st, repeat from * across.
Row 5: * K tog the yo and next k st of last row as 1 st, yo, sl 1, repeat from * across.
Row 6: K 1, * sl yo st, k 2, repeat from * across, end sl yo st, k 1. Repeat rows 3-6 for pattern stitch. To bind off, bind off in k on wrong side of pattern, knitting tog the yo and k 1 of last row as 1 st. Or, bind off in k on right side of pattern, knitting tog the k 1 and yo of last row as 1 st.

18. QUAKER STITCH OR RIDGING: This stitch forms horizontal ribs. It consists of stripes of stockinette stitch alternated with stripes (ridges) of reverse stockinette stitch. For example:
Row 1 (right side): Knit.
Row 2: Purl.
Row 3: Knit.
Row 4: Purl.
Row 5 (right side): Purl.
Row 6: Knit.
Row 7: Purl.
Row 8: Knit. Repeat rows 1-8 for pattern stitch.

19. GARTER STITCH AND LACE RIBS:
Rows 1-6: Knit.
Row 7: * K 1, yo, repeat from * across, end k 1.
Row 8: * K 1, drop yo off needle, repeat from * across, end k 1.
Rows 9-14: Knit. Repeat rows 7-14 for pattern. Bind off on last row of pattern.

20. EYELET PATTERN STITCH (Multiple of 8 sts):

Row 1 (right side): Knit.

Row 2 and All Even Rows: Purl.

Row 3: * K 6, yo, k 2 tog, repeat from * across.

Row 5: Knit.

Row 7: K 2, * yo, k 2 tog, k 6, repeat from * across, end last repeat k 4.

Row 8: Purl. Repeat rows 1-8 for pattern. Bind off on a purl row.

21. SMALL-PATTERNED LACE STITCH (Multiple of 6 sts plus 2): Sl all sl sts as if to k.

Row 1 and All Odd Rows (wrong side): Purl.

Row 2 (right side): * Yo, k 3, yo, sl 1 as if to k, k 2 tog, psso, repeat from * across, k 2.

Row 4: * Yo, sl 1, k 1, psso, k 1, k 2 tog, yo, k 1, repeat from * across, end yo, sl 1, k 1, psso.

Row 6: K 1, * yo, sl 1, k 2 tog, psso, yo, k 3, repeat from * across, end last repeat k 4.

Row 8: * K 2 tog, yo, k 1, yo, sl 1, k 1, psso, k 1, repeat from * across, end last repeat k 3.

Row 10: K 4, * yo, sl 1, k 2 tog, psso, yo, k 3, repeat from * across, end last repeat k 1. Repeat rows 3-10 for pattern. Bind off on a purl row.

22. LACE STRIPES (Multiple of 11 sts plus 3):

Row 1 (right side): * K 3, yo, sl 1, k 2 tog, psso, yo, p 2, yo, sl 1, k 2 tog, psso, yo, repeat from * across, end k 3.

Row 2: P 6, k 2, * p 9, k 2, repeat from * across, end p 6.

Row 3: K 6, p 2, * k 9, p 2, repeat from * across, end k 6.

Row 4: Repeat row 2. Repeat these 4 rows for pattern. Bind off on last row of pattern.

23. OPENWORK DIAMONDS (Multiple of 10 sts):

Row 1 and All Odd Rows (wrong side): Purl.

Row 2 (right side): K 3, * yo, sl 1 as if to p (throughout pattern), k 2 tog, psso, yo, k 7, repeat from * across, end last repeat k 4.

Row 4: K 2 tog, k 2, * yo, k 1, yo, k 2, sl 1, k 1, psso, k 1, k 2 tog, k 2, repeat from * across to last 6 sts, yo, k 1, yo, k 2, sl 1, k 1, psso, k 1.

Row 6: * K 2 tog, k 1, yo, k 3, yo, k 1, sl 1, k 1, psso, k 1, repeat from * across.

Row 8: K 2 tog, * yo, k 5, yo, sl 1, k 1, psso, k 1, k 2 tog, repeat from * across to last 8 sts, yo, k 5, yo, sl 1, k 1, psso, k 1.

Row 10: K 1, yo, * k 7, yo, sl 1, k 2 tog, psso, yo, repeat from * across to last 9 sts, k 7, yo, sl 1, k 1, psso—1 extra st.

Row 12: K 1, * yo, k 2, sl 1, k 1, psso, k 1, k 2 tog, k 2, yo, k 1, repeat from * across.

Row 14: K 2 tog, * yo, k 1, sl 1, k 1, psso, k 1, k 2 tog, k 1, yo, k 3, repeat from * across, end last repeat k 2. Extra st taken off.

Row 16: K 2, * yo, sl 1, k 1, psso, k 1, k 2 tog, yo, k 5, repeat from * across, end last repeat k 3. Repeat these 16 rows for pattern. Bind off on p row.

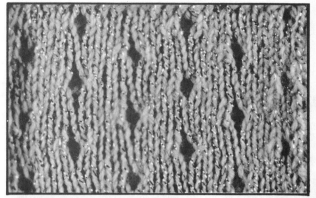

EYELET PATTERN STITCH

SMALL-PATTERNED LACE STITCH

LACE STRIPES

OPENWORK DIAMONDS

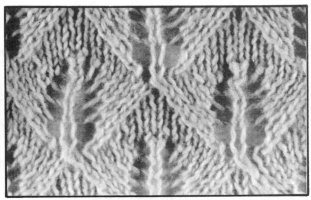

LEAF-PATTERNED LACE STITCH

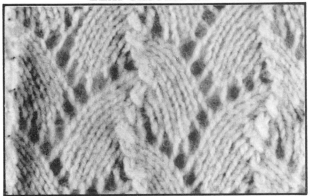

SHELL LACE PATTERN

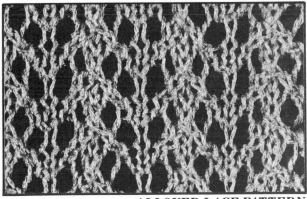

ALLOVER LACE PATTERN

24. LEAF-PATTERNED LACE STITCH (Multiple of 12 sts plus 1):

Row 1 and All Odd Rows (wrong side): Purl.

Row 2 (right side): * K 1, yo, sl 1, k 1, psso, k 7, k 2 tog, yo, repeat from * across, end k 1.

Row 4: * K 1, yo, k 1, sl 1, k 1, psso, k 5, k 2 tog, k 1, yo, repeat from * across, end k 1.

Row 6: * K 1, yo, k 2, sl 1, k 1, psso, k 3, k 2 tog, k 2, yo, repeat from * across, end k 1.

Row 8: * K 1, yo, k 3, sl 1, k 1, psso, k 1, k 2 tog, k 3, yo, repeat from * across, end k 1.

Row 10: * K 1, yo, k 4, sl 1, k 2 tog, psso, k 4, yo, repeat from * across, end k 1.

Row 12: K 4, k 2 tog, * yo, k 1, yo, sl 1, k 1, psso, k 7, k 2 tog, repeat from * across to last 7 sts, yo, k 1, yo, sl 1, k 1, psso, k 4.

Row 14: K 3, k 2 tog, k 1, * yo, k 1, yo, k 1, sl 1, k 1, psso, k 5, k 2 tog, k 1, repeat from * across to last 7 sts, yo, k 1, yo, k 1, sl 1, k 1, psso, k 3.

Row 16: K 2, k 2 tog, k 2, * yo, k 1, yo, k 2, sl 1, k 1, psso, k 3, k 2 tog, k 2, repeat from * across to last 7 sts, yo, k 1, yo, k 2, sl 1, k 1, psso, k 2.

Row 18: K 1, k 2 tog, k 3, * yo, k 1, yo, k 3, sl 1, k 1, psso, k 1, k 2 tog, k 3, repeat from * across to last 7 sts, yo, k 1, yo, k 3, sl 1, k 1, psso, k 1.

Row 20: K 2 tog, k 4, * yo, k 1, yo, k 4, sl 1, k 2 tog, psso, k 4, repeat from * across to last 7 sts, yo, k 1, yo, k 4, sl 1, k 1, psso. Repeat these 20 rows for pattern. Bind off on a purl row.

25. SHELL LACE PATTERN (Multiple of 11 sts plus 5):

Row 1 and All Odd Rows (wrong side): Purl.

Row 2 (right side): * K 1, yo, k 2, sl 1, k 2 tog, psso, k 5, yo, repeat from * across to last 5 sts, k 1, yo, k 2, sl 1, k 1, psso.

Row 4: K 2, * yo, k 1, sl 1, k 2 tog, psso, k 4, yo, k 3, repeat from *, end yo, k 1, sl 1, k 1, psso.

Row 6: K 3, * yo, sl 1, k 2 tog, psso, k 3, yo, k 5, repeat from * across, end yo, sl 1, k 1, psso.

Row 8: Yo, k 3, * sl 1, k 2 tog, psso, k 2, yo, k 1, yo, k 5, repeat from * across, end sl 1, k 1, psso.

Row 10: Yo, k 3, * sl 1, k 2 tog, psso, k 1, yo, k 3, yo, k 4, repeat from *, end sl 1, k 1, psso.

Row 12: * Yo, k 3, sl 1, k 2 tog, psso, yo, k 5, repeat from * across, end yo, k 3, sl 1, k 1, psso. Repeat these 12 rows. Bind off on a purl row.

26. ALLOVER LACE PATTERN (Multiple of 6 sts plus 3): Yarn in back, sl all sl sts as if to p.

Row 1 (right side): K 2, * yo, sl 1, k 1, psso, k 1, k 2 tog, yo, k 1, repeat from * across, end last repeat k 2.

Row 2: Purl.

Row 3: K 3, * yo, sl 1, k 2 tog, psso, yo, k 3, repeat from * across.

Row 4: Purl. Repeat these 4 rows for pattern.

27. WEDGE STITCH (Multiple of 7 sts):

Row 1: * P 6, k 1, repeat from * across.
Row 2: * P 2, k 5, repeat from * across.
Row 3: * P 4, k 3, repeat from * across.
Row 4: * P 4, k 3, repeat from * across.
Row 5: * P 2, k 5, repeat from * across.
Row 6: * P 6, k 1, repeat from * across. Repeat these 6 rows for pattern.

28. DIAMOND STITCH (Multiple of 8 sts plus 1):

Row 1 (right side): K 4, * p 1, k 7, repeat from * across, end p 1, k 4.
Row 2: P 3, * k 1, p 1, k 1, p 5, repeat from * across, end k 1, p 1, k 1, p 3.
Row 3: K 2, * p l, k 3, repeat from * across, end p 1, k 2.
Row 4: P 1, * k 1, p 5, k 1, p 1, repeat from * across.
Row 5: P 1, * k 7, p 1, repeat from * across.
Row 6: Repeat row 4.
Row 7: Repeat row 3.
Row 8: Repeat row 2. Repeat these 8 rows for pattern.

29. DIAMOND OVERLAY PATTERN (Multiple of 6 sts plus 2):

Note: Sl all sl sts as if to p. On even-numbered rows, sl all sl sts with yarn in back; on odd-numbered rows, sl all sl sts with yarn in front.

Row 1 (wrong side): P 1, * yo, p 5, yo, p 1, repeat from * across, end yo, p 2.
Row 2: K 1, * sl 1, drop yo off needle, k 4, sl 1, drop yo, repeat from * across, end k 1.
Row 3: P 1, sl 1, * p 4, sl 2, repeat from * across, end sl 1, p 1.
Row 4: K 1, sl 1, * k 4, sl 2, repeat from * across, end sl 1, k 1.
Row 5: Repeat row 3.
Row 6: K 1, * drop next st to front of work, k 2, pick up dropped st and k it; sl 2, drop next st to front of work, sl same 2 sl sts back to left-hand needle, pick up dropped st and k it, k 2, repeat from * across, end k 3.
Row 7: P 3, * yo, p 1, yo, p 5, repeat from * across, end yo, p 4.
Row 8: K 3, * (sl 1, drop yo) twice, k 4, repeat from * across, end k 3.
Row 9: P 3, * sl 2, p 4, repeat from * across, end p 3.
Row 10: K 3, * sl 2, k 4, repeat from * across, end k 3.
Row 11: Repeat row 9.
Row 12: K 1, * sl 2, drop next st to front of work, sl same 2 sts back on left-hand needle, pick up dropped st and k it, k 2, drop next st to front of work, k 2, pick up dropped st and k it, repeat from * across, end k 1. Repeat rows 1-12 for pattern.

30. EASY LACE PATTERN (Multiple of 9 sts):

Row 1 (right side): * K 2 tog, k 2, yo, k 1, yo, k 2, k 2 tog, repeat from * across.
Rows 2 and 4: Purl.
Row 3: * K 2 tog, k 1, yo, k 3, yo, k 1, k 2 tog, repeat from * across.
Row 5: * K 2 tog, yo, k 5, yo, k 2 tog, repeat from * across.
Row 6: Purl. Repeat rows 1-6 for pattern.

WEDGE STITCH

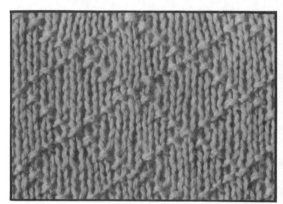

DIAMOND STITCH

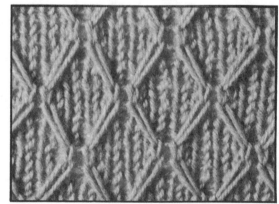

DIAMOND OVERLAY PATTERN

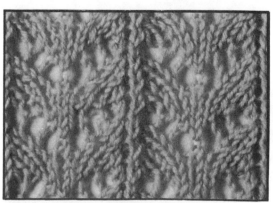

EASY LACE PATTERN

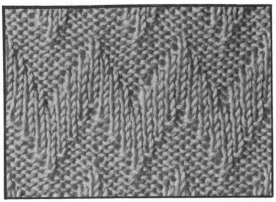

ZIGZAG PATTERN

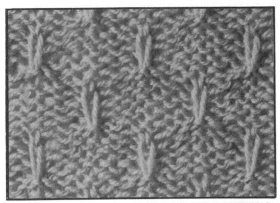

SLIP LOOP PATTERN

GULL STITCH RIB PATTERN

LACE AND CABLE PATTERN

31. ZIGZAG PATTERN (Multiple of 8 sts plus 1):

Row 1: K 1, * p 7, k 1, repeat from * across.
Row 2: P 1, * k 7, p 1, repeat from * across.
Row 2: P 1, * K 7, p 1, repeat from * across.
Row 3: K 2, * p 5, k 3, repeat from * across, and p 5, k 2.
Row 4: P 2, * k 5, p 3, repeat from * across, end k 5, p 2.
Row 5: K 3, * p 3, k 5, repeat from * across, and p 3, k 3.
Row 6: P 3, * k 3, p 5, repeat from * across, end k 3, p 3.
Row 7: K 4, * p 1, k 7, repeat from * across, end p 1, k 4.
Row 8: P 4, * k 1, p 7, repeat from * across, end k 1, p 4.
Row 9: Repeat row 2. Row 10: Repeat row 1.
Row 11: Repeat row 4. Row 12: Repeat row 3.
Row 13: Repeat row 6. Row 14: Repeat row 5.
Row 15: Repeat row 8. Row 16: Repeat row 7.
Repeat rows 1-16 for pattern.

32. SLIP LOOP PATTERN (Multiple of 6 sts plus 5):

Rows 1 and 3 (right side): P 2, * with yarn loosely in back, sl 1 as if to p, p 5, repeat from * across, end sl 1, p 2.
Rows 2 and 4: K 2, * with yarn loosely in front, sl 1 as if to p, k 5, repeat from * across, end sl 1, k 2. Row 5: P 2, * k 1, p 5, repeat from * across, end k 1, p 2.
Rows 6 and 8: K 5, * with yarn loosely in front, sl 1, k 5, repeat from * across.
Rows 7 and 9: P 5, * with yarn loosely in back, sl 1, p 5, repeat from * across.
Row 10: K 5, * p 1, k 5, repeat from * across. Repeat rows 1-10 for pattern.

33. GULL STITCH RIB PATTERN (Multiple of 9 sts plus 2): **Note:** Sl all sl sts as if to p.

Row 1 (wrong side): K 2, * p 7, k 2, repeat from * across.
Row 2 (right side): P 2, * k 2, sl 1 with yarn in back, k 1, sl with yarn in back, k 2, p 2, repeat from * across.
Row 3: K 2, * p 2, sl 1 with yarn in front, p 1, sl 1 with yarn in front, p 2, k 2, repeat from * across.
Row 4: P 2, * sl 2 with yarn in back, drop sl st to front of work, sl the same 2 sts back to left-hand needle, pick up dropped st and k it, k 3, drop sl st to front of work, k 2, pick up dropped st and k it, p 2, repeat from * across. Repeat rows 1-4

34. LACE AND CABLE PATTERN (Multiple of 11 sts plus 7): **Note:** Sl all sl sts as if to k.

Row 1 (right side): K 1, * yo, sl 1, k 1, psso, k 1, k 2 tog, yo, k 6, repeat from * across, end last repeat yo, k 1.
Row 2 and All Even Rows: Purl.
Row 3: K 2, * yo, sl 1, k 2 tog, psso, yo, k 8, repeat from * across, end last repeat yo, k 2.
Row 5: Repeat row 1.
Row 7: K 2, * yo, sl 1, k 2 tog, psso, yo, k 1, sl next 3 sts to a dp needle, hold in back of work, k next 3 sts, then k 3 sts from dp needle, k 1, repeat from * across to last 5 sts, yo, sl 1, k 2 tog, yo, k 2. Row 8: Purl. Repeat rows 1-8 for pattern.

35. CROSS-OVER LACE PATTERN (Multiple of 6 sts): **Row 1:** Knit.

Row 2: Putting yarn loosely around needle twice instead of once for each st, k across.

Row 3: * Sl 6 sts as if to p dropping extra lp of each st, insert left-hand needle under front lps of first 3 slipped sts, cross these sts over the last 3 and onto left-hand needle, sl last 3 of same group to left-hand needle, then k these 6 crossed sts, repeat from * across. **Row 4:** Knit.

Row 5: K 3, repeat row 2 to last 3 sts, k 3.

Row 6: K 3, work from first * to 2nd * of row 3 to last 3 sts, k 3. Repeat rows 1-6 for pattern.

36. BUTTERFLY STITCH (Multiple of 10 sts plus 9): **Note:** Sl all sl sts as if to p.

Rows 1, 3, 5, 7 and 9 (right side): K 2, * with yarn in front, sl 5, k 5, repeat from * across, end sl 5, k 2.

Rows 2, 4, 6 and 8: Purl.

Row 10: P 4, * insert right-hand needle down through the 5 loose strands, bring needle up and transfer the 5 strands to left-hand needle, p the 5 strands and next st tog as 1 st, p 9, repeat from * across, end p 4.

Rows 11, 13, 15, 17 and 19: K 7, * with yarn in front, sl 5, k 5, repeat from * across, end sl 5, k 7.

Rows 12, 14, 16 and 18: Purl.

Row 20: P 9, * insert right-hand needle down through the 5 loose strands, bring needle up and transfer the 5 strands to left-hand needle, p the 5 strands and next st tog as 1 st, p 9, repeat from * across. Repeat rows 1-20 for pattern.

37. PINE CONE LACE PATTERN (Multiple of 10 sts plus 3):

Row 1 (right side): K 2, * yo, k 3, k 3 tog, k 3, yo, k 1, repeat from * across, end yo, k 2.

Row 2: P 3, * yo, p 2, p 3 tog, p 2, yo, p 3, repeat from * across.

Row 3: K 4, * yo, k 1, k 3 tog, k 1, yo, k 5, repeat from * across, end yo, k 4.

Row 4: P 5, * yo, p 3 tog, yo, p 7, repeat from * across, end yo, p 5.

Row 5: K 1, k 2 tog, * k 3, yo, k 1, yo, k 3, k 3 tog, repeat from *, end last repeat k 2 tog, k 1.

Row 6: P 1, p 2 tog, * p 2, yo, p 3, yo, p 2, p 3 tog, repeat from *, end last repeat p 2 tog, p 1.

Row 7: K 1, k 2 tog, * k 1, yo, k 5, yo, k 1, k 3, tog, repeat from *, end last repeat k 2 tog, k 1.

Row 8: P 1, p 2 tog, * yo, p 7, yo, p 3 tog, repeat from * across, end last repeat p 2 tog, p 1. Repeat rows 1-8 for pattern.

38. LACY LEAF PATTERN (Multiple of 8 sts plus 1): **Note:** Sl all sl sts as if to k.

Row 1 (right side): K 1, * yo, sl 1, k 1, psso, k 3, k 2 tog, yo, k 1, repeat from * across.

Rows 2 and 4: Purl.

Row 3: K 2, yo, * sl 1, k 1, psso, k 1, k 2 tog, yo, k 3, yo, repeat from *, end last repeat yo, k 2.

Row 5: P 1, * k 2, yo, sl 1, k 2 tog, psso, yo, k 2, p 1, repeat from * across.

Rows 6 and 8: K 1, * p 7, k 1, repeat from * across.

Rows 7 and 9: P 1, * k 2 tog, (k 1, yo) twice, k 1, sl 1, k 1, psso, p 1, repeat from * across.

Row 10: Repeat row 6. Repeat rows 1-10.

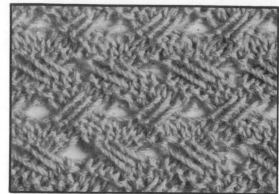

CROSS-OVER LACE PATTERN

BUTTERFLY STITCH

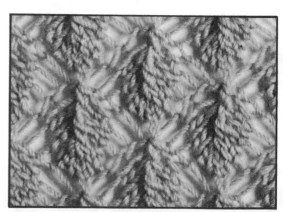

PINE CONE LACE PATTERN

LACY LEAF PATTERN

RAISED DIAMOND PULLOVER
Shown on page 46

SIZES: Directions for size 8-10. Changes for size 12-14 in parentheses.

Body Bust Size: 31½"-32½" (34"-36").

Blocked Bust Size: 34" (38").

MATERIALS: Knitting Worsted, 4 (5) 4-oz. skeins. Set of dp needles No. 5 for neckband; 14" knitting needles Nos. 5 and 7. One stitch holder.

GAUGE: 5 sts=1"; 20 rows=3" (pat before blocking, No. 7 needles).

PATTERN (multiple of 10 sts plus 5):

Row 1 (right side): K 5, * p 5, k 5, repeat from * across row.

Row 2: P 5, * k 5, p 5, repeat from * across row.

Row 3: P 1, k 4, * p 4, k 1, p 1, k 4, repeat from * across row.

Row 4: P 4, k 1, * p 1, k 4, p 4, k 1, repeat from * across row.

Row 5: P 2, k 3, * p 3, k 2, p 2, k 3, repeat from * across row.

Row 6: P 3, k 2, * p 2, k 3, p 3, k 2, repeat from * across row.

Row 7: P 3, k 2, * p 2, k 3, p 3, k 2, repeat from * across row.

Row 8: P 2, k 3, * p 3, k 2, p 2, k 3, repeat from * across row.

Row 9: P 4, k 1, * p 1, k 4, p 4, k 1, repeat from * across row.

Row 10: P 1, k 4, * p 4, k 1, p 1, k 4, repeat from * across row.

Row 11 (right side): P 5, * k 5, p 5, repeat from * across row.

Row 12: K 5, * p 5, k 5, repeat from * across row.

Row 13: K 1, p 4, * k 4, p 1, k 1, p 4, repeat from * across row.

Row 14: K 4, p 1, * k 1, p 4, k 4, p 1, repeat from * across row.

Row 15: K 2, p 3, * k 3, p 2, k 2, p 3, repeat from * across row.

Row 16: K 3, p 2, * k 2, p 3, k 3, p 2, repeat from * across row.

Row 17: K 3, p 2, * k 2, p 3, k 3, p 2, repeat from * across row.

Row 18: K 2, p 3, * k 3, p 2, k 2, p 3, repeat from * across row.

Row 19: K 4, p 1, * k 1, p 4, k 4, p 1, repeat from * across row.

Row 20: K 1, p 4, * k 4, p 1, k 1, p 4, repeat from * across row. Repeat these 20 rows for pat.

SLIP-ON: BACK: With No. 5 needles, cast on 84 (94) sts. Work in ribbing of k 1, p 1 for 1½", inc 1 st at end of last row-85 (95) sts. Change to No. 7 needles. Work in pat (**note**, beg with pat row 1 when working back; beg with pat row 11 when working front) until piece measures 15" from start or desired length to underarm, end wrong side.

Shape Armholes: Bind off in pat 4 (5) sts at beg of next 2 rows. Dec 1 st each side every other row 3 (5) times-71 (75) sts. Work even until armholes measure 7½" (8") above first bound-off sts.

Shape Shoulders: Bind off in pat 5 sts at beg of next 8 rows, 3 (5) sts next 2 rows. Put remaining 25 sts on a holder for neckband.

FRONT: Work as for back (see note) until piece measures ½" less than back to underarm, end on wrong side.

Divide sts for Neck: Work first 42 (47) sts, drop yarn, put next st on a safety pin, join another skein of yarn and work last 42 (47) sts.

Shape V Neck and Armholes: Working on both sides at once, dec 1 st at each neck edge every 4th row 12 times; at same time, when piece measures same as back to underarm, bind off 4 (5) sts at beg of each arm side once, then dec 1 st at each arm side every other row 3 (5) times. When neck decs are completed, work even on 23 (25) sts of each side until armholes measure same as back.

Shape Shoulders: Bind off in pat 5 sts at beg of each arm side 4 times, 3 (5) sts once.

SLEEVES: With No. 5 needles, cast on 38 (40) sts. Work in ribbing of k 1, p 1 for 2½", inc 7 (5) sts evenly spaced across last row-45 sts. Change to No. 7 needles. Beg with pat row 1, work in pat and inc 1 st each side every ¾" 1 (10) times, every 1" 11 (5) times, working added sts into pat-69 (75) sts. Check gauge: piece above last inc row should be 14" (15") wide. Work even until piece measures 17½" from start or desired length to underarm.

Shape Cap: Bind off in pat 4 (5) sts at beg of next 2 rows. Dec 1 st each side every other row 15 (17) times. Bind off 3 sts at beg of next 6 rows. Bind off remaining 13 sts.

FINISHING: Run in yarn ends on wrong side. Block pieces and sew seams with backstitch as follows: Sew shoulder seams. Sew in sleeves. Sew side and sleeve seams; weave cuffs and waistband ribbing from right side. Steam-press seams.

Neckband: Put back of neck sts on dp needle. Dividing sts on 3 dp needles, from right side, join yarn, k across back of neck sts, pick up and k 58 (60) sts on left neck edge to center front, put a marker on needle, k center st from safety pin, put a marker on needle, pick up and k 58 (60) sts on right neck edge to shoulder-142 (146) sts. Join, work in ribbing of p 1, k 1 and dec 1 st before first and after 2nd marker on every other rnd 4 times, keeping center st in k. Work even for 4 rnds. Inc 1 st in st before first and in st after 2nd marker on next rnd, then every other rnd 3 times. Work 1 rnd even. Bind off loosely in ribbing. Fold neckband in half to wrong side; sew loosely in place, matching center k st.

ZIPPED JACKET
Shown on page 35

SIZES: Directions for small size (34-36). Changes for medium size (38-40), large size (42-44) and extra large size (46-48) are in parentheses.

Body Chest Size: 34"-36" (38"-40"; 42"-44"; 46"-48").

Blocked Chest Size (closed); 38" (42"-46½"-50").

MATERIALS: Knitting Worsted, 6 (6-7-7) 4-oz. skeins. Knitting needles Nos. 6 and 8. Separating zipper.

GAUGE: 5 sts = 1"; 11 rows = 2" (pat, No. 8 needles).

PATTERN (worked on a multiple of 4 sts plus 1): **Row 1** (right side): K 4, * yo, sl 1 as if to p, k 3, repeat from * across, end last repeat k 4.

Row 2: P 4, * k 2 tog, p 3, repeat from * across, end last repeat p 4.

Rows 3-6: Repeat rows 1 and 2 twice.

Row 7: K 2, * yo, sl 1, k 3, repeat from * across, end last repeat k 2.

Row 8: P 2, * k 2 tog, p 3, repeat from * across, end last repeat p 2.

Rows 9-12: Repeat rows 7 and 8 twice. Repeat these 12 rows for pat. **Note:** When counting sts, always count yo and sl st as 1 st.

JACKET: BACK: Beg at lower edge, with No. 6 needles, cast on 79 (91-103-115) sts.

Twisted Ribbing: Row 1 (right side): * K in back lp of next st, p 1, repeat from * across, end k in back lp of next st.

Row 2: * P in back lp of next st, k 1, repeat from * across, end p in back lp of next st. Repeat these 2 rows for 2", end right side. P 1 row, inc 10 sts evenly spaced across–89 (101-113-125) sts. Change to No. 8 needles. Work in pat until piece measures 16½" from start or desired length to underarm, end wrong side. Note pat row. Check gauge; piece above ribbing should measure 18" (20"-22½"-25") wide.

Shape Raglan Armholes: Keeping to pat, bind off 4 (5-6-7) sts at beg of next 2 rows. Dec 1 st each side every other row 27 (26-23-22) times, every row 0 (6-14-20) times. Bind off remaining 27 sts.

LEFT FRONT: Beg at lower edge, with No. 6 needles, cast on 37 (41-45-49) sts. Work in twisted ribbing for 2", end right side. P 1 row, inc 4 sts evenly spaced across–41 (45-49-53) sts. Change to No. 8 needles. Mark end of right side row for front edge (**on right front, mark beg of right side row**

for front edge). Work in pat until piece measures same as back to underarm, end same pat row. Check gauge; piece above ribbing should measure 8" (9"-10"-10½") wide.

Shape Raglan Armhole: Bind off 4 (5-6-7) sts at beg of arm side once. Dec 1 st at beg of arm side every other row 18 (20-21-23) times, end front edge–19 (20-22-23) sts.

Shape Neck: Bind off 2 sts at beg of center edge once. Dec 1 st at center edge every other row 5 times; **at the same time**, continue to dec 1 st at arm side every other row 7 (6-4-3) times, then every row 4 (6-10-12) times. End off.

RIGHT FRONT: Work same as for left front, noting changes and reversing shaping.

SLEEVES: Beg at lower edge with No. 6 needles, cast on 47 (49-51-53) sts. Work in twisted ribbing for 2", end right side. P 1 row, inc 10 (12-10-12) sts evenly spaced–57 (61-61-65) sts. Change to No. 8 needles. Work in pat, inc 1 st each side every 8th row 8 (8-10-10) times, working added sts into pat–73 (77-81-85) sts. Work even until piece measures 19" from start or desired length to underarm. Check gauge; piece above last inc row should measure 14½" (15½"-16"-17") wide.

Shape Raglan Cap: Bind off 4 (5-6-7) sts at beg of next 2 rows. Dec 1 st each side every other row 27 (27-28-28) times, every 4th row 0 (1-1-2) times. Bind off remaining 11 sts.

Left Front Band: Beg at neck edge, from right side, with No. 6 needles, pick up and k 1 st in edge of each row down left front edge. Beg with row 2, work in twisted ribbing for 2". Bind off in ribbing.

Right Front Band: Beg at lower edge of right front edge, work same as for left front band.

COLLAR: Beg at neck edge, with No. 6 needles, cast on 99 sts. Work in twisted ribbing for 4", inc 1 st each side every 4th row, working added sts into ribbing. Bind off loosely in ribbing.

POCKET: Beg at lower edge, with No. 8 needles, cast on 21 sts. Work in pat for 24 rows. Change to No. 6 needles. Work in twisted ribbing for 6 rows. Bind off in ribbing.

FINISHING: Steam-press pieces lightly on wrong side; do not block ribbing. With back-stitch, sew caps of sleeves to back and fronts. Sew side and sleeve seams. With right side of collar facing wrong side of jacket, sew cast-on edge of collar to neck edge. Sew in zipper. Sew pocket to left front, 3" in from start of center band, with top of pocket 1" above start of underarm.

PUFF PATTERN PULLOVER
Shown on page 35

SIZES: Directions for size 6. Changes for sizes 8, 10, 12 and 14 are in parentheses.

Body Chest Size: 24″ (27″-28½″-30″-32″).

Blocked Chest Size: 26″ (28″-30″-32″-34″).

MATERIALS: Sport yarn, 5 (5-6-6-7) 2-oz. balls. Knitting needles Nos. 5 and 6; set of dp needles No. 5. Four stitch holders.

GAUGE: 5 sts = 1″; 7 rows = 1″ (pat, No. 6 needles).

PATTERN (worked on a multiple of 3 sts plus 2): Row 1 (right side): Knit.

Row 2: Purl.

Row 3: K 2, * yo, sl 1 as if to p, k 2, repeat from * across (yo and sl 1 count as 1 st).

Row 4: P 2, * k the yo and sl 1 tog, p 2, repeat from * across. Repeat rows 1-4 for pat.

PULLOVER: BACK: Beg at lower edge, with No. 5 needles, cast on 64 (70-74-80-86) sts. Work in ribbing of k 1, p 1 for 2″ (2″-2″-2½″-2½″), inc 1 (1-0-0-0) st at end of last row—65 (71-74-80-86) sts. Change to No. 6 needles. Work in pat until piece measures 11″ (11½″-12″-12½″-13″) from start or desired length to underarm, end wrong side. Check gauge; piece above ribbing should measure 13″ (14″-15″-16″-17″) wide.

Shape Raglan Armholes: Keeping to pat as established, bind off 2 (2-2-3-4) sts at beg of next 2 rows.

Next Row (right side): K 2, k 2 tog, work in pat to within last 4 sts, end sl 1 as if to k, k 1, psso, k 2—2 sts dec.

Next Row: P 3, work in pat to within last 3 sts, end p 3. Repeat last 2 rows 18 (20-21-22-23) times, Sl remaining 23 (25-26-28-30) sts on a holder.

FRONT: Work same as for back until 15 (17-17-18-19) raglan decs are completed—31 (33-36-38-40) sts, end wrong side.

Shape Neck: K2, k 2 tog, work next 5 (5-7-7-7) sts in pat, drop yarn, sl next 13 (15-14-16-18) sts on a holder, join another strand of yarn, work next 5 (5-7-7-7) sts in pat, sl 1, k 1, psso, k 2—8 (8-10-10-10) sts each side. Working on both sides at once, continue to work raglan decs every other row 3 (3-4-4-4) times more; at the same time, dec 1 st at each neck edge every other row 3 (3-4-4-4) times—2 sts each side. Bind off.

SLEEVES: Beg at lower edge, with No. 5 needles, cast on 34 (38-38-40-40) sts. Work in ribbing of k 1, p 1 for 2″ (2″-2″-2½″-2½″), inc 1 (0-0-1-1) st at end of last row—35 (38-38-41-41) sts. Change to No. 6 needles. Working in pat, inc 1 st each side every 1″ 8 (9-10-11-13) times, working

added sts into pat—51 (56-58-63-67) sts. Work even until piece measures 12″ (13″-14″-15″-16½″) from start or desired length to underarm, end wrong side. Check gauge; piece above last inc row should measure 10¼″ (11¼″-11½″-12½″-13½″) wide.

Shape Raglan Cap: Work same as for back armhole raglan shaping. Sl remaining 9 (10-10-11-11) sts on a holder.

FINISHING: Block pieces. Sew caps of sleeves to back and front. Sew side and sleeve seams.

Collar: From right side, with dp needles, k across left sleeve, pick up and k 8 (8-9-9-9) sts on left front neck edge, k across sts on front holder, pick up and k 8 (8-9-9-9) sts on right front neck edge, k across sts on right sleeve, k across sts on back holder—70 (76-78-84-88) sts. Divide sts on 3 dp needles. Join; work around in ribbing of k 1, p 1 for 5″ (5″-5″-5½″-6″). Bind off loosely in ribbing. Fold collar to right side.

TYROLEAN SWEATERS
Shown on page 34

SIZES: Directions for size 8. Changes for sizes 10, 12 and 14 are in parentheses.

Body Bust Size: 31½″ (32½″-34″-36″).

Blocked Bust Size: Pullover: 32″ (33″-36″-37″). Cardigan (closed): 34″ (35″-38″-39″).

MATERIALS: Sport yarn, 5 (5-6-6) 2-oz. skeins black for pullover, white for cardigan. For embroidery: Small amounts of red, blue, green, white and yellow. Knitting needles No. 5. Two stitch holders. Tapestry needle for embroidering.

GAUGE: 6 sts = 1″; 7 rows = 1″.

PULLOVER: BACK: Beg at lower edge, cast on 95 (99-107-111) sts.

Row 1: K 1, * p 1, k 3, repeat from * across, end p 1, k 1.

Row 2: * K 3, p 1, repeat from * across, end k 3. Repeat these 2 rows until piece measures 2½″ from start. Check gauge; piece should measure 16″ (16½″-18″-18½″) wide. Keeping to pat as established, dec 1 st each side of next row, then every other row 5 times—83 (87-95-99) sts. Work even until piece measures 4″ from start. Inc 1 st each side of next row, then every 4th row 5 times, working added sts into pat—95 (99-107-111) sts. Work even until piece measures 9″ from start, end pat row 2 (1-1-2). Mark next row for right side.

Popcorn: K in front and back of 1 st until there are 5 sts in 1 st, sl st worked in off left-hand needle, (with left-hand needle, pass 2nd st from tip of right-hand needle over and off needle) 4 times (1 st of group left).

Popcorn Pattern: Following chart, work from A to center st, then work back on same row to A. Continue in this manner until all sts are worked in popcorn pat: **at the same time,** when piece measures 15″ from start or desired length to underarm, shape armholes as follows: Bind off 6 (6-7-7) sts at beg of next 2 rows. Dec 1 st each side every other row 6 times–71 (75-81-85) sts. Keeping to popcorn pat as established, work even until armholes measure 7″ (7¼″-7½″-8″) above first bound-off sts.

Shape Shoulders: Bind off 7 (7-7-8) sts at beg of next 4 rows, 7 (8-9-8) sts next 2 rows. Sl remaining 29 (31-35-37) sts on a holder.

FRONT: Work same as for back until armholes measure 5½″ (5½″-5¾″-6″) above first bound-off sts–71 (75-81-85) sts.

Shape Neck and Shoulders: Keeping to popcorn pat, work 28 (29-31-32) sts, drop yarn, sl center 15 (17-19-21) sts on a holder, join another strand of yarn, finish row. Working on both sides at once, with separate strands of yarn, bind off 2 sts at beg of each neck edge twice. Dec 1 st at each neck edge every other row 3 (3-4-4) times; **at the same time,** when armholes measure same as back, bind off 7 (7-7-8) sts at beg of each arm side twice, 7 (8-9-8) sts once.

SLEEVES: Beg at lower edge, cast on 39 (39-43-43) sts. Work as for lower edge of back for 2 rows. Mark k side of center st for right side.

Continue in pat until piece measures 2½″ from start. Inc 1 st each side of next row, then every ¾″ 11 (12-12-13) times, working added sts into pat–63 (65-69-71) sts. Work even until piece measures 13½″ from start, end wrong side. Following chart work from B to center st, then work back on same row to B. Continue in this manner until piece measures 18″ from start or desired length to underarm.

Shape Cap: Keeping to pat, bind off 6 (6-7-7) sts at beg of next 2 rows. Dec 1 st each side every other row 14 (15-16-17) times. Bind off 3 sts at beg of next 4 rows. Bind off remaining 11 sts.

FINISHING: Block pieces; do not flatten popcorns. With back-stitch, sew left shoulder seam.

Neckband: From right side, k across 29 (31-35-37) sts on back holder, pick up and k 16 (14-13-13) sts on left front neck edge, k across sts on front holder, pick up and k 16 (14-13-13) sts on right front neck edge–76 (76-80-84) sts.

Row 1: * K 3, p 1, repeat from * across.

Row 2: K 2, * p 1, k 3, repeat from * across, end p 1, k 1. Repeat these 2 rows 4 times. Bind off loosely in pat.

Sew right shoulder and neckband seam; sew in sleeves. Sew side and sleeve seams after completing embroidery. Steam-press seams open flat.

EMBROIDERY: See page 282 for stitch details. Using single strand of sport yarn, with red, embroider 8 bullion stitches in a radiating circle, green stems in outline stitch, green leaves in straight stitch. For alternating flowers, with white, work 4 lazy daisy stitches having straight stitches in between; make yellow French knot centers.

☐ **PATTERN AS ESTABLISHED**   ◨ **P ON RIGHT SIDE**
                                  K ON WRONG SIDE   ◙ **POPCORN**

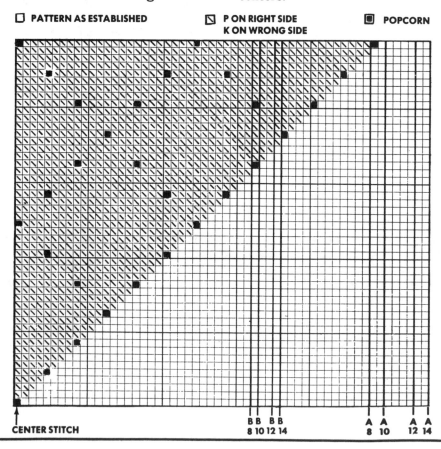

CENTER STITCH

B B   B B   A A   A A
8 10 12 14   8 10   12 14

TYROLEAN SWEATERS
Continued

CARDIGAN: BACK: Work as for pullover.

LEFT FRONT: Beg at lower edge, cast on 58 (60-64-66) sts.

Row 1 (wrong side): (P 1 k 1) 3 times, * p 1, k 3, repeat from * across, end p 1, k 3 (1-1-3).

Row 2: K 1 (3-3-1), p 1, * k 3, p 1, repeat from * to last 8 sts, end k 3, p 1, (k 1, p 1) twice. Mark end of row 2 for center front. Repeat these 2 rows until piece measures 2½" from start, end wrong side (side edge). Check gauge; piece should measure 9½" (10"-10½"-11") wide. Keeping to pat as established, dec 1 st at beg of next row, then dec 1 st at same edge every other row 5 times–52 (54-58-60) sts. Work even until piece measures 4" from start. Inc 1 st at side edge of next row, then every 4th row 5 times, working added sts into pat–58 (60-64-66) sts. Work even until piece measures 9" from start, end wrong side.

Popcorn Pattern: Next Row: Following chart, work from A to center st, end p 3, k 1, (k 1, p 1) 3 times.

Next Row: (P 1, k 1) 3 times, p 1, k 3, work from center st to A. Continue in this manner until all sts are worked in popcorn pat; at the same time, when piece measures same as back to underarm, shape armhole as follows: Bind off 6 (6-7-7) sts at beg of side edge once. Dec 1 st at same edge every other row 6 (6-7-7) times–46 (48-50-52) sts. Keeping to pat as established, work even until armhole measures 5" (5¼"-5½"-5¾") above first bound-off sts, end center edge.

Shape Neck and Shoulder: Work across first 7 sts, sl these sts on a holder, finish row. Keeping to pat, bind off 3 sts at beg of center edge 3 times. Dec 1 st at center edge every other row 9 (10-11-12) times; at the same time, when armhole measures same as back, bind off 7 (7-7-8) sts at beg of arm side twice, 7 (8-9-8) sts once.

With pins, mark position of 7 buttons evenly spaced on left center band, first one 1" above lower edge; 8th one to be made ½" above neck edge in neckband.

BUTTONHOLES: Beg at center edge, work 2 sts, bind off next 3 sts, finish row. **Next Row:** Cast on 3 sts over bound-off sts.

RIGHT FRONT: Beg at lower edge, cast on 58 (60-64-66) sts.

Row 1: (wrong side): K 3 (1-1-3), p 1, * k 3, p 1, repeat from * to last 6 sts, end (k 1, p 1) 3 times.

Row 2: (P 1, k 1) twice, * p 1, k 3, repeat from * across, end p 1, k 1 (3-3-1). Mark beg of row 2 for center front. Forming buttonholes (see Buttonholes) opposite markers, repeat these 2 rows until piece measures 2½" from start, end right side (side edge). Work as for left front until piece measures 9" from start, end wrong side.

Popcorn Pattern: Next Row: (P 1, k 1) 3 times, k 1, p 3; following chart, work from center st to A.

Next Row: Work from A to center st, end k 3, p 1, (k 1, p 1) 3 times. Complete as for left front.

SLEEVES: Work as for pullover.

FINISHING: Block pieces. Sew shoulder seams.

Neckband: From right side, work across sts on right front stitch holder, pick up and k 19 (19-18-18) sts on right front neck edge, work across 29 (31-35-37) sts on back holder, pick up and k 19 (19-18-18) sts on left front neck edge, work across sts on left front holder–81 (83-85-87) sts. Work in seed st as for center front bands for 1", forming buttonhole ½" above start of neckband. Bind off.

Sew in sleeves. Sew side and sleeve seams after completing embroidery.

EMBROIDERY: Embroider red roses as for pullover. For alternating flowers, work green outline stitch stems and blue straight stitch buds.

BUTTONS (make 8): Sc around ring; do not join.

Next Rnd: * Sk next sc, sc in next sc, repeat from * around. Cut yarn, leaving long end. Draw sts tog; sew buttons to left front band opposite buttonholes.

GIRL'S SNOW SET
Shown on page 45

SIZES: Directions for size 4. Changes for sizes 6 and 8 are in parentheses.

Body Chest Size: 23" (24"-26").

Blocked Chest Size: 26" (28"-30).

MATERIALS: Knitting worsted, 3 (3-4) 4-oz. skeins scarlet (MC), 1 skein each blue (B) and white (W). 14" straight knitting needles Nos. 6 and 8; 16" circular needle No. 6; 24" circular needle No. 8. Four stitch holders. Tapestry needle.

GAUGE: 5 sts = 1"; 7 rows = 1" (No. 8 needles).

Note: Triangle MC pat on B stripes and W pat on MC stripes are embroidered later in double duplicate stitch before assembling garment.

PULLOVER: BACK: Beg at lower edge, with MC and No. 6 straight needles, cast on 64 (70-74) sts. Work in ribbing of k 1, p 1 for 1½", inc 1 (0-1) st at end of last row–65 (70-75) sts. Change to No. 8 straight needles. Break off MC. With B, work in stockinette st (k 1 row, p 1 row) for 6 rows. Break off B. With MC, work in stockinette st until piece measures 10½" (11½"-12½") from start or desired length to underarm, end p row. Check gauge; piece should measure 13" (14"-15") wide.

Shape Underarms: Bind off 1 st at beg of every row 8 (10-12) times–57 (60-63) sts. Sl sts on a st holder for yoke.

FRONT: Work as for back. Sl sts on a st holder for yoke.

SLEEVES: Beg at lower edge, with MC and No. 6 straight needles, cast on 32 (34-36) sts. Work in ribbing of k 1, p 1 for 1½", inc 4 (2-0) sts evenly spaced across last row–36 sts. Change to No. 8 straight needles. Break off MC. With B, work in stockinette st for 6 rows. Break off B. With MC, work in stockinette st for 6 rows, then inc 1 st each side every inch 5 (7-9) times–46 (50-54) sts. Work even until piece measures 11½" (12½"-13½") from start or desired length to underarm. Check gauge; piece should measure 9" (10"-11") wide above last inc row.

Shape Underarm: Work same as back armholes. Sl remaining 38 (40-42) sts on a st holder for yoke. Make other sleeve.

Yoke: From wrong side, sl sts from holders of back, one sleeve, front and other sleeve to No. 8 circular needle–190 (200-210) sts. From right side, join MC at beg of back, k around for 1 rnd. Put a marker on needle at end of last rnd. Do not turn.

First Dec Rnd: K 1 rnd, dec 34 (38-42) sts evenly spaced (about 1 st every 5 sts)–156 (162-168) sts. * Break off MC. With B, k 6 rnds. Break off B. With MC, k 7 rnds *.

2nd Dec Rnd: With MC, k 1 rnd, dec 30 sts evenly spaced (about 1 st every 5 sts)–126 (132-138) sts. Repeat from first * to 2nd * of first dec rnd.

3rd Dec Rnd: With MC, k 1 rnd, dec 30 sts evenly spaced (about 1 st every 4 sts)–96 (102-108) sts.

Break off MC. With B, k 6 rnds. Break off B. Change to No. 6 circular needle.

4th Dec Rnd: With MC, k 1 rnd, dec 34 sts evenly spaced (about 1 st every 3 sts)–62 (68-74) sts. With MC, work around in ribbing of k 1, p 1 for 1". Bind off loosely in ribbing.

FINISHING: Steam-press pieces. Do not press ribbing. Sew raglan seams.

TRIANGLE PATTERN: To Embroider: With tapestry needle, work in double duplicate stitch, working each st over 2 rows of knitting.

For Front and Backs: Mark center of B stripe on lower edges. Following chart, start at center and work toward sides; work triangle pat, working V symbol with MC on B stripe, X symbol with W on MC stripe.

For Yoke: Mark center of first B stripe on front yoke. Work and repeat from A to C on chart around yoke.

For Sleeves: Starting at right side of work on B stripe, work and repeat across from A to C on chart.

Run in all yarn ends on wrong side. Sew side and sleeve seams. Steam-press seams.

HAT: With MC and No. 6 straight needles, cast on 78 (84-90) sts. Work in ribbing of k 1, p 1 for 9 rows. Break off MC. Change to No. 8 needles. * With B, work in stockinette st for 6 rows. Break off B. With MC, work in stockinette st for 8 rows. Repeat from * twice.

First Dec Row: With MC, k 2 tog across–39 (42-45) sts. P 1 row.

2nd Dec Row: K 2 tog across, end k 1 (0-1)–20 (21-23) sts. P 1 row.

3rd Dec Row: K 2 tog across, end k 0 (1-1)–10 (11-12) sts. P 1 row.

4th Dec Row: K 2 tog across, end k 0 (1-0)–5 (6-6) sts. P 1 row. Break yarn, leaving long end for sewing. With tapestry needle, pull yarn end through sts, draw sts up tightly and fasten securely on wrong side. Embroider as for sleeves. Sew back seam. Steam-press. With MC, make pompon. Attach to top of hat, trim to rounded shape.

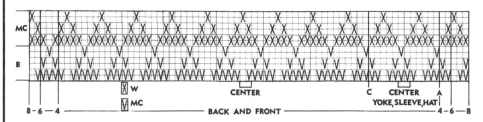

MC · B · 8-6-4 · W · MC · CENTER · BACK AND FRONT · C · CENTER · A · YOKE, SLEEVE, HAT · 4-6-8

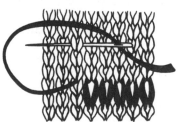

DOUBLE DUPLICATE STITCH

FLOWER-SPRAY CARDIGANS
Shown on page 36

SIZES: Directions for girl's size 4. Changes for girls' sizes 6 and 8, misses' sizes 10, 12, 14 and 16 are in parentheses.

Note: Before making garment, circle sts and measurements in size you plan to make.

Body Chest or Bust Size: 23" (24"-27"-32½"-34"-36"-38").

Blocked Chest or Bust Size (closed): 25½" (27"-29"-36"-37½"-39½"-41").

MATERIALS: Knitting worsted, 4 (5-6-8-9-9-10) 2-oz. skeins white; 1 ball each of pink, light blue, yellow and light green for embroidery. 14" knitting needles Nos. 6 and 8. Steel crochet hook No. 0. Six buttons for girl's cardigan; eight buttons for misses' cardigan. Tapestry needle. One stitch holder.

GAUGE: 9 sts = 2"; 6 rows = 1" (No. 8 needles).

Note: Bind off in p on wrong side; bind off in k (omit pat) on right side. Work all other sts in pat. When decreasing or increasing, k any sts of broken pats on right side keeping to correct number of sts.

CARDIGAN: BACK: Beg at lower edge with No. 6 needles and white, cast on 55 (59-63-77-81-85-89) sts.

Row 1 (right side): K 1, * p 1, k 1, repeat from * across.

Row 2: P 1, * k 1, p 1, repeat from * across. Repeat these 2 rows for 2" (2"-3"-3"-3"-3"), end right side. P 1 row, inc 1 st at beg and end of row–57 (61-65-79-83-87-91) sts. Change to No. 8 needles.

Pattern: Row 1: (right side): K 5 (7-9-5-7-9-11), * yo, sl 1 as if to k, k 2 tog, psso, yo, k 8, repeat from * across, end last repeat k 5 (7-9-5-7-9-11).

Row 2 and All Even Rows: Purl.

Row 3: K 4 (6-8-4-6-8-10), * yo, k 2 tog, k 1, k 2 tog, yo, k 6, repeat from * across, end last repeat k 4 (6-8-4-6-8-10).

Row 5: Repeat row 1.

Row 7: Knit.

Row 8: Purl. Repeat these 8 rows for pat until piece measures 10" (10½"-11"-14"-14"-14"-14") from start or desired length to underarm, end wrong side. Check gauge; piece above ribbing should measure 12½" (13½"-14½"-17½"-18½"-19¼"-20") wide.

Shape Armholes: Bind off 3 (3-3-5-5-5-5) sts at beg of next 2 rows. Dec 1 st each side every other row 3 (3-3-4-4-4-4) times–45 (49-53-61-65-69-73) sts. Work even until armholes measure 5" (5½"-5¾"-7"-7"-7¼"-7½"-8") above first bound-off sts, end p row.

Shape Shoulders: Bind off 5 (5-5-6-6-7-7) sts at beg of next 4 rows, 4 (5-6-7-8-7-8) sts next 2 rows. Sl remaining 17 (19-21-23-25-27-29) sts on a holder.

LEFT FRONT: Beg at lower edge with No. 6 needles and white, cast on 33 (35-37-45-47-49-51) sts. Work in ribbing as for back for 2" (2"-2"-3"-3"-3"-3"), end right side.

Next Row: Work first 6 (6-6-8-8-8-8) sts in ribbing, sl these sts on a safety pin to be worked later, p across, inc 0 (0-0-1-1-1-1) st in last st–27 (29-31-38-40-42-44) sts. Change to No. 8 needles.

Pattern: Row 1 (right side): K 5 (7-9-5-7-9-11), * yo, sl 1, k 2 tog, psso, yo, k 8, repeat from * across. P 1 row. Work in pat as established until piece measures same as back to underarm. Check gauge; piece above ribbing should measure 6" (6½"-7"-8½"-9"-9½"-10") wide.

Shape Armhole: Bind off 3 (3-3-5-5-5-5) sts at beg of arm side once. Dec 1 st at same edge every other row 3 (3-3-4-4-4-4) times–21 (23-25-29-31-33-35) sts. Work even until armhole measures 3¾" (4"-4¼"-5"-5¼"-5½"-5¾") above first bound-off sts, end center edge.

Shape Neck and Shoulder: Work 4 (5-6-6-7-8-9) sts, sl these sts on a safety pin, finish row. Dec 1 st at neck edge very other row 3 (3-3-4-4-4-4) times; at the same time, when armhole measures same as back, bind off 5 (5-5-6-6-7-7) sts at beg of arm side twice, 4 (5-6-7-8-7-8) sts once.

BUTTONHOLES: Work 2 (2-2-3-3-3-3) sts at beg of center edge, bind off next 2 sts, finish row. Next Row: Cast on 2 sts over bound-off sts.

RIGHT FRONT: Cast on and work ribbing same as for left front for 1" (1"-1"-1½"-1½"-1½"-1½"), end wrong side (center edge). Keeping to ribbing, form buttonhole on next 2 rows. Work in ribbing until piece measures 2" (2"-2"-3"-3"-3"-3") from start, end right side.

Next Row: Inc 0 (0-0-1-1-1-1) st in first st , p to last 6 (6-6-8-8-8-8) sts, sl these 6 (6-6-8-8-8-8) sts on a safety pin · 27 (29-31-38-40-42-44) sts. Change to No. 8 needles.

Pattern: Row 1 (right side): K 8, * yo, sl 1, k 2 tog, psso, yo, k 8, repeat from * across, end last repeat k 5 (7-9-5-7-9-11). P 1 row. Complete as for left front, reversing shaping.

SLEEVES: Beg at lower edge with No. 6 needles and white, cast on 27 (27-29-39-39-41-41) sts. Work in ribbing as for back for 2" (2"-2"-3"-3"-3"-3"), end right side. P 1 row, inc 2 (2-2-1-1-1-1) sts on row–29 (29-31-40-40-42-42) sts. Change to No. 8 needles.

Pattern: Row 1 (right side): K 2 (2-3-2-2-3-3), * yo, sl 1, k 2 tog, psso, yo, k 8, repeat from * across, end last repeat k 2 (2-3-2-2-3-3). P 1 row. Working in pat as established, inc 1 st each side every 1" 7 (8-8-10-11-11-12) times, working added sts into pat–43 (45-47-60-62-64-66) sts. Work even until piece measures 11" (12"-13"-17"-17"-17½"-17½") from start or desired length to underarm, end wrong side. Check gauge; piece above last inc row should measure 9½" (10"-10½"-13¼"-13¾"-14¼"-14¾") wide.

FLOWER-SPRAY CARDIGANS
Continued

Shape Cap: Keeping to pat, bind off 3 (3-3-5-5-5-5-) sts at beg of next 2 rows. Dec 1 st each side every other row 7 (8-9-11-12-13-14) times. Bind off 3 sts at beg of next 4 rows. Bind off remaining 11 (11-11-16-16-16-16) sts.

Left Center Band: Sl 6 (6-6-8-8-8-8) sts from safety pin above ribbing to No. 6 needle. From right side, join white at inner edge; work in ribbing as established until band, when slightly stretched, is same length as left front edge, end at inside edge. Cut yarn, sl sts on a safety pin.

With pins, mark position of 4 (4-4-6-6-6-6) buttons evenly spaced on left center band (last buttonhole will be on neckband).

Right Center Band: Work as for left front band, forming buttonholes opposite markers, end at inside edge. Do not cut yarn.

With backstitch, sew shoulder seams.

Neckband: From right side, with No. 6 needle of right center band, k across 4 (5-6-6-7-8-9) sts on safety pin, pick up and k 10 (10-10-14-14-14-14) sts on right neck edge, k across sts on back stitch holder, dec 2 sts evenly spaced, pick up and k 10 (10-10-14-14-14-14) sts on left neck edge, k across 4 (5-6-6-7-8-9) sts on safety pin, work in ribbing as established across left center band–57 (61-65-77-81-85-89) sts. Work in ribbing for 3 (3-3-5-5-5-5) rows, end right front edge. Keeping to ribbing, form buttonhole on next 2 rows. Work 2 (2-2-4-4-4-4) rows even. Bind off loosely in ribbing.

FINISHING: Sew center bands to front edges. Sew in sleeves; sew side and sleeve seams. Steampress lightly. Split yarn, work buttonhole stitch around buttonholes. From right side, with crochet hook and white, work 1 row sl st on left front edge. Do not turn. Working from left to right inserting hook from front to back, * ch 1, sk

next st, hdc in next st, repeat from * across. End off. Work same edging on right front edge. Sew on buttons.

Embroidery: On each 8-stitch stockinette panel, with green, embroider stems and leaves of flowers in straight stitches; for buds, work 3 lazy daisy stitches in graduated sizes. See page 282. Use yellow, blue and pink for alternate buds. Work flowers straight up on middle panel of misses' fronts and sleeves; slant others to right, and left.

LACE PATTERN BABY SET
Shown on page 37

SIZE: Infants to six months.

Fits Chest: Up to 19″.

MATERIALS: Baby yarn, 4 1-oz. balls. Knitting needles Nos. 1 and 2; set of dp needles No. 2. Steel crochet hook No. 2. Two stitch holders. Three buttons. Pink and white six-strand embroidery floss. Embroidery needle.

GAUGE: 8 sts = 1″; 11 rows = 1″ (pat, No. 2 needles).

Pattern Note: Sl all sl sts through back lp.

PATTERN (multiple of 8 sts plus 5): **Row 1** (right side); K 1, * yo, sl 1 (see Note), k 2 tog, psso, yo, k 1, repeat from * across.

Rows 2, 4 and 6: K 1, p across to last st, k 1.

Rows 3 and 5: K 1, * yo, sl 1, k 2 tog, psso, yo, k 5, repeat from * across, end last repeat yo, k 1.

Row 7: K 1, * k 3, yo, k 2 tog through back lps, k 1, k 2 tog through front lps, yo, repeat from * across, end k 4.

Row 8: Repeat row 2. Repeat these 8 rows for pat.

SWEATER: BODY: Beg at lower edge of back and fronts, with No. 2 needles, cast on 205 sts. Work in ribbing of k 1, p 1 for 1 row. Work the 8 rows of pat 8 times, then work row 1 (65 rows). Check gauge; piece should measure 25½″ wide, about 5½″ from start. Change to No. 1 needles.

Dec Row: K 1, p 15, * p 2 tog, p 8, repeat from * 16 times, p 2 tog, p 16, k 1 – 187 sts.

Divide Work: Right Front Yoke: K 1, yo, sl 1, k 2 tog, psso, yo, k 5, yo, sl 1, k 2 tog, psso, yo, k 32 – 44 sts. Sl next 99 sts to one holder (back), last 44 sts to another holder (left front). Working on right front, work as follows:

Shape Armhole: Bind off 2 sts, * p 1, k 1, repeat from * across to last 12 sts, p 11, k 1 – 42 sts.

Next Row: K 1, yo, sl 1, k 2 tog, psso, yo, k 5, yo, sl 1, k 2 tog, psso, yo, work in ribbing as established across.

Next Row: Bind off 2 sts, work in ribbing as established to last 12 sts, p 11, k 1 – 40 sts.

Next Row: K 4, yo, k 2 tog through back lps, k

1, k 2 tog through front lps, yo, k 3, finish row in ribbing.

Next Row: Work in ribbing to last 12 sts, p 11, k 1. Continue to work in this manner working 12 sts in pat, 28 sts in ribbing as established until 4 complete patterns plus rows 1 and 2 have been worked on the yoke, end center edge. (**On left front,** work 1 row less, end center edge.)

Shape Neck and Shoulder: Bind off 12 sts at beg of center edge once, finish row in ribbing – 28 sts. Work in ribbing until armhole measures 3¾". Bind off in ribbing for shoulder.

Left Front Yoke. Sl 44 sts from holder to No. 1 needle. Join yarn at underarm. K 32, yo, sl 1, k 2 tog, psso, yo, k 5, yo, sl 1, k 2 tog, psso, yo, k 1.

Next Row: K 1, p 11, work in k 1, p 1, ribbing across – 44 sts.

Shape Armhole: Working in pat and ribbing as established, bind off 2 sts at beg of arm side twice–40 sts. Complete left front yoke as for right front yoke reversing shaping and noting changes in directions.

Back Yoke: Sl 99 sts of back to No. 1 needles. Join yarn at right underarm.

Shape Armhole: Bind off first 6 sts, k across.

Next Row: Bind off first 6 sts, work in k 1, p 1 ribbing across – 87 sts. Working in ribbing as established, bind off 2 sts at beg of next 4 rows – 79 sts. Work even in ribbing until armholes measure 3½" above first bound-off sts.

Shape Neck and Shoulders: Work across first 28 sts, join another strand of yarn, bind off next 23 sts in ribbing for neck, finish row in ribbing – 28 sts each side. Work 3 more rows of ribbing on each shoulder. Bind off in ribbing.

SLEEVES: With No. 1 needles, cast on 53 sts. Work in ribbing as follows:

Row 1 (right side): K 1, * p 1, k 1, repeat from * across.

Row 2: P 1, * k 1, p 1, repeat from * across. Repeat these 2 rows for ¾", end row 2. Work in pat for 8 rows. Change to No. 2 needles and continue in pat until 8 complete patterns have been worked above ribbing (64 rows).

Shape Sleeve Cap: Keeping to pat, bind off 10 sts at beg of next 4 rows. Bind off remaining 13 sts.

FINISHING: Steam-press pieces lightly. With backstitch, sew shoulder and sleeve seams. Sew in sleeves.

With pins, mark position of 3 buttonholes evenly spaced on right front edge of yoke, first one 3 rows above start of yoke, last one 3 rows below neck edge.

Buttonholes: Join yarn with sc at lower edge of right front yoke. (Ch 3, sk 5 rows, work sc on front edge to within 2 rows of next pin) twice, ch 3, sk 5 rows, sc in last row. End off.

Edging: From right side, join yarn with sc in lower edge at right underarm. Work sc around outer edge of sweater, working 3 sc in each corner and 2 sc in each ch-3 buttonhole, keeping work flat. Join with sl st in first sc. Do not turn.

Row 2 (right side): Ch 1, working from **left** to **right**, sc in each sc around. End off. Sew on buttons.

BONNET: Beg at front edge, with No. 2 needles, cast on 101 sts. Work in pat for 17 rows, end row 1. Change to No. 1 needles. Work rows 1 and 2 of ribbing as for sleeve for 1". Change to No. 2 needles and continue in ribbing until piece measures 6¼" from start, end row 2, cast on 9 sts – 110 sts.

Shape Crown: Change to No. 2 dp needles. On first needle, (p 1, k 1) 4 times, p 1 across 9 cast-on sts; beg with k 1, work in ribbing as established across next 29 sts; work 36 sts in ribbing on each of 2nd and 3rd needles. Join, being careful not to twist sts.

Rnd 1: * (P 1, k 1) 4 times, k 2 tog, repeat from * around – 99 sts.

Rnd 2: * (P 1, k 1) 4 times, k 1, repeat from * around.

Rnd 3: * (P 1, k 1) 3 times, p 1, k 2 tog, repeat from * around–88 sts.

Rnd 4: (P 1, k 1) around.

Rnd 5: * (P 1, k 1) 3 times, k 2 tog, repeat from * around – 77 sts.

Rnd 6: * (P 1, k 1) 3 times, k 1, repeat from * around. Continue to dec 11 sts every other rnd having 1 st less between each dec until 11 sts remain. Cut yarn leaving 10" end; draw remaining sts tog, fasten neatly on wrong side.

Front Edging: From right side of cuff, work 1 row sc across cast-on edge. Do not turn.

Next Row: Working from left to **right**, sc in each sc across.

Bottom Edging and Beading: Fold cuff back at start of ribbing to right side. From right side, join yarn at front corner.

Row 1: Working through cuff and bonnet, work sc across bottom edge. Ch 1, turn.

Row 2: Sc in each of first 2 sc, * ch 3, sk 2 sc. Ch 1, turn.

Row 3: Sc in each sc, working 2 sc in each ch-3 sp. End off.

Cord: Using 2 strands of yarn, make a chain about 34" long. Draw through beading. Sew a pompon to cord ends (see page 283).

Embroidery: Make pink bullion stitch rosebuds, white lazy daisy stitch leaves as shown in illustration. See stitch details, page 282.

DIAGONAL STRIPE PILLOW
Shown on page 104

SIZE: About 14″ square.

MATERIALS: Knitting worsted, 1 4-oz. skein each of fuchsia (MC), pink (A), violet (B). Knitting needles No. 6. Two large bobbins. Knife-edge pillow form, 14″ square.

GAUGE: 5 sts = 1″.

Pattern Notes: Note 1: Wind bobbins with MC. First and last 7 sts are always worked in seed st with MC.

Note 2: When changing colors, pick up new strand from under dropped strand. Always change colors on wrong side of work; carry unused colors loosely up wrong side of work.

Note 3: Sl all sl sts as if to p with yarn in back of work on right side rows, in front of work on wrong side rows.

SEED STITCH: Row 1: K 1, * p 1, k 1, repeat from * across. Repeat this row for seed st, having k 1 over a p st and p 1 over a k st.

PILLOW COVER: With MC, cast on 85 sts. Work in seed st for 14 rows.

Row 15 (right side): With MC (on bobbin), work first 7 sts in seed st (border); with B, k 1, * sl 1 (see Note 3), k 1, repeat from * across to last 7 sts; with 2nd bobbin of MC, work last 7 sts in seed st (border).

Row 16: Work border; with A, sl 1 (see Note 3), * p 1, sl 1, repeat from * across to last 7 sts; work border.

Row 17: Work border; with MC, k 1, * sl 1, k 1, repeat from * across to last 7 sts; work border.

Row 18: Work border; with B, sl 1, * p 1, sl 1, repeat from * across to last 7 sts; work border.

Row 19: Work border; with A, k 1, * sl 1, k 1, repeat from * across to last 7 sts; work border.

Row 20: Work border; with MC, sl 1, * p 1, sl 1, repeat from * across to last 7 sts; work border.

Rows 21–32: Repeat rows 15–20 twice.

Row 33: Work border; with B, k across to last 7 sts; work border.

Rows 34–40: Work border; with B, k 1, * p 1, k 1, repeat from * across to last 7 sts; work border.

Row 41: Repeat row 17.

Row 42: Work border; with MC, p across to last 7 sts; work border.

Row 43: Repeat row 19.

Row 44: Work border; with A, p across to last 7 sts; work border.

Row 45: Repeat row 15.

Row 46: Work border; with B, p across to last 7 sts; work border.

Rows 47 and 48: Repeat rows 43 and 44.

Rows 49–64: Repeat rows 41–48 twice.

Rows 65 and 66: Repeat rows 41 and 42.

Rows 67–74: Repeat rows 33–40.

Row 75: Repeat row 33.

Rows 76–87: Work from row 20 back to row 15 twice.

Rows 88–92: Work from row 20 back to row 16.

Rows 93–152: Repeat rows 33–92. Cut off A and B.

Next Row: Work border; with MC, k across to last 7 sts; work border. With MC, work in seed st for 13 rows. Bind off loosely in seed st.

FINISHING: Run in all yarn ends. Block pillow cover square. Fold in half, wrong sides tog; weave top and bottom seams. Stretch cover over pillow form working seamed sides over two diagonal corners. Weave remaining seam, working from center to each corner.

REVERSE STRIPE PILLOW
Shown on page 104

SIZE: 14″ square.

MATERIALS: Knitting worsted, 1 4-oz. skein each of beige (MC), brick red (A), dark turquoise (B), off-white (C). Knitting needles No. 6. Knife-edge pillow form, 14″ square.

GAUGE: 5 sts = 1″.

Pattern Notes: Note 1: Sl all sl sts as if to p with yarn in back of work on k rows, in front of work on p rows.

Note 2: Cut and join colors as needed, leaving 8″ ends for weaving seams when pillow is completed.

PILLOW COVER: With MC, cast on 129 sts. P 1 row.

Pattern: Row 1 (right side): With A, k 1, sl 1 (see Note 1), * k 5, sl 1, repeat from * across, end k 1.

Row 2: With A, p 1, sl 1 (see Note 1), * p 5, sl 1, repeat from * across, end p 1.

Row 3: With MC, k 4, sl 1, * k 5, sl 1, repeat from * across, end k 4.

Row 4: With MC, p 4, sl 1, * p 5, sl 1, repeat from * across, end p 4.

Row 5: With A, k 3, * sl 1, k 1, sl 1, k 3, repeat from * across.

Row 6: With A, p 3, * sl 1, p 1, sl 1, p 3, repeat from * across.

Rows 7 and 8: Repeat rows 3 and 4.

Rows 9 and 10: Repeat rows 1 and 2.

Rows 11 and 12: With MC, knit. Cut A; join B.

Row 13 (right side): Working with B instead of A, repeat row 2 (pat stripe is reversed).

Row 14: With B, repeat row 1.

Row 15: Repeat row 4.

Row 16: Repeat row 3.

Row 17: With B, repeat row 6.

Row 18: With B, repeat row 5.

Continued on page 276

LILY POND BEDSPREAD
Shown on page 112

SIZES: Directions for afghan about 52″ × 73″. Changes for bedspreads about 83″ × 110″ and 94″ × 110″, including fringe are in parentheses.
MATERIALS: Bear Brand, Fleisher's or Botany Spectator, 25 (59–66) 2-oz. balls. Knitting needles No. 6. Crochet hook size F.
GAUGE: Each small square should measure about 4½″ before blocking.
SMALL SQUARE [make 96 (280–320)]: Cast on 3 sts.

Row 1 (wrong side): Knit.
Row 2: Inc 1 st in first st, k 1, inc 1 st in last st—5 sts.
Row 3: K 1, p 3, k 1.
Row 4: Inc 1 st in first st, k 1, yo, k 1, yo, k 1, inc 1 st in last st—9 sts.
Row 5: K 2, p 5, k 2.
Row 6: Inc 1 st in first st, k 3, yo, k 1, yo, k 3, inc 1 st in last st—13 sts.
Row 7: K 3, p 7, k 3.
Row 8: Inc 1 st in first st, k 5, yo, k 1, yo, k 5, inc 1 st in last st—17 sts.
Row 9: K 4, p 9, k 4.
Row 10: Inc 1 st in first st, k 7, yo, k 1, yo, k 7, inc 1 st in last st—21 sts.
Row 11: K 5, p 11, k 5.
Row 12: Inc 1 st in first st, k 9, yo, k 1, yo, k 9, inc 1 st in last st—25 sts.
Row 13: K 6, p 13, k 6.
Row 14: Inc 1 st in first st, k 11, yo, k 1, yo, k 11, inc 1 st in last st—29 sts.
Row 15: K 7, p 15, k 7.
Row 16: Inc 1 st in first st, k 6, k 2 tog, k 11, sl 1, k 1, psso, k 6, inc 1 st in last st—29 sts.
Row 17: K 8, p 13, k 8.
Row 18: Inc 1 st in first st, k 7, k 2 tog, k 9, sl 1, k 1, psso, k 7, inc 1 st in last st—29 sts.
Row 19: K 9, p 11, k 9.
Row 20: Inc 1 st in first st, k 8, k 2 tog, k 7, sl 1, k 1, psso, k 8, inc 1 st in last st.
Row 21: K 10, p 9, k 10.
Row 22: Inc 1 st in first st, k 9, k 2 tog, k 5, sl 1, k 1, psso, k 9, inc 1 st in last st.
Row 23: K 11, p 7, k 11.
Row 24: Inc 1 st in first st, k 10, k 2 tog, k 3, sl 1, k 1, psso, k 10, inc 1 st in last st.
Row 25: K 12, p 5, k 12.
Row 26: Inc 1 st in first st, k 11, k 2 tog, k 1, sl 1, k 1, psso, k 11, inc 1 st in last st.
Row 27: K 13, p 3, k 13.

Row 28: Inc 1 st in first st, k 12, k next 3 sts tog, k 12, inc 1 st in last st—29 sts.
Row 29: Purl.
Row 30: K 1, * yo, k 2 tog, repeat from * to end—29 sts.
Row 31: Purl.
Row 32: Inc 1 st in first st, k to within 1 st of end, inc 1 st in last st—31 sts.
Row 33: Knit.
Row 34: Inc 1 st in first st, p to within 1 st of end, inc 1 st in last st—33 sts.
Row 35: Knit
Row 36: K 2 tog, k to within 2 sts of end, k 2 tog—31 sts.
Row 37: Purl.
Row 38: K 2 tog, * k 2 tog, yo; repeat from * to within 3 sts of end, k 2 tog, k 1—29 sts.
Row 39: Purl.
Row 40: K 2 tog, k to within 2 sts of end, k 2 tog—27 sts.
Row 41: Knit.
Row 42: P 2 tog, p to within 2 sts of end, p 2 tog—25 sts.
Row 43: Knit.
Row 44: K 2 tog, k to within 2 sts of end, k 2 tog—23 sts.
Row 45: Purl.
Rows 46–61: Repeat rows 38–45 twice—7 sts.
Row 62: K 2 tog, k 2 tog, yo, k 2 tog, k 1—5 sts.
Row 63: Purl.
Row 64: K 2 tog, k 1, k 2 tog—3 sts. Bind off.

FINISHING: Arrange 4 small squares to form a large square, as shown on chart. From right side, with care to have rows matching and seams elastic, sew from outer edge to center through knots at ends of adjacent rows. Close center by inserting needle under center st in first row of each petal and drawing tog. End off. Block large squares to 10½″ × 10½″ with care not to flatten petals and ridges.

Arrange large squares as illustrated, having 4 (7–8) squares in width, 6 (10–10) squares in length. From right side, with care to have pat matching and to keep seams elastic, sew large squares tog. From right side, work 1 row sc around entire edge, with 3 sc in each corner; join with sl st in first st.

FRINGE: Wind yarn around an 11″ cardboard; cut at one end.
For Bedspread Only: Row 1: Knot a 6 strand fringe in upper right corner st and at each seam along both sides and lower edges only, with 6 6-

strand fringes evenly spaced between, end with last fringe in upper left corner st, leaving entire upper edge unfringed.

Row 2: From right side, leaving 6 strands free, knot 6 strands of first fringe and 6 strands of 2nd fringe tog, about 1″ below first row of knots; knot remaining 6 strands of 2nd fringe and 6 strands of 3rd fringe tog, about 1″ below first row of knots; continue across, knotting 6 strands of last fringe and 6 strands of next fringe tog, having knots 1″ below and midway between knots of last row, end with last 6 strands free.

Row 3: From right side, knot first 6 free strands and 6 strands under first knot of last row tog, 1″ below last row of knots; knot remaining 6 strands under last knot of last row and 6 strands under next knot of last row, continue across, end by knotting remaining 6 strands under last knot and last 6 free strands tog.

Trim fringe evenly.

For Afghan: Work fringe in same manner as for bedspread on all 4 sides.

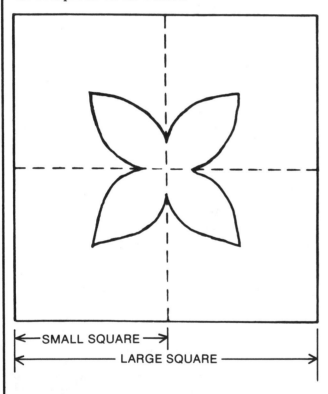

←— SMALL SQUARE —→

←———— LARGE SQUARE ————→

POPCORN PILLOWS
Shown on page 110

SIZES: 16″ square and 14″ × 20″.
MATERIALS: Columbia-Minerva Nantuk 4-Ply, 1 4-oz. skein each Winter White (W), Navy (N), Cranberry (C), Wood Brown (B), Birch Green (G), Sapphire (S). Circular knitting needle No. 7. Steel crochet hook size 00. Pillow form.

GAUGE: 4 sts = 1″; 6 rows = 1″.
SQUARE PILLOW (make 2 pieces): With N, cast on 64 sts. Work in stockinette st (k 1 row, p 1 row) for 8 rows, end p row. Cut N.

FIRST PAT STRIPE: Rows 1 and 2: With W, k 1 row, p 1 row. Drop W.

Row 3: Join C; with C, * with yarn in front, sl 1 as if to p; with yarn in back, k 1, repeat from * across. Drop C. Do not turn.

Rows 4–6: Pick up W. With W, k 1 row, p 1 row, k 1 row. Drop W.

Row 7: Pick up C. With C, * p 1; with yarn in back, sl 1 as if to p, repeat from * across. Cut C. Do not turn.

Rows 8 and 9: With W, p 1 row, k 1 row. Cut W.

Rows 10–18: With N, beg with p row, work 9 rows in stockinette st. Cut N.

Rows 19 and 20: With C, k 2 rows. Cut C.
Rows 21 and 22: With B, k 2 rows. Cut B.
2ND PAT STRIPE: Rows 23–36: With W, beg with a k row, work 14 rows in stockinette st. Cut W.

Rows 37 and 38: With B, k 2 rows. Cut B.
3RD PAT STRIPE: Rows 39–44: With N, beg with a k row, work 6 rows in stockinette st. Cut N.

Rows 45 and 46: With B, k 2 rows. Cut B.
4TH PAT STRIPE: Rows 47–60: Repeat rows 23–36.

Rows 61 and 62: With B, k 2 rows. Cut B.
Rows 63 and 64: With C, k 2 rows. Cut C.
Rows 65–73: With N, beg and ending with a k row, work in stockinette st for 9 rows. Cut N. Do not turn.

5TH PAT STRIPE: Rows 74–82: Join W, at beg of last row work as for First Pat Stripe, rows 1–9. Cut W. With N, work 8 rows in stockinette st. Bind off.

PICOT POPCORN PAT (worked on 2nd and 4th pat stripes): Cut 3-yard length of B. Make lp on hook, count off 7 sts from right-hand edge of 2nd pat stripe (14 rows of W stockinette st). Working around 8th st of 2nd row, insert hook in hole to right of 8th st, bring hook up in hole to left of same st, yo hook, bring yarn through st and lp on hook; * ch 5, sc in 5th ch from hook; drop lp from hook; bring hook up from wrong side in hole to left of same st, catch lp, bring complete length of B through to back of work (popcorn made). Sk 1 row above; bring complete length of B through to front in hole to right of next st (9th st) on 4th row; insert hook under st, bring lp of yarn up; repeat from * for popcorns, making diamond shaped design of 12 B popcorns as shown in Chart 1. At center, work 1 C popcorn. Sk 15 sts on 2nd row, work another diamond with S. Sk 15 sts on 2nd row, work another diamond with G. Sk 15 sts on 2nd row, work another diamond with B.

Work 4th pat stripe in same way changing position of G and S diamonds. Bring all hanging ends through to wrong side.

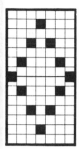 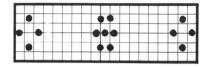

CHART 2

CHART 1

BOBBLE PAT (worked on 3rd pat stripe): Cut 3-yard length of S. Make lp on hook. Working on 6-row N stripe, following Chart 2, work 4-bobble pats directly in line with diamond pats on 2nd and 4th pat stripes. To work bobble, insert hook under st, pull lp through st and lp on hook; * (yo hook, pull up a lp in st) 4 times, yo and through all 9 lps on hook, ch 1; drop lp from hook; bring hook up from wrong side in same st, catch lp, bring complete length of S through to back of work (bobble made). To make next bobble, bring yarn up to right side of work in position for next bobble. Insert hook under st, pull lp through st, repeat from *. With C, work 7-bobble pat spaced evenly between 4-bobble pats. Bring all hanging ends through to wrong side.

FINISHING: Sew 2 pillow pieces tog from wrong side, leaving bottom edge open. Insert pillow form, close bottom opening.

Fringe: Cut W in 8″ lengths. Using 3 strands tog, knot fringe along top and bottom edges of pillow, placing fringes about ¾″ apart.

OBLONG PILLOW (make 2 pieces): With W, cast on 80 sts. Follow directions for square pillow from First Pat Stripe through 5th Pat Stripe. Bind off.

Work Picot Popcorn Pat on 2nd and 4th pat stripes and Bobble Pat on 3rd Pat Stripe same as for square pillow. See illustration for color arrangement. Finish as for square pillow.

ROSE AFGHAN
Shown on page 111

AFGHAN: SIZE: 56″ × 48″, plus fringe.
MATERIALS: Columbia-Minerva Nantuk 4-Ply, 15 4-oz. skeins Winter White (W). For Embroidery (afghan and pillow): 1 skein each of Scarlet, Imperial Blue, Kelly Green. Knitting needles No. 13. Crochet hook size I. Tapestry needle.

GAUGE: 11 sts = 4″; 4 rows = 1″ (double strand of yarn).

Note: Popcorn: K very loosely in front and back of 1 st until there are 5 sts in 1 st, sl st worked in off left-hand needle, (with left-hand needle, pass 2nd st from tip of right-hand needle over and off needle) 4 times (1 st of group left).

AFGHAN: Panels 1, 3 and 5: With double strand of W, cast on 29 sts. K 1 row, p 1 row.

Row 3 (right side): K 14, popcorn in next st (see Note), k 14.

Row 4: P 13, k 3, p 13.
Row 5: K 13, p 3, k 13.
Row 6: P 12, k 5, p 12.
Row 7: K 12, p 5, k 12.
Row 8: P 11, k 7, p 11.
Row 9: K 10, popcorn in next st, p 7, popcorn in next st, k 10.
Row 10: P 9, k 11, p 9.
Row 11: K 9, p 11, k 9.
Row 12: P 8, k 13, p 8.
Row 13: K 8, p 13, k 8.
Row 14: P 7, k 15, p 7.
Row 15: K 6, popcorn in next st, p 15, popcorn in next st, k 6.
Row 16: P 5, k 19, p 5.
Row 17: K 5, p 19, k 5.
Row 18: P 4, k 21, p 4.
Row 19: K 4, p 21, k 4.
Row 20: P 1, k 1, p 1, k 23, p 1, k 1, p 1.
Row 21: K 1, p 1, popcorn in next st, p 23, popcorn in next st, p 1, k 1.
Rows 22–39: Working back from row 20, work in pat to row 3. Repeat rows 4–39, 5 times more—6 diamonds in all. P 1 row, k 1 row. Bind off in p.

Panels 2 and 4: With double strand of W, cast on 23 sts. K 1 row, p 1 row.

Row 3 (right side): K 11, popcorn in next st, k 11.
Row 4: P 10, k 3, p 10.
Row 5: K 10, p 3, k 10.
Row 6: P 9, k 5, p 9.
Row 7: K 9, p 5, k 9.
Row 8: P 8, k 7, p 8.
Row 9: K 7, popcorn in next st, p 7, popcorn in next st, k 7.
Row 10: P 6, k 11, p 6.
Row 11: K 6, p 11, k 6.
Row 12: P 5, k 13, p 5.
Row 13: K 5, p 13, k 5.
Row 14: P 4, k 15, p 4.
Row 15: K 3, popcorn in next st, p 15, popcorn in next st, k 3.

Row 16: P 2, k 19, p 2.
Row 17: K 2, p 19, k 2.
Row 18: P 1, k 21, p 1.
Row 19: K 1, p 21, k 1.
Row 20: Knit.
Row 21: Purl.
Rows 22–39: Working back from row 20, work in pat to row 3. Repeat rows 4–39, 5 times more—6 diamonds in all. P 1 row, k 1 row. Bind off in p.

FINISHING: Steam-press panels. Embroider scarlet roses in center of purl diamonds as follows:

With double strand of scarlet, embroider 8 bullion stitches in a radiating circle. With single strand of green, embroider outline stitch stems. With triple strand of green, embroider straight stitch leaves (see stitch details, page 282). With backstitch, sew the 5 panels together in proper sequence, then embroider blue bullion stitch roses as for scarlet roses in center of knit diamonds.

With double strand of W, work a row of sc on each long edge, keeping work flat.

Fringe: Cut strands of W 22″ long. Using 6 strands for each fringe, pull through every 4th st on cast-on and bound-off edges. Knot ends of yarn close to edge of afghan. Trim.

PILLOW: SIZE: 20″ square.
MATERIALS: Columbia-Minerva Nantuk 4-Ply, 2 4-oz. skeins Winter White. Knitting needles No. 10. For Embroidery: See under Afghan, Materials. 20″ square pillow form, or stuffing. Tapestry needle.
GAUGE: 15 sts = 4″; 11 rows = 2″.
PILLOW: FRONT: Cast on 75 sts. K 1 row, p 1 row.

Row 3: K 13, popcorn in next st (see Note under afghan), (k 23, popcorn in next st) twice, k 13.
Row 4: P 12, (k 3, p 21) twice, k 3, p 12.
Row 5: K 12, (p 3, k 21) twice, p 3, k 12.
Row 6: P 11, (k 5, p 19) twice, k 5, p 11.
Row 7: K 11, (p 5, k 19) twice, p 5, k 11.
Row 8: P 10, (k 7, p 17) twice, k 7, p 10.
Row 9: K 9, (popcorn in next st, p 7, popcorn in next st, k 15) twice, popcorn in next st, p 7, popcorn in next st, k 9.
Row 10: P 8, (k 11, p 13) twice, k 11, p 8.
Row 11: K 8, (p 11, k 13) twice, p 11, k 8.
Row 12: P 7, (k 13, p 11) twice, k 13, p 7.
Row 13: K 7, (p 13, k 11) twice, p 13, k 7.
Row 14: P 6, (k 15, p 9) twice, k 15, p 6.
Row 15: K 5, (popcorn in next st, p 15, popcorn in next st, k 7) twice, popcorn in next st, p 15, popcorn in next st, k 5.

Row 16: P 4, (k 19, p 5) twice, k 19, p 4.
Row 17: K 4, (p 19, k 5) twice, p 19, k 4.
Row 18: P 3, (k 21, p 3) 3 times.
Row 19: K 3, (p 21, k 3) 3 times.
Row 20: P 2, (k 23, p 1) twice, k 23, p 2.
Row 21: K 1, (popcorn in next st, p 23) 3 times, popcorn in next st, k 1.
Rows 22–39: Working back from row 20, work in pat to row 3. Repeat rows 4–39 twice more. P 1 row. Bind off.

BACK: Cast on 75 sts. Work in stockinette st (k 1 row, p 1 row) until piece measures same length as front. Bind off.

FINISHING: Steam-press to measure 20″ square. Embroider front as for afghan. Sew three sides, insert pillow (or stuffing), close fourth side.

PLAID AFGHAN
Shown on page 38

SIZE: 44″ × 66″, plus fringe.
MATERIALS: Coats & Clark's Red Heart Fabulend, 8 4-oz. skeins navy, 3 skeins white, 1 skein each of red and green. 14″ knitting needles, 1 pair No. 9. Crochet hook size G.
GAUGE: 4 sts = 1″; 6 rows = 1″.
Note: Vertical stripes will be crocheted on after knitting has been completed.
AFGHAN: Beg at narrow edge, with navy, cast on 164 sts.
Rows 1–6: With navy, work in stockinette st (k 1 row, p 1 row). Drop navy. Tie in white. **Note:** Always carry navy loosely along side edge of work.
Row 7: With white, k. Drop white. Tie in green.
Rows 8 and 9: With green, p 1 row, k 1 row. Cut green.
Row 10: With white, p. Cut white.
Rows 11–24: With navy, work in stockinette st. Drop navy. Tie in white.
Rows 25–28: Using red instead of green, repeat rows 7–10. Cut white.
Rows 29–42: With navy, work in stockinette st.
Repeat rows 7–42 for pattern. Work in pat until total length is about 66″, end with 6 rows of navy.

Next Row: With navy, bind off first 9 sts, * drop next st off left-hand needle, pull out st on right hand needle to measure ½″, bind off 10 sts. Repeat from * across. Unravel each dropped st all the way down to cast-on edge. With navy and darning needle, secure st to cast-on edge. Ridges formed by dropped sts will be used to work vertical stripes.

Vertical Stripes: From right side, beg at cast-on edge, with hook attach white to base of first ridge formed by dropped st; holding yarn in back of work, * sl st over loose strand of next row above, repeat from * to top, sl st over st above at top edge. End off.

Attach red to base of same ridge at lower edge, work another line of sl sts close to first line. With white, work another line of sl sts close to 2nd line.

Alternating green and red for center line of stripes, always using white each side, work vertical stripe in each ridge across.

Edging: From right side, with navy and hook, join yarn in any corner st, ch 1, make 3 sc in corner st; being careful to keep work flat, sc evenly around outer edge, making 3 sc in each corner st. Sl st in first sc. End off.

Pin afghan to measurements on a padded surface; cover with a damp cloth and allow to dry. Do not press.

Fringe: Wind yarn around 6″ cardboard; cut at one edge to get 12″ strands. Using 2 strands tog for each fringe, knot a white fringe at both ends of each vertical white stripe. Matching colors, knot a fringe at both ends of each vertical red and green stripe. Knot a navy fringe in each free sc along same edges, knot fringe along long edges to correspond, working through end sts of rows. Trim fringe evenly.

PINWHEEL AFGHAN
Shown on page 39

SIZE: About 51″ × 68″.
MATERIALS: Knitting worsted, 7 4-oz. skeins black, 2 skeins each of yellow, red, blue and green. Knitting needles No. 8. Steel crochet hook No. 00.
GAUGE: 9 sts = 2″.
TRIANGLE: Cast on 1 st.
Row 1: K 1, yo, k 1 in same st.
Row 2: K 1, yo, k 2.
Row 3: K 1, yo, k 3.
Row 4: K 1, yo, k across. Repeat row 4 until there are 52 sts on needle. Bind off (yo after the first st, sl first st over the yo).

Work 48 black triangles, 12 triangles of each of the 4 colors.

TO JOIN 2 TRIANGLES: Sew a black triangle to a color triangle, joining the bound-off edges.

TO MAKE PINWHEEL SQUARE: Alternating black with colors and always having the same color sequence for each square, join side edge of black triangle to side edge of next color triangle, weaving through edge sts. Join 3 squares across and 4 squares in length.

BORDER: With black, work 2 rows of sc around afghan, working 3 sc in each corner st each row. Work 1 row of sl st around. End off.

HONEYCOMB BLOCKS
Shown on page 109

SIZE: 50″ × 58″, plus fringe.
MATERIALS: Bernat Berella "4", 6 4-oz. balls Natural (A), 5 balls Gazelle (B). Bernat-Aero circular needle No. 13. Bernat-Aero crochet hook size 6:50 mm (J).
GAUGE: 2 sts = 1″; 5 rows = 1″ (double strand).
AFGHAN: Strips 1 and 5: With 2 strands B, cast on 20 sts.
PATTERN: Row 1 (wrong side): Knit.
Row 2: * K 1, k 1 in row below (insert needle in hole below st on needle, bring yarn through, sl st above off needle), repeat from * across.
Row 3: Knit.
Row 4: * K 1 in row below, k 1, repeat from * across.

Repeat rows 1–4, 9 times more—40 rows. Cut 1 strand B; tie in 1 strand A. With A and B, work in pat for 40 rows. Cut B. Tie in 2nd strand of A. With 2 strands A, work in pat for 40 rows. Cut 1 strand A; tie in 1 strand B. With A and B, work in pat for 40 rows. Cut A. Tie in 2nd strand of B. With 2 strands B, work in pat for 40 rows. Cut 1 strand B; tie in 1 strand A. With A and B, work in pat for 40 rows. Cut B. Tie in 2nd strand of A. With 2 strands of A, work in pat for 40 rows. Bind off.

Strips 2 and 4: With 1 strand each of A and B, cast on 20 sts. Work in pat as for strips 1 and 5, working 40 rows A and B, 40 rows with 2 strands of A, 40 rows A and B, 40 rows with 2 strands of B, 40 rows A and B, 40 rows with 2 strands of A, 40 rows A and B. Bind off.

Strip 3: With 2 strands of A, cast on 20 sts. Work in pat as for other strips, working 40 rows with 2 strands of A, 40 rows A and B, 40 rows with 2 strands of B, 40 rows A and B, 40 rows with 2 strands of A, 40 rows A and B, 40 rows with 2 strands of B. Bind off.

FINISHING: Block all strips. Sew strips tog: 1, 2, 3, 4, 5. Steam seams. With 1 strand each of A and B, work 1 row sc across top and bottom edges of afghan.

FRINGE: Cut yarn in 16″ lengths. Using A and B tog, knot 4 or 5 strands in first sc, * sk 2 sc, knot a fringe in next sc, repeat from * across. Make another row of knots 1½″ from first row by dividing each fringe in half and knotting the halves tog.

ARAN BABY SET
Shown on page 108

SIZE: Fits up to 19″ chest.

MATERIALS: Knitting worsted, 3 2-oz. skeins. Knitting needles No. 9. Steel crochet hook size 00. One dp needle for cable. Five buttons. Satin ribbon, ¾ yard.

GAUGE: 11 sts = 2″; 7 rows = 1″.

Pattern Notes: Note 1: Sl all sl sts as if to p.

Note 2: Right Cross St (rc st): With dp needle, sl next p st and hold in back of work, k next 2 sts, then p st from dp needle.

Note 3: Left Cross St (lc st): With dp needle, sl next 2 sts and hold in front of work, p next st, then k 2 sts from dp needle.

PATTERN STITCHES: PATTERN 1: Seed Stitch: Row 1: K 1, * p 1, k 1, repeat from * across. Repeat this row for pat 1.

PATTERN 2 (worked on 12 sts): Row 1 (wrong side): P 1, k 1, p 8, k 1, p 1.

Row 2 (cable row): K 1, p 1, with dp needle, sl next 2 sts and hold in back of work, k next 2 sts, then k 2 sts from dp needle; with dp needle, sl next 2 sts and hold in front of work, k next 2 sts, then k 2 sts from dp needle, p 1, k 1.

Row 3: Repeat row 1.

Row 4: K 1, p 1, k 8, p 1, k 1.

Row 5: Repeat row 1.

Row 6: Repeat row 4. Repeat these 6 rows for pat 2.

PATTERN 3 (worked on 17 sts): Row 1 (wrong side): K 3, k very loosely in front and back of next st until there are 5 sts worked in 1 st, sl st worked in off left-hand needle (popcorn made), k 2, p 2, k 1, p 2, k 2, popcorn in next st, k 3.

Row 2: P 3, k tog the next 5 sts through back of loops as 1 st to complete popcorn, p 2, sl next 3 sts to dp needle, hold in back of work, k next 2 sts, sl p st from dp needle to left-hand needle, p this st, k the 2 sts from dp needle, p 2, complete next popcorn, p 3.

Row 3: K 6, p 2, k 1, p 2, k 6.

Row 4: P 5, rc on next 3 sts, p 1, lc on next 3 sts, p 5.

Row 5: K 5, p 2, k 3, p 2, k 5.

Row 6: P 4, rc on next 3 sts, p 3, lc on next 3 sts, p 4.

Row 7: K 4, p 2, k 2, popcorn in next st, k 2, p 2, k 4.

Row 8: P 3, rc on next 3 sts, p 2, complete popcorn, p 2, lc on next 3 sts, p 3.

Row 9: K 3, p 2, k 7, p 2, k 3.

Row 10: P 2, rc on next 3 sts, p 7, lc on next 3 sts, p 2.

Row 11: K 2, p 2, k 2, popcorn in next st, k 3, popcorn in next st, k 2, p 2, k 2.

Row 12: P 1, rc on next 3 sts, p 2, complete popcorn, p 3, complete popcorn, p 2, lc on next 3 sts, p 1.

Row 13: K 1, p 2, k 11, p 2, k 1.

Row 14: P 1, k 2, p 11, k 2, p 1.

Row 15: K 1, p 2, k 3, popcorn in next st, k 3, popcorn in next st, k 3, p 2, k 1.

Row 16: P 1, lc on next 3 sts, p 2, complete popcorn, p 3, complete popcorn, p 2, rc on next 3 sts, p 1.

Row 17: K 2, p 2, k 9, p 2, k 2.

Row 18: P 2, lc on next 3 sts, p 7, rc on next 3 sts, p 2.

Row 19: K 3, p 2, k 3, popcorn in next st, k 3, p 2, k 3.

Row 20: P 3, lc on next 3 sts, p 2, complete popcorn, p 2, rc on next 3 sts, p 3.

Row 21: K 4, p 2, k 5, p 2, k 4.

Row 22: P 4, lc on next 3 sts, p 3, rc on next 3 sts, p 4.

Row 23: K 5, p 2, k 3, p 2, k 5.

Row 24: P 5, lc on next 3 sts, p 1, rc on next 3 sts, p 5. Repeat these 24 rows for pat 3.

PATTERN 4 (worked on 11 sts): Note: On right front, work from first * to 2nd *; on left front, work from first # to 2nd #.

Row 1 (wrong side): * K 3, popcorn in next st, k 2, p 2, k 1, p 2 * # p 2, k 1, p 2, k 2, popcorn in next st, k 3 #.

Row 2: * Sl next 3 sts to dp needle, hold in back of work, k next 2 sts, sl p st from dp needle to left-hand needle, p this st, k the 2 sts from dp needle, p 2, complete popcorn, p 3 * # p 3, complete popcorn, p 2, sl next 3 sts to dp needle, hold in front of work, k next 2 sts, sl p st from dp needle to left-hand needle, p this st, k the 2 sts from dp needle #.

Row 3: * K 6, p 2, k 1, p 2 * # p 2, k 1, p 2, k 6 #.

Row 4: * K 2, p 1, lc on next 3 sts, p 1, k 2 #.

Row 5: * K 5, p 2, k 2, p 2 * # p 2, k 2, p 2, k 5 #.

Row 6: * K 2, p 2, lc on next 3 sts, p 4 * # p 4, rc on next 3 sts, p 2, k 2 #.

Row 7: * K 4, p 2, k 2, popcorn in next st, p 2 * # p 2, popcorn in next st, k 2, p 2, k 4 #.

Row 8: * K 2, complete popcorn, p 2, lc on next 3 sts, p 3 * # p 3, rc on next 3 sts, p 2, complete popcorn, k 2 #.

Row 9: * K 3, p 2, k 4, p 2 * # p 2, k 4, p 2, k 3 #.

Row 10: * K 2, p 4, lc on next 3 sts, p 2 * # p 2, rc on next 3 sts, p 4, k 2 #.

Row 11: * K 2, p 2, k 2, popcorn in next st, k 2, p 2 * # p 2, k 2, popcorn in next st, k 2, p 2, k 2 #.

Row 12: * K 2, p 2, complete popcorn, p 2, lc on next 3 sts, p 1 * # p 1, rc on next 3 sts, p 2, complete popcorn, p 2, k 2 #.

Row 13: * K 1, p 2, k 6, p 2 * # p 2, k 6, p 2, k 1 #.

Row 14: * K 2, p 6, k 2, p 1 * # p 1, k 2, p 6, k 2 #.

Row 15: * K 1, p 2, k 3, popcorn in next st, k 2, p 2 * # p 2, k 2, popcorn in next st, k 3, p 2, k 1 #.

Row 16: * K 2, p 2, complete popcorn, p 2, rc on next 3 sts, p 1 * # p 1, lc on next 3 sts, p 2, complete popcorn, p 2, k 2 #.

Row 17: * K 2, p 2, k 5, p 2 * # p 2, k 5, p 2, k 2 #.

Row 18: * K 2, p 4, rc on next 3 sts, p 2 * # p 2, lc on next 3 sts, p 4, k 2 #.

Row 19: * K 3, p 2, k 3, popcorn in next st, p 2 * # p 2, popcorn in next st, k 3, p 2, k 3 #.

Row 20: * K 2, complete popcorn, p 2, rc on next 3 sts, p 3 * # p 3, lc on next 3 sts, p 2, complete popcorn, k 2 #.

Row 21: * K 4, p 2, k 3, p 2 * # p 2, k 3, p 2, k 4 #.

Row 22: * K 2, p 2, rc on next 3 sts, p 4 * # p 4, lc on next 3 sts, p 2, k 2 #.

Row 23: * K 5, p 2, k 2, p 2 * # p 2, k 2, p 2, k 5 #.

Row 24: * K 2, p 1, rc on next 3 sts, p 5 * # p 5, lc on next 3 sts, p 1, k 2 #. Repeat these 24 rows for pat 4.

SWEATER: BACK: Cast on 51 sts. Work in pat 1 for 1″.

Pattern: Row 1 (wrong side): Work first five sts in pat 1, work next 12 sts in pat 2, work next 17 sts in pat 3, work next 12 sts in pat 2, work last 5 sts in pat 1.

Row 2: Work first 5 sts in pat 1, work next 12 sts in pat 2, work next 17 sts in pat 3, work next 12 sts in pat 2, work last 5 sts in pat 1. Work in pat as established until piece measures about 7″ from start, end row 20 of pat 3. Check gauge; piece should measure 9¼″ wide.

Shape Armhole: Keeping to pat as established, bind off 2 sts at beg of next 2 rows–47 sts. Work even until armhole measures about 4″ above first bound-off sts, end row 24 of pat 3.

Shape Shoulders: Keeping to pat, bind off 8 sts at beg of next 4 rows. Bind off remaining 15 sts for back of neck

Buttonhole Note: For boy's sweater, work right front first; for girl's, work left front first. When first front is completed, with pins mark position of 5 buttons evenly spaced on center band, first one ½″ above lower edge, last one ½″ below start of neck shaping. When making 2nd front, form buttonholes as follows:

Buttonholes: Beg at center edge, work first 2 sts, bind off next 2 sts, finish row. Next Row: Cast on 2 sts over bound-off sts.

RIGHT FRONT: Cast on 33 sts. Work in pat 1 for ½″. Form first buttonhole (see Buttonhole Note) on next row. Continue in pat 1 until piece measures 1″ from start, end arm side.

Pattern: Row 1 (wrong side): Work first 5 sts in pat 1, work next 12 sts in pat 2, work next 11 sts in pat 4, work last 5 sts in pat 1 (center band).

Row 2: Work first 5 sts in pat 1 (center band), work next 11 sts in pat 4, work next 12 sts in pat 2, work last 5 sts in pat 1. Work in pat as established, forming buttonholes opposite markers, until piece measures same as back to underarm, end arm side. Check gauge; piece should measure 6″ wide.

Shape Armhole: Keeping to pat as established, bind off 2 sts at beg of arm side once–31 sts. Work even until armhole measures 2¾″ above first bound-off sts, end center edge.

Shape Neck and Shoulder: Bind off 5 sts at beg of center edge once, 4 sts once, 3 sts twice; at the same time, when armhole measures same as back, bind off 8 sts at beg of arm side twice.

LEFT FRONT: Cast on, work in pat 1 as for right front for 1″, end center edge.

Pattern: Row 1 (wrong side): Work first 5 sts in pat 1 (center band), work next 11 sts in pat 4, work next 12 sts in pat 2, work last 5 sts in pat 1.

Row 2: Work first 5 sts in pat 1, work next 12 sts in pat 2, work next 11 sts in pat 4, work last 5 sts in pat 1 (center band). Keeping to pat as established, complete left front as for right front.

With backstitch, sew shoulder seams.

SLEEVES: Cast on 33 sts. Work in pat 1 for ¾″.

Pattern: Row 1 (wrong side): Work first 7 sts in pat 1, p 1, work next 17 sts in pat 3, p 1, work last 7 sts in pat 1.

Row 2: Work first 7 sts in pat 1, k 1, work next 17 sts in pat 3, k 1, work last 7 sts in pat 1. Continue in pat as established, inc 1 st each side every 1″ 5 times, working added sts into pat 1–43 sts. Work even until piece measures about 7″ from start, end row 22 of pat 3. Check gauge; piece above last inc row should measure 8″ wide.

Shape Cap: Bind off 2 sts at beg of next 6 rows. Bind off remaining 31 sts.

COLLAR: From wrong side, beg and ending ½″ in from each front edge, pick up and k 47 sts around neck edge. Work in pat 1 for 1¾″, inc 1 st each side every 4th row 3 times–53 sts. Bind off loosely.

FINISHING: Steam-press pieces lightly. Sew in sleeves. Sew side and sleeve seams. Beg at lower edge of right front, work 1 row sc around front edges and collar, working 3 sc at neck edge of fronts and points of collar; end at lower edge of left front. Work buttonhole st around buttonholes. Sew on buttons.

HAT: Front: Cast on 24 sts.

Row 1 (wrong side): Work first 5 sts in pat 1 (front band), p 1, work next 17 sts in pat 3, p last st.

Row 2: K 1, work next 17 sts in pat 3, k 1, work last 5 sts in pat 1. Repeat last 2 rows until 24 rows of pat 3 are completed, end right side. Work in pat, cast on 23 sts at end of next row for back piece–47 sts.

Back: Next Row (right side): Work first 23 sts in pat 1, finish row in pat as established. Working the 23 sts of back piece in pat 1 and remaining sts in pat as established, work even until 47 rows from start are completed, end row 23 of pat 3.

Next Row (right side): Bind off 23 sts (back piece), finish row–26 sts. Work even until 74 rows from start are completed, end row 2 of pat 3. Bind off.

FINISHING: Steam-press cap lightly. Sew sides of back piece to sides of front. Steam-press seams.

Neckband: From right side, pick up and k 45 sts around neck edge. Work in seed st for 5 rows, end wrong side.

Eyelet Row: K 1, p 1, * yo, k 2 tog, k 1, p 1, repeat from * across, end last repeat k 1. Work in seed st for 2 rows. Bind off in pat. Run ribbon through eyelet row, adjust ribbon; tack at sides.

FAIR ISLE SET
Shown on page 107

SIZES: Directions for size 10. Changes for sizes 12 and 14 are in parentheses.

Body Bust Size: 32½" (34"-36").

Blocked Bust Size: Pullover: 34" (35½"-37"). Cardigan (closed): 37" (39"-41").

MATERIALS: Unger Natuurwol, 1¾-oz. balls: Pullover: 3 (3-4) balls Camel (A), 2 (2-3) balls Natural (B) and 1 ball Brown (C); Cardigan: 10 (11-12) balls A. Knitting needles Nos. 5 and 6. One dp needle. Aluminum crochet hook size F. Seven plastic rings for buttons.

GAUGE: 5 sts = 1"; 6 rows = 1" (pullover pat, No. 6 needles). 6 sts = 1"; 7 rows = 1" (cardigan pat, No. 5 needles).

PULLOVER: Pattern Notes: Always change colors on wrong side, picking up new strand from under dropped strand. Carry unused colors across loosely; if more than 3 sts between colors, twist strands after every 3rd st. Always bring unused color to end of row and twist before beginning next row. Cut and join colors when necessary.

BACK: Beg at lower edge, with A and No. 5 needles, cast on 80 (84-88) sts. Work in ribbing of k 1, p 1 for 2½", inc 5 sts evenly spaced across last row–85 (89-93) sts. Change to No. 6 needles.

Pattern: Row 1: With C, knit.

Row 2: With C, purl.

Row 3: Following chart 1, k from A to B once, from B to C across.

Row 4: P from C to B to last st, p from B to A once.

Row 5-16: Repeat last 2 rows to top of chart 1.

Row 17: With C, knit.

Row 18: With C, purl.

Row 19: Following chart 2, k from A to B once, from B to C to last 2 (4-6) sts, from C to D once.

KNITTING WITH TWO COLORS

Knit all main color stitches in usual way: throw yarn around needle with right index finger. Knit design stitches as shown in illustration, pulling the yarn from left index finger through the stitch.

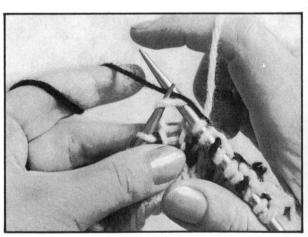

Catch in design color every fourth stitch to avoid loose strands on back between the stitches of design. Insert needle in the stitch, bring design color over needle as shown, knit stitch with the main color only.

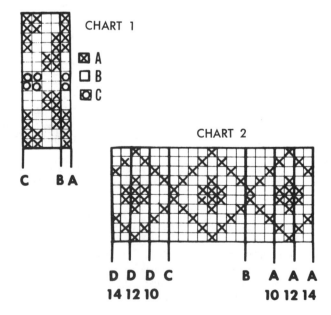

CHART 1

⊠ A
☐ B
▣ C

C   B A

CHART 2

D D D C   B   A A A
14 12 10   10 12 14

Row 20: Following chart 2, p from D to C once, from C to B to last 3 (5-7) sts, from B to A once.

Rows 21-28: Repeat last 2 rows to top of chart 2. Repeat these 28 rows for pat until piece measures 14″ (14″-14½″) from start or desired length to underarm, end wrong side. Check gauge; piece above ribbing should measure 17″ (17¾″-18½″) wide.

Shape Armholes: Keeping to pat, bind off 6 sts at beg of next 2 rows. Dec 1 st each side every row twice, then every other row 4 times-61 (65-69) sts. Work even until armholes measure 7½″ (8″-8½″) above first bound-off sts, end wrong side.

Shape Shoulders: Keeping to pat, bind off 5 sts at beg of next 4 rows, 5 (6-7) sts next 2 rows-31 (33-35) sts.

Neckband: Change to No. 5 needles. With A, k across, dec 1 st in center of row-30 (32-34) sts. Work in ribbing of k 1, p 1 for 5 rows. Bind off loosely in ribbing.

FRONT: Work same as for back until piece measures 2 rows less than back to underarm, end wrong side-85 (89-93) sts.

Shape V Neck and Armholes: Keeping to pat, work 42 (44-46) sts, drop yarn, sl next st on a safety pin; join strands of colors to be used, finish row. Working on both sides at once, with separate strands of yarn, work 1 row even. Dec 1 st at each neck edge of next row, then dec 1 st at each neck edge every 3rd row 14 (15-16) times more; at the same time, bind off 6 sts at beg of each arm side once. Dec 1 st at each arm side every row twice, then every other row 4 times-15 (16-17) sts each side. Work even until armholes measure same as back.

Shape Shoulders: Bind off 5 sts at beg of each arm side twice, 5 (6-7) sts once.

Front Neckband: From right side, with A and No. 5 needles, pick up and k 48 (50-52) sts down left front neck edge, k st from safety pin (mark this st for center front), pick up and k 48 (50-52) sts up right front neck edge--97 (101-105) sts.

Row 1: * K 1, p 1, repeat from * to within 2 sts of marked st, k 2 tog, p 1, k 2 tog; beg with p 1, work in ribbing across-2 sts dec.

Row 2: Working in ribbing as established, dec 1 st each side of marked st-2 sts dec. Repeat last row 3 times-87 (91-95) sts. Bind off in ribbing.

FINISHING: Run in yarn ends on wrong side. With backstitch, sew shoulder and neckband seams.

Armbands: From right side, with A and No. 5 needles, pick up and k 100 (104-108) sts around armhole. Work in ribbing of k 1, p 1 for 5 rows. Bind off loosely in ribbing.

Block pullover. Sew side and armband seams.

CARDIGAN: Note 1: Sl all sl sts as if to purl.

Note 2: Left Cross St (lc st): Sk next st, k in back lp of next st, k in front of skipped st, sl both sts off left-hand needle.

Note 3: Right Twist Stitch (rt st): With dp needle, sl next st and hold in back of work, k next 2 sts, then p st from dp needle.

Note 4: Left Twist Stitch (lt st): With dp needle, sl next 2 sts and hold in front of work, p next st, then k 2 sts from dp needle.

Note 5: Popcorn Stitch: K in front and back of 1 st until there are 6 sts in 1 st, sl st worked in off left-hand needle, (with left-hand needle, pass 2nd st from tip of right-hand needle over and off needle) 5 times (1 st of group left).

PATTERN STITCHES: PATTERN 1 (worked on 7 sts): **Row 1** (right side): P 1, lt st (see Note 4) on next 3 sts, p 3.

Row 2: K 3, p 2, k 2.

Row 3: P 2, lt st on next 3 sts, p 2.

Row 4: K 2, p 2, k 3.

Row 5: P 3, lt st on next 3 sts, p 1.

Rows 6 and 8: K 1, p 2, k 4.

Row 7: P 4, k 2, p 1.

Row 9: P 3, rt st (see Note 3) on next 3 sts, p 1.

Row 10: Repeat row 4.

Row 11: P 2, rt st on next 3 sts, p 2.

Row 12: Repeat row 2.

Row 13: P 1, rt st on next 3 sts, p 3.

Row 14: K 4, p 2, k 1. Repeat these 14 rows for pat 1.

PATTERN 2 (worked on 13 sts): **Row 1:** (right side): P 4; with dp needle, sl next 2 sts and hold in front of work, k 2, p 1, then k 2 sts from dp needle, p 4.

Row 2: K 4, p 2, k 1, p 2, k 4.

Row 3: P 3, rt st on next 3 sts, p 1, lt st on next 3 sts, p 3.

Row 4: (K 3, p 2) twice, k 3.

Row 5: P 2, rt st on next 3 sts, p 3, lt st on next 3 sts, p 2.

Row 6: K 2, p 2, k 5, p 2, k 2.

Row 7: P 1, rt st on next 3 sts, p 2, popcorn st (see Note 5) in next st, p 2, lt st on next 3 sts, p 1.

Row 8: K 1, p 2, k 7, p 2, k 1.

Row 9: P 1, lt st on next 3 sts, p 5, rt st on next 3 sts, p 1.

Row 10: Repeat row 6.

Row 11: P 2, lt st on next 3 sts, p 3, rt st on next 3 sts, p 2.

Row 12: Repeat row 4.

Row 13: P 3, lt st on next 3 sts, p 1, rt st on next 3 sts, p 3.

Row 14: Repeat row 2. Repeat these 14 rows for pat 2.

PATTERN 3 (worked on 2 sts): **Row 1** (right side): Work lc st (see Note 2) on 2 sts.

Row 2: P 2. Repeat these 2 rows for pat 3.

BACK: Beg at lower edge, with No. 5 needles,

cast on 99 (105-111) sts.

Ribbing: Row 1 (right side): K 1, * p 1, k 1, repeat from * across.

Row 2: P 1, * k 1, p 1, repeat from * across. Repeat these 2 rows for 2½", inc 10 sts evenly spaced across last row--109 (115-121) sts.

Pattern: Row 1 (right side): (P 1, work next 2 sts in pat 3) 1 (2-3) times, work next 7 sts in pat 1, * work next 2 sts in pat 3, work next 13 sts in pat 2, work next 2 sts in pat 3, work next 7 sts in pat 1, repeat from * 3 times, end (work next 2 sts in pat 3, p 1) 1 (2-3) times.

Row 2: (K 1, work next 2 sts in pat 3) 1 (2-3) times, work next 7 sts in pat 1, * work next 2 sts in pat 3, work next 13 sts in pat 2, work next 2 sts in pat 3, work next 7 sts in pat 1, repeat from * 3 times, end (work next 2 sts in pat 3, k 1) 1 (2-3) times. Working appropriate pat row, work in pat as established until piece measures 16½" from start or desired length to underarm, end wrong side. Check gauge; piece above ribbing should measure 18" (19"-20") wide.

Shape Armholes: Keeping to pat as established, bind off 7 sts at beg of next 2 rows. Dec 1 st each side every other row 5 times–85 (91-97) sts. Work even until armholes measure 7¼" (7½"-8") above first bound-off sts, end wrong side.

Shape Shoulders: Bind off 8 sts at beg of next 2 rows, 8 (9-10) sts next 4 rows. Bind off remaining 37 (39-41) sts.

LEFT FRONT: Beg at lower edge, with No. 5 needles, cast on 57 (61-63) sts. Work in ribbing as for back until piece measures 1 row less than back ribbing, end right side.

Next Row (wrong side): (P 1, k 1) 5 times (center band); finish row in ribbing, inc 5 (4-5) sts evenly spaced across–62 (65-68) sts.

Pattern: Row 1: (P 1, work next 2 sts in pat 3) 1 (2-3) times, * work next 7 sts in pat 1, work next 2 sts in pat 3, work next 13 sts in pat 2, work next 2 sts in pat 3, repeat from * once, p 1, (p 1, k 1) 5 times (center band).

Row 2: (P 1, k 1) 5 times, k 1, * work next 2 sts in pat 3, work next 13 sts in pat 2, work next 2 sts in pat 3, work next 7 sts in pat 1, repeat from * once (work next 2 sts in pat 3, k 1) 1 (2-3) times. Work in pat as established until piece measures 2" less than back to underarm, end side edge. Check gauge; piece above ribbing should measure 10" (10¾"-11¼") wide.

Shape V Neck and Armhole: Working in pat as established, work to within last 11 sts, p 2 tog, finish row ribbing–1 st dec. Continue to dec 1 st at center edge, inside of center band, every 4th row 15 (16-17) times more; at the same time, when piece measures same as back to underarm, bind off 7 sts at beg of arm side once. Dec 1 st at same edge every other row 5 times–34 (36-38) sts. Work even until armhole measures same as back, end

arm side.

Shape Shoulder and Neckband: Bind off 8 sts at beg of arm side once, 8 (9-10) sts twice–10 sts. Work in ribbing until piece measures 3" (3¼" - 3½"). Bind off in ribbing.

With pins, mark position of 7 buttons evenly spaced on left center band; first button ½" above lower edge, last button ½" below start of neck shaping.

Buttonholes: Keeping to ribbing, work 4 sts at beg of center edge, bind off next 3 sts at beg of center edge, bind off next 3 sts, finish row. Next Row: Cast on 3 sts over bound-off sts.

RIGHT FRONT: Cast on and work ribbing as for left front ½", end wrong side (center edge). Work buttonhole (see Buttonholes) on next 2 rows, then continue in ribbing until piece measures 1 row less than left front, end right side.

Next Row: Work in ribbing to within last 10 sts, inc 5 (4-5) sts evenly spaced; finish row in ribbing–62 (65-68) sts.

Pattern: Row 1 (right side): Work in ribbing across 10 sts (center band), p 1, * work next 2 sts in pat 3, work next 13 sts in pat 2, work next 2 sts in pat 3, work next 7 sts in pat 1, repeat from * once, (work next 2 sts in pat 3, p 1) 1 (2-3) times. Complete same as for left front, reversing shaping and forming buttonholes opposite markers.

SLEEVES: Beg at lower edge, with No. 5 needles, cast on 45 (47-49) sts. Work in ribbing as for back for 3", inc 16 (18-18) sts evenly spaced across last row–61 (65-67) sts.

Pattern: Row 1 (right side): P 0 (0-1); **for size 12 and 14 only,** work next 2 sts in pat 3; **for all sizes,** work next 13 sts in pat 2, * work next 2 sts in pat 3, work next 7 sts in pat 1, work next 2 sts in pat 3, work next 13 sts in pat 2, repeat from * once; **for sizes 12 and 14 only,** work next 2 sts in pat 3; **for size 14 only,** p 1. Work in pat as established, inc 1 st each side every 2" 6 times, working added sts into p 1, pat 3–73 (77-79) sts. Work even until piece measures 17" from start or desired length to underarm, end wrong side. Check gauge; piece above last inc row should measure 12" (13"-13½") wide.

Shape Cap: Keeping to pat, bind off 7 sts at beg of next 2 rows. Dec 1 st each side every row 4 times, then every other row 12 (13-14) times. Bind off 3 sts at beg of next 4 rows. Bind off remaining 15 (17-17) sts.

FINISHING: Block pieces; do not flatten pat. With backstitch, sew shoulder seams; sew in sleeves. Weave ends of neckband tog; sew to back of neck. Sew side and sleeve seams.

Buttons (make 7): With crochet hook, work sc around plastic ring until completely covered. Break yarn, leaving a 10" end. Thread needle with long end; draw sts tog. Sew on.

MOSAIC PULLOVER
Shown on page 106

SIZE: Directions for small size (6-8). Any changes for medium size (10-12) and large size (14-16) are in parentheses. Note: Needle size and gauge determine size.

Body Bust Size: 30½"-31½" (32½"-34"; 36"-38").

Blocked Bust Size: 33" (36"-39½").

MATERIALS: Sport yarn, 4 (4-5) 2-oz. balls blue, main color (MC); 2 balls white, contrasting color (CC). Knitting needles Nos. 4 (5-6) and 5 (6-7).

GAUGE: 6 sts = 1"; 17 rows = 2" (pat, No. 5 needles). 11 sts = 2"; 8 rows = 1" (pat, No. 6 needles). 5 sts = 1"; 15 rows = 2" (pat, No. 7 needles).

PATTERN NOTES: Sl all sl sts as if to p. Always have yarn in back of sl st on right side rows, in front of sl st on wrong side rows. Work 2 rows CC, 2 rows MC alternately for pat.

PATTERN (multiple of 16 sts, plus 3):

Row 1 (right side): With CC, k 1, * (k 1, sl 1, k 3, sl 1) twice, k 3, sl 1, repeat from * across, end k 2.

Row 2 And All Even Rows: With yarn to front, sl all sl sts and p all p sts.

Row 3: With MC, k 1, * sl 1, k 3, repeat from * across, end sl 1, k 1.

Row 5: With CC, k 4, * sl 1, k 1, (sl 1, k 3) twice, sl 1, k 5, repeat from * across, end last repeat k 4.

Row 7: With MC, k 2, * sl 2, k 3, (sl 1, k 3) twice, sl 2, k 1, repeat from * across, end last repeat k 2.

Row 9: With CC, k 4, * (sl 1, k 3) twice, sl 1, k 1, sl 1, k 5, repeat from * across, end last repeat k 4.

Row 11: With MC, repeat row 3.

Row 13: With CC, k 2, * (sl 1, k 3) twice, sl 1, k 1, sl 1, k 3, sl 1, k 1, repeat from * across, end last repeat k 2.

Row 15: With MC, k 3, * sl 1, k 3, repeat from * across.

Row 17: With CC, k 2, * (sl 1, k 1, sl 1, k 3) twice, sl 1, k 3, repeat from * across, end last repeat k 4.

Row 19: With MC, repeat row 3.

Row 21: With CC, k 4, * sl 1, k 1, sl 1, k 5, (sl 1, k 3) twice, repeat from * across, end last repeat k 2.

Row 23: With MC, k 3, * sl 1, k 3, sl 2, k 1, sl 2, k 3, sl 1, k 3, repeat from * across.

Row 25: With CC, k 2, * sl 1, k 3, sl 1, k 5, sl 1, k 1, sl 1, k 3, repeat from * across, end last repeat k 4.

Row 27: Repeat row 3.

Row 29: With CC, k 4, * (sl 1, k 3, sl 1, k 1) twice, sl 1, k 3, repeat from * across, end last repeat k 2.

Row 31: With MC, repeat row 15.

Row 32: Repeat row 2. Repeat these 32 rows for pat.

PULLOVER: BACK: Beg at lower edge, with MC and smaller needles, cast on 86 sts. Work in ribbing of k 1, p 1 for 1½".

Next Row (inc row): * (K 1, p 1) 5 times, k 1, inc 2 sts in next st (to inc 2 sts, k in front, back, front of next st), repeat from * 6 times, k 1, p 1–100 sts. Work in ribbing of k 1, p 1 until piece measures 5" from start. Change to larger needles. Work in ribbing until piece measures 15" from start or desired length to underarm. Check gauge; piece when slightly stretched measures 16¾" (18"-19¾") wide.

Shape Armholes: Keeping to ribbing, bind off 8 sts at beg of next 2 rows. Dec 1 st each side every other row 4 times–76 sts. Work even until armholes measure 7" (7¼"-7½") above first bound-off sts.

Shape Shoulders: Keeping to ribbing as established, bind off 7 sts at beg of next 6 rows–34 sts.

Neck Facing: Working in ribbing, inc 1 st each side every other row 3 times, working added sts into ribbing–40 sts. Bind off loosely in ribbing.

FRONT: Cast on and work same as for back for 1½"–86 sts.

Next Row (inc row): * Working in ribbing as established, work 5 sts, inc 1 st in next st, repeat from * 12 times, finish row in ribbing–99 sts. Change to larger needles. Work in pat until piece measures same as back to underarm.

Shape Armholes: Keeping to pat as established, bind off 8 sts at beg of next 2 rows. Dec 1 st each side every other row 4 times–75 sts. Work in pat as established until armholes measure 6¼" (6½"-6¾") above first bound-off sts, end wrong side. Cut CC; with MC only, work in ribbing of k 1, p 1 until armholes measure same as back.

Shape Shoulders: Keeping to ribbing as established, bind off 7 sts at beg of next 6 rows–33 sts.

Neck Facing: Working in ribbing, inc 1 st each side every other row 3 times–39 sts. Bind off loosely in ribbing.

SLEEVES: Beg at lower edge, with MC and smaller needles, cast on 44 sts. Work in ribbing of k 1, p 1 for 2½".

Next Row (inc row): * Work 6 sts in ribbing as established, inc 2 sts in next st, repeat from * 5 times, finish row in ribbing–56 sts. Change to larger needles. Working in ribbing, inc 1 st each side every 1" 10 times, working added sts into ribbing–76 sts. Work even until piece measures 16½" (17"-17½") from start or desired length to underarm. Check gauge; piece when slightly stretched, should measure 12½ (13¾"-15") wide.

Shape Cap: Bind off 6 sts at beg of next 2 rows. Dec 1 st each side every other row 13 times. Bind off 4 sts at beg of next 2 rows, 2 sts next 2 rows. Bind off remaining 26 sts.

FINISHING: Run in yarn ends on wrong side. Steam-press front pat on wrong side; do not press ribbing. Sew shoulder and facing seams; sew in sleeves. Sew side and sleeve seams. Fold neck facing to wrong side; tack facing seams to shoulder seams. Steam-press seams lightly on wrong side.

NORSE SWEATER DRESS
Shown on page 105

NOTE: Dress is worked from neck to lower edge. Body of dress to lower edge is tubular. Armholes are cut later.

SIZES: Directions for small size (8-10). Changes for medium size (12-14) and large size (16-18) are in parentheses.

Body Bust Size: 31½"-32½" (34"-36"; 38"-40").
Blocked Bust Size: 35" (38½" - 41½").

MATERIALS: Knitting worsted, 4 ply, 2 4-oz. skeins each of white (W), aqua (A) and green (G); 1 skein each of royal blue (B) and fuchsia (F). 29" circular needle No. 8; set of dp needles No. 8.

GAUGE: 5 sts = 1"; 5 rows = 1".

Pattern Notes: Always change colors on wrong side; pick up background color from under dropped pattern color; pick up pattern color over dropped background color. Carry color not being used loosely across back of work. Cut and join colors when necessary.

Length Note: Dress measures about 32" from lower edge to top of shoulders. For longer dress, repeat any desired pattern bands for desired length. More yarn may be needed.

DRESS: BODY: Beg at upper edge of back and front, with A and circular needle, cast on 176 (192-208) sts. Put and keep a marker on needle between last and first sts of rnd. Join, being careful not to twist sts.

Rnd 1: K 88 (96-104), put a marker on work for left armhole, k 88 (96-104), put a marker on work for right armhole.

Pattern: Rnds 2-54: Following chart, work pat in stockinette st (k each rnd) as follows: * K from A to B once, from B to C 10 times, from C to D once, put and keep a marker on needle, repeat from * once. Check gauge; piece should measure 35" (38½"-41½") around.

Rnd 55: Following chart, * k 1, inc 1 st (to inc, pick up horizontal strand between stitch just knitted and next st, place it on left-hand needle; k 1 st in back of this strand), work to marker, inc 1 st, sl marker, repeat from * once–4 sts inc. Work in pat, inc 4 sts every 6th rnd 13 times more–232 (248-264) sts. Work even to top of chart.

Next Rnd (eyelet rnd): With F, * yo, k 2 tog, repeat from * around.

Hem: With F, work in ribbing of k 1, p 1 for 2 rnds. Bind off loosely in ribbing.

SLEEVES: Beg at upper edge, with W and dp needles, cast on 76 (76-84) sts; divide on 3 dp needles. Mark end of rnds. Join, being careful not to twist sts.

Rnd 1: With W, k around.

Rnd 2: K around, dec 1 st beg and end of rnd–74 (74-82) sts.

Rnd 3: K around.

Rnd 4: K 1 W, k 1 A, k 8 W, * k 1 A, k 7 W, repeat from * around.

Rnd 5: K 3 A, k 6 W, * k 3 A, k 5 W, repeat from * around, end last repeat k 6 W.

Rnd 6: K 1 W, k 1 A; with W, k 2 tog, k 6, * k 1 A, k 7 W, repeat from * around, end last repeat k 1 A; with W, k 5, k 2 tog–72 (72-80) sts.

Rnds 7-83: Following chart, beg with rnd 69, repeat from B to C to end of rnds. Work to end of pat rnd 145.

Rnds 84 and 85: * K 1 W, k 1 A, repeat from * around.

Rnds 86 and 87: With W, k around, dec 27 (30) sts evenly spaced on last rnd–46 (50) sts.

Cuff: Work around in ribbing of k 1, p 1 for 2" or until sleeve is desired length. Bind off loosely in ribbing.

FINISHING: Run in yarn ends on wrong side. Block pieces.

Slash Armholes: With colored thread, run a basting line on dress from markers at right and left armholes straight down for 8½" (8½"-9"). Machine stitch twice ¼" each side of basting. Cut through basting line. Turn under ¾" on cut edges of armholes. With A, overcast top edges of dress together for shoulder seams for 20 (23-26) sts each side of armholes. With W, overcast cast-on sts of sleeves to armholes, placing end of sleeve rnds at underarms. Press seams.

Collar: Beg at front neck, from right side, with A, pick up and k 40 (42-44) sts on each of front and back neck on 3 dp needles--80 (84-88) sts. Join.

Rnd 1: With A, k around.

Rnds 2 and 3: K 2 A, * k 1 F, k 3 A, repeat from * around, end last repeat k 1 A.

Rnds 4 and 5: * K 1 A, k 3 F, repeat from * around.

Rnds 6 and 7: Repeat rnd 2.

Rnds 8 and 9: With A, knit around.

Rnd 10 (eyelet rnd): With A, * yo, k 2 tog, repeat from * around. With A, k 9 rnds. Bind off loosely.

Fold collar and hem on eyelet rnd to wrong side; sew in place loosely with matching yarn. Steampress hem and collar.

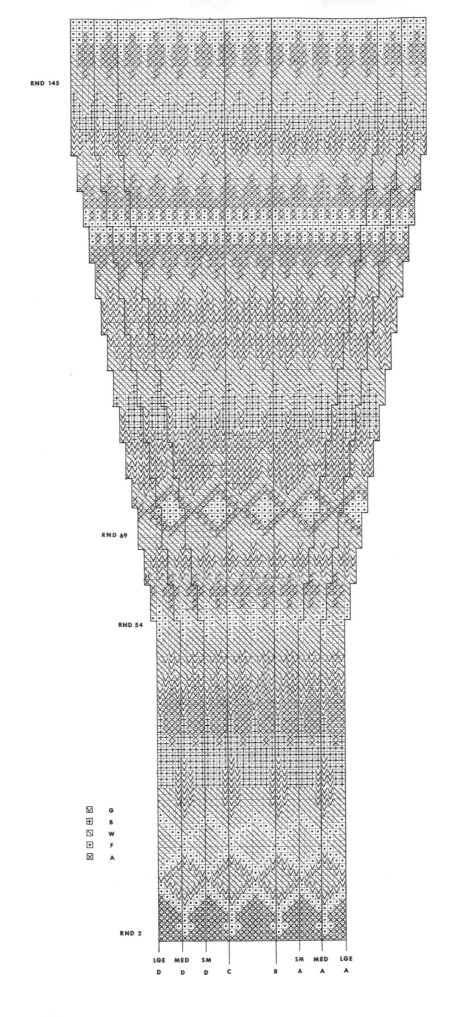

RND 145

RND 69

RND 54

RND 2

⊠	G
⊞	B
◩	W
⊡	F
⊠	A

LGE MED SM   SM MED LGE

D   D   D   C   B   A   A   A

KNITTING WITH FOUR NEEDLES

Four double-pointed needles are used to knit tubuar pieces which are too small to be made on circular needles. Socks, mittens, gloves, hats, and sleeves can all be knitted around and around without seams on double-pointed needles. Stitches are cast on loosely on one needle and divided evenly on three needles. The fourth needle is used for the actual knitting. Before starting to knit, hold tips of first and third needles together with the left hand so that the needles, stitches, and yarn from the ball are in the position shown in illustration at right.

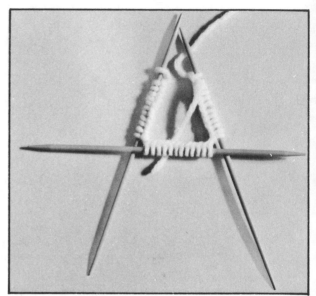

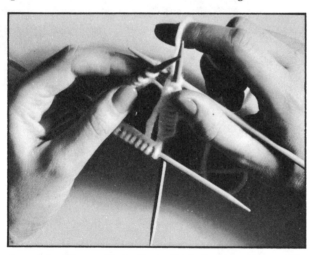

Insert fourth needle in first stitch, holding first and fourth needles and yarn in usual way, as shown.

CHILD'S REINDEER SET
Shown on page 33

NOTE: Body of pullover to shoulder is tubular. Armholes are cut later.

SIZES: Directions are for small size (3-4). Changes for medium size (6-8) are in parentheses.

Body Chest Size: 22″-23″ (24″-26″).

Blocked Chest Size: 24″ (28″).

MATERIALS: Knitting worsted, 3 (4) 4-oz. skeins green (A); 1 skein each of white (B) and scarlet (C), 24″ circular needle No. 10; set of dp needles No. 10. Aluminum crochet hook size G. Two stitch holders. Seam binding.

GAUGE: 4 sts = 1″; 11 rows = 2″.

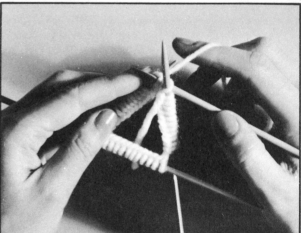

Yarn around needle, knit first stitch. Draw yarn tight to join the first and last stitches of the round.

Pattern Notes: Always change colors on wrong side; pick up background color from under dropped pattern color; pick up pattern color over dropped background color. Carry color not being used loosely across back of work. When more than 5 sts between colors, twist colors every 3rd or 4th st. Cut and join colors when necessary.

PULLOVER: BODY: Beg at lower edge of back and front, with A and circular needle, cast on 96 (112) sts. Put and keep a marker on needle between last and first sts of rnd. Join, being careful not to twist sts.

Hem: Work in ribbing of k 1, p 1 for 3 rnds.

Next Rnd (eyelet rnd): * Yo, k 2 tog, repeat from * around. K 2 rnds.

Pattern: Rnds 1-8: Following chart 1, work pat in stockinette st (k each rnd) starting at arrow on rnd 1. Repeat pat to end of rnd. Check gauge; piece should measure 24″ (28″) around. With A, k 2 rnds.

Next Rnd: Following chart 2, * k from A to B; with A, k 0 (3); k from B to C; with A, k 2 (3); k from C to D; with A, k 2 (3); k from D to E; with A, k 0 (3); k from E to F, repeat from * once. Repeat this rnd to top of chart. Following chart 3, repeat rnds 1-8 until piece measures 12″ (16″) above eyelet rnd or desired length from lower edge to top of shoulder.

Next Rnd: With A, bind off loosely 9 (11) sts for left front shoulder, k until 30 (34) sts from bound-off sts, sl these sts on a holder for front neck; bind off next 9 (11) sts for right front shoulder, put a marker on work in last st; bind off next 9 (11) sts for right back shoulder, k until 30 (34) sts from bound-off sts, sl these sts on a holder for back neck, bind off next 9 (11) sts for left back shoulder; leave marker on work.

SLEEVES (make 2): Beg at lower edge, with A and dp needles, cast on 32 (36) sts; divide on 3 dp needles. Mark end of rnd. Join, being careful not to twist sts. Work same as for body to end of rnd 8 on chart 1. Following chart 3, repeat rnds 1-8, inc 1 st at beg and end of rnd every 1″ 4 times, working added sts into pat—40 (44) sts. Work even until piece measures 11½″ (13½″) above eyelet rnd or desired sleeve length. Check gauge; piece above last inc rnd should be 10″ (11″) around. With A, bind off loosely.

FINISHING: Run in yarn ends on wrong side. Block pieces.

Slash Armholes: Baste a straight line from shoulder edge down for 5″ (5½″) at each arm side between sts of front and back (at marker and at last boundoff st). Machine stitch twice, using a loose tension and small sts; ¼″ each side of basting. Slash along basting line.

With A, sew shoulder seams. Fold armhole edge of sleeve in half between underarm incs; placing inc edge of sleeve at underarm of body and center top of sleeve at shoulder seam, sew in sleeves from right side, lapping sleeve over armhole (to conceal raw edge). Steam-press raw edges toward sleeves. Cover wrong side of armhole seams with seam binding. Turn hems to wrong side on eyelet rnds; sew in place.

Collar: Beg at front neck, from right side, sl 30 (34) sts each of front and back neck on 3 dp needles—60 (68) sts. Join; with A, k 1 rnd. Following chart 1, work rnds 1-8. With B, k 1 rnd.

Next Rnd ((eyelet rnd): With B, * yo, k 2 tog, repeat from * around. With B, k 1 rnd. With C, k 8 rnds. Bind off loosely.

Fold collar on eyelet rnd to wrong side; sew in place loosely. Steam-press.

PANTS: LEG: Beg at lower edge, with A and dp needles, cast on 52 (60) sts; divide on 3 dp needles. Mark end of rnd. Join, being careful not to twist sts. Work same as for pullover body to end of rnd 8 on chart 1. With A, work in stockinette st until piece measures 14″ (16″) above eyelet rnd or desired leg length to crotch. Check gauge; piece should measure 13″ (15″) around.

Shape Crotch: Next Rnd: Bind off 8 sts, finish rnd—44 (52) sts. Sl sts on a holder. Make other leg in same manner. Leave sts on dp needles.

Join Legs: From right side, sl sts from dp needles to circular needle. K around sts on holder—88 (104) sts. Work in stockinette st until piece measures 5½″ (6½″) above crotch.

Waistband: Work in ribbing of k 1, p 1 for 2 rnds.

Next Rnd (eyelet rnd): * Yo, k 2 tog, repeat from * around. K 1 rnd. Bind off loosely in k.

FINISHING: Run in yarn ends on wrong side. Block. Weave bound-off sts at crotch tog. Turn hem to wrong side on eyelet rnd; sew in place.

Cord: With double strand of A, work chain 45″ (50″) long. End off. Weave through eyelets at waist.

CAP: Cuff: Beg at top edge, with A and dp needles, cast on loosely and divide 64 (68) sts on 3 needles. Mark end of rnd. Join; work around in ribbing of k 1, p 1 for 3 rnds.

Next Rnd (eyelet rnd): * Yo, k 2 tog, repeat from * around. K 2 rnds. Following chart 1, work rnds 1-8. With B, k 1 rnd. With A, k 2 rnds. Repeat eyelet rnd. With A, k 2 rnds. With C, k 10 rnds. Turn work. Following chart 3, work and repeat rnds 1-8 three times, then work rnds 1-4. Cut B.

Shape Top: Next Rnd: With A, k 2 tog around—32 (34) sts. K 1 rnd. Repeat last 2 rnds. Cut A, leaving a 10″ end of yarn; draw remaining sts tog and fasten securely on wrong side.

POMPON: Wind C 100 times around a 2½″ piece of cardboard. Tie one end; cut other end. Trim; fasten to top.

FINISHING: Run in yarn ends on wrong side. Turn ribbing on eyelet rnd to wrong side of cuff; fold cuff on eyelet rnd to right side of cap; hem top edge of cuff to cap. Steam-press lightly.

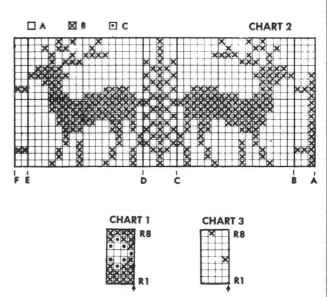

MOHAIR KITTEN
Shown on page 33

SIZE: About 10″ high.

MATERIALS: Mohair yarn, 1½ ozs.; fingering yarn, ½ oz. Small amount of knitting worsted for mittens. Set of double-pointed (dp) needles No. 5. Cotton batting for stuffing. Carpet thread. Scraps of felt: black, pink, green. All-purpose glue. Pipe cleaner. Stitch holder. Two ½″ buttons for attaching arms. Tapestry needle.

GAUGE: 5 sts = 1″ (using 1 strand each of mohair and fingering yarn).

Note: Kitten is knit with 1 strand each of mohair and fingering yarn throughout.

KITTEN: BODY: Beg at neck edge, with 2 strands (see Note), cast on 12 sts; divide on 3 dp needles. Join; work in stockinette st (k each rnd) for 2 rnds.

Rnd 3: Inc 1 st in each st-24 sts. K 2 rnds.

Rnd 6: Inc 1 st in each st-48 sts. K 21 rnds.

Next Rnd: (K 2, k 2 tog) 12 times-36 sts.

Divide for Legs: Sl next 18 sts on a holder (one leg); divide remaining 18 sts on 3 dp needles (2nd leg). Join; k 8 rnds.

Next Rnd: (K 2 tog, k 4) 3 times-15 sts. K 6 rnds.

Shape Heel; Sl front 7 sts on a safety pin; with 2 dp needles, work back and forth on remaining 8 sts in stockinette st (p 1 row, k 1 row) for 6 rows. Sl front 7 sts on a dp needle. Divide the 15 sts on 3 dp needles. Join; k 6 rnds. Bind off.

Sl the 18 sts from holder to 3 dp needles. Work other leg the same.

HEAD: Beg at top of head, cast on 9 sts; divide evenly on 3 dp needles. Join; k 2 rnds.

Rnd 3: Inc 1 st in each st around-18 sts. K 1 rnd.

Rnd 5: Inc 1 st in each st around-36 sts. K 2 rnds.

Rnd 8: * Inc 1 st in each of 2 sts, k 16, repeat from * once-40 sts. K 5 rnds.

Rnd 14: * Inc 1 st in each of 2 sts, k 18, repeat from * once-44 sts. K 5 rnds.

Rnd 20: * (K 2 tog) twice, k 18, repeat from * once-40 sts.

Rnd 21: * (K 2 tog) twice, k 16, repeat from * once-36 sts. K 1 rnd.

Rnd 23: K 2 tog around-18 sts. K 1 rnd.

Rnd 25: (K 1, k 2 tog) 6 times-12 sts. K 3 rnds. Bind off.

ARMS (make 2): Beg at upper edge, cast on 12 sts; divide on 3 dp needles. Join; k 12 rnds.

Shape Elbow: Sl next 6 sts on a holder. With 2 needles, work back and forth on remaining 6 sts in stockinette st for 4 rows. Sl sts from holder to dp needle. Divide 12 sts on 3 dp needles. Join; k 2 rnds.

Next Rnd: (K 2, k 2 tog) 3 times-9 sts. K 9 rnds.

Shape Paw: (K 2, inc 1 st in next st) 3 times-12 sts. K 1 rnd.

Next Rnd: (K 3, inc 1 st in next st) 3 times-15 sts. K 5 rnds.

Next Rnd: (K 2 tog, k 1) 5 times-10 sts. Bind off.

FACE: With 2 needles, cast on 10 sts. Work back and forth in stockinette st for 8 rows. Bind off.

TAIL: Cast on 9 sts; divide on 3 dp needles. Join; k 13 rnds.

Next Rnd: Dec 2 sts evenly spaced-7 sts. Work for 12″ or desired length.

Next Rnd: (K 2 tog) 3 times, k 1-4 sts. Cut yarn, leaving 8″ end; thread needle. Draw up sts; fasten securely.

EARS (make 2): Beg at lower edge, with 2 needles, cast on 7 sts. Work back and forth in stockinette st, dec 1 st each side every 4th row twice-1 st. End off.

MITTENS (make 2): With single strand of knitting worsted, cast on 12 sts; divide on 3 dp needles. Join; work in ribbing of k 2, p 2 for 6 rnds.

Next Rnd: (K 3, inc 1 st in next st) 3 times-15 sts. K 9 rnds.

Next Rnd: (K 2 tog, k 1) 5 times-10 sts. K 1 rnd.

Next Rnd: K 2 tog around-5 sts. Cut yarn, leaving 8″ end. Draw up sts; fasten securely.

Thumb: With 2 dp needles and single strand of knitting worsted, cast on 4 sts. Work in stockinette st for 6 rows.

Next Row: K 2 tog twice. Cut yarn, leaving 8″ end. Draw up sts, sew side. Sew thumb to side of mitten.

FINISHING: Sew heel to foot, elbow to arm. Weave front of foot; weave front of paws. Stuff lower body and legs firmly. Stuff lower arms. Using carpet thread, sew arms in place by sewing through body and inner arm, through button eyes and back, through arm and body. Fasten securely. Finish stuffing arms and body. Sew top of head; stuff firmly; sew to body. Stuff face; sew to head as shown. Using ear for pat, cut pink felt; glue to p side of ears. Sew ears to head. Run a few strands (loops) of mohair through top of head for hair. Trace patterns. Using patterns, cut black felt nose, mouth and pupils, pink tongue. Cut green felt bow and eyes. Attach bow to kitten with a strand of matching knitting worsted. Glue features in place. Glue 1″ oval felt pads to soles of feet and paws. With thread, embroider toes as shown in illustration, page 33. Insert pipe cleaner in tail; sew tail to back.

EYE

MOUTH

TONGUE

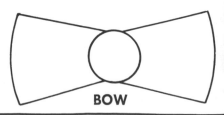

BOW

KNITTING WITH FOUR NEEDLES

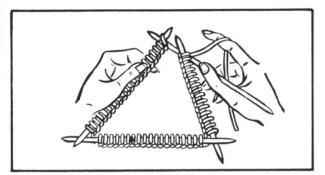

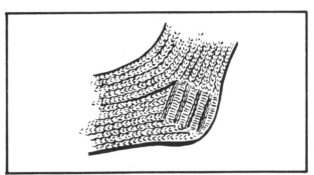

FRENCH HEEL

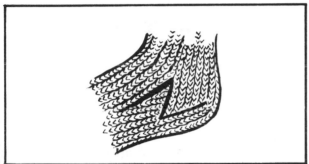

DUTCH OR SQUARE HEEL

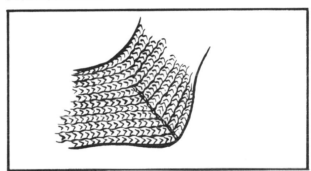

AUTO HEEL

Socks, mittens, gloves, hats, helmets, sleeves and necklines can all be knitted on four double-pointed needles in a tubular fashion. Stitches are cast on loosely and divided as evenly as possible on three needles; the fourth is used for the actual knitting. Stitch gauge is as important as in flat knitting; be sure the gauge agrees with that of the model for proper fit. As in flat knitting, shaping is accomplished by increasing or decreasing. Pattern stitches, including cables, are adaptable to four needle knitting. For twisting cables, an additional needle is required. Ribbing is worked by knitting over the knit stitches and purling over the purl stitches. Working round and round in plain knit stitch produces a seamless stockinette tube. Toes, fingers, etc. are finished by drawing the stitches together and sewing them securely or by weaving them in Kitchener stitch.

Socks are probably the most popular item made on four needles. A properly knitted sock fits well and wears well.

CUFFS: Cast on cuff stitches loosely so they will not bind or be broken in putting on the sock. Leave an extra long end in casting on. Carry this end with yarn and knit with a double strand for first row of ribbing. To insure a snug fit, an elastic thread may also be carried along with yarn for the first few rows. Cuffs are always ribbed and are usually 1″ to 2″ deep for the shorter lengths of men's socks and 2½″ to 4″ deep for regulation length.

LEGS: Slack length socks for men are about 4½″ from top of sock to top of heel; regulation length are 8″ to 9″ from top of sock to top of heel. When making these lengths, no decreases are necessary from top of heel to insure a smooth fit. If longer socks are made, more stitches must be cast on to fit the calf. These extra stitches are decreased 2 at a time at even intervals down center back of leg. The center 2 stitches are marked and decreases are made either side of the marked stitches.

HEELS: Reinforce the heels by carrying a matching nylon thread along with yarn unless sock is knitted of nylon or nylon and wool yarn.

French Heel: This is the most popular heel for men's and women's socks because it wears well and provides "cushion comfort." The heel stitches are worked in alternate rows of k 1, sl 1, repeated across, and purl, producing a ribbed effect.

Auto or Easy Heel is often suggested for children's socks. When the heel is reached, the yarn is dropped and the heel stitches are knitted across with a contrasting strand of yarn. These stitches are then slipped back on the left-hand needle and knitted again with the dropped yarn.

The sock is continued until the toe is completed. The heel stitches are then slipped on two needles as the contrasting yarn is pulled out. One needle will have one stitch less than the other. This stitch is picked up on the first round. The heel is then completed in the same manner as a toe, weaving the remaining stitches together after the shaping is completed.

Foot Length: Sizes for socks are measured in inches from center back of heel to tip of toe. A size 11 sock, for instance, is 11″ from front to back of foot. Tapering the toe section requires 2″ in length for men's and women's socks, 1½″ for children's socks; therefore, in making a size 11 sock, knit evenly around foot section until piece measures 9″ from back of heel straight forward to needles, then start toe decreases. When knitting a sock the same size as a ready-made one, mark off 2″ from toe. Measure back from this point to heel to determine how long foot should be before starting toe decreases.

TOES: Reinforce toes in same way as heels.

Round Toe: Stitches, evenly divided on three needles, are gradually decreased to a few stitches at the end which are drawn up and sewed together.

Pointed Toe: Instep and sole stitches are gradually decreased at sides. When sufficiently tapered, remaining stitches are woven together in Kitchener stitch.

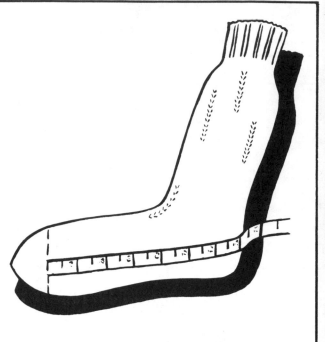

MEASURING FOR START OF TOE DECREASES

Replacing Heels and Toes

If the heels or toes of hand-knitted socks wear out and the rest of the socks are still in good condition, replace them as follows:

Toes: Run a line of basting thread through each stitch at the point where the toe shaping begins. Cut out worn area and ravel back the toe to the basting line, leaving a 2 to 3 inch yarn end. Using same size needles and weight of yarn as the original sock, pick up the stitches from the basting thread. Re-knit toe following any toe directions.

Heels: Run a line of basting around area to be replaced, carefully catching each stitch. Cut out the worn area and ravel the uneven edge up to the line of basting. Pick up the stitches along the back of the heel at the top and knit new heel section, shaping the same as original heel. When the heel is long enough to join rest of sock, do not cast off stitches, but weave them together using Kitchener stitch. Weave together the sides of the instep and edges of the heel replacement, working from wrong side.

KITCHENER STITCH

Stitches are evenly divided on two needles and held parallel. To weave them together, proceed as follows: Break off yarn, leaving about 12″ end on work. Thread this into a tapestry needle. Working from right to left, * pass threaded needle through first st on front needle as if to knit and slip st off needle; pass yarn through 2nd st on front needle as if to purl but leave st on needle; pass yarn through 1st st on back needle as if to purl and slip st off needle; pass yarn through 2nd st on back needle as if to knit but leave st on needle. Repeat from * until all sts are woven together. Fasten off yarn.

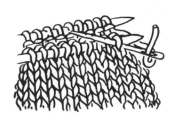

KITCHENER STITCH

SOCKS WITH FRENCH HEELS

MATERIALS: For lightweight socks: 3-ply sock and sport yarn, 3 1-oz. skeins. Set of dp needles No. 1. **For medium-weight socks:** 4-ply sport yarn, 2 2-oz. balls. Set of dp needles No. 2.

GAUGE: 17 sts = 2″ (3-ply yarn); 15 sts = 2″ (4-ply yarn).

Directions are written for lightweight yarn. Changes for medium-weight yarn are in parentheses.

CUFF: Cast on loosely 68 (64) sts; divide on 3 needles. Join, work in ribbing of k 2, p 2 for 4″. K 1 rnd, inc 1 st in every 17th st 4 times—72 sts (keep 64 sts for medium-weight yarn).

K even in stockinette st for 5½″. Mark space between first and last st of rnd as center back.

Dec Rnd: K 1, k 2 tog, k to within 3 sts of end of rnd, sl 1, k 1, psso, k 1. Work 1″ even. Repeat dec rnd—68 (60) sts. Work even until 12″ from beg or desired length to top of heel, end at center back.

FRENCH HEEL: K 18 (15), sl last 36 (30) sts worked to one needle for heel, hold remaining 32 (30) sts on 2 needles for instep.

Row 1: Working from wrong side, sl first st of heel needle as if to p, p to end.

Row 2: * Sl 1 as if to p, k 1, repeat from * to end of row. Repeat last 2 rows until there are 40 (32) rows on heel. Begin to turn heel on wrong side: sl 1, p 20 (16), p 2 tog, p 1, turn; sl 1, k 7 (5), sl 1, k 1, psso, k 1, turn; sl 1, p 8 (6), p 2 tog, p 1, turn; sl 1, k 9 (7), sl 1, k 1, psso, k 1, turn; sl 1, p 10 (8), p 2 tog, p 1, turn; sl 1, k 11 (9), sl 1, k 1, psso, k 1, turn; sl 1, p 12 (10), p 2 tog, p 1, turn; sl 1, k 13 (11), sl 1, k 1, psso, k 1, turn. Contunue in this way to work towards sides of heel, having 1 st more before dec on each row until there are 22 (18) sts left, end k row.

GUSSETS AND FOOT: With free needle, pick up and k 20 (16) sts on side edge of heel; k 32 (30) instep sts to one needle; with free needle, pick up and k 20 (16) sts on other side of heel and k 11 (9) sts of heel to same needle. Sl remaining 11 (9) sts of heel to same needle. Sl remaining 11 (9) heel sts to first needle. There will be 31 (25) sts on first and 3rd needles; 32 (30) sts on 2nd or instep needle. K 1 rnd.

Next Rnd: K to within 3 sts of end of first needle, k 2 tog, k 1; k across instep needle; on 3rd needle, k 1, sl 1, k 1, psso, k to end of rnd. Repeat last 2 rnds until 18 (13) sts remain on each of first and 3rd needles—68 (56) sts. K until foot is 9″ or desired length from tip of heel allowing 2″ for toe.

TOE: Beg at center of sole, place 17 (14) sts on first needle, 34 (28) sts on 2nd needle, 17 (14) sts on 3rd needle.

First Dec Rnd: K to within 3 sts of end of first needle, k 2 tog, k 1; on 2nd needle, k 1, sl 1, k 1, psso, k to last 3 sts, k 2 tog, k 1; on 3rd needle, k 1, sl 1, k 1, psso, k to end. K 1 rnd even. Repeat these last 2 rnds until 20 (16) sts remain. K 5 (4) sts of first needle to 3rd needle. Break off leaving an end. Weave 10 (8) sts of sole and 10 (8) upper sts tog in Kitchener st, page 84. Steam-press socks.

Plain stockinette stitch is used for these basic socks to make in any length, any size, in lightweight or medium-weight yarns.

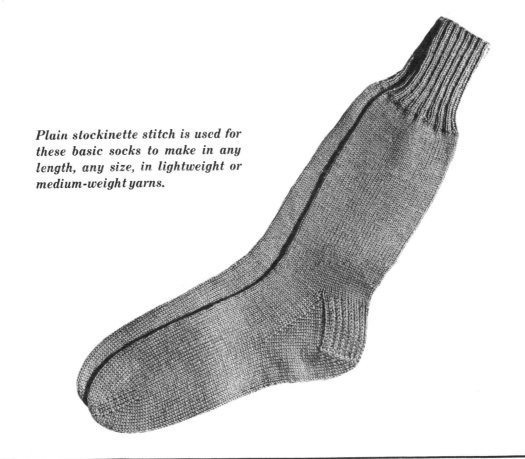

B

A

■BLACK ⊡SCARLET □MC ⊠WHITE

ARGYLE SOCKS

SIZE: Adjustable length, men's sizes.

MATERIALS: Fingering yarn, 3-ply, 3 1-oz. skeins oxford, main color (MC), 1 skein each of scarlet, white and black. Straight knitting needles Nos. 1 and 2; set of dp needles No. 2. Set of bobbins.

GAUGE: 15 sts = 2″; 11 rows = 1″ (stockinette st, No. 2 needles).

Pattern Note: Use a separate bobbin for each white, MC and scarlet diamond. Use separate bobbin wound with MC between diamond panels. Use separate strands of black for diamond outline sts. Always change colors on wrong side, picking up new strand from under dropped strand. Following chart, work pat in stockinette st (k 1 row, p 1 row). **On K Rows** (right side): Read chart from A to B. **On P Rows:** Read chart from B to A.

CUFF AND LEG: With MC and No. 1 needles, cast on loosely 64 sts. Work in ribbing of k 2, p 2 for 2½″. Change to No. 2 straight needles. Work in pat (see Pat Note) to top of chart. With MC bobbin at edge, k 1 row. With dp needle, p 1 row. Break off all bobbins.

Divide Sts for Heel: Sl first and last 16 sts on one dp needle, having back seam at center of heel; divide and leave center 32 sts on 2 dp needles for instep.

HEEL: From right side, join MC at beg of heel sts, work back and forth on 32 heel sts as follows: **Row 1** (right side): * K 1, sl 1, repeat from * across.

Row 2: Purl. Repeat these 2 rows until 33 rows are completed, ending k row.

Turn Heel: P 17 sts, p 2 tog, p 1, turn; sl 1, k 3, sl 1, k 1, psso, k 1, turn; sl 1, p 4, p 2 tog, p 1, turn; sl 1, k 5, sl 1, k 1, psso, k 1, turn; sl 1, p 6, p 2 tog, p 1, turn. Continue in same way, working 1 st more before dec on each row until all sts are worked, ending k row—18 sts.

INSTEP: With same heel needle, pick up and k 16 sts on side of heel piece; with 2nd dp needle, k across 32 instep sts; with 3rd dp needle, pick up and k 16 sts on other side of heel piece and with same needle k 9 sts from heel needle. Mark last st for end of rnd. There are 25 sts on each of first and 3rd needles, 32 sts on 2nd needle. K around as follows:

Shape Gussets: Rnd 1: K to last 3 sts on first needle, k 2 tog, k 1; k across 2nd needle; on 3rd needle, k 1, sl 1, k 1, psso, k to end of rnd.

Rnd 2: K even. Repeat these 2 rnds until 16 sts remain on each of first and 3rd needles. Work even on 64 sts until foot measures 2″ less than desired finished length from center back of heel.

Shape Toe: Rnd 1: K to last 3 sts on first needle, k 2 tog, k 1; on 2nd needle, k 1, sl 1, k 1, psso, k to last 3 sts, k 2 tog, k 1; on 3rd needle, k 1, sl 1, k 1, psso, k to end of rnd. **Rnd 2:** K even. Repeat these 2 rnds until 20 sts remain in rnd. With 3rd needle, k across first needle. Break off yarn, leaving about 12″ end on work. Thread this into a tapestry needle and, holding needles parallel, weave sole and instep sts together in Kitchener stitch (page 84). Sew back seam. Steam-press, using steam iron or damp cloth and dry iron.

Argyle-patterned socks, unlike most socks, are worked back and forth on two needles until diamonds are completed; then socks are finished in four-needle knitting. Each colorful diamond is knitted from a separate bobbin of yarn as described in directions.

REVERSIBLE DOUBLE-THICK MITTENS

SIZE: Men's medium size.

MATERIALS: 6 ozs. knitting worsted. Knitting needles No. 6.

GAUGE: 4 k sts = 1".

MITT: Cast on 48 sts. Work in ribbing of k 2, p 2 for 4".

Inc Row: (Inc 1 st in each of 2 k sts, p 2) 5 times, (inc 1 st in each of 2 k sts, inc 1 st in each of 2 p sts) twice, (inc 1 st in 2 k sts, p 2) 5 times—76 sts.

Double Knitting Pat: Row 1: * K 1, yarn in front of work, sl 1 as if to p allowing yarn to cross in front of st, repeat from * across. Repeat row 1 for pat. This pat forms a double thickness of knitting.

Work in pat for 10 rows (looks like 5 rows).

First Inc for Thumb: Work in pat on 35 sts, put marker on needle, inc 1 st in each of next 2 sts, work in pat on 2 sts, inc 1 st in each of next 2 sts, put a marker on needle, work in pat on 35 sts. Work in pat for 3 rows, slipping markers.

2nd Inc for Thumb: Work in pat to marker, sl marker, inc 1 st in each of next 2 sts, work in pat on 6 sts, inc 1 st in each of next 2 sts, sl marker, work in pat to end. Work in pat for 3 rows, slipping markers. Continue in this manner, increasing 2 sts after first marker and 2 sts before 2nd marker every 4th row until there are 30 sts between markers for thumb. Work in pat for 3 rows.

Thumb: Work in pat on 35 sts, place these sts on a holder. Inc 1 st in first st of thumb, work in pat to last st of thumb, inc 1 st—32 sts for thumb. Place remaining 35 sts on a holder. Work even in pat on 32 thumb sts for 2½".

First Dec Row: * Work pat on 4 sts, k 2 tog twice, repeat from * across. Work back in pat.

2nd Dec Row: * Work pat on 2 sts, k 2 tog twice, repeat from * across. Work back.

3rd Dec Row: K 2 tog across row. Break yarn, leaving end for sewing. Draw end through sts; fasten. Sew thumb seam.

HAND: Place sts from first holder on needle, join yarn, pick up and k 6 sts under thumb, work pat on 35 sts of 2nd holder. Work even in pat on these 76 sts for 4".

First Dec Row: * Work pat on 6 sts, k 2 tog twice, repeat from * across, work pat on 6 sts. Work 3 rows in pat—62 sts.

2nd Dec Row: * Work pat on 5 sts, k 2 tog twice, repeat from * across to last 8 sts, work pat on 4 sts, k 2 tog twice. Work 3 rows in pat—48 sts.

3rd Dec Row: * Work pat on 4 sts, k 2 tog twice, repeat from * across. Work 3 rows in pat—36 sts.

4th Dec Row: * Work pat on 3 sts, k 2 tog twice, repeat from * across, sl last st. Work 1 row in pat—26 sts.

5th Dec Row: * Work pat on 2 sts, k 2 tog twice, repeat from * across, k 1, sl 1. Work 1 row in pat—18 sts. K 2 tog across next row. Break yarn, leaving end for sewing. Draw end through sts. Sew side seam.

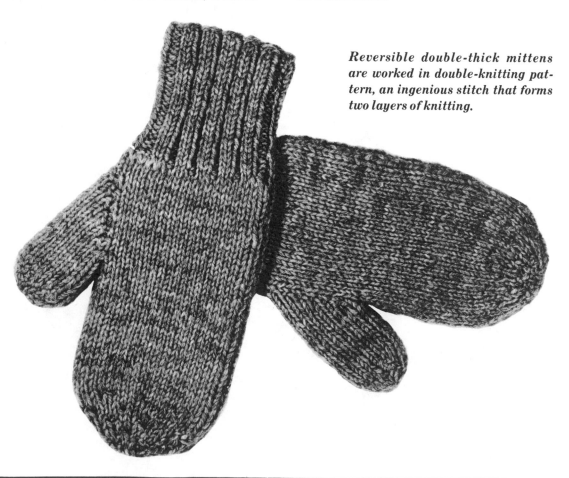

Reversible double-thick mittens are worked in double-knitting pattern, an ingenious stitch that forms two layers of knitting.

Colored patterns can be worked in four-needle knitting, as in these authentic Norwegian gloves. Pattern color forming large snowflakes on backs and smaller motifs on fingers and palms is carried around with background color.

SNOWFLAKE PATTERN GLOVES

SIZE: 8-8½.

MATERIALS: Sport yarn, 2 2-oz. balls blue, main color (MC); 2 balls white, contrasting color (CC). One set of dp needles No. 2. One stitch holder.

GAUGE: 15 sts = 2″ (pat).

Pattern Note: Always change colors on wrong side, picking up new strand from under dropped strand. Carry colors across loosely; when there are more than 5 sts, twist colors every 3rd st.

RIGHT GLOVE: CUFF: With MC, cast on 45 sts, divide sts evenly on 3 needles. Mark end of rnd. Join, working in ribbing of k 2, p 1 for 7 rnds.

Striped Pat: Rnds 1-10: Continue in ribbing, working 1 rnd CC, 1 rnd MC alternately. Break off CC. With MC, continue in ribbing for 6 rnds.

HAND: Work in stockinette st (k each rnd) for 4 rnds, inc 12 sts evenly spaced on last rnd—57 sts.

Thumb Gore: Rnd 1: Following Chart 1 from right to left, k first 37 sts, put a marker on needle, with MC, k in front and back of next st (thumb inc made), put a marker on needle, k 2 CC, continue in pat to end of rnd.

Rnd 2: Following Chart 1, work rnd 2 of pat, having 2 MC sts in thumb gore and 2 CC sts each side of thumb gore.

Rnd 3: Following Chart 1, work rnd 3 of pat to first marker, with MC, k 1, inc 1 st in next st, k 2 CC, continue in pat to end of rnd.

Rnd 4: Following Chart 1, work rnd 4 of pat, having 3 MC sts in thumb gore and 2 CC sts each side of thumb gore.

Rnds 5-11: Continue to inc 1 st in st after first and before 2nd marker on next rnd, then every other rnd 3 times as shown on chart—11 sts between markers for thumb gore, 67 sts.

Rnds 12-14: Following Chart 1, work even.

Row 5: Following Chart 1, work to within 2 sts of first marker, sl next 15 sts on a holder for thumb, with MC, cast on 15 sts, work in pat to end of rnd. Remove markers.

Rnd 16: Following Chart 1, k first 33 sts, with MC, k 2 tog, work in pat to end of rnd—66 sts.

Rnds 17-27: Following Chart 1, work in pat.

Rnd 28: Following Chart 1, sl first 22 sts on a colored thread for back of hand side of other fingers, break off yarn; join MC and k next 19 sts as shown on chart for first finger, with MC, cast on 5 sts on inner side, sl remaining 25 sts on another colored thread for palm side of other fingers.

First Finger: Divide these 24 sts on 3 needles. Join, following Chart 2 from right to left for right glove (from left to right for left glove). K around in pat to end of rnd 20.

Shape Tip: Rnd 21: Following Chart 2, k to after first CC stripe, sl 1, k 1, psso, k to last 4 sts of rnd, k 2 tog, k 2 CC.

Rnds 22-24: * Sl 1, k 1, psso, k to within 2 sts of CC stripe, k 2 tog, k 2 CC, repeat from * once—10 sts remain at end of rnd 24.

Rnd 25: * With MC, sl 1, k 2 tog, psso, k 2 CC, repeat from * once—6 sts. Break off MC.

Rnd 26: With CC, k 2 tog 3 times—3 sts.

Rnd 27: With CC, sl 1, k 2 tog, psso. End off last st. Break off CC, pull CC strand to wrong side and fasten securely.

Second Finger: Sl next 6 sts from back of hand to needle. From right side, join MC at beg of back finger, k sts on needle, pick up and k 5 sts on cast-on sts of last finger, sl next 8 sts of palm on a spare needle, on palm needle, (k 3 MC, k 1 CC) twice, with MC, cast on 5 sts. Divide these 24 sts on 3 needles.

Join, following Chart 2, k around in pat to end of rnd 20. Shape tip as for first finger.

Third Finger: Work as for second finger.

Fourth Finger: Sl last 10 sts from back of hand to needle. From right side, join CC at beg of back finger, k 2 CC, k 8 MC, with MC, pick up and k 5 sts on cast-on sts of last finger, sl last 9 sts of palm on a spare needle, on palm needle, (k 3 MC, k 1 CC) twice, k 1 MC. Divide these 24 sts on 3 needles. Join, following Chart 2, k around in pat to end of rnd 14.

Shape Tip: Rnds 15-18: Following Chart 2, work rnds 15-18, shaping tip as for rnds 21-24 of directions on first finger.

Rnds 19-21: Work as for rnds 25-27 of directions on first finger.

THUMB: Sl 15 sts from holder to 2 needles, join MC, pick up and k 15 sts on cast-on sts. Divide these 30 sts on 3 needles. Join, with CC, k 2 CC sts, mark last st for end of rnd. Following Chart 3 from right to left, k around in pat to end of rnd 12.

Shape Tip: Rnds 13 and 14: Following Chart 3,

k to after first CC strip, sl 1, k 1, psso, k to last 4 sts fo rnd, k 2 tog, k 2 CC (these 2 CC sts are part of back sts) 26 sts.

Rnds 15-18: Following Chart 3, work rnds 15-18, shaping tip as for rnd 22 of directions on first finger–10 sts.

Rnds 19-21: Work as for rnds 25-27 of first finger.

LEFT GLOVE: Work as for right glove to thumb gorè.

Thumb Gore: Rnd 1: Following Chart 1, from left to right, k first 19 sts, put a marker on needle, with MC, k in front and back of next st (thumb inc made), put a marker on needle, k 2 CC, work in pat to end of rnd.

Rnds 2-27: Repeat rnds 2-27 as for right glove.

Rnd 28: Following Chart 1, sl first 25 sts on a colored thread for palm, break yarn; join CC, k next 19 sts as shown on chart for first finger; with MC, cast on 5 sts on inner side, sl remaining 22 sts on another colored thread for back of hand.

Work fingers as for right glove, beg fingers from palm side; work thumb as for right glove. Steam-press gloves; stretch fingers if necessary.

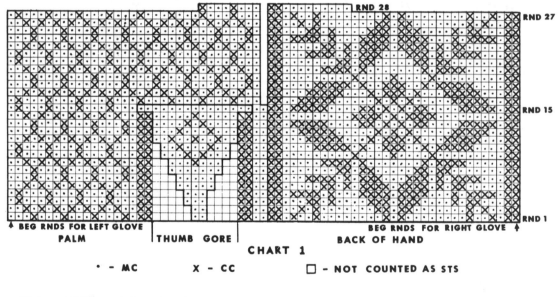

CHART 1

• - MC   X - CC   ☐ - NOT COUNTED AS STS

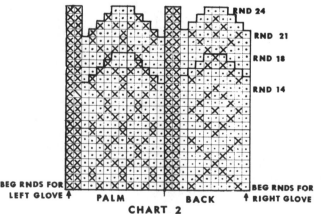

CHART 2

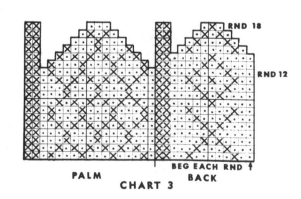

CHART 3

Double-thick rug is knit with a slip-stitch pattern that makes the front and back at the same time. The simple striped pattern is worked in three colors of rug yarn—we selected orange, yellow, and gold, but darker colors would be just as effective. Rug measures 20″ × 34″, plus the tricolor fringe, which is added last. Tubular Knit Rug, page 92.

DOUBLE-KNIT PILLOWS
Shown on page 40

SIZE: 16" square.

MATERIALS: Knitting worsted, 4 ozs. each of Kelly green (A) and sapphire (B) for each pillow. 14" knitting needles No. 10. Yarn needle.

GAUGE: 14 sts = 2" (7 sts each side).

Note: Both pillows are made the same. One pillow uses Side A as right side, other pillow uses Side B.

PILLOW (make 2 pieces): With color A, looping sts on with single strand, cast on 114 sts. Join B.

Note: When knitting the k sts, hold both colors in back of work; when purling the p sts, hold both colors in front of work. Twist yarns tog at beg of rows for a firm edge.

Border: Row 1 (Side A): * K 1 A, p 1 B, repeat from * across.

Row 2 (Side B): * K 1 B, p 1 A, repeat from * across. Repeat these 2 rows until piece is 2" from start, end row 2. Check gauge; piece should be 16" wide.

Narrow Stripe: Row 1 (Side A): (K 1 A, p 1 B) 7 times for side border, place a marker on needle; * k 1 B, p 1 A, repeat from * across to last 14 sts, place a marker on needle; (k 1 A, p 1 B) 7 times.

Note: Sl markers every row.

Row 2 (Side B): (K 1 B, p 1 A) 7 times; * k 1 A, p 1 B, repeat from * to marker; (k 1 B, p 1 A) 7 times.

Row 3: Repeat row 1 of narrow stripe.

BLOCK PATTERN: Row 1 (Side B): Work border; (k 1 A, p 1 B) 3 times, * k 1 B, p 1 A, repeat from * to last 20 sts, (k 1 A, p 1 B) 3 times; work border.

Row 2 (Side A): Work border; (k 1 B, p 1 A) 3 times, k 1 A, * (p 1 B, k 1 A) twice; skip first 2 sts on **right-hand** needle, insert **left-hand** needle in front of 3rd st and sl it over the 2 skipped sts and off needle (cluster), repeat from * to last 21 sts, p 1 B, (k 1 B, p 1 A) 3 times; work border.

Row 3 (Side B): Work border; (k 1 A, p 1 B) 3 times, * k 1 B, p 1 A, k 1 B; with A, yo; passing B under the yo st, repeat from * to last 22 sts, k 1 B, p 1 A, (k 1 A, p 1 B) 3 times; work border.

Row 4 (Side A): Work border; (k 1 B, p 1 A) 3 times, k 1 A, p 1 B, k 1 A, * (p 1 B, k 1 A) twice, work cluster as on row 2, repeat from * to last 23 sts, p 1 B, k 1 A, p 1 B, (k 1 B, p 1 A) 3 times; work border.

Row 5 (Side B): Work border; (k 1 A, p 1 B) 3 times, k 1 B, p 1 A, * k 1 B, p 1 A, k 1 B; with A, yo; passing B under the yo st, repeat from * to last 24 sts, (k 1 B, p 1 A) twice, (k 1 A, p 1 B) 3 times; work border.

Repeat rows 2-5 10 times more, or until block pattern is square, end on Side B. Repeat Narrow Stripe rows 1-3, end on Side A. Beg on Side B, work border for 2". Bind off on side to be used for right side by knitting 1 A and 1 B st tog with right side color.

FINISHING: Steam-press pieces to 16" squares. Sew three sides, insert pillow, close fourth side.

TUBULAR-KNIT RUG
Shown on page 91

SIZE: 20" x 34", plus fringe.

MATERIALS: Rayon and cotton rug yarn, 7 70-yard skeins orange, main color (MC), 2 skeins each of gold (A) and yellow (B). 18" knitting needles or 29" circular needle No. 10. Steel crochet hook No. 00. Large-eyed rug needle.

GAUGE: 6 sts = 1" (3 sts on front, 3 sts on back); 9 rows = 1" (9 rows = 2" on front or back).

TUBULAR KNITTING PATTERN (multiple of 2 sts): **Row 1:** * Bring yarn to front, sl 1 as if to p, bring yarn to back, k 1, repeat from * across. Repeat row 1 for pattern.

RUG: With MC, cast on 120 sts. Work in tubular knitting pattern for 36 rows (18 rows on front, 18 rows on back). Check gauge; piece should measure 20" wide, 4" deep. Cut MC.

Striped Pattern: Tie in A. With A, work in pattern for 10 rows (5 rows on front, 5 rows on back). Cut A.

Tie in MC. With MC, Work 2 rows (1 row on front, 1 row on back). Cut MC.

Tie in B. With B, work 28 rows (14 rows on front, 14 rows on back). Cut B.

Tie in MC. With MC, work 2 rows (1 row on front, 1 row on back). Cut MC.

Tie in A. With A, work 10 rows (5 rows on front, 5 rows on back). Cut A.

Center: Tie in MC. With MC, work 116 rows (58 rows on front, 58 rows on back). Cut MC.

Repeat striped pattern.

Tie in MC. With MC, work 36 rows (18 rows on front, 18 rows on back). Bind off as follows: (K 2 tog) twice, * pass first st over 2nd st, k 2 tog, repeat from * across. Cut yarn; pull end through last lp.

FINISHING: Run in ends of yarn on inside of rug. Thread rug needle with long strand of MC. Starting in 3rd row of B stripe, draw yarn under first st at edge. Leave 4 end hanging at side. Go back around same st. Working through both thicknesses, make running st across 3rd B row, going over 1 st, under 1 st. Be sure running st on reverse side is over 1 st and under 1 st. Stitch over edge st at end of row and work back in running st, covering alternate sts. Repeat running st stripe in corresponding row at other end of B stripe. Repeat stripes in 2nd B stripe. Run in yarn ends.

Fringe: Cut strands 6½" long: 62 MC, 62 A, 32 B. Hold one strand of each color together. Insert hook in first st on cast-on edge, catch center of 3 strands, pull loop through st, pull ends of strands through loop; tighten knot. Repeat in last cast-on st. Alternating fringe of 3 colors with fringe of 2 colors (MC and A), knot fringe in every other st across–31 fringe knots. Repeat fringe on bound-off edge. Steam-press.

*No beginner's project, the knitted doily with
its intricate lace patterns in circular knitting is
a challenge even to the experienced knitter.
Directions on page 102.*

CHRYSANTHEMUM MATS

LARGE MAT: SIZE: 15″ diameter.

MATERIALS: Star Mercerized Crochet Cotton, size 20, two 200-yd. balls. Set of steel dp needles No. 1. (Or English size 12.) Steel crochet hook No. 8.

Note: K in front lp of st as usual, unless otherwise directed. Sl sts as if to p.

Beg at center, cast on 8 sts. Divide on 3 needles. Sl and keep a marker on needle between last and first sts of rnd by placing end and beg of rnd at center of a needle.

Rnds 1 and 2: Join, knit around.

Rnd 3: * Yo (an inc), k 1, repeat from * around—16 sts.

Rnd 4 and All Even Rnds: Knit, unless otherwise directed.

Rnd 5: * Yo, k 2 tog, repeat from * around—16 sts.

Rnd 7: * Yo, k 2, repeat from * around—24 sts.

Rnd 9: * Yo, k 3, repeat from * around—32 sts.

Rnd 11: * Yo, k 2, k 2 tog, repeat from * around—32 sts.

Rnd 13: * Yo, k 4, repeat from * around—40 sts.

Rnd 15: * Yo, k 2, yo, k 2 tog, k 1, repeat from * around— 48 sts.

Rnd 17: * Yo, k 4, k 2 tog, repeat from * around—48 sts.

Rnd 19: * Yo, k 6, repeat from * around—56 sts.

Rnd 21: * Yo, k 3, yo, k 2 tog, k 2, repeat from * around—64 sts.

Rnd 23: * Yo, k 1, yo, k 7, repeat from * around—80 sts.

Rnd 25: * Yo, k 3, yo, k 2, sl 1, k 2 tog, psso, k 2, repeat from * around—80 sts.

Rnd 27: * Yo, k 5, yo, k 1, sl 1, k 2 tog, psso, k 1, repeat from * around—80 sts.

Rnd 29: * Yo, k 7, yo, sl 1, k 2 tog, psso, repeat from * around—80 sts.

Rnd 31: * Yo, sl 1, k 1, psso, k 2, yo, k 2 tog, k 1, k 2 tog, yo, k 1 in back lp, repeat from * around—80 sts.

Rnd 33: * K 1, yo, sl 1, k 1, psso, k 3, k 2 tog, yo, k 2, repeat from * around—80 sts.

Rnd 35: * K 2, yo, sl 1, k 1, psso, k 1, k 2 tog, yo, k 3, repeat from * around—80 sts.

Rnd 37: * K 3, yo, sl 1, k 2 tog, psso, yo, k 4, repeat from * around—80 sts.

Rnd 39: * Yo, k 1 in back lp, k 3, yo, sl 1, k 1, psso, k 2, k 2 tog, repeat from * around—80 sts.

Rnd 41: * Yo twice, k 1 in back lp, yo twice, k 1 in back lp, k 7, k 1 in back lp, repeat from * around—96 sts, always counting yo-twice as 1 st.

Note: In all following even rnds, always k 1 yo st of each yo-twice and drop 2nd yo off needle, thus making a long st.

Rnd 43: * Yo twice, k 3, yo twice, k 1 in back lp, k 7, k 1 in back lp, repeat from * around—112 sts.

Rnd 45: * Yo twice, k 5, yo twice, k 1 in back lp, k 3, yo, k 2 tog, k 2, k 1 in back lp, repeat from * around—128 sts.

Rnd 47: * Yo twice, k 7, yo twice, sl 1, k 1, psso, k 5, k 2 tog, repeat from * around—128 sts.

Rnd 49: * Yo twice, k 9, yo twice, sl 1, k 1, psso, k 3, k 2 tog, repeat from * around—128 sts.

Rnd 51: * Yo twice, k 5, yo twice, k 1, yo twice, k 5, yo twice, sl 1, k 1, psso, k 1, k 2 tog, repeat from * around—144 sts.

Rnd 53: * Yo twice, k 5, k 1 in back lp, yo twice, k 3, yo twice, k 1 in back lp, k 5, yo twice, sl 1, k 2 tog, psso, repeat from * around—160 sts.

Rnd 55: * Yo twice, k 1 in back lp, k 5, k 1 in back lp, yo twice, k 5, yo twice, k 1 in back lp, k 5, k 2 tog, repeat from * around—176 sts.

Rnd 57: * K 7, k 1 in back lp, yo twice, k 7, yo twice, k 1 in back lp, k 6, repeat from * around—192 sts.

Rnd 59: * K 6, k 2 tog, yo twice, k 9, yo twice, sl 1, k 1, psso, k 5, repeat from * around to within last st of rnd, move marker back to after last st worked.

Rnd 61: * Yo, sl 1, k 2 tog, psso, yo, k 3, k 2 tog, yo twice, k 5, yo twice, k 1, yo twice, k 5, yo twice, sl 1, k 1, psso, k 3, repeat from * around—208 sts.

Rnd 63: K 1, move marker up to after last st worked, * k 4, k 2 tog, yo twice, k 5, k 1 in back lp, yo twice, k 3, yo twice, k 1 in back lp, k 5, yo twice, sl 1, k 1, psso, k 3, repeat from * around—224 sts.

Rnd 65: * K 3, k 2 tog, yo twice, k 6, k 1 in back lp, yo twice, k 5, yo twice, k 1 in back lp, k 6, yo twice, sl 1, k 1, psso, k 2, repeat from * around—240 sts.

Rnd 67: * K 2, k 2 tog, yo twice, k 6, k 2 tog, yo twice, k 7, yo twice, sl 1, k 1, psso, k 6, yo twice, sl 1, k 1, psso, k 1, repeat from * around—240 sts.

Rnd 69: * K 1, k 2 tog, yo twice, k 6, k 2 tog, yo twice, k 4, yo 3 times, sl 1, k 1, psso, k 3, yo twice, sl 1, k 1, psso, k 6, yo twice, sl 1, k 1, psso, repeat from * around—256 sts, always counting yo-twice as 1 st and yo-3 times as 3 sts.

Rnd 70: Working off, as before, yo-twice as 1 st, * k to the 3 yo-sts, drop the 3 yo-sts off needle, yo 3 times, repeat from * around.

Rnd 71: K 2 sts, move marker up to after last st worked, * yo twice, k 6, k 2 tog, yo twice, k 3, k 2 tog, drop the 3 yo-sts off needle, yo 3 times, sl 1, k 1, psso, k 3, yo twice, sl 1, k 1, psso, k 6, yo twice, sl 1, k 2 tog, psso, repeat from * around—240 sts, counting yo-3 times as 3 sts.

Rnd 72: Repeat rnd 70.

Rnd 73: * Yo twice, k 8, yo twice, k 3, k 2 tog, yo 4 times, drop the 3 yo-sts off left-hand needle, from back insert left-hand needle under the 4 rows of dropped strands and with right-hand needle k

Continued on page 100

Small mat, 5½" in diameter, shown at right, is the center motif for the larger doily, below. For a 15" mat, use mercerized crochet cotton, size 20; for larger sizes, use thicker cottons. Row upon row of petal-like patterns suggest the name for these Chrysanthemum Mats. Two rounds of chain-loop crochet edge doilies. Directions on opposite page.

CORNFLOWER DOILY

SIZE: 16″ diameter, No. 30 thread, 14½″ diameter, No. 50 thread.

MATERIALS: Six Cord Mercerized Crochet Thread, size 30 or 50. Steel dp needles No. 1. Steel crochet hook No. 12.

Beg at center, cast on 7 sts. Divide on 3 needles: 3-2-2.

Rnd 1: Join, k around. Sl and keep a marker on needle between last and first sts of rnd.

Rnd 2: (Yo, k 1) 7 times; 14 sts.

Rnd 3 and All Uneven Rnds: Knit, unless otherwise directed.

Rnd 4: (Yo, k 1) 14 times; 28 sts.

Rnd 6: (Yo, k 2) 14 times; 42 sts.

Rnd 8: (Yo, k 3) 14 times; 56 sts.

Rnd 10: (Yo, k 4) 14 times; 70 sts.

Rnd 12: (Yo, k 5) 14 times; 84 sts.

Rnd 14: (Yo, k 6) 14 times; 98 sts.

Rnd 16: (Yo, k 7) 14 times; 112 sts.

Rnd 18: (Yo, k 8) 14 times; 126 sts.

Rnd 20: (Yo, k 9) 14 times; 140 sts.

Rnd 22: (Yo, k 10) 14 times; 154 sts.

Rnd 24: (Yo, k 11) 14 times; 168 sts.

Rnd 26: (Yo, sl 1 as if to p always, k 1, psso, k 10) 14 times; 168 sts.

Rnd 28: (Yo, k 1, yo, sl 1, k 1, psso, k 9) 14 times; 182 sts.

Rnd 30: (Yo, k 3, yo, sl 1, k 1, psso, k 8) 14 times; 196 sts.

Rnd 32: (Yo, k 5, yo, sl 1, k 1, psso, k 2 tog, sl 1, k 1, psso, k 3) 14 times; 182 sts.

Rnd 34: (Yo, k 1, yo, sl 1, k 1, psso, k 1, k 2 tog, yo, k 1, yo, k 2 tog, sl 1, k 1, psso, k 2) 14 times; 182 sts.

Rnd 35: * K 4, make a butterfly drop-st in next st (*butterfly drop-st:* With crochet hook, sl st off left-hand needle and ravel it down for 5 rows, place this st back on left-hand needle, with hook in back of work, pick up the 5 strands and place them on left-hand needle, then k the st and 5 strands off tog), k 8, repeat from * 13 times more; 182 sts.

Rnd 36: (Yo, k 1, yo, k 2 tog, k 3, sl 1, k 1, psso, yo, k 1, yo, k 1, yo, sl 1, k 1, psso, k 1) 14 times; 210 sts.

Rnd 38: * (Yo, k 2 tog) twice, yo, sl 2, k 1, pass 2 sl-sts over k-st, yo (sl 1, k 1, psso, yo) 3 times, sl 1, k 1, psso, repeat from * 13 times more; 196 sts.

Rnd 40: * (Yo, k 2 tog) twice, yo, k 3, yo, (sl 1, k 1, psso, yo) 3 times, k 1, repeat from * 13 times more; 224 sts.

Rnd 42: * (Yo, k 2 tog) twice, yo, k 5, yo, (sl 1, k 1, psso, yo) twice, sl 2, k 1, pass 2 sl-sts over k-st, repeat from * 13 times more; 224 sts.

Rnd 44: * (Yo, k 2 tog) twice, yo, k 1, yo, sl 1, k 1, psso, k 1, k 2 tog, yo, k 1, yo, (sl 1, k 1, psso, yo) twice, k 1, repeat from * 13 times more; 252 sts.

Rnd 45: * K 8, make butterfly drop-st in next st, k 9, repeat from * 13 times more; 252 sts.

Rnd 46: Sl 1, * (yo, sl 1, k 1, psso) 3 times, k 3, (k 2 tog, yo) 3 times, k 3, repeat from * 13 times more, moving 1 st up at end of rnd; 252 sts. Move marker up. This will happen on every even rnd.

Rnd 48: Sl 1, * (yo, sl 1, k 1, psso) twice, yo, k 1, yo, sl 2 sts, k 1, pass 2 sl-sts over k-st, yo, k 1, (yo, k 2 tog) twice, yo, k 5, repeat from * 13 times more; 280 sts.

Rnd 50: Sl 1, * (yo, sl 1, k 1, psso) 3 times, k 1, (k 2 tog, yo) 3 times, k 7, repeat from * 13 times more; 280 sts.

Rnd 51: * K 16, make butterfly drop-st in next st, k 3, repeat from * 13 times; 20 sts in each pat and 280 sts.

Rnd 52: Sl 1, * (yo, sl 1, k 1, psso) twice, yo, sl 2, k 1, pass 2 sl-sts over k-st, (yo, k 2 tog) twice, yo, sl 2, k 1, pass 2 sl-sts over k-st, yo, k 3, yo, sl 2, k 1, pass 2 sl-sts over k-st, repeat from * 13 times more; 252 sts.

Rnd 54: Sl 1, * (yo, sl 1, k 1, psso) twice, k 1, (k 2 tog, yo) twice, k 3, yo, k 3, yo, k 3, repeat from * 13 times more; 280 sts.

Rnd 56: Sl 1, * yo, sl 1, k 1, psso, yo, sl 2, k 1, pass 2 sl-sts over k-st, yo, k 2 tog, yo, k 5, yo, sl 2, k 1, pass 2 sl-sts over k-st, yo, k 5, repeat from * 13 times more; 280 sts.

Rnd 58: Sl 1, * yo, sl 1, k 1, psso, k 1, k 2 tog, yo, k 7, yo, k 1, yo, k 7, repeat from * 13 times more; 308 sts.

Rnd 59: * K 8, make butterfly drop-st in next st, raveling down 6 rows, k 9, butterfly drop-st in next st, k 3, repeat from * 13 times more; 308 sts.

Rnd 60: Sl 1, * yo, sl 2, k 1, pass 2 sl-sts over k-st, yo, (k 4, yo, k 1, yo) 3 times, k 4; 392 sts.

Rnd 62: * (Yo, k 3, yo, sl 2, k 1, pass 2 sl-sts over k-st, yo, k 5, yo, sl 2, k 1, pass 2 sl-sts over k-st) twice, repeat from * 13 times more; 392 sts. Keep marker between last and first sts of rnd hereafter.

Rnd 64: * (Yo, k 5, yo, sl 1, k 1, psso, yo, k 5, yo, k 2 tog) twice, repeat from * 13 times more; 448 sts.

Rnd 66: * (Yo, sl 1, k 1, psso, k 3, k 2 tog, yo, sl 1, k 1, psso, yo, sl 1, k 1, psso, k 1, k 2 tog, yo, k 2 tog) twice, repeat from * 13 times more; 392 sts.

Rnd 68: * (Yo, k 1, yo, sl 1, k 1, psso, make butterfly drop-st in next st, raveling down 5 rows, k 2 tog, yo, k 1, yo, sl 1, k 1, psso, yo, sl 2, k 1, pass 2 sl-sts over k-st, yo, k 2 tog) twice, repeat from * 13 times more; 392 sts.

Rnd 70: † * (Yo, k 3) 3 times, yo, sl 1, k 1, psso, k 1, k 2 tog, repeat from * once more, then repeat from † 13 times more; 448 sts.

Rnd 72: * (Yo, k 1, yo, sl 2, k 1, pass 2 sl-sts over k-st) 8 times, repeat from * 13 times more; 448 sts.

Rnd 74: Sl last st of rnd on crochet hook, * ch 7, sl next 3 sts from needle to hook, yo, through 3 lps on hook, yo, through 2 lps, ch 7, sl next st from needle to hook, yo, through 1 lp on hook, yo, through 2 lps, repeat from * to end of rnd, ch 7, sl st in first st. End off. If desired, draw center cast-on sts tog at beg of doily. Starch lightly.

Cornflower doily combines a center of solid sections with a deep border of beautiful openwork patterns, including butterfly drop-stitch patterns. In size 30 cotton, doily is 16" in diameter; in size 50 cotton, 14½" in diameter. On last round, groups of stitches are worked off together on a crocket hook for finishing edge. Directions, opposite.

GOTHIC COBWEB DOILY

SIZE: About 12½″ diameter.

MATERIALS: Six Cord Crochet Cotton, No. 30, 2 220-yard balls. Set of steel dp needles No. 1.

Note: K in front lp of sts, unless otherwise directed. Sl sts as if to p.

Beg at center, cast on 8 sts. Divide on 3 needles.

Rnd 1: Join, k around. Sl and keep a marker on needle between last and first sts of rnd, placing end and beg of rnd at center of a needle.

Rnd 2: * Yo (an inc), k 1, repeat from * around—16 sts.

Rnd 3: Knit.

Rnd 4: * Yo, k 1 in back lp, repeat from * around—32 sts.

Rnd 5: Knit.

Rnd 6: * K 1, yo, k 2, yo, k 1, repeat from * around—48 sts.

Rnd 7: * K 1, yo, k 1, p 1, repeat from * around—64 sts.

Rnd 8: * K 2, yo, k 1, p 1, repeat from * around—80 sts.

Rnd 9: * Sl 1, k 1, psso, yo, k 2, p 1, repeat from * around—80 sts.

Rnd 10: * K 2, yo, k 2 tog, p 1, repeat from * around—80 sts.

Rnds 11–15: Repeat rnds 9 and 10 alternately—80 sts.

Rnd 16: * K 2, yo twice, k 2 tog, p 1, repeat from * around—80 sts (always counting yo-twice as 1 st).

Note: In all following rnds, always k 1 yo st of each yo-twice or of each yo-3 times and drop 2nd or 2nd and 3rd yo off needle, thus making a long st.

Rnd 17: * Sl 1, k 1, psso, yo twice, k 2, p 1, repeat from * around—80 sts.

Rnds 18–22: Repeat rnds 16 and 17 alternately—80 sts.

Rnd 23: * Sl 1, k 1, psso, yo, 3 times, k 2, p 1, repeat from * around—80 sts.

Rnd 24: * K 2, yo 3 times, k 2 tog, p 1, repeat from * around—80 sts, counting yo-3 times as 1 st.

Rnds 25–28: Repeat rnds 23 and 24 alternately—80 sts.

Rnd 29: * K 1, k 1 in back lp, yo 11 times, k 1 in back lp of yo-st, drop 2 yo off needle, k 1, p 1, repeat from * around— 80 sts.

Rnd 30: * K 2, k 1 in back lp of each of the 11 yo sts, k 2, p 1, repeat from * around—256 sts.

Rnd 31: * K 15, p 1, repeat from * around.

Rnd 32: * K 15, yo, p 1, yo, repeat from * around—288 sts.

Rnd 33: * K 15, p 3, repeat from * around.

Rnd 34: * Sl 1, k 1, psso, k 11, k 2 tog, yo, p 3, yo, repeat from * around—288 sts.

Rnd 35: * K 13, p 5, repeat from * around.

Rnd 36: * Sl 1, k 1, psso, k 9, k 2 tog, yo, p 5, yo, repeat from * around—288 sts.

Rnd 37: * K 11, p 7, repeat from * around.

Rnd 38: * Sl 1, k 1, psso, k 7, k 2 tog, yo, p 2, yo, (k 1, yo) 3 times, p 2, yo, repeat from * around—352 sts.

Rnd 39: * K 9, p 3, yo (k 2, yo) 3 times, k 1, p 3, repeat from * around—416 sts in rnd.

Rnd 40: * Sl 1, k 1, psso, k 5, k 2 tog, yo, p 3, (k 1, yo, k 2 tog) 3 times, k 1, yo, k 1 in back lp, p 3, yo, repeat from * around—432 sts.

Rnd 41: * K 7, p 4, k 1, (yo, k 1, k 2 tog) 3 times, yo, k 2, p 4, repeat from * around—448 sts.

Rnd 42: Sl 1, k 1, psso, k 3, k 2 tog, yo, p 3, p 2 tog, (k 1, yo, k 2 tog) 3 times, k 1, yo, k 1 in back lp, p 2 tog, p 3, yo, repeat from * around—432 sts.

Rnd 43: * K 5, p 4, p 2 tog, (yo, k 1, k 2 tog) 3 times, yo, k 1, p 2 tog, p 4, repeat from * around—416 sts.

Rnd 44: * Sl 1, k 1, psso, k 1, k 2 tog, yo, p 3, p 2 tog, (k 1, yo, k 2 tog) 3 times, k 1, yo, p 2 tog, p 4, yo, repeat from * around—400 sts.

Rnd 45: * K 3, p 4, p 2 tog, (yo, k 1, k 2 tog) 3 times, yo, k 1, p 2 tog, p 4, repeat from * around—384 sts.

Rnd 46: * Sl 1, k 2 tog, psso, yo, p 3, p 2 tog, (k 1, yo, k 2 tog) 3 times, k 1, yo, p 2 tog, p 4, yo, repeat from * around—368 sts in rnd.

Rnd 47: * K 1, p 4, p 2 tog, (yo, k 1, k 2 tog) 3 times, yo, k 1, p 2 tog, p 4, repeat from * around—352 sts.

Rnd 48: * P 4, p 2 tog, (k 1, yo, k 2 tog) 3 times, k 1, yo, p 2 tog, p 4, repeat from * around—336 sts.

Rnd 49: * P 4, p 2 tog, (yo, k 1, k 2 tog) 3 times, yo, k 1, p 2 tog, p 3, repeat from * around—320 sts.

Rnd 50: * P 1, p 2 tog twice, (k 1, yo twice, k 2 tog) 3 times, k 1, yo twice, p 2 tog twice, p 1, repeat from * around—272 sts (always counting yo-twice as 1 st).

Note: In following rnds, always k 1 yo st of each yo-twice and drop 2nd yo off needle.

Rnd 51: * P 2 tog twice, (yo twice, k 1, k 2 tog) 3 times, yo twice, k 1, p 2 tog, p 1, repeat from * around—240 sts.

Rnd 52: * P 2 tog, (k 1, yo twice, k 2 tog) 3 times, k 1, yo twice, p 3 tog, repeat from * around—208 sts.

Rnd 53: K 2 sts, move marker up to after last st worked, * (k and p 5 times in first yo st, drop next yo off, k 1, k 1 in back lp) 3 times, k and p 5 times in first yo st, drop next yo off, p 3 tog, repeat from * around—432 sts.

Rnd 54: K in each st around. Bind off loosely. Wash, starch, pin out. Let dry.

The gossamer cobweb of white lace at the center of this unusual doily and the cobwebby border are made by dropping yarn-over stitches. Unlike many knitted doilies, last round of work is bound off in knitting, rather than crocheted. In size 30 cotton, piece is 12½″ in diameter. See Gothic Cobweb Doily on opposite page.

CHRYSANTHEMUM MATS

Continued from page 94

them off as 1 st (butterfly st made), yo 4 times, sl 1, k 1, psso, k 3, yo twice, k 8, yo twice, k 1 in back lp, repeat from * around—304 sts, counting yo-4 times as 4 sts.

Rnd 74: * K 14, k 1 in back lp of each of the 4 yo-sts, k 1, k in back lp of each of the 4 yo-sts, k 15, repeat from * around—304 sts.

Shape Points: From now on, each of the 8 points is worked separately, working back and forth as follows:

Row 1: (right side): Bind off 2 sts, k 5 (there are 6 sts counting 1 st after binding off), sl 1, k 1, psso, yo twice, sl 1, k 1, psso, k 13, k 2 tog, yo twice, sl 1, k 1, psso, k 9, place the remaining sts of same needle onto next needle. Turn.

Row 2: Bind off 3 sts, p 30 sts. Turn.

Row 3: Sl 1, k 1, psso, k 6, yo twice, sl 1, k 1, psso, k 4, sl 1, k 2 tog, psso, k 4, k 2 tog, yo twice, k 8—28 sts. Turn.

Row 4: Sl 1, p 1, psso, p 26—27 sts. Turn.

Row 5: Sl 1, k 1, psso, k 6, yo twice, sl 1, k 1, psso, k 7, k 2 tog, yo twice, k 8—26 sts. Turn.

Row 6: Sl 1, p 1, psso, p 24—25 sts. Turn.

Row 7: Sl 1, k 1, psso, k 6, yo twice, sl 1, k 1, psso, k 1, sl 1, k 2 tog, psso, k 1, k 2 tog, yo twice, k 8—22 sts. Turn.

Row 8: Sl 1, p 1, psso, p 20. Turn.

Row 9: Sl 1, k 1, psso, k 6, yo twice, sl 1, k 1, psso, k 1, k 2 tog, yo twice, k 8—20 sts. Turn.

Row 10: Sl 1, p 1, psso, p 18. Turn.

Row 11: Sl 1, k 1, psso, k 6, yo twice, sl 1, k 2 tog, psso, yo twice, k 8—18 sts. Turn.

Row 12: Sl 1, p 1, psso, p 16. Turn.

Row 13: Sl 1, k 1, psso, k 15. Turn.

Row 14: Sl 1, p 1, psso, p 14. Turn.

Row 15: Bind off 2 sts, k to end. Turn.

Row 16: Bind off 2 sts, p to end. Turn.

Row 17: Sl 1, k 1, psso, k 9. Turn.

Row 18: Sl 1, p 1, psso, p 8. Turn. Bind off remaining 9 sts. End off. ** Join thread in next st of rnd 74 and shape next point in same way. Repeat from ** 6 times; do not end off at end of last point; work as follows:

Edging: Rnd 1: From right side, sl last st of last point on crochet hook, ch 8 (lp), * sk 3 sts, sc in next st, ch 7 (lp), repeat from * around entire edge of mat. Join with sl st in first ch of ch 8.

Rnd 2: Sl st in each of next 3 ch of ch 8, ch 8, * sc in next lp, ch 7, repeat from * around, join in first ch of ch 8. End off. Wash, starch lightly and stretch mat to size while damp, pinning out to a point every other lp around outside edge. Let dry.

SMALL MAT (center motif): SIZE: 5½″ diameter. Work as for mat through rnd 30.

Point: Row 1: Sl 1, k 1, psso, k 2, yo, k 2 tog, k 2, k 2 tog.

Row 2 and All Even Rows: Sl first st, p back.

Row 3: Sl 1, k 1, psso, k 3, k 3 tog.

Row 5: Sl 1, k 1, psso, k 1, k 2 tog.

Row 7: Sl 1, k 2 tog, psso. End off. ** Join thread in next st of rnd 30 and shape next point in same way. Repeat from ** 6 times; do not end off at end of last point; work as follows:

Edging: Rnd 1: From right side, sl last st of last point on crochet hook, * sl st loosely in each of the next 2 sts, ch 1, repeat from * around.

Rnd 2: Ch 6, * sk 3 sts, sc in next st, ch 5, repeat from * around. Join with sl st in first ch of ch 6.

Rnd 3: Sl st in each of next 2 ch of ch 6, sc in same lp, * ch 6, sc in next lp, repeat from * around, join in first sc. End off.

KNITTED PLACE MAT

SIZE: Approx. 12″ × 18″.

MATERIALS: Crochet cotton, size 10, 2 20-gram balls. Knitting needles No. 3. Steel crochet hook No. 6.

Gauge: 6 sts = 1″; 11 rows = 1″.

Note: Always sl first st of row and k last st through back lp of st—referred to as "edge st."

BORDER: Cast on 70 sts.

Rows 1 to 8: Working edge sts each side (see note) work in garter st.

Row 9: Edge st, k 3, * k 2 tog, yo, repeat from * to last 8 sts, k 2, yo, k 2 tog, k 3, edge st.

Row 10: Edge st, k across, end edge st.

Row 11: Edge st, k 3, k 2 tog, yo, k to last 6 sts, yo, k 2 tog, k 3, edge st.

Row 12: Repeat row 10.

Rows 13 to 16: Repeat rows 11 and 12 twice.

PATTERN (Multiple of 10 sts plus 2):

Row 1: Edge st, k 3, k 2 tog, yo, k 3 (border);

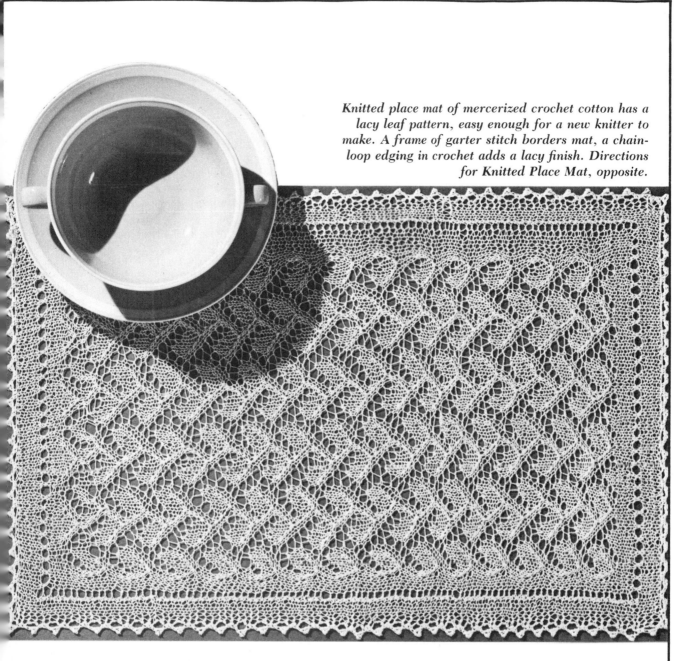

Knitted place mat of mercerized crochet cotton has a lacy leaf pattern, easy enough for a new knitter to make. A frame of garter stitch borders mat, a chain-loop edging in crochet adds a lacy finish. Directions for Knitted Place Mat, opposite.

k 2, * yo, k 1, yo, k 1, sl 1, k 1, psso, k 3, k 2 tog, k 1, repeat from * across to last 9 sts; k 3, yo, k 2 tog, k 3, edge st.

Row 2 and All Even Rows: Edge st, k 8, p 52, k 8, edge st.

Row 3: Work border; k 2, * yo, k 3, yo, k 1, sl 1, k 1, psso, k 1, k 2 tog, k 1, repeat from * across to last 9 sts, work border.

Row 5: Border; k 2, * yo, k 5, yo, k 1, sl 1, k 2 tog, psso, k 1, repeat from * across to last 9 sts; border.

Row 7: Border, * sl 1, k 1, psso, k 3, k 2 tog, k 1, yo, k 1, yo, k 1, repeat from * across to last 11 sts, k 2; border.

Row 9: Border; * sl 1, k 1; repeat from * across to last 11 sts, k 2; border.

Row 11: Border; * sl 1, k 2 tog, psso, k 1, yo, k 5, yo, k 1, repeat from * to last 11 sts, k 2; border.

Row 12: Repeat row 2 of pat. Repeat rows 1 through 12 for pat until piece measures 17″ from start, end row 11 of pat.

Next row: Edge st, k across, end edge st. Repeat rows 11 and 10 of border alternately for 6 rows.

Next row: Repeat row 9 of border. Repeat rows 1 to 7 of border. Bind off loosely, do not end off last lp, work as follows:

EDGING: Insert crochet hook in last lp, ch 1, working along side, sc in next st (in st between knots at end of rows on side edges), * ch 3, sc in 2nd ch from hook, dc in next ch (p made), sk 1 st, sc in each of next 2 sts, repeat from * around, do not sk sts between p's each side of each corner, join rnd with sl st in first ch. End off. Starch and block mat. Repeat this process after each washing.

KNITTED ASTER DOILY

Shown on page 93

SIZE: 20″ diameter.

MATERIALS: Six Cord Mercerized Crochet Cotton, size 30, 3 220-yd. balls. Five dp aluminum needles No. 1. Steel crochet hook No. 13.

Note: Circular needles may be substituted for dp needles after Rnd 21 as follows: Rnd 22 (11″ needle), Rnd 28 (16″ needle), Rnd 38 (24″ needle).

STITCHES AND ADDITIONAL ABBREVIATIONS:

C 2–Cross 2 Stitches: Sk 1 st, k in front lp of next st, k in front lp of skipped st, sl both sts from lefthand needle.

T 1–Turn 1 Stitch: K in back lp of st.

D 1–Butterfly Drop Stitch: With crochet hook, sl st off left-hand needle and unravel it for 5 or 3 rows as specified, place this st back on left-hand needle; with hook in back of work, pick up the 5 or 3 strands and place them on left-hand needle, then k the st and 5 or 3 strands off tog.

R 2 decs–Reverse 2 Decreases: Sl 1, k 1, psso (1 dec), sl remaining k st to left-hand needle and pass next st on left-hand needle over this slipped st (1 dec), then sl the slipped st back to right-hand needle.

DOILY: Beg at center, cast on 12 sts. Divide on 3 needles (4 sts on each needle) and work with 4th needle.

Rnd 1: Join, k around. Sl and keep a marker on needle between last and first st of rnd.

Rnd 2: Knit.

Rnd 3 and all odd rnds: Knit.

Rnd 4: (Yo, k 1) 12 times–24 sts.

Rnd 6: (Yo, C 2) 12 times–36 sts.

Rnd 8: (Yo, k 1, C 2) 12 times–48 sts.

Rnd 10: (Yo, k 2, C 2) 12 times–60 sts.

Rnd 12: (Yo, k 1, C 2 twice) 12 times–72 sts.

Rnd 14: (Yo, k 1, C 2, k 1, C 2) 12 times–84 sts.

Rnd 16: (Yo, k 1, C 2, k 2, C 2) 12 times–96 sts.

Rnd 18: (Yo, k 1, C 2, k 3, C 2) 12 times–108 sts.

Rnd 20: (Yo, k 1, C 2, k 4, C 2) 12 times–120 sts.

Rnd 22: (Yo, k 1, C 2, k 5, C 2) 12 times–132 sts.

Rnd 24: (Yo, sl, k 1, psso, C 2, k 5, C 2) 12 times–132 sts.

Rnd 26: (Yo, k in back and front of next st, yo, sl 1, k 1, psso, C 2, k 4, C 2) 12 times–156 sts.

Rnd 28: (Yo, k 4, yo, sl 1, k 1, psso, C 2, k 3, C 2) 12 times–168 sts.

Rnd 30: * (Yo, p 3, pass the first p st over 2 remaining p sts) twice, yo, sl 1, k 1, psso, C 2, k 2, C 2, repeat from * 11 times more–168 sts.

Rnd 32: * Yo, k 2, yo, p 3, pass first p st over 2 remaining p sts, yo, k 2, yo, sl 1, k 1, psso, C 2, k 1, C 2, repeat from * 11 times more–192 sts.

Rnd 34: * Yo, k 2, (yo, p 3, pass first p st over remaining 2 p sts) twice, yo, k 2, yo, sl 1, k 1, psso, C 2 twice, repeat from * 11 times more–216 sts.

Rnd 36: * Yo, k 2, (yo, p 3, pass first p st over 2 remaining p sts) 3 times, yo, k 2, yo, sl 1, k 1, psso, k 1, C 2, repeat from * 11 times more–240 sts.

Rnd 38: * Yo, C 2, (yo, p 3, pass first p st over 2 remaining p sts) 4 times, yo, C 2, yo, sl 1, k 1, psso, C 2, repeat from * 11 times more–264 sts. Divide sts on 4 needles and work with 5th needle.

Rnd 40: * (Yo, k 2 tog) 4 times, yo, sl 2, k 1, pass 2 sl sts over k st, yo, (sl 1, k 1, psso, yo) 4 times, sl 1, k 1, psso, k 1, repeat from * 11 times more–252 sts.

Rnd 42: *(Yo, k 2 tog) 4 times, yo, sl 2, k 1, pass 2 sl sts over k st, yo, (sl 1, k 1, psso, yo) 4 times, C 2, repeat from * 11 times more–252 sts.

Rnd 44: * K 2 tog, (yo, k 2 tog) 3 times, yo, k 3, yo, (sl 1, k 1, psso, yo) 3 times, sl 1, k 1, psso, C 2, repeat from * 11 times more–252 sts.

Rnd 46: Remove marker, sl 1 st, insert marker, * k 2 tog, (yo, k 2 tog) twice, yo, k 5, yo, (sl 1, k 1, psso, yo) twice, sl 1, k 1, psso, C 2 twice, repeat from * 11 times more–252 sts.

Rnd 48: Remove marker, sl 1, insert marker, * (yo, k 2 tog) twice, yo, k 3, yo, D 1 for 5 rows, yo, k 3, yo, (sl 1, k 1, psso, yo) twice, sl 1, k 1, psso, C 2, k 2 tog, repeat from * 11 times more–276 sts.

Rnd 50: * K 2 tog twice, yo, k 5, yo, k 1, yo, k 5, yo, (sl 1, k 1, psso) 3 times, k 2 tog, repeat from * 11 times more–252 sts.

Rnd 52: Remove marker, sl 2 sts, insert marker, * yo, k 3, yo, D 1 for 5 rows, yo, k 3, yo, T 1, yo, k 3, yo, D 1 for 5 rows, yo, k 3, yo, sl 1, k 1, psso, k 2, k 2 tog, repeat from * 11 times more–324 sts.

Rnd 54: * Yo, k 5, yo, k 1, yo, k 5, yo, T 1, yo, k 5, yo, k 1, yo, k 5, yo, sl 1, k 1, psso, k 2 tog, repeat from * 11 times more–396 sts.

Rnd 56: * Sl 1, k 1, psso, k 11, k 2 tog, yo, T 1, yo, sl 1, k 1, psso, k 11, k 2 tog, C 2, repeat from * 11 times more–372 sts.

Rnd 58: * Sl 1, k 1, psso, k 9, k 2 tog, yo, k 1, yo, T 1, yo, k 1, yo, sl 1, k 1, psso, k 9, k 2 tog, yo, C 2, yo, repeat from * 11 times more–396 sts.

Rnd 60: * Sl 1, k 1, psso, k 7, k 2 tog, yo, k 3, yo, T 1, yo, k 3, yo, sl 1, k 1, psso, k 7, k 2 tog, yo, sl 1, k 1, psso, k 2 tog, yo, repeat from * 11 times

KNITTED ASTER DOILY

Continued

more-396 sts.

Rnd 62: * Sl 1, k 1, psso, k 5, k 2 tog, yo, k 2, yo, D 1 for 3 rows, yo, k 2, yo, T 1, yo, k 2, yo, D 1 for 3 rows, yo, k 2, yo, sl 1, k 1, psso, k 5, k 2 tog, yo, sl 1, k 1, psso, k 2 tog, yo, repeat from * 11 times more-444 sts.

Rnd 64: * Sl 1, k 1, psso, k 3, k 2 tog, yo, k 9, yo, T 1, yo, k 9, yo, sl 1, k 1, psso, k 3, k 2 tog, yo, sl 1, k 1, psso, k 2 tog, yo, repeat from * 11 times more-444 sts.

Rnd 66: * Sl 1, k 1 psso, k 1, k 2 tog, yo, sl 1, k 1, psso, k 7, k 2 tog, yo, k 1, yo, sl 1, k 1, psso, k 7, k 2 tog, yo, sl 1, k 1, psso, k 1, k 2 tog, yo, sl 1, k 1, psso, yo, repeat from * 11 times more-408 sts.

Rnd 68: *Sl 1, k 2 tog, psso, yo, k 1, yo, sl 1, k 1, psso, k 5, k 2 tog, yo, k 3, yo, sl 1, k 1, psso, k 5, k 2 tog, yo, k 1, yo, R 2 decs, yo, k 2 tog, yo, k 1, yo, sl 1, k 1, psso, yo, repeat from * 11 times more-408 sts.

Rnd 70: Remove marker, sl 1, insert marker, * yo, k 2 tog, yo, k 1, yo, sl 1, k 1, psso, k 3, k 2 tog, yo, k 2 tog, yo, k 1, (yo, sl 1, k 1, psso) twice, k 3, k 2 tog, yo, k 1, yo, (sl 1, k 1, psso, yo) 3 times, k 1, (yo, k 2 tog) twice, repeat from * 11 times more-432 sts.

Rnd 72: * (Yo, k 2 tog) twice, yo, k 1, yo, sl 1, k 1, psso, k 1, k 2 tog, yo, k 2 tog, (yo, k 1) 3 times, yo, sl 1, k 1, psso, yo, sl 1, k 1, psso, k 1, k 2 tog, yo, k 1, yo, (sl 1, k 1, psso, yo) 4 times, k 1, (yo, k 2 tog) twice, repeat from * 11 times more-480 sts.

Rnd 74: * (K 2 tog, yo) 3 times, k 1, yo, sl 1, k 2 tog, psso, (yo, k 2 tog) twice, yo, k 3, yo, (sl 1, k 1, psso, yo) twice, R 2 decs, yo, k 1, (yo, sl 1, k 1, psso) 5 times, yo, k 1, yo, (k 2 tog, yo) twice, repeat from * 11 times more-504 sts.

Rnd 76: * (Sl 1, k 1, psso, yo) 7 times, sl 2, k 1, pass 2 sl sts over k st, (yo, k 2 tog) 9 times, yo, k 3, yo, (sl 1, k 1, psso, yo) twice, repeat from * 11 times more-504 sts.

Rnd 78: * (Sl 1, k 1, psso, yo) 5 times, (sl 1, k 1, psso) twice, k 1, (k 2 tog) twice, (yo, k 2 tog) 7 times, yo, k 5, yo, (sl 1, k 1, psso, yo) twice, repeat from * 11 times more-480 sts.

Rnd 80: * (Sl 1, k 1, psso, yo) 4 times, (sl, k 1, psso) twice, k 1, (k 2 tog) twice, (yo, k 2 tog) 6 times, yo, k 3, yo, D 1 for 5 rows, yo, k 3, yo, (sl 1, k 1, psso, yo) twice, repeat from * 11 times more-480 sts.

Rnd 82: Remove markers, sl 1, insert marker, * (k 2 tog, yo) 3 times, k 1, yo, sl 1, k 1, psso, k 1, k 2 tog, yo, k 1, (yo, sl 1, k 1, psso) 7 times, k 5, (k 2 tog, yo) 4 times, repeat from * 11 times more-480 sts.

Rnd 84: Remove marker, sl 1, insert marker, * (k 2 tog, yo) twice, k 3, yo, sl 2, k 1, pass 2 sl sts over k st, yo, k 3, (yo, sl 1, k 1, psso) 7 times, k 3, (k 2 tog, yo) 5 times, repeat from * 11 times-480 sts.

Rnd 86: Remove markers, sl 1, insert marker, * k 3, yo, sl 1, k 2 tog, psso, yo, (k 1, yo) 3 times, sl 1, k 2 tog, psso, yo, k 3, (yo, sl 1, k 1, psso) 6 times, k 1, (k 2 tog, yo) 6 times, repeat from * 11 times more-504 sts.

Rnd 88: Remove marker, sl 2, insert marker, * k 1, k 2 tog, (yo, k 1, yo, k 3) twice, yo, k 1, yo, sl 1, k 1, psso, k 1, k 2 tog, (yo, sl 1, k 1, psso) 5 times, yo, sl 2, k 1, pass 2 sl sts over k st, yo, (k 2 tog, yo) 5 times, sl 1, k 1, psso, repeat from * 11 times more-528 sts.

Rnd 90: Remove marker, sl 1, insert marker, * (k 3, yo, sl 1, k 2 tog, psso, yo) 3 times, k 1, yo, (sl 1, k 1, psso, yo) 4 times, sl 1, k 1, psso, k 1, k 2 tog, (yo k 2 tog) 4 times, yo, k 1, yo, sl 1, k 2 tog, psso, yo, repeat from * 11 times more-528 sts.

Rnd 92: * (Yo, sl 1, k 2 tog, psso, yo, k 3) 3 times, (yo, k 1) twice, yo, (sl 1, k 1, psso, yo) 4 times, sl 2, k 1, pass 2 sl sts over k st, (yo, k 2 tog) 4 times, yo, (k 1, yo) twice, k 3, repeat from * 11 times more-576 sts.

Rnd 94: * K 3, yo, sl 1, k 2 tog, psso, yo, (k 1, yo) 3 times, (sl 1, k 2 tog, psso, yo, k 3, yo) twice, (k 1, yo) twice, (sl 1, k 1, psso, yo) twice, (sl 1, k 1, psso) twice, k 1, (k 2 tog) twice, (yo, k 2 tog) twice, yo, (k 1, yo) twice, k 3, yo, sl 1, k 2 tog, psso, yo, repeat from * 11 times more-624 sts.

Rnd 96: * Yo, sl 1, k 2 tog, psso, yo, k 3, (yo, k 1, yo, k 3) twice, (yo, sl 1, k 2 tog, psso, yo, k 3) twice, (yo, k 1) twice, yo, (sl 1, k 1, psso) 3 times, k 1, (k 2 tog) 3 times, yo, (k 1, yo) twice, k 3, yo, sl 1, k 2 tog, psso, yo, k 3, repeat from * 11 times more-672 sts.

Rnd 98: Sl last st of rnd on crochet hook, * sl first 3 sts from left-hand needle on crochet hook, yo and through 3 lps on hook, yo and through 2 lps on hook (sc on 3 sts tog), ch 8, sc next 3 sts tog as before, ch 9, sc next 3 tog, (ch 10, sc next 3 tog) twice, ch 9, sc next 3 tog, ch 8, sc next 3 tog, ch 7, sc next 3 tog, ch 6, sc next 3 tog, ch 5, sc next 3 tog, ch 4, sc next 3 tog, ch 3, sc next 2 tog, ch 3, (sc 1 st off at a time, no ch between) 7 times, ch 3, sc 2 tog, ch 3, sc 3 tog, ch 4, sc 3 tog, ch 5, sc 3 tog, ch 6, sc 3 tog, ch 7, repeat from * around, end last repeat sc 2 tog, ch 7, sl st in first sc. End off. If desired, draw cast-on sts tog at center. Wash, starch and pin out to size, let dry.

Textured pillow in beige, brick, blue, and white uses the right and "wrong" sides of the same pattern stripe to create this handsome design. Directions for Reverse Stripe Pillow, page 66.

Fuchsia, pink, and violet, knit in seed stitch and two slip stitch patterns, make a jewel-like combination in the striped and tasseled pillow, below. Diagonal Stripe Pillow, page 66.

Norse sweater dress in the cool colors of the sea with flashes of warm rose can be made in any length. Knit it as a tube in the Scandinavian way on a circular needle; stitch, then slash the armholes and sew in the tubular sleeves. Norse Sweater Dress, sizes 8 to 18, on page 78.

Two-color pullover is knit in the "key and basket" pattern of mosaic knitting, using only one color at a time. Sleeves, top and bottom edges are ribbed. Sizes 6–16. See Mosaic Pullover, page 77.

Fair Isle knitting, characterized by a horizontal pattern stripe worked in stockinette, may be in as many colors as you please. Here, three tones create the patterned vest that combines with an Aran cardigan. For Fair Isle Set, see page 74.

The Aran Isles at the entrance of Galway Bay have given their name to the Irish knits that are a tour de force of beautiful raised pattern stitches. Cables, popcorns, and diamonds are worked in panels on this warm and cozy infant's sweater and its matching ribbon-tied cap. Directions for Aran Baby Set are on page 72.

The same honeycomb pattern is used throughout in this easy-to-knit afghan, worked in five strips. Yarn in white and brown is used double, making solid blocks of a color alternating with tweeded blocks. See Honeycomb Blocks, page 71.

DESIGNED BY VIOLA SYLBERT FOR COLUMBIA-MINERVA YARNS

Striped pillows in oblong and square shapes are knit the same back and front in pleasing bands of navy, cranberry and white. Popcorn patterns are crocheted in after the knitting is finished; fringe is knotted on. Popcorn Pillows, page 68.

Knit a cozy afghan for winter warmth, then embellish it with pretty Alpine flowers. In this pattern, diamonds, marked off with popcorn puffs, alternate in stockinette and reverse stockinette stitch. Red and blue flowers are embroidered in bullion stitch. Afghan, 56" × 48", can be made longer. Matching pillow is 20" square. Rose Afghan Set, page 69.

PART 11

CROCHET

Who was the first crocheter? We do not know; the origins of crochet are obscure. The word "crochet" itself comes from the French word for hook "croche". Possibly France deserves the credit for the first written instructions and it may be because of the instructions that the French word for this craft is used. Crochet is a development of tambour work, embroidery worked in chain stitch with a small hook. Crochet eliminated the use of background material and became the art of working chains and loops in the air.

It is possible that crochet was invented to simulate fine needle laces. The earliest date we have for crochet is the 16th century, when fine laces were worked by nuns in Europe. Nuns carried the craft to Ireland where it was developed into an elaborate form with raised roses, leaves and picot lace fillings.

Crochet has had many ups and downs in popularity. Today it is as popular as it has ever been because of the great upsurge in fashion crochet. Starting in Italy and picked up in France, England and other countries of Europe, the use of crochet for beautiful clothes has created a new demand for crocheters and a new desire on the part of women everywhere to learn how to crochet.

ABBREVIATIONS AND STITCHES

STITCHES

Treble or Triple Crochet (tr): With 1 loop on hook put yarn over hook twice, insert in 5th chain from hook, pull loop through. Yarn over and draw through 2 loops at a time 3 times. At end of a row, chain 4 and turn. Chain 4 counts as first treble of next row.

Double Treble (dtr): Put yarn over hook 3 times and work off 2 loops at a time as for treble.

Treble Treble (tr tr): Put yarn over hook 4 times and work off 2 loops at a time as for treble.

HOW TO TURN YOUR WORK

In crochet a certain number of ch sts are needed at the end of each row to bring work into position for the next row. Then work is turned so reverse side is facing the crocheter. Follow the stitch table below for the number of ch sts required to make a turn.

Single crochet (sc)	Ch 1 to turn
Half double crochet (half dc or hdc)	Ch 2 to turn
Double crochet (dc)	Ch 3 to turn
Treble crochet (tr)	Ch 4 to turn
Double treble crochet (dtr)	Ch 5 to turn
Treble treble crochet (tr tr)	Ch 6 to turn

CROCHET HOOKS (STEEL)														
U.S.	1	2	3	4	5	6	7	8	9	10	11	12	13	14
English	3/0	2/0	1/0	1	1½	2	2½	3	4	5	5½	6	6½	7
Continental—mm.	3	2.5		2		1.75	1.5	1.25	1	0.75		0.6		

CROCHET HOOKS (ALUMINUM OR PLASTIC)									
U.S.	1/B	2/C	3/D	4/E	5/F	6/G	8/H	9/I	10/J	10½/K
English	12	11	10	9	8	7	6	5	4	2
Continental—mm.	2½	3		3½	4	4½	5	5½	6	7

CROCHET ABBREVIATIONS

ch–chain stitch
st–stitch
sts–stitches
lp–loop
inc–increase
dec–decrease
rnd–round
beg–beginning
sk–skip
p–picot
tog–together
lp–loop

sc–single crochet
sl st–slip stitch
dc–double crochet
hdc–half double crochet
tr–treble or triple crochet
dtr–double treble crochet
tr tr–treble treble crochet
bl–block
sp–space
cl–cluster
pat–pattern
yo–yarn over hook

HOW TO FOLLOW DIRECTIONS

An asterisk (*) is often used in crochet directions to indicate repetition. For example, when directions read "* 2 dc in next st, 1 dc in next st, repeat from * 4 times" this means to work directions after first * until second * is reached, then go back to first * 4 times more. Work 5 times in all.

When ( ) (parentheses) are used to show repetition, work directions within parentheses as many times as specified. For example, "(dc, ch 1) 3 times" means to do what is within ( ) 3 times altogether.

"Work even" in directions means to work in same stitch without increasing or decreasing.

CROCHET HOOKS-THEIR SIZES AND USES

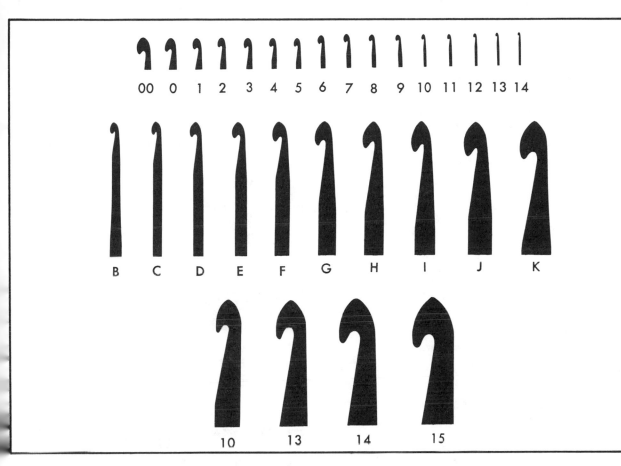

Crochet hooks come in a large range of sizes, from the very fine No. 14 steel hook for fine crochet cotton to larger hooks of aluminum, or plastic for coarser cotton, wool or other yarns.

STEEL CROCHET HOOKS

These are 5″ long and come in size 00 (large) to 14 (very fine). Steel hooks are generally used for cotton threads, but the larger sizes are often used for other yarns.

PLASTIC AND ALUMINUM HOOKS

Plastic crochet hooks are 5½″ long and come in sizes D to K. These hooks sometimes carry a number, too. The numbers, however, are not standardized.

"Bone" crochet hooks are 5″ long and come in sizes 1 to 6, roughly the equivalent of B to G shown in illustration.

Aluminum crochet hooks are 6″ long and come in sizes B to K.

Afghan hooks of aluminum and plastic are 9″ to 18″ long and have a straight, even shaft. They range from sizes 4 to 10½ and E to K. When afghan hooks are sized by number, the shaft of each hook is roughly equal to the same size in knitting needles. When they are sized by letter, they are equivalent to crochet hooks sized in the same way.

WOODEN CROCHET HOOKS

These are 9″ or 10″ long in sizes 10 to 16, and are used for jiffy work. For extra bulky crochet, hollow plastic hooks are available in sizes Q and S.

STEP-BY-STEP LESSON FOR RIGHT-HANDED CROCHETERS

GETTING READY TO CROCHET

1. Use a ball of knitting worsted for practicing your stitches when learning to crochet and a crochet hook size H or 6 in a contrasting color.

If you have never learned to crochet, you can teach yourself from this step-by-step lesson. On these pages, we show, in a series of photographs, basic information on crochet—how to hold your yarn and hook, how to make chain stitch, single crochet, double crochet, half double crochet, and slip stitch, how to turn your work at the end of a row, how to increase and decrease, how to end off. After you have finished the lesson, turn to page 114. On that page, we give Abbreviations used in our crochet directions, other information you will need to follow directions; the importance of gauge in making any crocheted fashion is on page 128.

2. Grasp the yarn about 2" from the end between your thumb and forefinger. With your right hand, lap the long strand over the short, forming a loop.

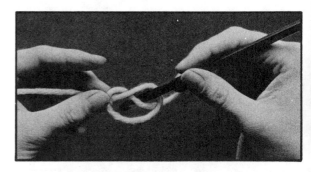

3. Hold this loop in place between your left thumb and forefinger. Grasp the hook in your right hand like a pencil. Insert the hook through the loop.

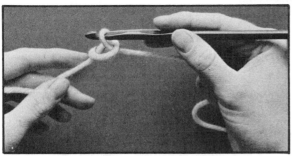

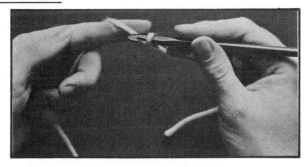

CHAIN STITCH (ch)

4. Catch the strand with the hook and draw it through loop. Pull end of yarn and strand coming from ball in opposite directions to close loop.

7. Hold the hook in your right hand as shown. Bend the little finger, ring finger, and middle finger of left hand to control strand of yarn.

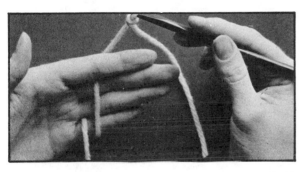

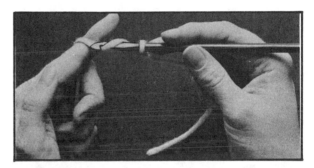

5. Loop yarn from ball around base of little finger of left hand. Bring yarn across front of three fingers and back under forefinger.

8. Pass the hook under the strand of yarn on index finger. Catch yarn with hook and draw it through loop on hook. This makes one chain stitch (1 ch).

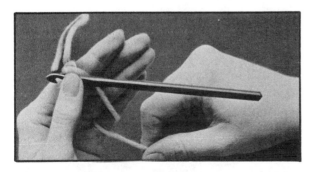

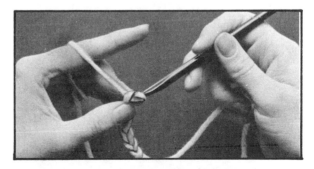

6. To adjust the tension of your yarn, grasp the hook and loop in your left hand. Pull strand from ball firmly down to tighten around fingers.

9. Make as many chains as needed. (One loop remains on hook, but does not count as a chain.) Practice until you can make chains even in size.

STEP-BY-STEP LESSON FOR RIGHT-HANDED CROCHETERS

SINGLE CROCHET (sc)

10. Chain 20 stitches for practice piece. Hold chain with right side toward you. Insert hook under two top threads of 2nd chain from hook.

13. Insert hook under two top threads of next chain and repeat: yarn over hook, draw loop through, yarn over and through two loops.

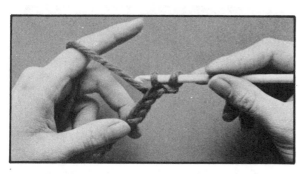

11. Pass hook under yarn on index finger and catch yarn with hook as you did for chain stitch. Draw yarn through chain — two loops on hook.

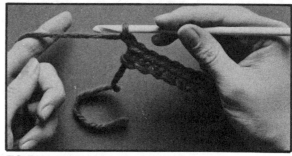

TO TURN SINGLE CROCHET

14. Work a single crochet in each chain to end of row. You will have one single crochet less than number of chains. At end of row, chain one.

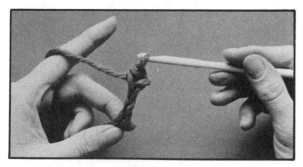

12. Yarn over hook again and draw it through the two loops on hook. This completes one single crochet (1 sc). One loop is left on the hook.

15. Turn work so that reverse side faces you. Insert hook under two top threads of first stitch. Work single crochet as before in each stitch.

118

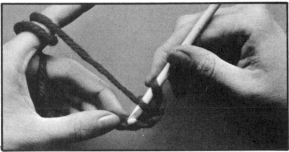

DOUBLE CROCHET (dc)

16. Chain 20 stitches for practice piece. Yarn over hook, insert hook under two top threads of 4th chain from hook (do not count loop on hook).

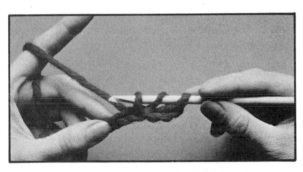

17. Pass the hook under the strand of yarn on index finger. Catch yarn with hook and draw it through the chain stitch — three loops on hook.

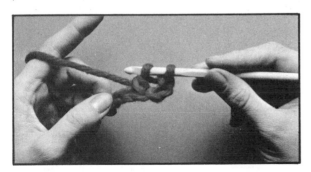

18. Pass hook under yarn on index finger again, catch yarn with hook and draw it through the two loops on hook. There are now two loops remaining.

19. Yarn over hook again and draw through the last two loops on hook. This completes one double crochet (1 dc). Work double crochet in each chain.

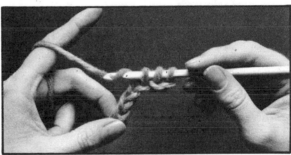

HALF DOUBLE CROCHET (hdc)

20. Yarn over hook, insert hook under two top threads of 3rd chain from hook, catch yarn with hook, draw through chain three loops on hook.

21. Pass hook under yarn on index finger again, catch yarn with hook and draw through all three loops on hook—one half double crochet.

STEP-BY-STEP LESSON FOR RIGHT-HANDED CROCHETERS

SLIP STITCH (sl st)
22. Slip stitch is often used as an edge stitch on crochet and knitting. Insert hook, yarn over, pull through stitch and loop in one motion.

TO INCREASE 1 STITCH (inc 1 st)
25. When directions say "increase one stitch", make two stitches in one. In hats and other round pieces, increases are made every round.

SLIP STITCH FOR JOINING
23. Slip stitch is also used for joining chains into rings and joining rounds of crochet. For joining ring, insert the hook in the last chain from hook.

TO DECREASE 1 SINGLE CROCHET (dec 1 sc)
26. When directions say "decrease one single crochet", work one single crochet until there are two loops on hook. Begin next single crochet.

24. Pass the hook under strand of yarn on index finger, draw yarn through chain and loop on hook with one motion—ring is joined with slip stitch.

27. Yarn over hook and draw through all three loops on hook with one motion. There is now only one stitch to work in on the next row.

STEP-BY-STEP LESSON FOR RIGHT-HANDED CROCHETERS

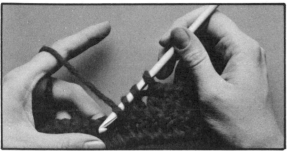

TO DECREASE 1 DOUBLE CROCHET (dec 1 dc)
28. Work one double crochet until there are two loops on hook. Begin next double crochet : yarn over hook, insert in stitch, draw loop through.

TO END OFF
31. When directions say "end off", cut the yarn 3" or more from your last stitch. Insert hook in final loop, yarn over hook and draw through last loop.

29. With four loops on hook, pass hook under strand of yarn on index finger, catch yarn, draw through two loops, leaving three loops on hook.

32. Pull yarn end to tighten stitch. This fastens the end of your work. To hide yarn end, thread it in a yarn needle and weave it into the back of work.

30. Yarn over hook and draw through all three loops on hook with one motion. There is now only one stitch to work in on the next row.

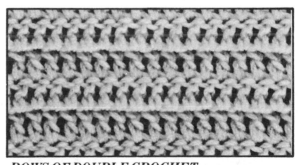

ROWS OF DOUBLE CROCHET
33. Photograph shows double crochet worked back and forth. When turning work at end of row, ch 3 to count as first double crochet of next row.

STEP-BY-STEP LESSON FOR LEFT-HANDED CROCHETERS

GETTING READY TO CROCHET

1. Use a ball of knitting worsted for practicing your stitches when learning to crochet and a crochet hook size H or 6 in a contrasting color.

If you have never learned to crochet, you can teach yourself from this step-by-step lesson. On these pages, we show, in a series of photographs, basic information on crochet—how to hold your yarn and hook, how to make chain stitch, single crochet, double crochet, half double crochet, and slip stitch, how to turn your work at the end of a row, how to increase and decrease, how to end off. After you have finished the lesson, turn to page 114. On that page, we give Abbreviations used in our crochet directions, other information you will need to follow directions; the importance of gauge in making any crocheted fashion is on page 128.

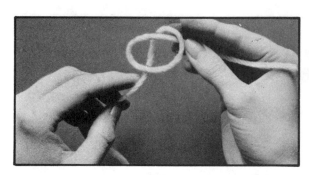

2. Grasp the yarn about 2" from the end between your thumb and forefinger. With your left hand, lap the long strand over the short, forming a loop.

3. Hold this loop in place between your right thumb and forefinger. Grasp the hook in your left hand like a pencil. Insert hook through loop.

STEP-BY-STEP LESSON FOR LEFT-HANDED CROCHETERS

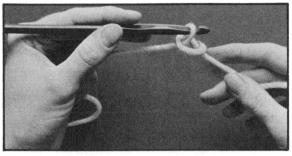

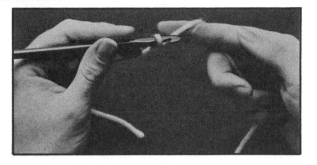

CHAIN STITCH (ch)

4. Catch the strand with the hook and draw it through loop. Pull end of yarn and strand coming from ball in opposite directions to close loop.

7. Hold the hook in your left hand as shown. Bend the little finger, ring finger, and middle finger of right hand to control strand of yarn.

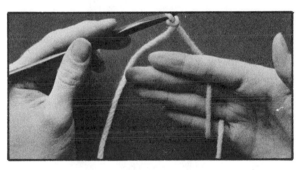

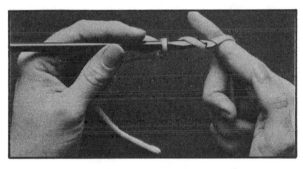

5. Loop yarn from ball around base of little finger of right hand. Bring yarn across front of three fingers and back under forefinger.

8. Pass the hook under the strand of yarn on index finger. Catch yarn with hook and draw it through loop on hook - one chain stitch (1 ch).

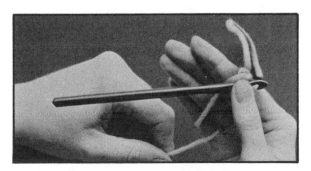

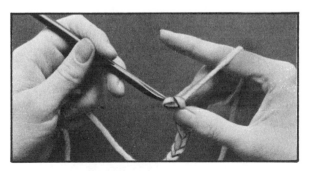

6. To adjust tension of your yarn, grasp the hook and loop in your right hand as shown. Pull strand from ball firmly down to tighten around fingers.

9. Make as many chains as needed. (One loop remains on hook, but does not count as a chain.) Practice until you can make chains even in size.

STEP-BY-STEP LESSON FOR LEFT-HANDED CROCHETERS

SINGLE CROCHET (sc)

10. Chain 20 stitches for practice piece. Hold chain with right side toward you. Insert hook under two top threads of 2nd chain from hook.

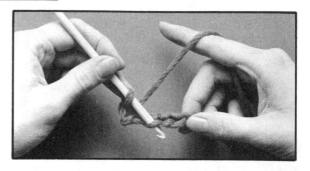

13. Insert hook under two top threads of next chain and repeat : yarn over hook, draw loop through, yarn over and through two loops.

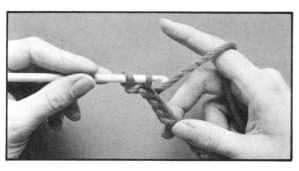

11. Pass hook under yarn on index finger and catch yarn with hook as you did for chain stitch. Draw yarn through chain—two loops on hook.

TO TURN SINGLE CROCHET

14. Work a single crochet in each chain to end of row. You will have one single crochet less than number of chains. At end of row, chain one.

12. Yarn over hook again and draw it through the two loops on hook. This completes one single crochet (1 sc). One loop is left on the hook.

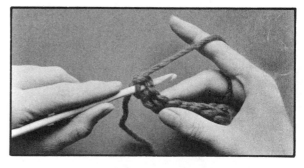

15. Turn work so that reverse side faces you. Insert hook under two top threads of first stitch. Work single crochet as before in each stitch.

STEP-BY-STEP LESSON FOR LEFT-HANDED CROCHETERS

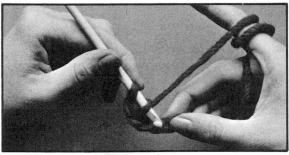

DOUBLE CROCHET (dc)

16. Chain 20 stitches for practice piece. Yarn over hook, insert hook under two top threads of 4th chain from hook (do not count loop on hook).

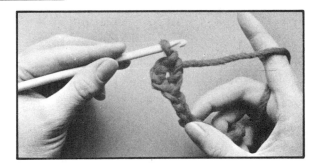

19. Yarn over hook again and draw through the last two loops on hook. This completes one double crochet (1 dc). Work double crochet in each chain.

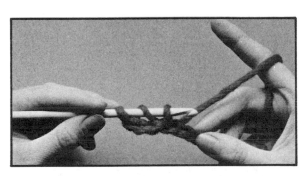

17. Pass the hook under the strand of yarn on index finger. Catch yarn with hook and draw it through the chain stitch — three loops on hook.

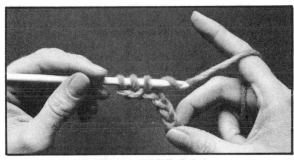

HALF DOUBLE CROCHET (hdc)

20. Yarn over hook, insert hook under two top threads of 3rd chain from hook, catch yarn with hook, draw through chain—three loops on hook.

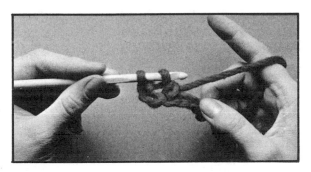

18. Pass hook under yarn on index finger again, catch yarn with hook and draw it through the two loops on hook. There are now two loops remaining.

21. Pass hook under yarn on index finger again, catch yarn with hook and, draw through all three loops on hook—one half double crochet.

STEP-BY-STEP LESSON FOR LEFT-HANDED CROCHETERS

SLIP STITCH (sl st)

22. Slip stitch is often used as an edge stitch on crochet and knitting. Insert hook, yarn over, pull through stitch and loop in one motion.

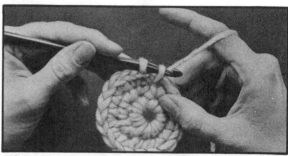

TO INCREASE 1 STITCH (inc 1 st)

25. When directions say "increase one stitch", make two stitches in one. In hats and other round pieces, increases are made every round.

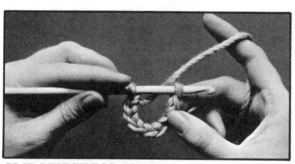

SLIP STITCH FOR JOINING

23. Slip stitch is also used for joining chains into rings and joining rounds of crochet. For joining ring, insert the hook in the last chain from hook.

TO DECREASE 1 SINGLE CROCHET (dec 1 sc)

26. When directions say "decrease one single crochet", work one single crochet until there are two loops on hook. Begin next single crochet.

24. Pass the hook under strand of yarn on index finger, draw yarn through chain and loop on hook with one motion—ring is joined with slip stitch.

27. Yarn over hook and draw through all three loops on hook with one motion. There is now only one stitch to work in on the next row.

STEP-BY-STEP LESSON FOR LEFT-HANDED CROCHETERS

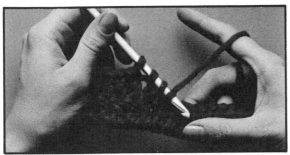

TO DECREASE 1 DOUBLE CROCHET (dec 1 dc)
28. Work one double crochet until there are two loops on hook. Begin next double crochet: yarn over hook, insert in stitch, draw loop through.

TO END OFF
31. When directions say "end off", cut the yarn 3" or more from your last stitch. Insert hook in final loop, yarn over hook and draw through last loop.

29. With four loops on hook, pass hook under strand of yarn on index finger, catch yarn, draw through two loops, leaving three loops on hook.

32. Pull yarn end to tighten stitch. This fastens the end of your work. To hide yarn end, thread it in a yarn needle and weave it into the back of work.

30. Yarn over hook and draw through all three loops on hook with one motion. There is now only one stitch to work in on the next row.

ROWS OF DOUBLE CROCHET
33. Photograph shows double crochet worked back and forth. When turning work at end of row, ch 3 to count as first double crochet of next row.

THE IMPORTANCE OF GAUGE IN CROCHET

Before crocheting a garment, make a swatch to check your gauge using the yarn and hook called for in the directions.

Start with a chain about four inches long and work the swatch in the pattern stitch of the garment until piece is about three inches deep. Block swatch by smoothing it out, pinning it down along edges and steam-pressing it. Measure across two inches, counting the number of stitches to the inch. If you have **more** stitches to the inch than directions call for , you are working too tightly; try a new swatch with a larger hook or work more loosely. If you have **fewer** stitches to

the inch, you are working too loosely; try a smaller hook or work more tightly.

If you wish to substitute one yarn for another, be sure the substitute yarn produces the proper gauge. By crocheting a swatch you will be able to check your gauge and determine the texture of the substitute yarn in the pattern stitch.

In crocheting household designs, you may wish to alter the appearance of the design by choosing a different thread from the one recommended. In this case be sure to work a small sample first, then check the appearance and gauge to be sure you will obtain the result you wish.

Actual-size photograph of box stitch shell pattern worked very tightly with steel crochet hook No. 0.

Same yarn and stitch were used for this swatch, worked very loosely with plastic hook size H or 8.

BOX STITCH

Multiple of 6 ch.

Row 1: Dc in 3rd ch from hook, dc in each of next 2 ch, sk 2 ch, sl st in next ch, * ch 2, dc in each of next 3 ch, sk 2 ch, sl st in next ch; repeat from * across, ending last shell with dc in the last 4 ch. Turn.

Row 2: Sl st across top of 4 dc, sl st under ch-2 loop of shell, * ch 2, 3 dc under same ch-2 loop, sl st under ch-2 loop of next shell; repeat from * across to last shell, make shell in ch-2 loop of last shell. Turn.

Repeat row 2 for pattern, having same number of shells in each row.

BEGINNERS' PROJECTS IN SINGLE CROCHET

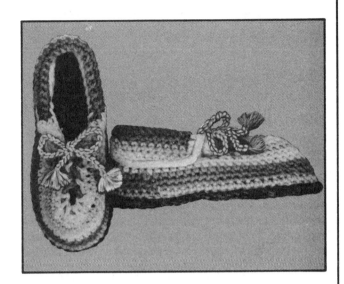

A rainbow of color rings slippers, to crochet for sizes 6", 7", or 8" in sport yarn. Slippers have turn-down cuffs, lace with tasseled ties.

CHILDREN'S SLIPPERS

SIZE: Directions for 6" foot. Changes for 7" and 8" feet in parentheses.

MATERIALS: Sport yarn, approx. ½ oz. each of 4 colors. Steel crochet hook No. 00.

GAUGE: 3½ sc = 1" (4 strands). 4 sc = 1" (2 strands).

SOLE: Using 1 strand of each color, beg at center, with 4 strands of yarn, ch 17 (20-23).

Rnd 1: Sc in 2nd ch from hook and in each of 14 (17-20) ch, 3 sc in last ch; working along other side of ch, sc in each of next 15 (18-21) ch, 3 sc in turning ch–36 (42-48) sc. Mark last sc end of rnd.

Rnd 2: Sc in each of 4 (5-6) sc, sl st in each of 5 (6-7) sc, sc in next sc, hdc in next sc, dc in each of 4 (5-6) sc, 2 dc in each of 3 sc (toe), dc in each of 4 (5-6) sc, hdc in next sc, sc in next sc, sl st in each of 5 (6-7) sc, sc in next sc, hdc in next sc, dc in each of 2 (3-4) sc, 2 dc in each of 3 sc–42 (48-54) sts.

Rnd 3: Dc in each of 2 (3-4) sc, hdc in next sc, sc in each of 14 (16-18) sts, 2 sc in each of 3 sts, sc in each of 18 (21-24) sts, 2 sc in each of 3 sts, sc in last st–48 (54-60) sts.

Rnd 4: Sc in each of 16 (19-22) sts, (2 sc in each of 2 sc, sc in next sc) twice, 2 sc in each of 2 sc, sc in each of 18 (21-24) sc, 2 sc in each of 3 sc, sc in each of 3 sc–57 (63-69) sc. Join with sl st in first sc, end off.

UPPER SECTION: Note: Change colors every 2 or 3 rows.

Rnd 1: Holding wrong side of sole toward you, with 2 strands of one color yarn, join yarn in center sc at back of heel by bringing hook up through 2 lps of first sc and down through 2 lps of next sc, yarn in front, pull yarn through and ch 1, * bring hook up through same sp with last st and down through 2 lps of next sc, work a sc, repeat from * around–57 (63-69) sc. Mark end of rnd.

Rnd 2: Sc in each sc around.

Rnd 3: Work in sc, dec 2 sc evenly spaced at edge of toe. Continue in sc and repeat decs every 3rd rnd twice more–51 (57-63) sc. Work even for 1 (2-2) rnds. End off.

Cuff: Row 1: From wrong side, join yarn in 11th (12th-13th) sc from end of last rnd, sc in same st and in each of 21 (23-25) sc. Ch 1, turn.

Row 2: Sc in each sc–22 (24-26) sc. Ch 1, turn.

Rows 3-7: Repeat row 2. End off. From right side, join yarn at edge of first row of cuff, work 1 row sc around edge of cuff. Join and end off.

From right side of sole, with 4 strands of yarn, same as sole, work 1 rnd of sl st loosely in both lps of each sc on last rnd of sole. End off.

CORD: With 2 strands of same color yarn, make a 20" ch. Weave cord through every other sc across center 12 sc, then lace ends of cord across instep through remaining sc to tie.

RIPPLE BAND POT HOLDER
Shown on page 133

SIZE: 6½" square.

MATERIALS: Coats & Clark's O.N.T. Speed-Cro-Sheen, 1 100-yard ball each of Chartreuse, main color (MC) and Hunter's Green contrasting color (CC), few yards of Killarney (K). Steel crochet hook size 0.

GAUGE: 5 sc = 1"; 6 rows = 1".

POT HOLDER: FRONT: With CC, ch 43. **Row 1:** Sc in 2nd ch from hook and in each of next 3 ch, * 3 sc in next ch, sc in each of next 4 ch, sk 2 ch, sc in each of next 4 ch, repeat from * twice, 3 sc in next ch, sc in each of last 4 ch. Ch 1, turn each row.

Row 2: Sk first sc, sc in each of next 4 sc, * 3 sc in next sc, sc in each of next 4 sc, sk 2 sc, sc in each of next 4 sc, repeat from * twice, 3 sc in next sc, sc in each of next 4 sc. Drop CC. With K, ch 1, turn.

Rows 3 and 4: With K, repeat row 2. At end of row 4, cut K; pick up CC, ch 1, turn.

Rows 5 and 6: With CC, repeat row 2. At end of row 6, cut CC. Draw MC through lp on hook, ch 1, turn.

Row 7: With MC, sk first sc, * dc in next sc, hdc in next sc, sc in each of next 5 sc, hdc in next sc, dc in next sc; holding back on hook last lp of each dc, dc in each of next 2 sc, yo and through 3 lps on hook (2-dc cluster), repeat from * across, end sc in 5 sc, hdc in next sc, dc in next sc. Ch 1, turn.

Row 8: Sk first dc, * dc in hdc, hdc in next sc, sc in each of next 3 sc, hdc in next sc, dc in next hdc; holding back on hook last lp of each dc, dc in each of next 3 sts, yo and through 4 lps on hook, repeat from * across, end sc in 3 sc, hdc in next sc, dc in next hdc. Ch 1, turn.

Row 9: Sc in each st across. Ch 1, turn. Work even on 31 sc for 3½".

Lower Band: Row 1: Turn piece so that starting ch is up. Join MC with sc in first ch, sc in next ch, * hdc in next ch, dc in next ch, 2-dc cluster in next 2 ch, dc in next ch, hdc in next ch, sc in each of 5 ch, repeat from * across, end sc in each of last 2 ch. Ch 1, turn.

Row 2: Sc in first st, * hdc in next st, 2-dc cluster in next 2 sts, dc in next st, 2-dc cluster in next 2 sts, hdc in next st, sc in each of 3 sts, repeat from * across, end sc in last st—31 sts. Ch 1, turn. Work 3 rows of 31 sc. End off.

BACK: With CC, ch 32. Work even on 31 sc until back is same as front.

FINISHING: Place pieces tog. Join CC in upper right-hand corner. Sc pieces tog, working 3 sc in each corner. Ch 25 starting corner for hanger, sl st in first sc. End off.

EMBROIDERED POT HOLDERS
Shown on page 133

SIZE: 7" square.

MATERIALS: Coats & Clark's O.N.T. Speed-Cro-Sheen, 1 100-yard ball each of 2 colors for each pot holder, a few yards of white for embroidery. (If white is used for second color, 1 ball is enough for back, edging and embroidery.) Steel crochet hook size 0. Large-eyed embroidery needle.

GAUGE: 5 sc = 1"; 6 rows = 1".

POT HOLDER: FRONT: With main color, ch 33. **Row 1:** Sc in 2nd ch from hook and in each ch across—32 sc. Ch 1, turn.

Row 2: Sc in each sc across. Ch 1, turn each row. Repeat row 2 until piece is square, about 38 rows. End off.

BACK: With contrasting color, work as for front.

EMBROIDERY: Embroider front before finishing pot holder. Thread white in embroidery needle. Beginning and ending 1" in from sides, embroider 1 line of chain st across center front. Beginning and ending 1" from top and bottom, embroider 1 line of chain st down center. Make 2 more lines of chain st crossing at center, same length as first 2 lines, equidistant between them. Follow illustration for additional lines of chain st. On green pot holder, embroider 2 lazy daisy sts at end of each "spoke" and 1 lazy daisy st in the V-shaped decorations between the "spokes".

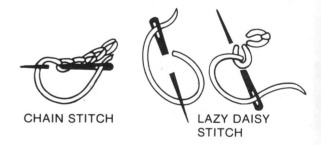

CHAIN STITCH   LAZY DAISY STITCH

FINISHING: Place front and back of pot holder wrong sides tog. Join contrasting color in one corner. Working through both thicknesses, crochet front and back tog with sc, working 3 sc in each corner. Ch 20 for hanger, sl st in first sc. End off.

ROUND POT HOLDER
Shown on page 133

SIZE: 7¼″ diameter.

MATERIALS: Coats & Clark's O.N.T. Speed-Cro-Sheen, 1 100-yard ball each of Spanish Red, main color (MC) and Killarney, contrasting color (CC). Crochet hook size E. Red felt circle, 7⅛″ diameter. Matching sewing thread.

GAUGE: 5 sts = 1″; 2 dc rnds = 1″.

POT HOLDER: FRONT: Beg at center with MC, ch 6. Join with sl st in first ch to form ring.

Rnd 1: Ch 1, 16 sc in ring. Sl st in first sc.

Rnd 2: Ch 3, dc in next sc, * ch 5, dc in each of next 2 sc, repeat from * around, end ch 5, sl st in top of ch 3—8 lps.

Rnd 3: Sl st in next dc, ch 1, * 9 sc in next lp, repeat from * around, sl st in first sc. End off.

Rnd 4: Join CC in same sc with sl st, sc in st, * ch 5, sk 2 sc, sc in next sc, repeat from * around, end ch 5, sl st in first sc—24 lps.

Rnd 5: Sl st in first lp, ch 1, sc, hdc and dc in same lp, * yo hook, insert hook in next lp and draw up a lp to measure ½″, complete a dc—long dc made; 1 more long dc in same lp, yo hook twice, draw up a lp in same lp to measure ½″, complete a tr—long tr made; in same lp make 7 more long tr and 2 long dc; in next lp, make dc, hdc and sc; in next lp make sc, hdc and dc, repeat from * around, end dc, hdc and sc in last lp. Sl st in first sc—8 scallops. End. Stretch out scallops.

BACK: Beg at center with MC, ch 5. Sl st in first ch to form ring. **Rnd 1:** Ch 1, 8 sc in ring.

Rnd 2: Ch 1, 2 sc in same sc as sl st, 2 sc in each sc around. Sl st in first sc—16 sc.

Rnd 3: Ch 3, dc in same sc as sl st, 2 dc in each sc around. Sl st in top of ch 3—32 dc.

Rnds 4 and 5: Ch 3, dc in same st as sl st, * dc in next dc, 2 dc in next dc, repeat from * around, end dc in last dc. Sl st in top of ch 3—72 dc.

Rnd 6: Ch 3, dc in same st as sl st, * dc in each of next 8 dc, 2 dc in next dc, repeat from * around, end dc in last 8 dc. Sl st in top of ch 3—80 dc.

Rnd 7: Ch 3, dc in same st as sl st, * dc in each of next 9 dc, 2 dc in next dc, repeat from * around, end dc in last 9 dc. Sl st in top of ch 3—88 dc.

Rnd 8: Ch 1, 2 sc in same st as sl st, * sc in each of next 10 dc, 2 sc in next dc, repeat from * around, end sc in each of last 10 dc. Sl st in first sc—96 sc.

Rnd 9: Ch 1, sc in same st as sl st, sc in each of next 10 sc; pick up front section and hold in front of work, right side up; insert hook in sp be-tween center 2 tr of any scallop and through next sc on back, work 1 sc, work another sc in same sp and st, * sc in each of next 11 sc, make 2 joining sc through next scallop and sc, repeat from * around. Sl st in first sc.

Rnd 10: Ch 1, 2 sc in same st as sl st, * sc in next 12 sc, 2 sc in next sc, repeat from * around, end sc in last 12 sc. Sl st in first sc—112 sc. End off.

EDGING: Join CC in same sc as sl st. Ch 1, sc in same sc, sc in each sc around. Sl st in first sc. Ch 14 for hanger, sl st in same st as sl st; turn, sl st in each of 14 ch. End off.

Pin felt circle to wrong side just inside top of edging sts. With matching sewing thread, sew lining in place.

CLUSTER STITCH MAT
Shown on page 134

SIZE: 10″ diameter.

MATERIALS: Knitting and crochet cotton, 1 175-yard ball each of yellow, orange, dark orange, red, rose, pale green, aqua, lavender and purple. Steel crochet hook No. 0.

GAUGE: 6 sts = 1″ (double strand).

Note: Use double strand of cotton throughout.

MAT: With 2 strands of yellow held tog, ch 5, sl st in first ch to form ring.

Rnd 1: 8 sc in ring. Sl st in first sc.

Rnd 2: Ch 1, 2 sc in each sc around—16 sc. Sl st in first sc. End off.

Rnd 3: Join orange in any sc, ch 3 (counts as 1 dc), * 2 dc in next sc, dc in next sc, repeat from * around, end 2 dc in last sc, sl st in top of ch 3—24 dc. End off.

Rnd 4: With lavender, make lp on hook, (sc in each of 3 dc, 2 sc in next dc) 6 times—30 sc. Join; end off.

Rnd 5: Turn piece to wrong side. With purple, make lp on hook, * sc in each of 2 sc, yo, pull up a lp in next sc, (yo, pull up a lp in same sc) 4 times, yo and through all 11 lps on hook, ch 1 for eye of cluster, (cluster st made), repeat from * around, sl st in first sc—10 cluster sts. End off.

Rnd 6: Turn piece to right side. With red, make lp on hook, sc in each st around (do not work in eye of cluster), inc in every other st—45 sc. Join; end off.

Rnd 7: With yellow, sc around, inc in every 3rd st—60 sc. Join; end off.

Rnd 8: Join dark orange in any sc, ch 3, dc in each of next 3 sc, 2 dc in next sc, * dc in each of next 4 sc, 2 dc in next sc, repeat from * around—72 dc. Join; end off.

Rnd 9: Turn piece to wrong side. With orange, repeat rnd 5—24 cluster sts. End off.

Rnd 10: Turn piece to right side. With yellow, sc around, inc in every 9th st—80 sc.

Rnd 11: Join aqua in any sc, ch 3 for first dc, dc around, inc in every 8th st—90 dc.

Rnd 12: Turn to wrong side. With rose, repeat rnd 5—30 cluster sts.

Rnd 13: Turn to right side. With green sc around, inc 6 sts in rnd—96 sc.

Rnd 14: With orange, work in dc around, inc 6 sts in rnd—102 dc.

Rnd 15: With lavender, work in sc around, inc 6 sts in rnd—108 sc.

Rnd 16: Turn piece to wrong side. With purple, repeat rnd 5—36 cluster sts.

Rnd 17: Turn piece to right side. With red, work in sc around, inc 6 sts in rnd—114 sc.

Rnd 18: With yellow, work in sc around, inc 6 sts in rnd—120 sc.

Rnd 19: With dark orange, work in dc around, inc 6 sts in rnd—126 dc.

Rnd 20: Turn to wrong side. With orange, repeat rnd 5—42 cluster sts.

Rnd 21: Turn to right side. With green, sc in any st after a cluster, * sk 1 st, work sc, dc, ch 2, dc, sc in cluster st, sc in next st, repeat from * around. End off.

KITCHEN HOT MAT
Shown on page 148

SIZE: 9″ diameter.

MATERIALS: Pearl cotton, size 5, 1 50-yard ball of light yellow (LY), 2 balls each of red (R), dark yellow (DY) and black (B). Steel crochet hook No. 1. Felt for backing (optional).

GAUGE: 6 dc = 1″; 3 dc rows = 1″.

Note: Use double strand of cotton throughout.

HOT MAT: With 2 strands of LY, ch 5. Sl st in first ch to form ring.

Rnd 1: 7 sc in ring.

Rnd 2: 2 sc in each sc around—14 sc.

Rnd 3: Pull up a lp in next sc, draw 2 strands of R through 2 lps on hook to complete sc; working over strands of LY (always work over color not in use), and ends of R, R sc in next st, LY sc in same st, LY sc in each of next 2 sts changing to R to complete last sc, R sc in same st, LY sc in next st, 2 LY sc in next st changing to R to complete last sc, R sc in next st, 2 LY sc in next st, LY sc in next st changing to R to complete sc, R sc in next st, LY sc in same st, LY sc in next 2 sts changing to R to complete last sc, R sc in same st, LY sc in each of next 2 sts changing to R to complete last sc—20 sc.

Rnd 4: Work 2 R sc in each R sc, 1 LY sc in each LY sc around—25 sc. Cut LY.

Rnd 5: With R, work (2 dc in each of next 2 sc, 1 dc in each of next 3 sc) 5 times—35 dc.

Rnd 6: Dc in each of first 2 dc changing to DY to complete last dc (always change colors in this way), * DY dc in each of next 2 sts, 2 R dc in next st, repeat from * around, end DY dc in last 2 sts—44 dc.

Rnd 7: (2 R dc in next st, 1 R dc in next st, 1 DY dc in each of next 2 sts) 11 times.

Rnd 8: (R dc in next st, 2 R dc in next st, R dc in next st, DY dc in each of next 2 sts) 11 times. Cut R.

Rnd 9: (DY dc in next st, 2 DY dc in next st, B dc in next st, DY dc in each of next 3 dc) 11 times.

Rnd 10: (DY dc in next st, 2 DY dc in next st, B dc in each of next 3 sts, 2 DY dc in next st, DY dc in next st) 11 times.

Rnd 11: (2 DY dc in next st, DY dc in next st, B dc in each of next 2 sts, R dc in next st, B dc in each of next 2 sts, DY dc in each of next 2 sts) 11 times.

Rnd 12: (DY dc in each of next 2 sts, B dc in each of next 2 sts, R dc in each of next 3 sts, B dc in each of next 2 sts, 2 DY dc in next st) 11 times.

Rnd 13: (DY dc in next st, B dc in each of next 2 sts, R dc in each of next 5 sts, B dc in each of next 2 sts, 2 DY dc in next st) 11 times, end last repeat B dc in each of next 2 sts, DY hdc in next st, DY sc in next st, changing to R. Cut DY and B.

Rnd 14: With R, ch 3, dc in same st as sc, dc around, inc as necessary to keep work flat. Sl st in top of ch 3. End off.

Rnd 15: Join DY in any dc, * ch 7, sl st in next dc, repeat from * around. End off.

Steam-press mat flat. If desired, cut a circle of felt same size as mat inside looped edge. Sew to wrong side.

*Five cheery pot holders add color to your kitchen.
Round pattern has a flower-shaped piece in two colors
on a solid background. Chain-stitch embroidery deco-
rates three of the square pot holders. Ripple band em-
bellishes design at bottom. Directions on pages 130–131.*

Brightly colored hot mat alternates nine colors in a pleasing variety of stitch patterns. Made of mercerized knitting and crochet cotton, used double, mat design offers you the perfect opportunity to use up your leftover cottons from other crochet projects. Directions for Cluster Stitch Mat are on page 131.

PICTURE POT HOLDERS

Shown on page 149

SIZE: 6½" square.

MATERIALS: Rayon and cotton rug yarn, 1 70-yard skein each of the following colors: white, evergreen and medium green for pine tree pot holder; medium blue, white, yellow and evergreen for star flower pot holder; national blue, medium blue, red and white for sailboat pot holder; white, cerise and dark green for tulip pot holder, light yellow, turquoise and black for butterfly pot holder; white, black, dark green, medium blue and national blue for cottage pot holder. Aluminum crochet hook size G or H. Large-eyed sewing needle.

GAUGE: 4 sts = 1"; 7 rows = 2".

GENERAL DIRECTIONS: Design Note: When a row has more than one color, start extra color or colors at beginning of row. Work over color or colors not being used.

When changing colors, work last sc or reverse sc of one color until there are 2 lps on hook, drop strand to wrong side. Pick up new color and finish sc.

POT HOLDER: See chart for desired pot holder. With color of first row of chart, ch 24.

Row 1 (right side): Sc in 2nd ch from hook and in each ch across–23 sc. Ch 1, turn.

Row 2: Following next row of chart from left to right, work in reverse sc as follows: Insert hook from back to front in first sc, yarn around hook from back to front, pull lp through and complete sc; work reverse sc in each sc across. Ch 1, turn.

Row 3: Following next row of chart from right to left, sc in each sc. Ch 1, turn. Repeat rows 2 and 3 to top of chart, changing colors as directed above. End off.

BORDER: Rnd 1: With border color (see illustration), from right side, work in sc around edge of pot holder, making 3 sc in each corner. Join with sl st in first sc.

Rnd 2: Working in back lp of sts, work sl st in each sc around. Join in first sl st. End off.

RING HANGER: Ch 8, join with sl st in first ch. Cut yarn, leaving an end for sewing. Sew ring to top of pot holder.

EMBROIDERY DETAILS: Untwist a piece of black rug yarn and, with 2 strands, embroider mast of sailboat, antennae of butterfly, and tree trunk of cottage pot holder in outline st. If red chimney of cottage was not crocheted in, embroider chimney in satin st with red cotton.

CHARTS FOR MAKING PICTURE POT HOLDERS

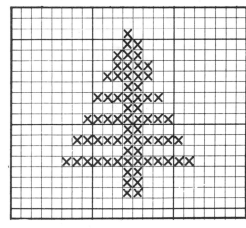

WHITE ☐   EVERGREEN ☒

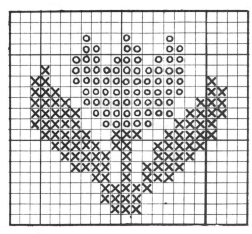

WHITE ☐   CERISE ◉   DK. GREEN ☒

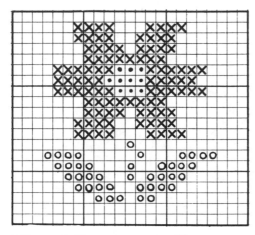

MED. BLUE ☐ EVERGREEN ◙ YELLOW ⊡ LT. YELLOW ☐ BLACK ■ TURQUOISE ⊠
WHITE ⊠

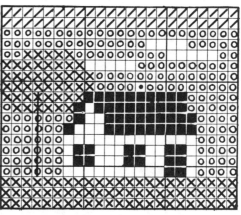

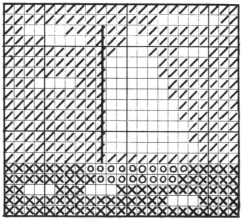

WHITE ☐ RED ◙ MED. BLUE ⊘
NATIONAL BLUE ⊠

WHITE ☐ NATIONAL BLUE ⊘
MED. BLUE ◙ RED ⊡ DK. GREEN ⊠ BLACK ■

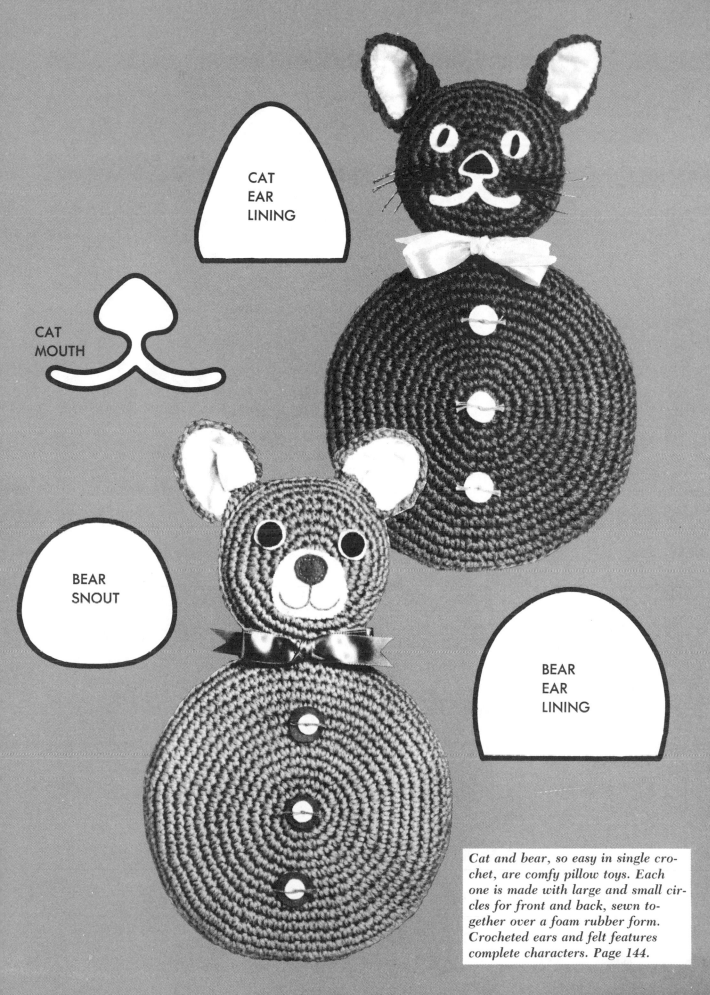

CAT EAR LINING

CAT MOUTH

BEAR SNOUT

BEAR EAR LINING

Cat and bear, so easy in single crochet, are comfy pillow toys. Each one is made with large and small circles for front and back, sewn together over a foam rubber form. Crocheted ears and felt features complete characters. Page 144.

Alligator, lion, and kangaroo wear sweaters that are crocheted as part of body. All in single crochet; cotton-stuffed. Embroidered features add to their personalities. Directions for Toy Menagerie begin opposite.

KANGAROO
Shown opposite

SIZE: 11″ high

MATERIALS: Wintuk sport yarn, 2 2-oz. skeins camel (A), 1 oz. cerise (B) and few yards white (C). Steel crochet hook No. 00. Six-strand embroidery floss, black, white, light blue and rose. Scrap of black felt. Embroidery and yarn needles. Polyester filling.

GAUGE: 5 sc = 1″; 5 rnds = 1″.

KANGAROO: HEAD: Beg at tip of nose with A, ch 4, join with a sl st to form ring.

Rnd 1: 4 sc in ring. Do not join rnds; mark end of each rnd.

Rnd 2: 2 sc in each sc around–8 sc.

Rnd 3: * Sc in next sc, 2 sc in next sc, repeat from * around–12 sc.

Rnd 4: * Sc in each of 2 sc, 2 sc in next sc, repeat from * around–16 sc.

Rnds 5-9: Continue to inc 4 sc evenly spaced every rnd–36 sc. Work even until piece measures 3¼″ from rnd 1.

Next Rnd: * Sc in each of 4 sc, dec 1 sc (**to dec:** draw up a lp in each of 2 sc, yo hook and through 3 lps on hook), repeat from * around–30 sc. Continue to dec 6 sc evenly spaced every rnd until 6 sc remain, stuffing head before opening becomes too small. End off leaving an 8″ end. Thread needle; sew opening.

SWEATER: Beg at neck edge with B, ch 4, join with a sl st to form ring.

Rnd 1: 7 sc in ring. Do not join rnds; mark end of each rnd.

Rnd 2: 2 sc in each sc around–14 sc.

Rnds 3-6: Sc in each sc around, inc 1 sc at end of rnd 6–15 sc.

Rnd 7: Sc in each sc around, inc 1 sc around – 18 sc.

Rnds 8-14: Continue to inc 3 sc evenly spaced around, being careful not to work inc over inc of previous rnd–39 sc. Inc 3 sc evenly spaced every other rnd until 57 sc around. Work even until piece measures 5½″ from start. End off.

Body: Join A in last sc; work even until piece measures 6¾″ from start of sweater.

First Leg: Rnd 1: Sc in next sc, put a marker on last sc, sc in each of 22 sc, ch 6 for crotch, sl st in marked sc–29 sts. Mark end of rnds.

Rnd 2: Sc in same sc, sc in each st around–29 sc. Work even until piece measures 1″ from crotch.

Fold leg in half, having the 6 crotch sts at center of inner part of body. Mark sc at one fold (center front leg).

Foot: Rnd 1: Sc in each sc to marked sc, sc in marked sc, move marker to this sc, ch 19 for foot, sc in 2nd ch from hook and in each ch, sc in each sc on leg–47 sc.

Rnd 2: Sc in each sc to marked sc, sc in marked sc, remove marker; working on opposite side of foot ch, sc in each of 18 sc, sc in each sc on foot, finish rnd–65 sc. Work even until foot measures 1¾″ from start of foot. Fold in half and mark each end for toe and heel.

Next Rnd: Sc around, dec 3 sc across toe and heel–59 sc. Repeat last rnd–53 sc. Sl st in next sc. End off.

2nd Leg: Sk next 4 sc on last rnd of body, join A in next sc.

Rnd 1: Sc in each of next 23 sc on body, ch 6 for crotch, sl st in first sc. Mark end of rnds. Beg with rnd 2, work same as first leg, being careful to mark sc at front fold when marking for foot. Stuff body, legs and feet. Sew lower edges of each foot tog.

Crotch: With A, ch 5. Sc in 2nd ch from hook and in each ch across–4 sc. Ch 1, turn. Work even for 1″. End off. Sew crotch in place to body and legs.

Foreleg (make 2): Beg at paw with A, ch 4, join with a sl st to form ring.

Rnd 1: 6 sc in ring. Do not join rnds; mark end of rnds.

Rnd 2: * Sc in next sc, 2 sc in next sc, repeat from * around–9 sc.

Rnds 3-6: Sc in each sc around. Cut A, join B.

Sleeve: With B, work even until piece measures 2½″ from start of leg. End off. Stuff. With C, make chain to fit around sleeve. End off, leaving an 8″ end. Sew chain around sleeve edge above paw.

Collar: With B, ch 4. Work back and forth on 3 sc until piece measures same as neck. End off. With C, make chain same length as collar. End off leaving an 8″ end. Sew chain along center of collar.

TAIL: Beg at tip with A, ch 4, join with a sl st to form ring.

Rnd 1: 6 sc in ring. Do not join rnds; mark end of rnds.

Rnd 2: Sc in each sc around, inc 2 sc evenly spaced–8 sc. Work 1 rnd even. Repeat last 2 rnds until 18 sc around, being careful not to work inc over previous inc. Work even until piece measures 9" from start. End off. Stuff tail and sew to back of body just below lower edge of sweater.

Pocket: Beg at lower edge with B, ch 16.

Row 1: Sc in 2nd ch from hook and in each ch across—15 sc. Ch 1, turn. Work even for 2". End off. With C, make chain same length as width of pocket. End off, leaving an 8" end. Thread needle, sew chain across 2nd row from top of pocket. Sew pocket to front of Kangaroo with lower edge along 3rd rnd below lower edge of sweater.

Sew head securely to 3rd rnd of sweater. Place collar around neck and weave ends tog. Sew forelegs to sweater about 2½" below neck, 2" apart.

EARS (make 2): Beg at center with A, ch 10.

Row 1: Sc in 2nd ch from hook and in each of 7 ch, 3 sc in last ch; working along opposite side of ch, sc in each of 8 ch—19 sc. Ch 1, turn.

Row 2: Sc in each of next 9 sc, 3 sc in next sc, sc in each of next 9 sc—21 sc. Ch 1, turn.

Row 3: Sc in each of next 10 sc, 3 sc in next sc, sc in each of next 10 sc; do not turn, sc in edge of each row—29 sc. Ch 1, turn; dec 1 st 3 times across straight end. End off. Sew dec edge of ears to head.

EMBROIDERY: See stitch details, page 282. With white floss, embroider oval eyes in satin stitch as pictured; with blue, embroider short stitches across back edge of eyes. With black, outline eyes. Tack ¼" black felt circle to each eye for pupil. With black, work nose in satin stitch across tip of head. Cut three 2" lengths of black for whiskers. Hold strands tog, fold in half. Draw fold end through crochet ¼" to side of nose. Draw free ends through loop; pull tightly. Repeat on other side of nose.

Tongue: With pink floss, ch 3. 2 sc in 2nd ch from hook, sc in next ch. End off, leaving a long end. Thread needle, sew tongue 2 rnds below nose. Embroider mouth each side of tongue in outline stitch.

BABY KANGAROO: HEAD: Beg at tip of nose, work as for tail of kangaroo until 10 sc around. Work 2 rnds even.

Next Rnd: Dec 5 sc around. End off. Stuff head and sew opening.

Body: With A, ch 11.

Row 1: Sc in 2nd ch from hook and in each ch across—10 sc. Ch 1, turn.

Row 2: Sc in each of first 6 sc, ch 1, turn. Remaining 4 sc form front leg.

Row 3: Sc in each of 6 sc. Ch 1, turn.

Row 4: Sc in each of 6 sc, ch 5, turn.

Row 5: Sc in 2nd ch from hook, sc in each of 3 ch forming 2nd front leg, sc in each of next 6 sc. End off.

Fold body in half over a bit of stuffing, sew 6 sts of last row to 6 sts of starting ch, leaving front legs free. Sew head to body, above legs.

Hind Legs: With A, ch 8. Sc in 2nd ch from hook and in each ch across. End off. Sew center of row to rear of body forming hind legs.

Ears (make 2): With A, ch 4. Sc in 2nd ch from hook and in each of next 2 ch. End off. Sew to head.

With black floss, embroider nose and eyes with short stitches.

PANDA
Shown on page 138

SIZE: About 11" high.

MATERIALS: Wintuk sport yarn, 1 2-oz. skein each of black (B) and white (W). Steel crochet hook No. 00. Small amount of rose and aqua six strand embroidery floss. ½ yard rose satin ribbon. Yarn and embroidery needles. Polyester filling.

GAUGE: 5 sc = 1"; 5 rnds = 1".

PANDA: HEAD: Beg at nose with W, ch 2.

Rnd 1: 5 sc in 2nd ch from hook. Do not join rnds; mark end of each rnd.

Rnd 2: 2 sc in each sc around—10 sc.

Rnd 3: * Sc in next sc, 2 sc in next sc, repeat from * around—15 sc.

Rnd 4: * Sc in each of 2 sc, 2 sc in next sc, repeat from * around—20 sc.

Rnds 5-7: Continue to inc 5 sc evenly space every rnd—35 sc. Mark next 15 sc for forehead.

Rnd 8: (2 sc in next sc, sc in each of 2 sc) 5 times, sc in each of 20 sc—40 sc.

Rnd 9: Sc in each sc around.

Rnd 10: (2 sc in next sc, sc in each of 3 sc) times, sc in each of 20 sc—45 sc.

Rnd 11: (2 sc in next sc, sc in each of 4 sc) times, sc in each of 20 sc—50 sc.

Rnd 12: (2 sc in next sc, sc in each of 5 sc) times, sc in each of 19 sc, 2 sc in next sc—56 sc. Work even until piece measures 3¾" from rnd 1.

PANDA
Continued

Next Rnd: * Sc in each of 6 sc, dec 1 sc (**to dec:** draw up a lp in each of 2 sc, yo hook and through 3 lps on hook), repeat from * around–49 sc. Continue to dec 7 sc evenly spaced every rnd until 7 sc remain, stuffing head before opening becomes too small. End off leaving an 8″ end. Thread needle; sew opening.

Body: Beg at neck with W, ch 4. Join with a sl st in first ch to form ring.

Rnd 1: 6 sc in ring. Do not join; mark end of each rnd.

Rnd 2: * Sc in next sc, 2 sc in next sc, repeat from * around–9 sc.

Rnd 3: * Sc in each of 2 sc, 2 sc in next sc, repeat from * around–12 sc.

Rnd 4: Repeat rnd 2–18 sc.

Rnds 5-8: Continue to inc 6 sc evenly spaced every rnd – 42 sc. Work even until piece is 5″ from start. Stuffing body as work progresses, dec 6 sc evenly spaced on each of next 6 rnds – 6 sc. End off, leaving an 8″ end. Thread needle; sew opening.

Hind Leg (make 2): Beg at lower edge with B, work same as head through rnd 2 - 10 sc.

Rnd 3: 2 sc in each sc around–20 sc. Work even until piece measures 3½″ from start. End off. Cut circle of cardboard 1″ in diameter. Insert in bottom of leg; stuff firmly.

Foreleg (make 2): Work as for hind leg until piece measures 3″ from start. Finish as for hind leg.

Eyes (make 2): Beg at center with B, work same as body through rnd 1-6 sc.

Rnd 2: 2 sc in each sc around–12 sc. Sl st in next sc. End off, leaving a 10″ end.

Ears (make 2): Beg at center with B, ch 5.

Row 1: Sc in 2nd ch from hook, sc in each of 2 ch, 3 sc in last ch; working on opposite side of starting ch, sc in each of 3 ch–9 sc. Ch 1, turn.

Row 2: Sc in each of 3 sc, 2 sc in each of next 3 sc, sc in each of 3 sc–12 sc. Ch 1, turn.

Row 3: Sc in each of 3 sc, (2 sc in next sc, sc in next sc) 3 times, sc in each of next 3 sc–15 sc. Ch 1, turn.

Row 4: Sc in each sc. End off, leaving a 10″ end.

Finishing: Sew head to neck, placing forehead uppermost. With aqua embroidery floss, embroider pupil in center of eye, using satin stitch (see page 282). Sew ears and eyes to head as pictured. With rose floss, embroider nose in satin stitch.

Tongue: With rose floss, ch 3. Work 2 sc in 2nd ch from hook, sc in next ch. End off. With rose floss, work 2 long stitches under nose for mouth; sew tongue at side of mouth.

ALLIGATOR
Shown on page 138

SIZE: About 24″ long.

MATERIALS: Wintuk sport yarn, 2 2-oz. skeins each of apple green (A) and baby aqua (B); ½ oz. light pink (C). Steel crochet hook No. 00. Six-strand embroidery floss, 1 skein each of red, green, black and white. Scrap of red yarn for bow. ½ yard medium white rickrack. Embroidery and yarn needles. Polyester filling.

GAUGE: 5 sc = 1″; 5 rnds = 1″.

ALLIGATOR: SNOUT: Top Front Section: Beg at front edge, with A, ch 11.

Row 1: Sc in 2nd ch from hook and in each ch across–10 sc. Ch 1, turn.

Row 2: Sc in each sc across. Ch 1, turn. Repeat row 2 until piece measures 2½″. End off.

Bottom Front Section: Work as for top front section: do not end off. Ch 1, turn.

Head: Rnd 1 (joining rnd): Sc in each sc across bottom front section; with wrong side of last row facing you, sc in each sc on last row of top front section–20 sc. Sl st in first sc.

Rnd 2: * 2 sc in first sc, (sc in each of 2 sc, 2 sc in next sc) 3 times, repeat from * once–28 sc. Do not join rnds; mark end of each rnd.

Rnd 3: Sc in next sc, 2 sc in next sc, sc in each of 10 sc, 2 sc in next sc; sc in next sc, repeat from * once–32 sc.

Rnd 5: * Sc in next sc, 2 sc in next sc, sc in each of 12 sc, 2 sc in next sc, sc in next sc, repeat from * once–36 sc. Work even until head measures 3½″ above joining rnd.

Shape Neck: Rnd 1: * Sc in each of 4 sc, dec 1 sc (**to dec:** draw up a lp in each of 2 sc, yo hook and through 3 lps on hook), repeat from * around – 30 sc.

Rnd 2: Repeat rnd 1-25 sc.

Rnd 3: * Sc in each of 3 sc, dec 1 st, repeat from * around–20 sc.

Rnd 4: (Sc in each of 8 sc, dec 1 sc) twice–18 sc. Work 3 rnds even. Cut A; join B.

Sweater: Rnds 1 and 2: With B, sc in each sc around.

Rnd 3: (Sc in each of 2 sc, 2 sc in next sc) 6 times–24 sc. Work 2 rnds even.

Rnd 6: (Sc in each of 2 sc, 2 sc in next sc) 8 times–32 sc. Work 1 rnd even.

Rnd 8: (Sc in each of 3 sc, 2 sc in next sc) 8 times–40 sc. Work even until sweater measures 5¾". Cut B; join A.

Rear Body: With A, work even until rear body measures 2".

Next Rnd: (Sc in each of 8 sc, dec 1 sc) 4 times–36 sc.

Next Rnd: (Sc in each of 4 sc, dec 1 sc) 6 times–30 sc. Continue to dec 6 sc evenly spaced every rnd until 12 sc remain, stuffing body before opening becomes too small. Sl st in next sc. End off.

Stuff head. Holding top and bottom of snout tog, stitch across first rnd of head.

TAIL: Beg at tip, with A, ch 2.

Rnd 1: 5 sc in 2nd ch from hook. Do not join rnds; mark end of each rnd.

Rnds 2 and 3: Sc in each sc around.

Rnd 4: Sc in each sc around, inc 1 sc–6 sc. Continue to inc 1 sc every rnd, being careful not to work inc over inc of previous rnd until there are 20 sc, then inc 1 st every other rnd until there are 25 sc. Work even until piece measures 9" from start. End off, leaving a 10" end. Stuff tail firmly. Gather sts of last rnd to fit back edge of body, sew tail to body.

Hind Leg (make 2): Beg at back with A, ch 6, join with a sl st to form ring.

Rnd 1: 6 sc in ring. Do not join rnds; mark end of each rnd.

Rnd 2: 2 sc in each sc around–12 sc.

Rnd 3: * Sc in each of 2 sc, 2 sc in next sc, repeat from * around–16 sc. Work even until piece measures 1½" from start.

Next Rnd: * Sc in each of 2 sc, dec 1 sc, repeat from * around–12 sc. Work 2 rnds even.

Paw: Row 1: Sc in each of 6 sc. Ch 1, turn.

Rows 2-6: Sc in each of 6 sc. Ch 1, turn. End off. Stuff leg; sew bottom of leg to paw.

Front Leg (make 2): With B, work as for hind leg until end of dec rnd–12 sc. Work 1 rnd even. Cut B; join A.

Paw: With A, work as for hind leg paw. Complete as for hind leg.

Pad (make 4): With C, ch 7.

Row 1: Sc in 2nd ch from hook and in each ch across–6 sc. Work 5 rows even. End off, leaving a 10" end. Thread needle; sew a pad under each paw.

Sew hind legs to sides of back of body about 3" from start of sweater.

MOUTH: With C, ch 11.

Row 1: Sc in 2nd ch from hook and in each ch across–10 sc. Ch 1, turn. Work even until piece measures 5". End off. Open snout; sew mouth to inside of top and bottom snout. Sew rickrack around outer edges of snout. With double strand of B, work a chain to fit first rnd of sweater, a chain to fit around 7th and last rnds of sweater, a chain for first B rnd of each front leg. With wrong side of chain up, sew chains in place.

EMBROIDERY: See page 282 for stitch details. With red floss, embroider 10 French knots evenly spaced around 3rd rnd of sweater. With green, embroider 2 small lazy daisy stitches next to each French knot for leaves. With black, embroider eyes in satin stitch on each side of head about 1¾" above snout. With white, embroider a ½" V in front of each eye. Tie a red yarn bow to top of sweater.

LION
Shown on page 138

SIZE: About 11" long.

MATERIALS: Wintuk sport yarn, 1 2-oz. skein yellow (A); about ½ oz. each of cerise (B) and white (C); few yards pink. Steel crochet hook No. 00. Six-strand embroidery floss, 1 skein each of red, green and black. Embroidery and yarn needles. Polyester filling.

GAUGE: 5 sc = 1"; 5 rnds = 1"

LION: HEAD: Beg at center front with C, ch 4; join with a sl st to form ring.

Rnd 1: 6 sc in ring. Do not join rnds; mark beg of each rnd.

Rnd 2: 2 sc in each sc around–12 sc.

Rnd 3: * Sc in next sc, 2 sc in next sc, repeat from * around–18 sc.

Rnd 4: * Sc in each of 2 sc, 2 sc in next sc, repeat from * around–24 sc.

Rnd 5: Sc in each sc around. Cut C; join A.

Rnds 6-9: With A, sc around, inc 6 sc evenly

LION
Continued

spaced around, being careful not to work inc over inc of previous rnd-48 sc.

Rnd 10: Sc in each sc around.

Rnd 11: Repeat rnd 6-54 sc. Work even until piece measures 8″ in diameter.

Shape Back: Rnd 1: * Sc in each of 7 sc, dec 1 sc (to dec: draw up a lp in each of 2 sc, yo hook and through 3 lps on hook), repeat from * around-48 sc. Continue to dec 6 sc evenly spaced every rnd until 6 sc remain, stuffing head before opening becomes too small. End off, leaving an 8″ end. Thread needle, sew opening.

First Front Leg: Beg at center of pad with A, work same as head rnds 1-4-24 sc. Work 2 rnds even.

Rnd 7: Sc in each of 7 sc, (sc in next sc, dec 1 sc) 3 times, sc in each of 8 sc-21 sc.

Rnds 8-11: Sc in each sc around. Cut A; join B.

Rnds 12 and 13: With B, sc in each sc around. Drop B.

Rnds 14 and 15: With C, sc in each sc around. Drop C. Repeat last 4 rnds once. Repeat rnds 12 and 13. Sl st in next st. End off.

2nd Front Leg: Work as for first leg, do not end off. Drop B.

Body: Rnd 1: With C, sc in each of 16 sc on 2nd front leg; sk first 5 sc on first front leg, sc in each of next 16 sc on first front leg. Join with a sl st in first sc on 2nd leg. Sew free 5 sc on each leg tog for inner legs. Mark first st for beg of rnd.

Rnd 2: With C, sc in each sc around-32 sc. Drop C.

Rnds 3 and 4: With B, sc in each sc around. Drop B.

Rnds 5 and 6: With C, sc in each sc around. Drop C. Repeat rnds 3-6 4 times. Repeat rnds 3 and 4. Cut B and C; join A. With A, work 1 rnd even. Stuff front legs and body.

Next Rnd: Sc in each of 8 sc, (2 sc in next sc, sc in each of 2 sc) 6 times, sc in each of next 6 sc-38 sc. Work even until piece measures 6″ from start of body.

First Back Leg: Rnd 1: Beg at underside of body, sc in each of 19 sc, ch 4, sk remaining 19 sc, join with a sl st in first sc.

Rnd 2: Ch 1, sc in same sc, sc in each of 18 sc, sc in each of 4 ch-23 sc. Mark beg of rnds.

Rnd 3: Sc in each sc around.

Rnd 4: Sc in each of 10 sc, (2 sc in next sc, sc in next sc) 3 times, sc in each of next 7 sc-26 sc. Work 2 rnds even.

Rnd 7: Sc in each of 10 sc, (2 sc in next sc, sc in each of 2 sc) 3 times (mark these sts for toe), sc in each of next 7 sc-29 sc. Work 2 rnds even.

Rnd 10: Sc in each of 10 sc, (dec 1 sc, sc in next sc) 5 times, sc in each of 4 sc-24 sc.

Rnd 11: Dec 6 sc evenly spaced around-18 sc. Stuffing leg before opening becomes too small, repeat last rnd twice-6 sc. End off leaving an 8″ end. Thread needle; sew opening.

2nd Back Leg: From right side, join A in sc on body before ch-4 of first back leg.

Rnd 1: Ch 1, sc in same sc, sc in each ch of ch-4 of first back leg, sc in each of next 18 sc on body. Join with a sl st in first sc-23 sc.

Rnd 2: Ch 1, sc in same sc, sc in each sc around. Beg with rnd 3, work same as first back leg.

Tail: Beg at tip with A, ch 2.

Rnd 1: 4 sc in 2nd ch from hook. Do not join rnds.

Rnd 2: Sc in each sc.

Rnd 3: Sc in each sc around, inc 1 st-5 sc.

Rnd 4: Sc in each sc around. Repeat last 2 rnds once-6 sc. Work even until piece measures 5″, stuffing tail as work progresses. End off.

Tassel: Wind A 15 times around 1¾″ piece of cardboard. Tie one end; cut other end. Tie a strand of A around tassel ¼″ from tied end. Trim ends; fasten to tip of tail; sew tail to back of body.

Ears (make 2): Beg at center with A, ch 5.

Row 1: Sc in 2nd ch from hook and in each of next 3 ch-4 sc. Ch 1, turn.

Row 2: Sc in each of 3 sc, 3 sc in last sc; working on opposite side of ch, sk first ch, sc in each of next 3 ch-9 sc. Ch 1, turn.

Row 3: Sc in each of 2 sc, 2 sc in next sc, (sc in next sc, 2 sc in next sc) twice, sc in each of 2 sc-12 sc. Ch 1, turn.

Row 4: Sc in each of 3 sc, 2 sc in next sc, (sc in next sc, 2 sc in next sc) twice, sc in each of 4 sc-15 sc. End off, leaving an 8″ end.

Mane: Cut about 150 6″ strands of A. Using 3 strands tog, insert hook in a sc on 14th rnd of head, catch center of 3 strands, pull loop through st, pull ends of strands through loop; tighten knot. Repeat in every 3rd sc around 14th rnd. Mark half of rnd for top of head. Sew an ear in front of tassels just inside each marker for top section. Tie a tassel in every other sc between ears on 13th rnd of head. Tie a tassel in every other sc on top half of 16th rnd.

EMBROIDERY: See stitch details, page 282. With red floss, embroider nostrils across center of face in satin stitch, as pictured. With black, make a long straight stitch from center of nose down to mouth; embroider mouth in satin stitch. Embroider round eyes with green directly above white section of face and pupils with black in satin stitch. With black, outline eyes in backstitch. With pink yarn, embroider nose in long straight stitches, running from center of space between eyes to top edge of nostrils. Run four 3½" strands of black floss through sts above mouth for whiskers.

Sew head securely in place as pictured. Pinch toe end of back leg; with double red floss, make 5 overcast sts covering 3 rnds of crochet and having ¼" between sts. Embroider other toes in same manner.

TOY PILLOWS
Shown on page 137

SIZE: Each toy about 11" high, plus ears.
MATERIALS: Knitting worsted, 2 ozs. for each toy. Crochet hook size G or 5. Foam rubber, 1" thick, piece 7" x 11" for each toy. Small pieces of felt: yellow and black for cat; red, white and black for bear. Sewing threads to match felt. Six-strand embroidery floss, black and red. Ribbon for bows, ¾" wide: ½ yard red for bear, ½ yard yellow for cat.

GENERAL DIRECTIONS: BODY (make 2 pieces): Ch 2.
Rnd 1: 6 sc in 2nd ch from hook. Do not join rnds; mark end of each rnd.
Rnd 2: 2 sc in each sc around–12 sc.
Rnd 3: * Sc in next sc, 2 sc in next sc, repeat from * around–18 sc.
Rnd 4: * 2 sc in next sc, sc in each of 2 sc, repeat from * around–24 sc.
Rnd 5: * Sc in each of 3 sc, 2 sc in next sc, repeat from * around–30 sc. Continue to inc 6 sc evenly in each rnd until piece measures 7" in diameter. Sl st in next st; end off.
Make second piece with same number of sts in last rnd.
HEAD (make 2 pieces): Work as for Body until piece is 4" in diameter.
Sew about 8 sts on edge of one body piece over edge of one head piece for neck. Repeat for back of toy. Place front on foam rubber, trace around outline. Cut out foam rubber. Place between front and back. Pin crocheted pieces tog around edge,

sew front and back tog with matching yarn, overcasting back lps of sc.

TO MAKE PATTERNS: Place tracing paper over patterns and trace needed patterns. Cut out paper patterns.

CAT: Ears: Ch 3. **Row 1:** 2 sc in 2nd ch from hook, 2 sc in last ch. Ch 1, turn each row.
Row 2: Sc in each sc–4 sc. **Row 3:** 2 sc in first sc, sc in next 2 sc, 2 sc in last sc–6 sc.
Row 4: Sc in each sc.
Row 5: 2 sc in first sc, sc in next 4 sc, 2 sc in last sc–8 sc.
Row 6: Sc in each sc.
Row 7: 2 sc in first sc, sc in next 6 sc, 2 sc in last sc–10 sc.
Row 8: Sc in each sc. End off.
Features: From yellow felt, using patterns, cut two pieces for ear linings; cut nose and mouth in one. Cut two circles for eyes, three for buttons, ⅝" diameter. Sew linings inside ears. Curve inner edges of ears toward inside; sew in place. Cut two narrow black felt pupils; sew to eyes. Cut black triangle smaller than nose; sew in place on yellow nose. Sew on mouth and nose piece; sew on eyes. Make whiskers each side of nose with black embroidery thread; stiffen with glue.
Tie buttons in place with yarn or thread. Tie ribbon bow around neck.

BEAR: Ears: Ch 4. **Row 1:** 2 sc in 2nd ch from hook, sc in next ch, 2 sc in last ch. Ch 1, turn each row.
Row 2: 2 sc in first sc, sc in next 3 sc, 2 sc in last sc.
Row 3: Sc in each sc–7 sc.
Row 4: 2 sc in first sc, sc in next 5 sc, 2 sc in last sc.
Row 5: Sc in each sc–9 sc.
Row 6: 2 sc in first sc, sc in next 7 sc, 2 sc in last sc.
Rows 7-9: Sc in each sc–11 sc. End off at end of row 9, leave end for sewing.
Features: From white felt, using patterns, cut two pieces for ear linings and one piece for snout. Sew linings to crocheted ears. Gather ears along bottom edge; sew to head. Cut two black felt circles, ½" diameter, and two white felt circles slightly larger, for eyes. Sew black circles over white, sew to head. Cut red felt circle, ¾" diameter, for nose, sew to top of white snout with red embroidery floss; embroider red mouth in outline stitch below nose; see illustration and detail, page 282. Sew snout to face.
Cut three red felt circles, ¾" diameter, and three white circles, ⅜" diameter, for buttons. Tie in place with red floss. Tie ribbon bow around neck.

Popular fisherman's knit patterns are adapted in crochet for this unusual cardigan, worked in panels of raised stitches. For a more authentic look, make it in natural wool color. Sizes 8 to 18. See Aran-Pattern Cardigan, page 220.

*Small, close shaping of
an easy-crochet pullove_
repeats itself in the bac_
with one slight change—
neck is higher and
slightly rounded.
Sweater is all single cro_
chet. For Peach Pastels
see page 154.*

Granny squares, in winter white and three-color versions, join together neatly to make a charming blouse. Color motifs stripe the sleeves, form bottom border, and go up front and back in pairs. A feminine note: the little bows tied on sleeves. Directions for Bow-Tied Blouse on page 155.

Here's a colorful hot mat for informal meals—a bright wheel pattern of yellow, red and black pearl cotton. The cotton is used double for extra thickness; backing the mat with a circle of felt adds more protection. Pattern is mostly double crochet; chain loops make a ruffled edge. Kitchen Hot Mat, page 132.

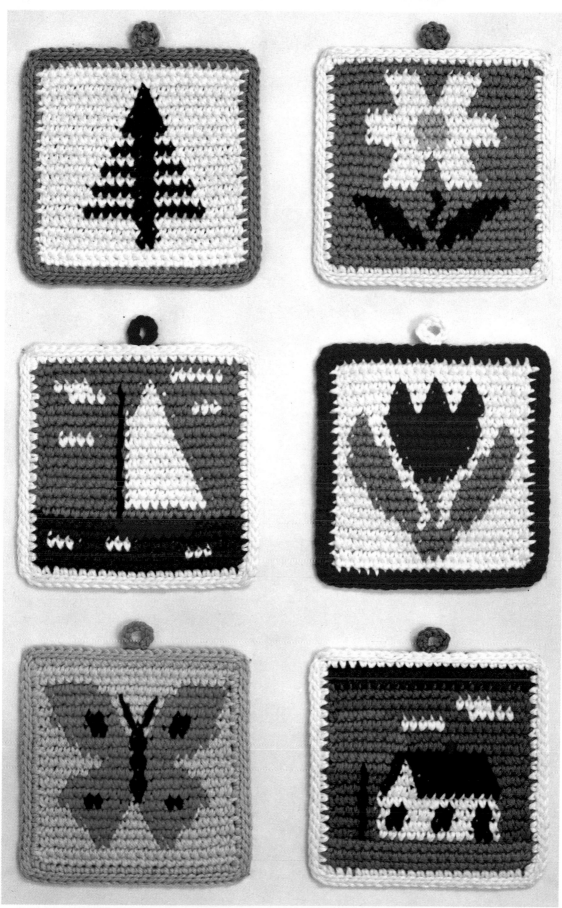

Picture Pot Holders, combining single crochet and reverse single crochet, make jiffy-quick gifts! Designs are worked in as you go, with embroidered details added. Directions, page 135.

Favorite of all afghan motifs is the granny square, elaborated below in soft and fluffy mohair for an extra luxurious effect. The pattern can be used for more usual yarns. Mohair Granny Squares, page 160.

Easy-to-make couch cover is a variation of the popular ripple pattern, this one starting at long edge and worked in one piece to opposite edge. Use a profusion of colors in random striping, one row to a color, or crochet to a set plan in a few favorite colors. Couch cover, page 160.

Made all in one piece of frosty white yarn in afghan-stitch crochet, the elegant coverlet is embroidered with cross-stitched "tiles" and "lace" patterns in four blues. Blue Tiles Afghan, page 161.

USEFUL CROCHET PATTERN STITCHES

FILET MESH

Make a ch of desired length. **Row 1:** Dc in 8th ch from hook (1 sp), * ch 2, sk 2 ch, dc in next ch, repeat from * across ch. Ch 5, turn.

Row 2: Dc in next dc, * ch 2, dc in next dc, repeat from * across to last dc, ch 2, sk 2 ch of turning-ch, dc in next ch. Ch 5, turn.

Repeat row 2 for pattern.

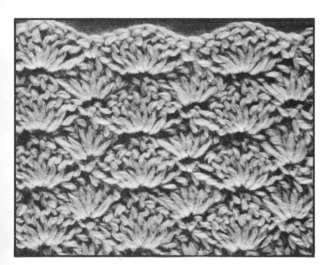

FAN SHELL STITCH

Multiple of 6 ch.

Row 1: Work 2 dc in 3rd ch from hook, ch 1, 3 dc in same ch, sk 2 ch, 1 sc in next ch, * sk 2 ch, 3 dc in next ch, ch 1, 3 dc in same ch, sk 2 ch, 1 sc in next ch, repeat from * across row, ch 3, turn.

Row 2: 2 dc in first sc, * sk 3 dc, 1 sc in ch-1 sp, sk 3 dc, 3 dc in sc between 2 shells, ch 1, 3 dc in same st, repeat from * across row, end sk 3 dc, 1 sc in ch-1 sp, sk 2 sc, 3 dc in last st, ch 1, turn.

Row 3: * 3 dc in next sc (between shells), ch 1, 3 dc in same st, sk 3 dc, sc in next ch-1 sp, sk 3 dc, repeat from * across row, end with shell in last sc, sk 2 dc, 1 sc in last st (top of turning-ch), ch 3, turn.

Repeat rows 2 and 3 for pattern.

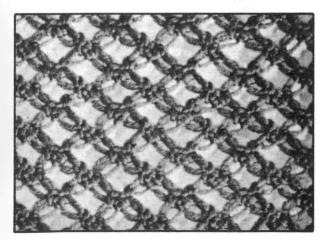

KNOT STITCH

Multiple of 6 ch. Make ch desired length.

Row 1: * Pull up loop on hook to ½" length, draw yarn through this loop and hold single strand at back of loop between thumb and middle finger; insert hook under this single strand and work sc; repeat from * once (double knot st made); sk 3 ch, 1 sc in each of next 3 ch, repeat from first * across, end 1 sc in each of last 3 ch.

Row 2: Work double knot st to turn. * Work 1 sc in loop on one side of knot st of previous row, work 1 sc in loop on other side of same knot st; work double knot st, repeat from * across row.

Repeat row 2 for pattern.

PEACH PASTELS
Shown on page 146

SIZE: Directions for size 8. Changes for sizes 10, 12 and 14 are in parentheses.

Body Bust Size: 31½″ (32½″-34″-36″).

Blocked Bust Size: 35″ (36″-37½″-39″).

MATERIALS: Wintuk sport yarn, 6 (6-7-7) 2-oz. skeins peach (A); 1 skein coral (B). Crochet hook size F.

GAUGE: 4 sc = 1″; 5 rows = 1″.

To Bind Off: At beg of row, sl st loosely across specified number of sts, ch 1, work in sc across; at **end of row,** leave specified number of sts unworked. Ch 1, turn.

To Dec 1 Sc: Pull up a lp in each of 2 sc, yo and through 3 lps on hook.

To Inc 1 Sc: Work 2 sc in same sc.

STRIPED PATTERN: Working in sc, (work 2 rows B, 4 rows A) 3 times, 2 rows B. When working striped pat, carry color loosely up side edge when not being used. When changing colors, work off last 2 lps with new color.

SWEATER: BACK: Beg at lower edge, with A, ch 67 (69-72-75).

Row 1 (wrong side): Sc in 2nd ch from hook and in each ch across–66 (68-71-74) sc. Ch 1, turn.

Row 2: Sc in each sc across. Ch 1, turn each row. Check gauge; piece should measure 16½″ (17″-17¾″-18½″) wide. Work in sc, working 5 more A rows, then work the 20 rows of striped pat, then work with A until piece measures 9″ (9″-9½″-10″) from start, then repeat the 20 rows of striped pat; at the same time, when piece measures 1″ (1″-1½″-1½″) from start, dec 1 st each side of next row, then dec 1 st each side every 1½″ 3 times more–58 (60-63-66) sc. Work even until piece measures 6½″ (6½″-7″-7″) from start. Inc 1 st each side of next row, then inc 1 st each side every 6th (6th-7th-7th) row 5 times more–70 (72-75-78) sc. Check gauge; when 2nd striped pat is completed, piece should measure about 13″ (13″-13½″-14″) from start; 17½″ (18″-18¾″-19½″) wide.

Shape Armholes: Working with A only, bind off (see To Bind Off) 4 sts each side of next row. Dec 1 sc each side every other row 4 (5-5-5) times–54 (54-57-60) sc. Work even until armholes measure 7″ (7¼″-7½″-7¾″) above first bound-off sts.

Shape Neck and Shoulders: Next Row: Sc in each of 19 (19-19-20) sc, drop yarn; join another strand of A, sl st in each of next 16 (16-19-20) sc, sc in each of next 19 (19-19-20) sc. Working on both sides at once, with separate strands of yarn, dec 1 sc each neck edge every row twice. Bind off 3 sts at each arm side of next row, then bind off 3 sts at each arm side every other row 2 (2-1-0) times, 4 sts 1 (1-2-3) times; at the same time, dec 1 st at each neck edge every row 2 (2-1-1) times more. End off.

FRONT: Work same as for back until armholes measure 4½″ (4½″-5″-5″) above first bound-off sts–54 (54-57-60) sc.

Shape Neck: Next Row: Sc in each of 13 (13-14-15) sc, drop yarn; join another strand of A, sl st in each of next 28 (28-29-30) sc, sc in each of next 13 (13-14-15) sc. Working on both sides at once, with separate strands of yarn, work even until armholes measure same as back.

Shape Shoulders: Bind off 3 sts at each arm side of next row, then bind off 3 sts at each arm side every other row 2 (2-1-0) times, 4 sts 1 (1-2-3) times. End off.

SLEEVES: Beg at lower edge, with A, ch 31 (31-33-33). Sc in 2nd ch from hook and in each ch across–30 (30-32-32) sc. Work in sc, working 6 more A rows, then work the 20 rows of striped pat, then complete piece with A only; at the same time, inc 1 sc each side every 6th row 9 (10-9-10) times–48 (50-50-52) sc. Work even until piece measures 16″ (16″-16½″-17″) from start or desired length to underarm. Check gauge; piece above last inc row should be 12″ (12½″-12½″-13″) wide.

Shape Cap: Bind off 4 sts each side of next row. Dec 1 sc each side every other row 2 (2-2-0) times, every 3rd row 8 (8-8-10) times, every other row 2 (2-4-4) times, every row 3 (4-1-2) times–10 (10-12-12) sts. End off.

FINISHING: Run in yarn ends on wrong side. With backstitch, sew in sleeves, easing in top of cap. Sew side and sleeve seams.

Lower Edging: Beg at lower side seam, from right side, with A, work 1 row sc around lower edge, join with a sl st in first sc. Do not turn.

Next Rnd: Sl st in each sc around. End. Work same edging around each sleeve edge.

Neck Edging: From right side, beg at right shoulder seam, with B, work 1 rnd sc around neck edge, holding in to desired fit. Join with a sl st in first st.

Rnd 2: Sl st in each sc around. End off. Steam-press lightly.

BOW-TIED BLOUSE
Shown on page 147

SIZES: Directions for small size (6-8). Changes for medium size (10-12) are in parentheses.

NOTE: Both sizes are made the same; only the hook size and gauge are different.

Body Bust Size: 30½"-31½" (32½"-34").

Blocked Bust Size: 32" (36").

MATERIALS: Knitting worsted, 2 4-oz. skeins winter white, main color (MC); 2 ozs. each of light yellow, orange, pink, green, red, turquoise and purple or any desired colors. Crochet hook size H (J).

GAUGE: Each motif = 4" (4½") square.

BLOUSE: MOTIF A (make 30): With first color, ch 4, sl st in first ch to form ring.

Rnd 1: Ch 3, 2 dc in ring, (ch 3, 3 dc in ring) 3 times, ch 3; join with sl st in top of first ch 3; end off.

Rnd 2: Join 2nd color in any ch-3 sp, ch 3, 2 dc in same sp, ch 3, 3 dc in same sp, (3 dc, ch 3, 3 dc in next sp) 3 times; join end off.

Rnd 3: Join 3rd color in any corner ch-3 sp, ch 3, 2 dc in same sp, ch, 3 dc in same sp, (3 dc in next sp between 3-dc groups; 3 dc, ch 3, 3 dc in next ch-3 sp) 3 times, 3 dc in next sp between 3-dc groups; join; end off. Check gauge; motifs should measure 4" (4½") square.

MOTIF B (make 28): With MC only, work same as for motif A. Do not end off each rnd; sl st to corner sp.

Joining: Arrange motifs as shown on diagram. From wrong side, with color matching one side, keeping seams elastic, sew motifs tog through top lps only.

Gussets: From right side, join MC in first corner sp at lower edge of 2nd sleeve motif (X on diagram), 2 sc in same sp, 3 hdc in next sp, 3 dc in next sp, 2 dc in next sp, dc in corner sp of next motif, 3 dc in each of next 2 sps, 3 dc in corner sp. End off. Beg in corner sp on opposite edge of sleeve, work gusset to correspond, end with 2 sc in corner sp at lower edge of 2nd motif.

FINISHING: Run in yarn ends on wrong side. Weave sleeve and sides tog.

Neck Edging: With MC, make lp on hook, dc in corner ch-3 sp at center front neck, * ch 1, sk next dc, dc in next dc, repeat from * to neck corner, yo hook, pull up a lp in corner sp, yo and through 2 lps on hook, yo hook, pull up a lp in corner sp of next motif, yo hook and through 2 lps on hook, yo and through 3 lps, repeat from * around. End off.

TIES (make 2): With MC, make ch 18" long. Tie into bow around center 3 dc group at center top of each sleeve. Make one 30" chain. Tie at front neck edge.

Steam-press lightly.

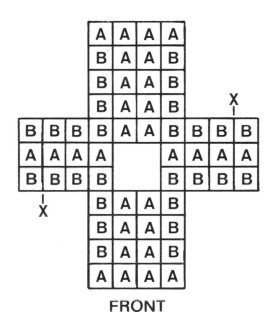

FRONT

MAN'S MOTIF PULLOVER
Shown on page 224

SIZES: Directions are for size 36. Any changes for sizes 38, 40 and 42 are in parentheses. Note: Directions are the same for all sizes; only the hook size and gauge are different.

Body Chest Size: 36" (38"-40"-42").

Blocked Chest Size: 37½" (40"-42½"-45").

MATERIALS: Knitting worsted, 7 (7-8-8) 4-oz. skeins. Crochet hook sizes E (F-G-H) and G (H-I-J).

GAUGE: Each Square = 3¾" (4"-4¼"-4½") square with size G (H-I-J) crochet hook.

PULLOVER: SQUARE (make 98): Beg at center of square with larger crochet hook, ch 5, join with a sl st to form ring.

Rnd 1: Ch 5 (counts as dc, ch 3), (3 dc in ring, ch 3) 3 times, end 2 dc in ring; join with a sl st in 2nd ch of ch 5–4 groups of 3 dc.

Rnd 2: Ch 2 (counts as 1 dc), * (2 dc, ch 3, 2 dc) in ch-3 sp, dc in each of next 3 dc, repeat from * twice, end (2 dc, ch 3, 2 dc) in ch-3 sp, dc in each of next 2 dc, sl st in top of ch 2.

Rnd 3: Ch 2, dc in each of next 2 dc, * (2 dc, ch 3, 2 dc) in ch-3 sp, dc in each of next 7 dc, repeat from * twice, end (2 dc, ch 3, 2 dc) in ch-3 corner, dc in each of next 4 dc; join with a sl st in top of ch 2; end off leaving a 10" end for sewing.

TRIANGLE (make 4): With larger crochet hook, ch 4, join with a sl st to form ring.

Row 1: Ch 5 (counts as 1 dc, ch 3), 3 dc in ring, ch 3, 3 dc, ch 3, dc in ring; end off; do not turn.

Row 2: Join yarn in 2nd ch of ch 5 at beg of row, ch 5 (counts as 1 dc, ch 3), 2 dc in same sp, dc in each of next 3 dc, (2 dc, ch 3, 2 dc) in ch-3 sp, dc in each of next 3 dc, (2 dc, ch 3, dc) in last sp; end off; do not turn.

Row 3: Join yarn in 2nd ch of ch 5 at beg of row, ch 5 (counts as 1 dc, ch 3), 2 dc in same sp, dc in each of next 7 dc, (2 dc, ch 3, 2 dc) in ch-3 sp, dc in each of next 7 dc, (2 dc, ch 3, dc) in last sp. End off.

Joining: Arrange squares and triangles as shown in diagram. From wrong side, keeping seams elastic, sew squares tog through top lps only.

Shape Back Neck: From right side, join yarn in 3rd dc at upper edge of squares.

Row 1: With larger hook, * sc in each dc to corner sp, sc in corner sp, sc in seam, sc in next corner sp, repeat from * to within last 3 dc–47 sc. Turn.

Row 2: Sl st in each of next 3 sc, sc in each sc to within last 3 sc–41 sc. Turn.

Rows 3 and 4: Repeat last row–29 sc. End off.

Shape Front Neck: Work same as for back neck.

FINISHING: Sew side seams. Sew one motif at each upper edge of front and back tog for shoulder. Sew sleeve seam. With center of top square of sleeve at shoulder seams, sew in sleeves.

Waistband: With smaller hook, ch 12.

Row 1: Sc in 2nd ch from hook and in each ch across–11 sc. Ch 1, turn.

Row 2: Sc in back lp of each sc across. Ch 1, turn. Repeat last row until piece, when slightly stretched, fits around lower edge of pullover. End off. Weave ends tog; sew to lower edge of body, easing in to fit.

Sleeve Band (make 2): With smaller hook, ch 8. Working on 7 sc, work same as for waistband until bands measure 9" (9½"-9¾"-10") from start. End off. Weave ends tog; sew to lower edge of sleeve, easing in sleeve to fit.

Steam-press lightly.

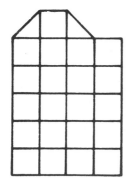

SLEEVE

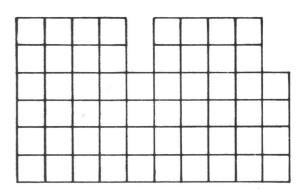

FRONT AND BACK

BATH SET
Shown on page 237

SIZE: Mat, 32″ × 26″.

MATERIALS: One towel set (bath towel, hand towel, face cloth). For mat, 1 yard broadcloth (cotton or cotton and polyester) to match towels; 1 yard heavy unbleached muslin; 1 yard batting. For crochet, 4-ply butcher's twine, 1 cone. Steel crochet hook No. 1. Sewing thread, natural color.

GAUGE: 2 bls or sps = 1″; 3 rows = 1″.

GENERAL DIRECTIONS:

Space (sp): Each sp is dc, ch 2, sk 2 sts, dc in next st; for each additional sp, ch 2, sk 2 sts, dc in next st. Ch 5 for first sp of row.

Block (bl): Each bl is dc in each of 4 sts; for each additional bl, dc in each of 3 sts. When working bl over sp, work 2 dc in sp.

Double Space (double sp): Each double sp is dc, ch 5, sk 5 sts, dc in next st; for each additional double sp, ch 5, sk 5 sts, dc in next st.

To Inc 1 Sp: At beg of row, ch 8, dc in first dc. Add 3 ch for each additional sp to be increased; dc in 9th ch from hook for first sp. At end of row, ch 2, dtr in same st with last dc. For each additional sp, ch 2, dtr in center of last dtr.

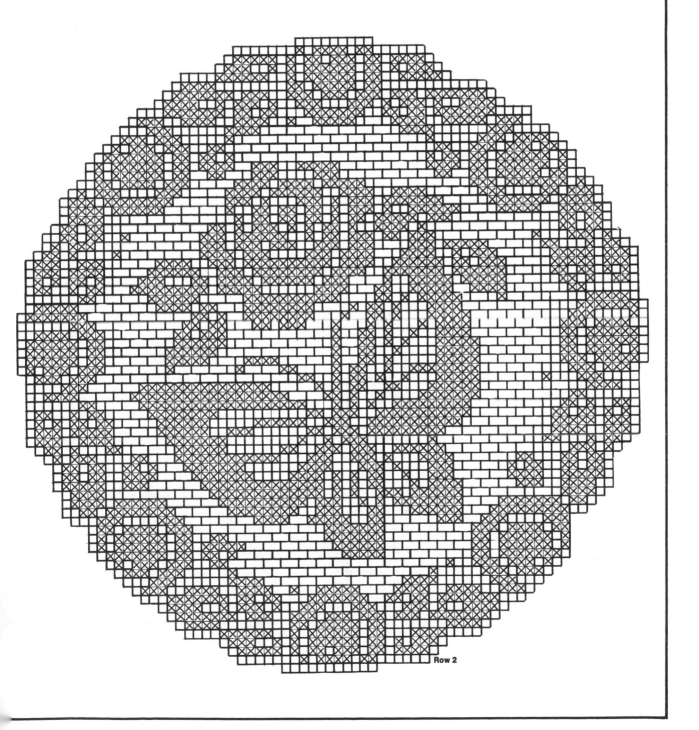

Row 2

To Dec 1 Sp: At beg of row, sl st across first sp to next dc, ch 5 for first sp, sk 2 sts, dc in next dc. **At end of row,** leave last sp unworked.

MAT: With twine, beg at lower edge of mat, ch 39.

Row 1: Dc in 9th ch from hook (1 sp), * ch 2, sk 2 ch, dc in next ch, repeat from * across—11 sps. Ch 23, turn.

Row 2: Dc in 9th ch from hook, (ch 2, sk 2 ch, dc in next ch) 4 times, ch 2, sk 2 ch, dc in dc (6 sps made), (2 dc in next sp, dc in next dc) twice (2 bls made), ch 2, dc in next dc (1 sp made), (2 dc in next sp, dc in next dc) 4 times (4 bls made), ch 2, dc in next dc (1 sp), 2 dc in next sp, dc in next dc (1 bl), ch 2, dc in next dc, ch 2, sk 2 ch of end ch, dc in next ch (2 sps); now add on 5 sps as follows: ch 2, dtr in same st with last dc (1 sp added), (ch 2, dtr in center of last dtr) 4 times (4 more sps added). Ch 8, turn.

Row 3: Dc in first dtr (1 sp added), (2 dc in next sp, dc in next st) 5 times, ch 2, dc in next dc, 2 dc in next sp, dc in next dc, ch 2, sk 2 dc, dc in next dc, 2 dc in next sp, dc in each of next 4 dc, ch 2, sk 2 dc, dc in each of next 7 dc, 2 dc in next sp, dc in next dc, ch 2, sk 2, dc, dc in each of next 4

dc, 2 dc in next sp, dc in next dc, ch 2, dc in next dc, (2 dc in next sp, dc in next dc) 3 times, 2 dc in end sp, sk 2 ch of end sp, dc in next ch; ch 2, dtr in same ch with last dc (1 sp added). Ch 8, turn.

Row 4: Working from chart, add 1 sp, work in bls and sps across, add 1 sp at end of row. Continue to work from chart to top. End off.

FINISHING: Cut broadcloth, muslin and 2 layers of batting, slightly larger than filet piece. Back filet with broadcloth, batting and muslin, in that order. Baste layers together. With natural color sewing thread, working from center to edge, machine stitch layers together, stitching around outlines of pattern (outline of butterfly, outline of rose, outline of border). Stitch all around edge. Cut 3″ wide bias strip from muslin, long enough to go around mat. Stitch one edge to mat, right sides together, taking ½″ seam. Turn to back of mat, turn under raw edge, hem down. Steam lightly.

BATH TOWEL: MOTIF: Beg at one end, ch 12.

Row 1: Dc in 9th ch from hook, ch 2, sk 2 ch, dc in next ch—2 sps. Ch 8, turn.

BATH TOWEL MOTIF

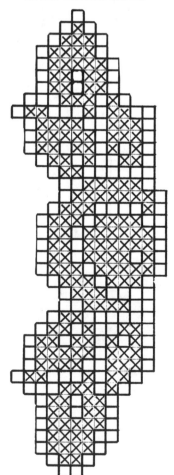

BATH TOWEL EDGING

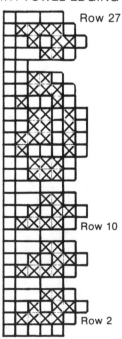

Row 27

Row 10

Row 2

HAND TOWEL MOTIF

HAND TOWEL EDGING

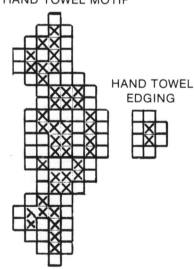

Row 2: Dc in first dc (1 sp inc), 2 dc in next sp, dc in dc, 2 dc in next sp, sk 2 ch, dc in next ch, ch 2, dtr in same ch with last dc (1 sp inc). Working from chart, beg with third row, continue to top, adding and decreasing sps at each edge as indicated.

With natural color sewing thread, sew motif to towel.

EDGING: Beg at one end, ch 21.

Row 1: Dc in 9th ch from hook, (ch 2, sk 2 ch, dc in next ch) 4 times—5 sps. Ch 8, turn.

Row 2: Dc in first dc (1 sp inc), (2 dc in next sp, dc in next dc) 4 times, ch 2, sk 2 ch, dc in next ch. Ch 5, turn.

Row 3: Dc in next dc, ch 2, sk 2 dc, dc in each of next 4 dc, ch 2, sk 2 dc, dc in each of next 4 dc, 2 dc in end sp, sk 2 ch, dc in next ch, ch 2, dtr in same ch with last dc. Turn.

Row 4: Sl st to first dc, ch 5, sk 2 dc, dc in next dc for first sp; continue to work from chart to row 27; repeat rows 10–27 twice more, then continue until edging fits edge of towel. Sew top edge of edging inside bound edge of towel.

HAND TOWEL: MOTIF: Beg at one end, ch 12. Sl st in first ch to form end sp. Ch 8. Dc in same ch with sl st, 2 dc in ch-12 sp, sk 2 ch, dc in next ch, ch 2, dtr in same ch with last dc—2 rows completed. Continue to work from chart to top. With natural color sewing thread, sew motif to towel.

EDGING: Beg at one end, ch 12.

Row 1: Dc in 9th ch from hook, ch 2, sk 2 ch, dc in last ch—2 sps. Ch 5, turn.

Row 2: Dc in next dc, 2 dc in next sp, sk 2 ch of sp, dc in next ch, ch 2, dtr in same ch with dc. Ch 5, turn. Working from chart, repeat 4 rows of chart until edging is same length as towel edge. Sew top edge of edging inside bound edge of towel.

FACE CLOTH EDGING: Ch 9. Dc in 9th ch from hook. Ch 5, turn.

Row 1: Dc in 4th ch from hook, dc in next ch, dc in dc, ch 2, sk 2 ch, dc in next ch. Ch 5, turn.

Row 2: Sk first dc, dc in next dc. Ch 5, turn. Repeat rows 1 and 2 until piece is 11″ long, end row 2. Ch 5, turn.

Corner: Dc in 4th ch from hook, dc in next ch, dc in dc, ch 3, yo hook, draw up a lp in last dc worked in, yo and through 1 lp on hook (this ch is base for next dc), (yo and through 2 lps) twice, yo hook, draw up a lp in base st, yo and through 1 lp on hook, (yo and through 2 lps) twice, ch 3, sl st in last base st made, ch 2, sl st in 3rd ch of corner ch-5 sp. Ch 5, turn. Dc in same base st with sl st. Ch 5, turn. Repeat from row 1 until 4 corners have been made, end with sl st in 3rd ch of corner ch-5 sp. End off. Sew edging to face cloth with natural color sewing thread.

FLOWER STRIPED AFGHAN
Shown on page 233

SIZE: About 50″ × 60″.

MATERIALS: Unger's Nanette, 1¾ oz. balls, 5 balls Rose (A), 4 balls each of Lt. Orange (B), Purple (C), Yellow (D), Red (E). Crochet hooks sizes H and I.

GAUGE: 1 flower = 2¾″; 4 flowers = 11″.

Note: Afghan is worked from side edge to side edge.

AFGHAN: With size I hook and A, ch 172 loosely.

Row 1: 3-tr cluster in 8th ch from hook (to make 3-tr cluster, work 3 tr in 1st holding back last lp of each tr, yo and through all 4 lps on hook)—1 petal made—ch 7, 3-tr in same ch with last petal, * ch 3, sk 3 ch, sc in next ch, ch 3, sk 3 ch, 3-tr cluster, ch 7, 3-tr cluster in next ch, repeat from * across, end ch 3, sk 3 ch, sc in last ch—21 half-flowers. End off. Turn.

Row 2: Join B in ch before first petal, ch 4, 2-tr cluster in same ch (to make 2-tr cluster, work 2 tr in 1st holding back last lp of each tr, yo and through all 3 lps on hook), ch 4, 2-tr cluster in top of petal just made, sc in 4th ch of next ch 7, * ch 4; holding back last lp of each tr, work 2 tr in last sc made (3 lps on hook); holding back last lp of each tr, work 3 tr in ch after next petal (6 lps on hook); holding back last lp of each tr, work 3 tr in ch before next petal (9 lps on hook); yo and through 9 lps on hook, ch 4, 2-tr cluster in center of 3-petal group just formed, sc in 4th ch of next ch 7, repeat from * across, end ch 4; holding back last lp of each tr, work 2 tr in last sc made; end 3 tr in ch after last petal, yo and through 6 lps on hook. Ch 4, turn.

Row 3: 2-tr cluster in top of petal group, * ch 3, sc in next sc, ch 3, 3-tr cluster in center of next flower, ch 7, 3-tr cluster in center of same flower, repeat from * across, end 3-tr cluster in st at center of last 2 petals. There are 20 6-petal flowers and a 3-petal half-flower at each end. End off. Turn.

Row 4: Join C in first st, ch 7; holding back on hook last lp of each tr, work 2 tr in 4th ch from hook, 3 tr in ch after first petal and 3 tr in ch before next petal, yo and through 9 lps on hook, * ch 4, 2-tr cluster in center of group just completed, sc in 4th ch of ch 7, ch 4; holding back last lp of each tr, work 2 tr in sc just made, 3 tr in ch after next petal and 3 tr in ch before next petal, yo and through 9 lps on hook, repeat from * across, end ch 4, 2-tr cluster in center of group just completed, tr in last st—21 flowers of 4 petals each. Ch 3, turn.

Row 5: * 3-tr cluster in center of flower, ch 7, 3-tr cluster in same place, ch 3, sc in next sc, ch 3, repeat from * across, end 3-tr cluster, ch 7, 3-

tr cluster in center of last flower, ch 3, sc in tip of last petal—21 flowers of 6 petals each. End off. Turn. Repeat rows 2–5 for pattern. Work 2 rows D, 2 rows E, 2 rows A, 2 rows B, 2 rows C and repeat color sequence until 5th E flower is completed. End off E. Join A.

Last Row: With A, ch 3, 3-tr cluster in ch before first petal, ch 3, sc in 4th ch of ch 7, ch 3, * holding back last lp of each tr, work 3 tr in ch after next petal, 3 tr in ch before next petal, yo and through 7 lps on hook, ch 3, sc in 4th ch of ch 7, ch 3, repeat from * across, end 3-tr cluster in st after last petal. End off.

BORDER: Rnd 1: From right side, with size H hook, join A in corner, ch 2, hdc in corner, hdc around 4 sides of afghan, working 3 hdc in each corner, end hdc in starting corner, sl st in top of ch 2. Make sure work lies flat and opposite sides have same number of sts. Work 2 more rnds of hdc in same manner.

Last Rnd: Working from left to right, ch 1, hdc in last st worked, * ch 1, sk 1 st, hdc in next st, repeat from * around, making sure to keep work flat. End off.

FINISHING: Steam. Do not press.

COUCH COVER
Shown on page 151

SIZE: About 60″ × 90″.

MATERIALS: Coats & Clark's Red Heart 4-Ply Handknitting yarn, about 80 ozs. of assorted colors. In cover shown, the following colors were used: Paddy Green, Light Olive, Yellow, Orange, Eggshell, Coffee, Wood Brown, Pink Rose, Lavender, Amethyst, Lilac, Vermillion, Burnt Orange, Dark Turquoise, Blue Jewel, Skipper Blue. Include 8 ozs. of one dark color for border. Crochet hook size H.

GAUGE: 4 dc = 1″. Each chevron = 4½″ across.

COVER: With any desired color, beg at side edge, ch 444.

Row 1: 2 dc in 4th ch from hook and in each of next 8 ch, * sk 2 ch, dc in next ch, sk 2 ch, dc in each of next 8 ch, 5 dc in next ch, dc in each of next 8 ch, repeat from * across, end sk 2 ch, dc in next ch, sk 2 ch, dc in each of next 8 ch, 3 dc in last ch, working off last 2 lps of last dc with new color. With new color, ch 3, turn.

Row 2: 2 dc in first dc, dc in each of next 8 dc, * sk 2 dc, dc in next dc, sk 2 dc, dc in each of next 8 dc, 5 dc in next dc (center dc of 5-dc group), dc in each of next 8 dc, repeat from * across, end sk 2 dc, dc in next dc, sk 2 dc, dc in each of next 8 dc, 3 dc in top of ch 3, changing color as before.

Ch 3, turn. Check gauge; piece should be about 90″ long. Repeat row 2 for desired width of cover.

FINISHING: Rnd 1: Join dark color for border in last ch of starting ch. Working across starting ch, sc in each ch across, 2 sc in each point, 3 sc in last (corner) ch; working up side, 3 sc in end of each row, 3 sc in top of last row; working across last row, sc in each dc, sk 1 dc at V's, work 2 sc in dc at each point, 3 sc in last st; work last side as for first side, 2 sc in same ch with first sc, sl st in first sc.

Rnd 2: Ch 3, dc in each sc around, working 2 dc in 1 st at each point, sk 1 sc at each V, 4 dc in each corner st. Sl st in top of ch 3.

Rnd 3: Working from left to right, sc in each dc around. End off.

MOHAIR GRANNY SQUARES
Shown on page 150

SIZE: 50″ × 65″.

MATERIALS: Mohair or mohair type yarn, 17 ozs. of assorted colors, 7 ozs. black. Crochet hook size G.

GAUGE: Each square = 7″.

GRANNY SQUARE (make 63): With first color, ch 3, sl st in first ch to form ring.

Rnd 1: Ch 3 (counts as 1 dc), 2 dc in ring, (ch 3, 3 dc in ring) 3 times, ch 3, sl st in top of ch 3, sl st in each of next 2 dc, sl st in next ch. End off.

Rnd 2: Join another color in any ch-3 sp. Working over end of new color, ch 3, 2 dc in ch-3 sp, ch 3, 3 dc in same ch-3 sp, (ch 2; in next corner sp work 3 dc, ch 3, 3 dc) 3 times, ch 2, sl st in top of ch 3, sl st in each of next 2 dc, sl st in next ch. End off.

Rnd 3: Join another color in any ch-3 sp. Working over end of new color, ch 3, 2 dc in ch-3 sp, ch 3, 3 dc in same ch-3 sp, (ch 2, 3 dc in ch-2 sp, ch 2; in next corner sp work 3 dc, ch 3, 3 dc) 3 times, ch 2, 3 dc in next ch-2 sp, ch 2, sl st in top of ch 3, sl st in each of next 2 dc, sl st in next ch. End off.

Rnd 4: With another color, work as for rnd 3, working 2 groups of 3 dc on each side of square.

Rnd 5: With black, work as for rnd 3, working 3 groups of 3 dc on each side of square.

FINISHING: Overcast squares tog with black, sewing through back lps of sts. Make afghan 7 squares wide by 9 squares long.

BORDER: With black, work 1 rnd of dc around afghan, working dc in each dc and in each ch and working 3 dc, ch 3, 3 dc in each corner. Sl st in first dc. End off.

BLUE TILES AFGHAN
Shown on page 152

SIZE: About 60″ square.

MATERIALS: 4-Ply Knitting Worsted Weight Orlon Acrylic Yarn, 12 4-oz. balls white, 2 balls each of Ice Blue and Cadet Blue, 1 ball each of Baby Blue and Dark Blue, 20″ aluminum afghan hook or flexible hook size G. Plastic crochet hook size G. Tapestry needles.

GAUGE: 4 sts = 1″; 7 rows = 2″.

AFGHAN: With white and afghan hook, ch 234.

Row 1: Pull up a lp in 2nd ch from hook and in each ch across, keeping all lps on hook.

To Work Lps Off: Yo hook, pull through first lp, * yo hook, pull through next 2 lps, repeat from * across until 1 lp remains. Lp that remains on hook always counts as first st of next row.

Row 2: Keeping all lps on hook, pull up a lp under 2nd vertical bar and under each vertical bar across. Work lps off as before. Repeat row 2 until there are 203 rows. Sl st loosely under 2nd vertical bar and in each vertical bar across. End

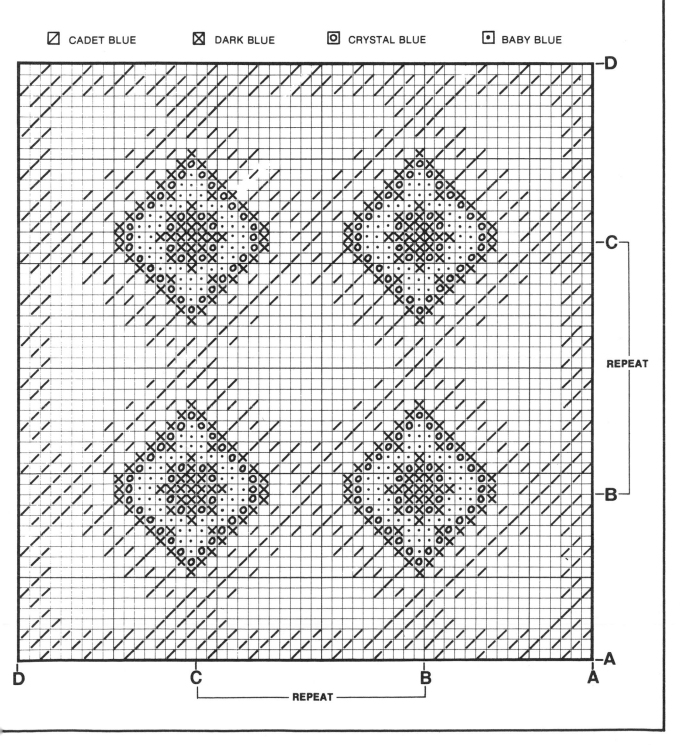

CADET BLUE   DARK BLUE   CRYSTAL BLUE   BABY BLUE

off. Weave in ends on reverse side. Steam top and bottom edges lightly so that edges lie flat.

EMBROIDERY: Following chart and color key, embroider design in cross-stitch. Working horizontally, work from A to B, repeat from B to C 9 times, work from C to D. Working vertically, work from A to B, repeat from B to C 7 times, work from C to D.

FINISHING: With white and crochet hook, work 1 row of sc around afghan, working 1 sc in each st or row and 3 sc in each corner. Join with sl st in first sc. End off.

FRINGE: Wrap crystal blue around 5″ cardboard; cut at one end. Using 2 strands tog, fold strands in half, insert hook from wrong side through sc on edge, draw fold through, draw ends through loop. Tighten knot. * Skip 1 sc, knot a fringe in next sc, repeat from * around. Trim fringe evenly.

CROSS-STITCH ON AFGHAN STITCH

AFGHAN CROCHET STITCHES

PLAIN AFGHAN STITCH: Work with afghan hook. Make a ch desired length.

Row 1: Keeping all lps on hook, sk first ch from hook (lp on hook is first st), pull up a lp in each ch across; Figure 1.

To Work Lps Off: Yo hook, pull through first lp, * yo hook, pull through next 2 lps, repeat from * across until 1 lp remains; Figure 2. Lp that remains on hook always counts as first st of next row.

Row 2: Keeping all lps on hook, sk first vertical bar (lp on hook is first st), pull up a lp under next vertical bar and under each vertical bar across; Figure 3. Work lps off as before. Repeat row 2 for plain afghan stitch.

EDGE STITCH: Made at end of rows only to make firm edge. Work as follows: Insert hook under last vertical bar and in lp at back of bar, pull up 1 lp; Figure 4.

TO INC 1 AFGHAN ST: Pull up 1 lp under ch between 2 vertical bars; Figure 5.

TO DEC 1 AFGHAN ST: At beg of a pat row, keep to pat, insert hook under 2nd and 3rd vertical bars and pull up 1 plain lp for plain or cross st, or pull up 1 purl lp for purl st; keep lp on hook; Figure 6. At end of a pat row, insert hook under 3rd and 2nd vertical bars from end and dec as for beg row, then make edge stitch, as described above.

PURL STITCH: Holding yarn with thumb in front, and below hook, pull up a lp under vertical bar; keep lp on hook; Figure 7.

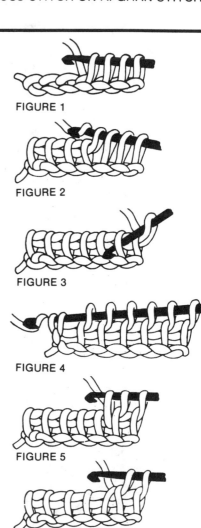

FIGURE 1

FIGURE 2

FIGURE 3

FIGURE 4

FIGURE 5

FIGURE 6

FIGURE 7

"PATCHWORK" IN EASY CROCHET

Beginners in crochet can make attractive accessories for the home with only two stitches, basic chain stitch and single crochet. By crocheting two-color squares, all the same size, and sewing them together according to a planned pattern, many colorful extras for the home are possible. On the next four pages, we show several favorite patchwork quilt designs based on triangles. These patchwork patterns, rendered in crochet, are the basis for pillows, small and large, floor cushions, afghans of all sizes, even bedspreads. The module we have used is a 6" square crocheted in yarn of knitting worsted weight. You can use other materials for smaller or larger squares and for projects other than those illustrated. Directions for making squares are below.

CROCHETED PATCHWORK

SIZE OF SQUARE: 6".

MATERIALS: Knitting worsted weight yarn (one 4-oz. skein will make at least 5 complete squares of one color or 10 halves). Aluminum or plastic crochet hook size 5 or G. Tapestry needle.

GAUGE: 4 sc = 1"; 4 rows = 1".

SQUARE: First Half: With first color, leaving 12" end for sewing, ch 35 to measure 9".

Row 1: Sc in 2nd ch from hook and in each ch across—34 sc. Check gauge; piece should measure 8½" wide. Ch 1 loosely, turn.

Row 2: Sk first st, sc in each sc across to last 2 sts, sk 1 st, sc in last sc—32 sc. Ch 1 loosely, turn.

Rows 3–17: Repeat row 2–2 sc remain. Ch 1, turn.

Last Row: Sk first sc, sc in last sc. End off; leave end for sewing.

Second Half: Row 1 (right side): With second color, leaving end for sewing, make lp on hook. Working on opposite side of starting chain and beg at same end as hanging end, sc in each of 34 ch. Work as for first half.

FINISHING: Steam squares lightly to same 6" square size. Arrange squares in any desired pattern, sew squares tog on wrong side with hanging ends. After sewing, weave in ends on wrong side for 1" or 2"; cut ends close to work.

Two-color square of worsted weight yarn is crocheted on the diagonal, each half worked from the center to the corner in easy single crochet. 6" squares, when sewn together, offer an endless variety of patterns for your household crochet.

Star quilt pattern is worked in orange, red, an lemon yellow. Repeat is a 24" square. Use this combination of crocheted two-color blocks to make the pair of pretty pillows.

164

Two lively patterns in patchwork can be worked out in 36"-square repeats— a perfect size for floor cushions. At upper left, the familiar Ohio Star pattern is planned for three colors. Left, triangles in four colors combine for a prismatic square-in-square design.

Double the simple triangle for a square, then multiply the square in a repeating pattern—and you have "patchwork." Try one of the patterns here for an afghan, baby blanket, car robe, bedspread or pillow. Choose your colors first, then decide on the size of your basic unit—such as a 6″ square. The pinwheel design at right and the overlapping pyramids below work out to a 12″ repeat. Motif at lower right has 24″ repeat.

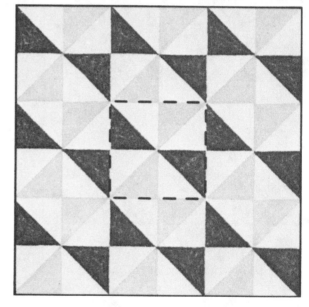

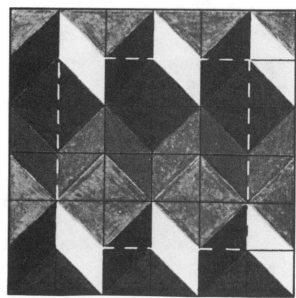

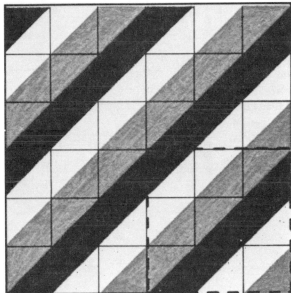

Patchwork geometrics work beautifully for pillows or a handsome bedspread that doubles as a blanket. With a 6" square as the basic unit, the hourglass pattern has a 24"-square repeat. Using the same size unit, stripes in red, white, and blue form an 18" square.

Gaily colored and styled, these mats are designed for all your oven-to-table ware. They are made of sturdy rug yarn for practicality, trimmed with rickrack. Pineapple Hot Mat, 15" × 8", has separate fruit and leaf sections. Round mat is a good beginners' project. Hen-in-a-basket has a shell pattern body, rickrack details. Oval Hot Mat, 9½" × 12½", is adjustable to larger and smaller sizes. Directions, page 173, 174.

Directions for
Gay 90s Potholders
are on page 174.

Directions for Shamrock Doily, page 178.

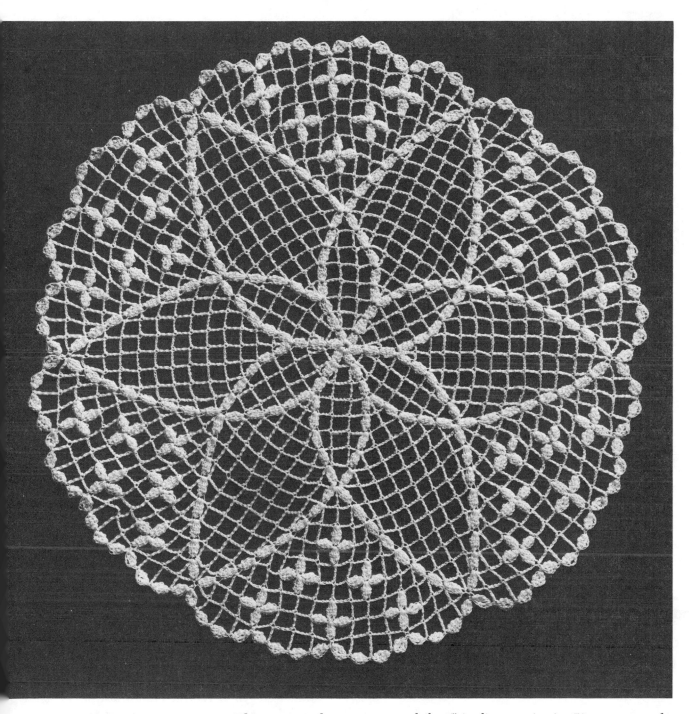

This smart and contemporary doily, 7" in diameter in size 70 cotton, can be made larger by using heavier thread. It is made in an unusual way, with a minimum of directions, by following the chart of symbols for crocheting the pretty flower-and-leaf patterns in rice stitch clusters on an openwork mesh.
Directions on page 179.

This cheery yellow centerpiece in filet crochet is easy to make in knitting and crochet cotton. The simple blocks and spaces that form the checkerboard center and flower-patterned border are worked from a chart.
Flower Filet Mat, directions on page 180.

PINEAPPLE HOT MAT
Shown on page 168

SIZE: 15″ × 8″.

MATERIALS: Coats & Clark Craft and Rug Yarn, 1 4-oz. skein each of orange and hunter's green. Crochet hook size G. Boiltex Rick Rack, 1 card each of jumbo and medium size, yellow; 1 card medium size, dark nile.

MAT: Beg at base, with orange, ch 12.

Row 1: Sc in 2nd ch from hook and in each ch across—11 sc. Ch 1, turn.

Row 2: 2 sc in first sc, sc in each sc across to last sc, 2 sc in last sc—13 sc. Ch 1, turn.

Row 3: Sc in each sc. Ch 1, turn. Repeat rows 2 and 3 until there are 25 sc on row. Place marker on last row.

Work even on 25 sc for 10 more rows.

Next Row: Dec 1 sc (**to dec:** draw up a lp in each of 2 sc, yo hook and through all 3 lps on hook), sc in each sc across to last 2 sc, dec 1 sc. Ch 1, turn.

Following Row: Sc in each sc across. Repeat last 2 rows until there are 13 sc on row. Dec 1 sc at both sides of next 3 rows. End off.

LEAVES: First Leaf: With green, ch 9; dc in 4th ch from hook, dc in next ch, hdc in next ch, sc in each of next 3 ch. End off.

2nd Leaf: Ch 11; dc in 4th ch from hook, dc in next ch, hdc in next 3 ch, sc in next 3 ch.

3rd and 4th Leaves: Ch 14; 2 dc in 4th ch from hook, dc in next ch, hdc in next 6 ch, sc in next 3 ch.

Work 5th leaf as for 2nd leaf; work 6th leaf as for first leaf. Sew base of leaves across top edge of pineapple. Tack first few sts at base of each leaf to adjoining leaf.

Sew green rickrack around leaves. Sew strips of medium yellow rickrack diagonally across pineapple to form diamonds; sew jumbo rickrack around edge.

ROUND HOT MAT
Shown on page 168

SIZE: 10½″ in diameter.

MATERIALS: Coats & Clark Craft and Rug Yarn, 1 4-oz. skein blue. Crochet hook size G. Boiltex Rick Rack, 1 card each medium and baby size, purple.

MAT: Beg at center, ch 2. **Rnd 1:** 7 sc in 2nd ch from hook. Do not join rnds; mark end of rnds.

Rnd 2: 2 sc in each sc around—14 sc.

Rnd 3: * Sc in next sc, 2 sc in next sc, repeat from * around—21 sc.

Rnds 4–6: Sc in each sc, inc 7 sc evenly around—42 sc.

Rnd 7: Sc in each sc, inc 6 sc evenly around. Repeat rnd 7 until piece measures 10½″ in diameter or desired size. Sl st in next sc. End off.

Sew medium rickrack around edge, baby size around 4th rnd from edge.

CHICKEN HOT MAT
Shown on page 168

SIZE: 15″ long × 14½″ high.

MATERIALS: Coats & Clark Craft and Rug Yarn, 1 4-oz. skein white, 1 skein each red and yellow. Crochet hook size G. Boiltex Rick Rack, 1 card each of medium and baby size, turquoise; 1 card medium size, red; few inches of dark blue.

BODY: Beg at base with white, ch 30.

Row 1: Sc in 2nd ch from hook, * sk next ch, 3 dc in next ch (shell made), sk next ch, sc in next ch, repeat from * across—7 shells. Ch 3, turn.

Row 2: 2 dc in first sc (starting shell), *sc in center dc of next shell, shell in next sc, repeat from * across—8 shells. Ch 3, turn.

Row 3: Dc in first dc (half shell), sc in next dc of same shell, * shell in next sc, sc in center dc of next shell, repeat from * across, ending with sc in center of last shell, 2 dc in top of turning ch. Ch 1, turn.

Row 4: Sc in first dc, * shell in next sc, sc in next shell, repeat from * across, ending with sc in top of turning ch. Ch 3, turn.

Rows 5–10: Repeat rows 2–4 twice—10 shells on last row. Ch 3, turn.

Row 11: Dc in first sc, * sc in center of next shell, shell in next sc, repeat from * across, ending with sc in last shell, 2 dc in last sc. Ch 1, turn.

Row 12: Repeat row 4.

Rows 13 and 14: Repeat rows 11 and 12. Do not ch to turn at end of last row.

Rows 15–20: Sl st in first dc of shell, sc in center dc of same shell, shell in next sc, sc in next shell, work in pat across, ending with sc in last shell, turn—4 shells on last row. End off.

HEAD: Beg at center with white, ch 2.

Rnd 1: 7 sc in 2nd ch from hook.

Rnd 2: 2 sc in each sc around—14 sc.

Rnd 3: * Sc in next sc, 2 sc in next sc, repeat from * around—21 sc.

Rnd 4: * Sc in next 2 sc, 2 sc in next sc, repeat from * around—28 sc. Ch 1, turn. Work in rows for neck.

Row 1: Sc in first 10 sc. Ch 1, turn.

Rows 2–5: Sc in each sc. Ch 1, turn.

Row 6: 2 sc in first sc, sc in next 8 sc, 2 sc in last sc. Ch 1, turn.

Row 7: Repeat row 2. Ch 3, turn.

Row 8: Dc in first sc, hdc in next 3 sc, sc in next 2 sc, sl st in next 2 sc. End off. Sew neck to body.

TAIL: Place a marker on curved edge of body 4″ from lower edge and another marker 6″ above first marker, measured along edge.

Row 1: Attach white at first marker, work 25 sc evenly across to next marker. Ch 1, turn.

Row 2: Sc in first sc, * sk next sc, shell in next sc, sk next sc, sc in next sc. Repeat from * across— 6 shells. Ch 3, turn.

Row 3: Work as for row 11 of body, ch 1, turn.

Row 4: Work as for row 4 of body until 4 shells have been made, sc in next shell. Turn.

Row 5: Sl st in next dc, sc in center dc of same shell, shell in next sc, work in pat across ending with 2 dc in last sc.

Ch 1, turn.

Row 6: Work as for row 4 of body until 2 shells have been made, sc in next shell. Turn.

Row 7: Sl st in next dc, sc in center dc of same shell, shell in next sc, sc in next shell, 2 dc in last sc. End off.

BEAK: Attach yellow yarn to 5th free sc on head preceding neck.

Row 1: Draw up a lp in same sc and in next sc, yo hook and through all 3 lps on hook (1 dec), sc in next sc, dec 1 sc over next 2 sc. Ch 1, turn.

Row 2: Sc in first sc, dec 1 sc over next 2 sc. Ch 1, turn.

Row 3: Dec 1 sc over remaining 2 sc. End off.

WATTLE: Attach red yarn just below beak, sc in same st, make (5 dc in end of next row, sc in next sc) 3 times. End off.

COMB: Mark off 13 sc at top of head, attach red yarn to first of these sts, sc in same sc, (sk next sc, 5 dc in next sc, sk next sc, sc in next sc) 3 times. End off.

FINISHING: Sew red rickrack around comb and wattle. With medium size blue rickrack, out-line tail, cut small strips for neck and tail and sew in place as illustrated; make an oval 7½″ long and sew to body for wing. Sew a strip across lower edge and 2 strips across body about 3″ from lower edge. With baby rickrack, make 3 sets of spirals on wing. Gather 4 points of dark blue rickrack for eye and sew in place.

OVAL HOT MAT
Shown on page 168

SIZE: 9½″ × 12½″.

MATERIALS: Coats & Clark Craft and Rug Yarn, 1 4-oz. skein Robinette. Crochet hook size G. Boiltex Rick Rack, 1 card each of jumbo and medium size, white.

MAT: Beg at center, ch 14. **Rnd 1:** 2 sc in 2nd ch from hook, sc in each ch across, 3 sc in last ch; working across opposite side of starting ch, sc in each ch across, sc in same ch as first 2 sc. Do not join rnds; mark end of rnds.

Rnd 2: 2 sc in each of next 2 sc, sc in each sc across to 3-sc group, 2 sc in each of 3 sc, sc in each remaining sc to last sc, 2 sc in last sc.

Rnd 3: Sc in each sc around, inc 3 sc evenly across each end. Repeat rnd 3 until piece measures 9½″ × 12½″, keeping center inc at tip of each end and spreading side incs wider apart. Sl st in next sc. End.

Sew jumbo rickrack around edge, medium size around 4th rnd from edge.

GAY 90's POT HOLDERS
Shown on page 169

SIZE: 7″ × 10″.

MATERIALS: Mercerized knitting and cro-chet cotton (bedspread cotton), 3 balls white (A); 1 ball each of ecru (B), aqua (C) and coral (D); small amount of black, for both pot holders. Cro-chet hook No. 7. Two plastic rings. Toweling or flannel for padding. Large-eyed embroidery needle.

GAUGE: 7 sts = 1″; 10 rows = 1″.

Note: Ch 1, turn each row.

POT HOLDER (make 4): Beg at side corner, with A, ch 2.

Row 1: 3 sc in 2nd ch from hook.

Row 2: 2 sc in first sc, long sc inserting hook at base of next sc, 2 sc in last sc—5 sc.

Row 3: 2 sc in first sc, * long sc in base of next sc, sc in next sc, repeat from * across, end 2 sc in last sc—7 sts. Repeat last row until there are 71 sts across row. Work 3 rows even.

Next Row: Dec 1 sc (**to dec:** pull up a lp in each of 2 sts, yo hook and through 3 lps on hook), work in pat to last 2 sts, dec 1 sc—69 sts. Re-peat last row until 3 sts remain. End off.

For Man Pot Holder: Face: Beg at chin, with B, ch 3.

Row 1: Sc in 2nd ch from hook, sc in last ch—2 sc.

Row 2: 2 sc in each sc—4 sc.

Row 3: Inc 1 sc (**to inc:** work 2 sc in same sc), sc in each sc to last sc, inc 1 st—6 sc.

Rows 4–6: Repeat row 3—12 sc.

Rows 7–15: Work even. End off.

Hat: Beg at lower edge, with C, ch 19.

Row 1: Sc in 2nd ch from hook and in each ch across—18 sc.

Row 2: Sc in each sc across.

Row 3: Sl st in each of 3 sc, ch 1, sc in each sc to within 2 sc of end—14 sc. Work 5 rows even. End off.

Moustache: Beg at side edge, with black, ch 2.

Row 1: Sc in 2nd ch from hook.

Row 2: 2 sc in sc—2 sc. Work 3 rows even.

Row 6: Dec 1 sc—1 sc.

Row 7: Sc in sc.

Row 8: 2 sc in sc—2 sc. Work 3 rows even.

Row 12: Dec 1 sc—1 sc.

Row 13: Sc in sc. End off.

Bow Tie: Beg side edge, with black, ch 6.

Row 1: Sc in 2nd ch from hook and in each ch across—5 sc.

Row 2: Work even.

Row 3: Dec 1 sc each side—3 sc.

Row 4: Work even.

Row 5: Inc 1 sc each side—5 sc. Work 2 rows even. End off.

Shirt: Beg at lower edge, with D, ch 13.

Row 1: Sc in 2nd ch from hook, sc in each ch across—12 sc. Work 7 rows even.

Rows 9 and 10: Dec 1 sc each side—8 sc. Work 4 rows even. End off.

Jacket: Beg at lower edge, with C, ch 5.

Row 1: Sc in 2nd ch from hook and in each ch across—4 sc.

Row 2: Inc 1 sc each side—6 sc.

Rows 3–5: Inc 2 sc each side—18 sc.

Rows 6–12: Inc 1 sc each side—32 sc. Work 5 rows even.

Lapel: Row 18: Sc in each of 16 sc. Ch 1, turn.

Row 19: Sc in each of 14 sc, dec 1 sc—15 sc.

Row 20: Dec 1 sc, finish row—14 sc.

Rows 21–32: Continue to dec 1 sc at side edge every row—2 sc. Work 1 row even.

Row 34: Dec 1 sc—1 sc.

Row 35: Sc in sc. End off. Join D in next st at center of last long row, sc in each sc across—16 sc. Dec 1 sc at side edge every row until 2 sc remain. Finish same as first lapel. Join black about 1″ below outside point of lapel. Work 1 row sc around each lapel ending 1″ below point of other lapel and working 3 sc in each point. End off.

Flower: With D, ch 4. Join with a sl st in first ch to form ring.

Rnd 1: 7 sc in ring; join with a sl st.

Rnd 2: * Ch 2, sc in next sc, repeat from * around.

Rnd 3: * Work sc, dc, sc in next ch-2 lp, repeat from * around. End off.

For Lady Pot Holder: Face: Beg at neck edge, with B, ch 9.

Row 1: Sc in 2nd ch from hook and in each ch across—8 sc. Work 4 rows even.

Rows 6 and 7: Inc 1 sc each side—12 sc. Work 13 rows even. End off.

Hat: With D, work same as for man through row 4.

Rows 5–7: Sc in each of 4 sc, sl st in next 6 sts, sc in each of 4 sc. End off.

Blouse: Beg at lower edge, with C, ch 13.

Row 1: Sc in 2nd ch from hook and in each ch across—12 sc. Work 9 rows even.

Row 11: Dec 1 sc each side—10 sc.

Row 12: Repeat row 11—8 sc. Ch 3, turn.

Row 13: Dc in first sc, hdc in next sc, sc in each sc to last 2 sc, hdc in next sc, dc in next sc. Cut C; join D.

Row 14: * Ch 3, sc in next st, repeat from * across. End off.

Flower: With C, work same as for man.

Jacket: With D, work same as for man.

FINISHING: With black, embroider eyes, nose and mouth on each face as pictured. Sew moustache on man's face. Sew hat to each face, overlapping hat ⅛″ on top of head. Sew flower to woman's hat. With black, embroider 2 lines on man's hat for hatband; with D, make small dots on hatband. Sew woman's head to one pot holder piece; sew on blouse. With D, embroider four buttons on center front of blouse. Sew on jacket as pictured. With black, work outline st down center front of jacket; make 3 lazy daisy sts on each side for frogs. Sew man's shirt to head, overlapping chin ⅛″ over shirt. Sew to one pot holder piece. With black, embroider 4 buttons on jacket front; with outline st, embroider a curved line from center to lower edge of jacket. Sew jacket in place; sew flower to lapel. Sew on bow tie. With black, embroider hair on each head. Cut padding to fit each pot holder; tack to back pot holder pieces. With wrong sides together, with D, crochet woman's pot holder together with sc, working 3 sc in each corner. With c, crochet man's pot holder together. Sew a ring to top corner of each pot holder.

HOT MITTS

MATERIALS: Rayon and cotton rug yarn, 2 70-yard skeins of white, yellow, or cerise, main color (MC), 1 skein cerise, contrasting color (CC) for white and yellow mitts, 1 skein each of yellow and white for cerise mitt. Aluminum afghan hook size 9. Rug needle.

GAUGE: 7 sts = 2″; 3 rows = 1″.

MITT: First Half: With MC, ch 20. Work in afghan st as follows:

Row 1: Sk first ch (lp on hook is first st), pull up a lp in each ch across, keeping all lps on hook.

To Work Lps Off: Yo hook, pull through first lp, * yo hook, pull through next 2 lps, repeat from * across until 1 lp remains. Lp that remains on hook always counts as first st of next row.

Row 2: Sk first vertical bar, pull up a lp under next vertical bar and under each vertical bar across, keeping all lps on hook. Work lps off as before. Repeat row 2 for afghan st.

Rows 3–5: Work even—20 sts.

Row 6: Insert hook under 2nd and 3rd vertical bars, pull up a lp (1 st dec), work to 3rd st from end, insert hook under 3rd and 2nd vertical bars from end, pull up a lp (1 st dec), pull up a lp in last vertical bar. Work lps off—18 sts.

Rows 7 and 8: Work even.

Row 9: Work across to last st, insert hook under top strand of horizontal bar between last 2 sts, pull up a lp (1 st inc), work last st—19 sts. Work lps off.

Row 10: Work even.

Rows 11–16: Repeat rows 9 and 10.

Row 17: Repeat row 9—23 sts.

Divide for Thumb: Row 18: Work across 16 sts. Working on these sts only, work even until there are 25 rows from start. Dec 1 st each side every other row 3 times—10 sts. Sl st in each st across. End off.

Thumb: Row 1: Join yarn in 17th st of last long row, work across—7 sts. Work lps off.

Row 2: Dec 1 st at beg of row, inc 1 st at end of row.

Row 3: Work even.

Row 4: Repeat row 2.

Row 5: Dec 1 st at beg of row, work across—6 sts. Sl st in each st across. End off.

Second Half: Work as for first half through row 8.

Row 9: Inc 1 st at beg of row—19 sts.

Row 10: Work even.

Rows 11–16: Repeat rows 9 and 10.

Row 17: Repeat row 9.

Divide for Thumb: Row 1: Work first 7 sts.

Row 2: Inc 1 st at beg of row, dec 1 st at end of row.

Row 3: Work even.

Row 4: Repeat row 2.

Row 5: Dec 1 st at end of row—6 sts. Sl st in each st across. End off.

Join yarn in next free st of row 17, work as for first half from row 18.

EMBROIDERY: White Mitt: Thread strand of CC in rug needle. Beg in row 1 on back of mitt, following chart, embroider cross-stitch design, working 1 cross-stitch over each afghan st except first and last sts of row.

Yellow Mitt: First Row: Thread strand of CC in rug needle; make knot in end. Bring needle up from wrong side through back of mitt between first and 2nd sts, between rows 2 and 3. Weave under 3rd st of row 1, 5th st of row 3, 7th st of row 1, 9th st of row 3, 11th st of row 1, 13th st of row 3, 15th st of row 1, 17th st of row 3, 19th st of row 1. Bring needle down to wrong side before last st in sp between rows 2 and 3.

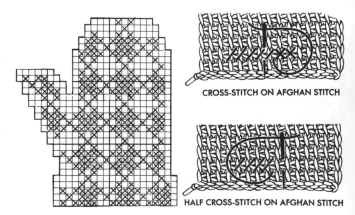

CROSS-STITCH ON AFGHAN STITCH

HALF CROSS-STITCH ON AFGHAN STITCH

2nd Row: Bring needle up between rows 4 and 5, between 20th and 19th sts. Weave under 17th st of row 3, 15th st of row 5, 13th st of row 3, etc., end in same sp with knot. Continue in this manner, always weaving through last row woven through and 2 rows above.

Cerise Mitt: Working half cross-stitch over each afghan st except first and last sts of each row, embroider first 2 sts at right edge in white for 4 rows, * next 4 sts in yellow for 4 rows, next 4 sts in white for 4 rows, repeat from * once. On next 4 rows above, reverse colors for checkerboard design and continue reversing colors every 4 rows.

EDGING: With CC, make lp on hook. From right side, beg at outer edge of mitt, sc pieces tog along sides and top, working 2 sc at each top corner of palm and thumb, and 1 sl st at inner corner of thumb. When bottom of mitt is reached, sc around bottom edge. End off.

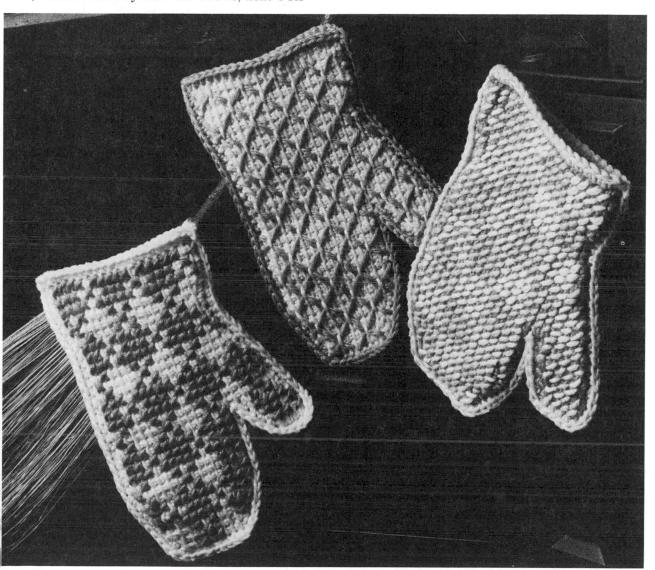

Three chunky hot mitts are all crocheted the same in afghan stitch, but backs are embroidered in three different ways. White mitt at left has a cross-stitch "gingham" design. Yellow mitt, center, is woven to resemble smocking. Cerise mitt at right has a yellow and white checkerboard pattern.

SHAMROCK DOILY
Shown on page 170

SIZE: 16″ diameter.

MATERIALS: Mercerized crochet cotton size 10, 2 200-yard balls. Steel crochet hook No. 8.

DOILY: Ch 10. Sl st in first ch to form ring.

Rnd 1: Ch 1, 24 sc in ring. Sl st in first sc.

Rnd 2: Ch 3, dc in next sc, (ch 3, dc in each of next 2 sc) 11 times, ch 3, sl st in top of ch 3.

Rnd 3: Sl st in first dc and in ch-3 sp, ch 1, sc in sp, (ch 4, sc in next sp) 11 times, ch 4, sl st in first sc.

Rnd 4: Sl st in first sp, ch 4; holding back on hook last lp of each tr, work 4 tr in sp, yo and through 5 lps on hook (cluster made), (ch 5, 5-tr cluster in same sp) twice, * sk next sp, (5-tr cluster, ch 5, 5-tr cluster, ch 5, 5-tr cluster) in next sp, repeat from * around, sl st in top of first cluster.

Rnd 5: Sl st in first sp, ch 1, (sc, ch 5, sc) in first sp, * ch 5, (sc, ch 5, sc) in next sp, repeat from * around, end ch 5, sl st in first sc—24 sps.

Rnds 6–9: Sl st to center of first sp, ch 1, sc in sp, (ch 5, sc in next sp) 23 times, ch 5, sl st in first sc.

Rnd 10: Sl st in next sp, ch 4, 3-tr cluster in same sp, * ch 3, sc in same sp, ch 3, 3-tr cluster in same sp, ch 3, sc in same sp, ch 3, 4-tr cluster in same sp, sk next sp, 4-tr cluster in next sp, repeat from * around, end 4-tr cluster, sl st in top of first cluster.

Rnd 11: Ch 10, * sc in next (center) cluster, ch 6, tr in sp between groups of clusters, ch 6, repeat from * around, end sc in center cluster, ch 6, sl st in 4th ch of ch 10.

Rnd 12: Sl st in first sp, ch 3, 6 dc in sp, * 7 dc in next sp, repeat from * around, sl st in top of ch 3.

Rnd 13: Ch 5, * sk 1 dc, dc in next dc, ch 2, repeat from * around, end ch 2, sl st in 3rd ch of ch 5—84 sps.

Rnd 14: Sl st in next sp, ch 5, dc in same sp, * ch 1, sk next sp, (dc, ch 2, dc) in next sp, repeat from * around, end ch 1, sk last sp, sl st in 3rd ch of ch 5.

Rnd 15: Sl st in next ch-2 sp, ch 3, dc in same sp, ch 2, 2 dc in same sp, * ch 3, sk ch-1 sp, sc in next ch-2 sp, ch 3, sk next ch-1 sp, (2 dc, ch 2, 2 dc) in next ch-2 sp, repeat from * around, end sl st in top of ch-3—21 pats.

Rnd 16: Sl st in next dc and in ch-2 sp, ch 3, dc, ch 2, 2 dc in same sp, * ch 4, sc in next sc, ch 4, 2 dc, ch 2, 2 dc in next ch-2 sp, repeat from * around; end ch 4, sl st in top of ch 3.

Rnd 17: Sl st in next dc and in ch-2 sp, ch 3, 2 dc, ch 3, 3 dc in same sp, * ch 3, 3 dc, ch 3, 3 dc in next ch-2 sp, repeat from * around, end ch 3, sl st in top of ch 3 at beg of rnd.

Rnd 18: Sl st in each of next 2 dc, sl st in ch-3 sp, ch 7, sc in 3rd ch from hook for picot, tr in same sp, (ch 3, sc in 3rd ch from hook for picot, tr is same sp) 5 times, * ch 3, sc in next sp, ch 3, tr in next sp, (picot, tr) 6 times in same sp, repeat from * around, end ch 3, sl st in ch below first picot. End off.

RICE STITCH DOILY
Shown on page 171

SIZE: 7″ in diameter.

MATERIALS: Tatting cotton, 1 ball white. Steel crochet hook No. 13. (For larger doily, use heavier cotton and larger hook.)

GENERAL DIRECTIONS: This doily is worked from a chart of stitch symbols rather than from row by row directions. The symbols are given with the chart. The doily has six equal sections or repeats; the chart gives one complete section.

At right of chart are numbers marking begin-ning of each rnd. Start at number for each rnd, work sts for that rnd to the left-hand edge of chart and repeat sts 5 times. This completes one rnd. Rnd 1 is shown in its entirety on chart.

Ch 4 at beg of each rnd to count as 1 tr. Join all rnds with sl st in top of ch 4.

DOILY: Ch 8, join with sl st to form ring.

Rnd 1: Ch 4 (counts as 1 tr), 3 tr in ring leaving last lp of each tr on hook, thread over and through all lps on hook, * ch 4, 4 tr cluster in ring, repeat from * 4 times, ch 4, join. Complete doily from chart.

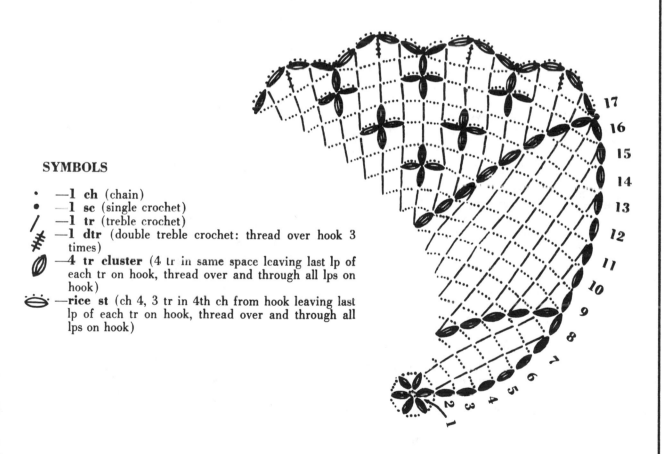

SYMBOLS

- **·** —**1 ch** (chain)
- **●** —**1 sc** (single crochet)
- **/** —**1 tr** (treble crochet)
- **‡** —**1 dtr** (double treble crochet: thread over hook 3 times)
- **⌀** —**4 tr cluster** (4 tr in same space leaving last lp of each tr on hook, thread over and through all lps on hook)
- **⊝** —**rice st** (ch 4, 3 tr in 4th ch from hook leaving last lp of each tr on hook, thread over and through all lps on hook)

FLOWER FILET MAT
Shown on page 172

SIZE: 20″ × 18″.

MATERIALS: Mercerized knitting and crochet cotton, 4 175-yd balls. Steel crochet hook No. 7.

GAUGE: 7 sps or bls = 2″.

MAT: Ch 176.

Row 1: Dc in 8th ch from hook, * ch 2, sk 2 ch, dc in next ch, repeat from * across—57 sps. Ch 5, turn each row.

Row 2: Dc in next dc, (ch 2, dc in next dc) 6 times, * dc in each of next 2 ch, dc in next dc (1 bl), (ch 2, dc in next dc) 13 times, repeat from * twice, dc in each of next 2 ch, dc in next dc, (ch 2, dc in next dc) 6 times, ch 2, sk 2 ch of turning ch, dc in next ch.

Row 3: Dc in next dc, (ch 2, dc in next dc) twice, * (dc in each of next 2 ch, dc in next dc) twice, (ch 2, dc in next dc) twice, dc in each of next 3 dc (bl over bl), (ch 2, dc in next dc) twice, (dc in each of next 2 ch, dc in next dc) twice, (ch 2, dc in next dc) 5 times, repeat from * across, end (ch 2, dc in next dc) twice, ch 2, sk 2 ch of turning ch, dc in next ch.

Working from chart, beg with row 4, follow chart from right edge to center, then work back to right edge for each row, working center sp or bl only once. Each empty square on chart is 1 sp, each x square is 1 bl. Work to top of chart. At end of last row, ch 3, do not turn.

Border: Rnd 1: Working down side of mat, * 2 dc in sp, dc in end of row, repeat from * to lower corner; in corner sp work 2 dc, (dc, ch 1, dc) in corner st, 2 dc; working across lower edge, dc in each ch in which dc or row 1 was worked, 2 dc in each sp, work corner as for first corner; working up side of mat, work as for first side, work corner as for first corner; working across top, dc in each dc, 2 dc in each sp across, 2 dc in corner sp, dc in same st with ch 3, ch 1, sl st in top of dc 3.

Rnd 2: Ch 5, sk 2 sts, dc in next st, * ch 2, sk 2 sts, dc in next st, repeat from * to corner, ch 2, dc, ch 2, dc, ch 2 in ch-1 sp, dc in next dc; work in same way around all 4 sides, end ch 2, dc, ch 2, dc, ch 2 in last corner sp, sl st in 3rd ch of ch 5.

Rnd 3: Ch 3, 2 dc in next sp, dc in next dc, * ch 2, dc in next dc, 2 dc in next sp, dc in next dc, repeat from * around, working 3 dc, ch 1, 3 dc in each corner sp. At last corner, work 3 dc, ch 1, 3 dc in corner sp, dc in last dc, ch 2, sl st in top of ch 3.

Rnd 4: Ch 3; holding back on hook the last lp of each dc, dc in each of next 3 dc, yo and through all 4 lps on hook (cluster), * ch 3, sl st in top of cluster for picot, ch 2; holding back on hook the last lp of each dc, dc in each of next 4 dc, yo and through all 5 lps on hook (cluster), repeat from * around, working ch 3, cluster, picot, ch 3, in each corner sp. At end of rnd, after last cluster and picot, ch 2, sl st in top of ch 3 at beg of rnd, end off.

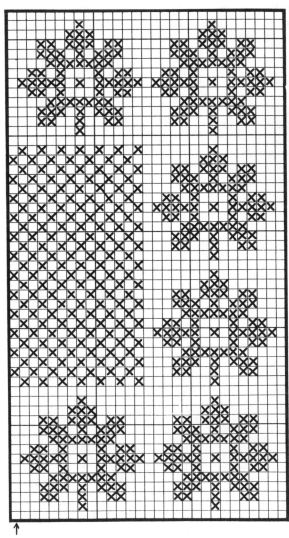

↑
CENTER

EMBOSSED DAISY MAT
Shown on page 183

SIZE: 20" x 15½".
MATERIALS: Mercerized Crochet Cotton, size 30. Steel crochet hook No. 13. Piece of linen, 13" x 8½".
GAUGE: 6 sps = 1"; 6 rows = 1".
Note: Daisies are made separately.
LACE EDGING: Rnd 1: Beg at inner edge, * (ch 8, tr in 8th ch from hook) 19 times across one end, ch 4, tr in 4th ch from hook (corner), (ch 8, tr in 8th ch from hook) 35 times, ch 4, tr in 4th ch from hook (corner), repeat from * once, join with sl st (with work untwisted) in base of first tr at A on chart. Keep lps on inner edge. Turn.

Rnd 2 (right side): Ch 3, 2 dc over tr-bar of last corner, * 7 dc through 2 threads in center of same bar, 2 dc over balance of same bar, dc between bars, make (5 dc over next tr-bar, dc between bars) across to next corner, 2 dc over bar of corner, repeat from * 3 times, end 5 dc over last tr-bar, join in top of ch 3. Sl st in next 6 dc (corner). Turn.

Rnd 3: Ch 6, sk next 2 dc, sc in next dc, ch 3, sk 2 dc, dc in next dc (lacet st), * make (ch 3, sk 2 dc, sc in next dc, ch 3, sk 2 dc, dc in dc between bars) across to center dc at corner (21 lacet sts), ch 5, dc in same corner dc, make 37 lacet sts to next corner *, ch 5, dc in same corner dc, repeat from first * to 2nd * once, ch 2, join with dc in 3rd ch of ch 6, ending at exact corner. Turn.

Rnd 4: Ch 9, sk first sp, dc in next dc, * (ch 5, dc in next dc) across to first dc at corner, ch 5, dc in corner sp, ch 5, dc in next dc, repeat from * around, end ch 5, sl st in 4th ch of ch 9. Turn.

Rnd 5: Ch 5, dc in center of first sp, ch 2, dc in next dc, * (ch 2, dc in next sp, ch 2, dc in next dc) 8 times, (ch 3, sc in next sp, ch 3, dc in next dc for lacet st) 5 times, (ch 2, dc in next sp, ch 2, dc in next dc) 9 times to corner dc, ch 5, dc in same dc, following chart across wide end, make 32 sps, 7 lacet sts, 32 sps to next corner dc *, ch 5, dc in same dc, ch 2, dc in center of next sp, ch 2, dc in next dc, repeat from first * to 2nd * once, end ch 2, dc in 3rd ch of ch 5 (exact corner). Turn.

Rnd 6: Ch 5, sk first sp, dc in next dc, * following chart from C to B, make 15 ch-2 sps, (2 dc in next sp, dc in next dc for 1 bl) 5 times, make 12 sps, 7 ch-5 sps, 12 sps, 5 bls, 16 ch-2 sps to corner sp, ch 5, 3 dc in balance of corner sp, dc in next dc, 4 bls, 14 ch-2 sps, 5 ch-5 sps, 14 ch-2 sps, 5 bls *, ch 5, dc in corner sp, ch 2, dc in next dc, repeat from first * to 2nd once, end ch 2, dc in 3rd ch of ch 5 (corner). Turn.

Rnd 7: Ch 4, 3 dc in top of corner dc (½ corner shell), * following chart from B across narrow end, 2 dc in corner sp, dc in next dc, 4 sps, continue across, make 2 dc in next corner sp, 7 dc in 3rd ch of same sp, 4 sps, continue across wide end

*, make 6 more dc in same corner ch, repeat from first * to 2nd * once, end ch 2, 3 dc in same st with first half shell, join with sl st in top of ch 4. Turn.

Rnds 8 and 9: Ch 4, 3 dc in corner dc, * following chart from C to B, work across wide end to next corner, make 6 more dc in corner dc (7 in all), continue across narrow end *, make 6 more dc in corner dc (7 in all), repeat from first * to 2nd * once, end ch 2, 3 dc in same st with first half shell, join top of ch 4. Turn.

Rnd 9 (wrong side): Following chart from B to C, begin work corners, and end as for rnd 8. Turn.

Rnd 11: Ch 3, dc in each of next 3 dc (1 bl), * following chart from B to C, work across narrow end to next corner (ending 2 sps), dc in each of next 3 corner dc, ch 5, dc in dc last worked in, dc in each of next 3 corner dc (1 bl), continue across wide end (ending 3 sps) *, work corner as before, repeat from first * to 2nd * once, end 1 bl, ch 2, join with dc in top of ch 3 (exact corner). Turn.

Rnd 12: Ch 5, sk first sp, dc in next dc, * following chart from C to B, work across wide end to 3rd ch of corner sp, ch 5, dc in same ch, continue across narrow end to 3rd ch of next corner sp *, ch 5, dc in same ch, repeat from first * to 2nd * once, end ch 2, join with dc in 3rd ch of ch 5 (exact corner). Turn.

Rnd 13 (wrong side): Following chart from B to C, begin, work corners, and end as for rnd 12. Turn.

Rnds 14-23: Repeat rnds 12 and 13 alternately.

Rnd 24: Ch 6, sk first sp, sc in next dc, ch 3, dc in next dc, * continue in lacet st to center ch of next corner sp, ch 3, dc in same ch, repeat from * around, end ch 3, join with sl st in 3rd ch of ch 6. Do not turn.

Rnd 25: * Ch 7, sc in next dc, repeat from * around, end ch 7, sl st in first lp. Do not turn.

Rnd 26: In each lp around, make (4 sc, ch 4, sl st in last sc for p, 4 sc); join end of rnd and end off.

DAISY (make 8): * Ch 20, sk 2 ch, sc in next 2 ch, hdc in next ch, dc in next 2 ch, (tr in next 2 ch; holding back last lp of each of the following tr, make tr in next 2 ch, yo and through 3 lps on hook) twice, dc in next 3 ch, hdc in next ch, sl st in end ch, repeat from * 5 times more–6 petals. Ch 1, make sc in base of each of 6 petals. Ch 5, turn. Holding back last lp of each tr, make tr in each of 5 sc, 2 tr in last sc, yo and through 8 lps on hook. End off.

FINISHING: Turn daisies right side up, sew in place on edging as shown on chart. Stretch and pin edging, right side down, in true shape, pinning out each lp on inner and outer edges. Steam and press dry through a damp cloth.

Place edging, right side up, over linen. Baste inner edge of edging to linen. Hem down inner edge of rnd 2 (dc row) and lps of rnd 1. Cut linen ¼" outside stitching, turn under edge next to edging and hem.

Actual-size detail

CHART FOR EMBOSSED DAISY MAT

⊙	**BL**	☐	**CH-2 SP**
⋈	**LACET ST**	▭	**CH-5 SP**

Leaf-and-scroll design of filet crochet borders a linen place mat. Flowers are worked separately and sewn to the background for a three-dimensional effect. Lacet stitch, a variation of filet crochet, adds interest to the border 4″ deep; mat measures 20″ by 15½″. Chart and directions for Embossed Daisy Mat are on pages 181–182.

WHITE ROSE CENTERPIECE

SIZE: 40″ × 52″.

MATERIALS: Pearl cotton, size 5, 73 50-yd. balls white, 3 balls yellow. Steel crochet hook No. 6.

GAUGE: Motif = 4″.

ROUND MOTIF: ROSE: With yellow, ch 8. Sl st in first ch to form ring. **Rnd 1:** Ch 1, 16 sc in ring. Cut yellow. Insert hook in first sc, draw white through st and lp on hook.

Rnd 2: Ch 1, (sc, hdc, dc) in first st, * (dc, hdc, sc) in next st, (sc, hdc, dc) in next st, repeat from * around, end (dc, hdc, sc) in last st—8 petals. Sl st in first sc.

Rnd 3: * Ch 3; working behind petals, sc between next 2 petals, repeat from * around.

Rnd 4: Sc, hdc, 3 dc, hdc, sc in each lp around. Sl st in first sc.

Rnd 5: Repeat rnd 3. End off.

LEAF (make 8): With white, ch 10.

Row 1: Sc in 2nd ch from hook and in each of next 7 ch, 3 sc in last ch. Working on opposite side of starting ch, sc in each of next 7 ch. Ch 1, turn each row.

Row 2: Sk first sc, sc in each of next 7 sc, 3 sc in next sc, sc in each of next 7 sc.

Rows 3 and 4: Repeat row 2.

Row 5: Sc in first sc, (ch 3, sk 1 sc, sc in next sc) 3 times, sc in each of next 4 sc, (ch 3, sk 1 sc, sc in next sc), ch 3, sc in last st of preceding row, (ch 3, sc in tip of leaf) twice, ch 3, sc in first st of preceding row. Sl st in first st of row 5. End off.

Sew the rounded end of a leaf to each of the 8 ch-3 lps of rnd 5 of a rose to make the round motif.

CENTERPIECE: Make 104 round motifs. Arrange in 13 rows of 8 motifs each, join them by the tips of the leaves, as pictured. Fill in spaces between 4 motifs with Fill-In Motif.

Fill-In Motif: Make a rose as for round motif through rnd 4.

Rnd 5: * Ch 3, join with sc to next leaf, ch 3, sc between next 2 petals, repeat from * around.

Three-dimensional roses imbedded in leaves are sewn together for a charming centerpiece. More little yellow-centered roses fill in the spaces between the larger leaf-ringed motifs. Made of pearl cotton, centerpiece has a rich and glossy appearance. Directions for White Rose Centerpiece, above.

WHEAT PATTERN RUNNER

SIZE: 18″ × 32″.

MATERIALS: Mercerized crochet cotton, size 30, 3 400-yard balls. Steel crochet hook No. 10.

GAUGE: Each Motif = 4½″ square.

FIRST MOTIF: Beg at center, ch 8. Sl st in first ch to form ring.

Rnd 1: Ch 3, 23 dc in ring. Sl st in top of ch 3.

Rnd 2: Ch 7, tr in same place as sl st, * ch 3, sk 2 sts, tr in next st, ch 3, sk 2 sts, (tr, ch 3, tr) in next st (corner), repeat from * twice, ch 3, sk 2 sts, tr in next st, ch 3, sl st in 4th ch of ch 7.

Rnd 3: Sl st in next sp, ch 4, 4 tr, ch 3, 5 tr in same sp, * ch 2, sk 1 sp, (tr, ch 3, tr) in next tr, ch 2, sk 1 sp, (5 tr, ch 3, 5 tr) in corner sp, repeat from * twice, ch 2, sk 1 sp, (tr, ch 3, tr) in next tr, ch 2, sl st in top of ch 4.

Rnd 4: Ch 4; holding back on hook last lp of each tr, tr in each of next 4 tr, yo and through all 5 lps on hook (cluster made), * ch 3, (5 tr, ch 3, 5 tr) in corner ch-3 sp, ch 3, 5-tr cluster over next 5 tr, ch 3, (tr, ch 3, tr) in next ch-3 sp, ch 3, 5-tr cluster over next 5 tr, repeat from * around, end ch 3, sl st in top of first cluster.

Rnd 5: Sl st across next 3 ch, sl st in next tr, 5-tr cluster over 5 tr (ch 4 for first tr), * ch 3, (5 tr, ch 3, 5 tr) in corner sp, ch 3, 5-tr cluster over next 5 tr, ch 3, sk next 2 sps, (tr, ch 3) 4 times in next (center) sp, sk 2 sps, 5-tr cluster over next 5 tr, repeat from * around, end (tr, ch 3) 4 times in last center sp, sl st in top of cluster.

Rnd 6: Sl st across next 3 ch, sl st in next tr, * 5-tr cluster over 5 tr, (ch 4 for first tr), ch 3, (5 tr, ch 3, 5 tr) in corner sp, ch 3, 5-tr cluster over next 5 tr, ch 3, sk 2 sps, (tr, ch 3, tr, ch 3 in next sp) 3 times, sk 2 sps, repeat from * around, sl st in top of cluster.

Rnd 7: Sl st across next 3 ch, sl st in next tr, * 5-tr cluster over 5 tr, ch 5, 5 tr in corner sp, ch 5, 5-tr cluster over next 5 tr, ch 5, sc in top of next cluster, ch 5, sk next sp, (tr, ch 3, tr, ch 3 in next sp) 4 times, tr, ch 3, tr in next sp, ch 5, sc in top of next cluster, ch 5, repeat from * around, sc in top of first cluster of rnd.

Rnd 8: * Ch 11, 5 tr cluster over next 5 tr, ch 7, sc in top of cluster, ch 11, sc in top of next cluster, ch 9, sk 2 sps, sc in next sp, (ch 5, sc in next sp) 8 times, ch 9, sc in top of next cluster, repeat from * around, end ch 9, sl st in sc. End off.

SECOND MOTIF: Work as for first motif until 7 rnds have been completed.

Rnd 8: * Ch 11, 5-tr cluster over next 5 tr, ch 3, sl st in corner lp of first motif, ch 3, sc in same cluster on second motif, ch 6, sl st in ch-11 lp of first motif, ch 5, sc in top of next cluster, ch 5, sl st in ch-9 lp of first motif, ch 4, sk 2 sps of second motif, sc in next sp, (ch 2, sl st in next ch-5 lp of first motif, ch 2, sc in next sp of second motif) 8 times, ch 4, sl st in ch-9 lp of first motif, ch 5, sc in top of next cluster, ch 5, sl st in ch-11 lp of first motif, ch 6, 5-tr cluster over next 5 tr of second motif, ch 3, sl st in corner lp of first motif, ch 3, sc in same cluster on second motif. Complete motif as for first motif.

Make 4 × 7 motifs, joining as second motif was joined to first motif. Where 4 corners meet, join 3rd and 4th corners to joining of previous 2 corners.

Versatile wheat pattern motif, 4½" square in size 30 cotton, is adaptable to place mats, tablecloths, and runners. In heavier cotton, this attractive motif can be used for bedspreads, too. The squares are joined in the crochet. Outer edges of squares, left free, form decorative scallops. Directions opposite.

Rich and beautiful design for a tablecloth of heirloom quality has flower-like patterns formed by cluster stitches on a tracery of lace. Smaller square motifs fill in spaces between the main motifs and help to highlight them. Trianon Tablecloth, below.

TRIANON TABLECLOTH

SIZE: 62″ × 86″.

MATERIALS: D.M.C. Cordonnet Special Six-Cord Crochet Cotton, Art. 151, Size 20, 57 174-yard balls. Steel crochet hook No. 7. Or size 10, 84 124-yard balls. Steel crochet hook No. 9.

GAUGE: Round Motif = 4¾″ in diameter; Square Motif = 2¼″ across center from picot to picot.

ROUND MOTIF: Ch 8; sl st in first ch to form ring.

Rnd 1: Ch 1, (sc in ring, ch 4) 8 times, sl st in first sc—8 lps.

Rnd 2: Sl st in first lp, ch 4, 4-tr cluster in lp (to make 4-tr cluster, holding back last lp of each tr on hook, work 4 tr in lp, yo and through 5 lps on hook), ch 7, * 5-tr cluster in next lp (to make 5-tr cluster, holding back last lp of each tr on hook, work 5 tr in lp, yo and through 6 lps on hook), ch 7, repeat from * around, end sl st in top of first cluster.

Rnd 3: Sl st in each of next 4 ch (center ch of ch 7), ch 4, 3 tr in same center ch, ch 7, (4 tr in center ch of next lp, ch 7) 7 times, sl st in top of ch 4.

Rnd 4: Ch 4, 2 tr in each of next 2 tr, tr in next tr, ch 4, sc in center ch of next lp, ch 4, * tr in next tr, 2 tr in each of next 2 tr, tr in next tr, ch 4, sc in center ch of next lp, ch 4, repeat from * around, end sl st in top of ch 4.

Rnd 5: Ch 1, sc in same ch as sl st, * ch 5, 4-tr cluster over next 4 tr, ch 5, sc in next tr, ch 7, sk next 2 lps, sc in next tr, repeat from * around, end ch 7, sl st in first sc.

Rnd 6: Sl st in each of next 3 ch of ch 5, ch 7, * (tr, ch 3, tr, ch 3, tr) in top of next cluster, ch 3, tr in center ch of next ch 5, ch 2, tr in next sc, sk ch 7, tr in next sc, ch 2, tr in center ch of next ch 5, ch 3, repeat from * around, end ch 2, sl st in 4th ch of ch 7.

Rnd 7: Ch 3, * (3 dc in next sp, dc in next tr) 4 times, (2 dc in next sp) twice, dc in next tr, repeat from * around, end 2 dc in each of last 2 sps, sl st in top of ch 3.

Rnd 8: Ch 1, sc in same ch with sl st, * (ch 8, sc in 4th ch from hook for picot, ch 4, sk next 7 dc, sc in next dc) twice, ch 6, sc in 4th ch from hook, ch 2, sk next 4 dc, sc in next dc, repeat from * around, sl st in first sc. End off.

TABLECLOTH: Make 234 round motifs arranging them as shown in diagram, 18 × 13 motifs. Motifs may be tacked tog or joined tog in the crochet through the picots.

To Crochet Motifs Together: Work motif through rnd 7.

Rnd 8: Ch 1, sc in same ch with sl st, ch 8, sc in 4th ch from hook for picot, ch 4, sk next 7 dc, sc in next dc, ch 6, drop lp from hook, insert hook in corresponding picot of previous motif, draw lp through, ch 2, sc in 4th ch from hook for picot, ch 4, sk next 7 dc, sc in next dc, ch 4, drop lp from hook, join as before to next picot of previous motif, ch 2, sc in 4th ch from hook for picot, ch 2, sk next 4 dc, sc in next dc, ch 6, drop lp from hook, join as before to next picot of previous motif, ch 2, sc in 4th ch from hook for picot, ch 4, sk next 7 dc, sc in next dc, finish motif as for previous motif.

SQUARE MOTIF: Ch 8, sl st in first ch to form ring.

Rnd 1: Ch 4; in ring work tr, (5 dc, 3 tr) 3 times, 5 dc and tr; sl st in top of ch 4.

Rnd 2: Ch 3, 2 dc in same ch with sl st, dc in each of next 7 sts, (5 dc in next tr, dc in each of next 7 sts) 3 times, 2 more dc in st with 2 dc at beg of rnd, sl st in top of ch 3.

Rnd 3: Ch 7, tr in same ch with sl st, * (ch 2, sk 2 sts, tr in next st) 3 times, ch 2, (tr, ch 3, tr, ch 3, tr) in center dc of 5-dc group, repeat from * around, end 1 more tr in same ch with first tr, ch 3, sl st in 4th ch of ch 7.

Rnd 4: Ch 3, 3 tr and 1 dc in same ch with sl st, ** 3 dc in next sp, dc in next tr, ch 3, sl st in 3rd ch from hook for a picot, * (2 dc in next sp, dc in next tr) twice, ch-3 picot, repeat from * once, 3 dc in next sp, (dc, 3 tr, dc) in center tr at corner, repeat from ** around, sl st in top of ch 3. End off.

Make 204 square motifs, placing them in spaces between 4 round motifs and joining them through the picots as shown in diagram.

⧫ **TACKED PICOTS**

SUNBURST TABLECLOTH
Shown opposite

SIZE: 55″ × 70″.

MATERIALS: Mercerized crochet cotton, size 20, 26 300-yard balls. Steel crochet hook No. 11.

GAUGE: Motif measures about 5″ in diameter.

LARGE MOTIF: Ch 7, sl st in first ch to form ring.

Rnd 1: Ch 1, 11 sc in ring. Join in ch 1.

Rnd 2: Ch 5, dc in first sc, * ch 2, dc in next sc, repeat from * 9 times, ch 2, join in 3rd ch of ch 5—12 sps.

Rnd 3: Sl st in next sp, ch 3, 2 dc in same sp, 3 dc in each sp around. Join each rnd.

Rnd 4: * Ch 5, long sc in next dc of rnd 2 (between dc groups of rnd 3), repeat from * around—12 ch-5 lps.

Rnd 5: Sl st to center of first lp, ch 11, tr in next lp, * ch 7, tr in next lp, repeat from * around, end ch 7, join in 4th ch of ch 11.

Rnd 6: Ch 3, 2 dc in same ch as joining, * ch 4, sl st in center ch of next lp, ch 4, 3 dc in next tr, repeat from * around, end ch 4, join in top of ch 3.

Rnd 7: Ch 3, dc in same st as sl st, dc in next dc, 2 dc in next dc, * ch 7, 2 dc in first dc of next group, dc in next dc, 2 dc in next dc, repeat from * around, end ch 7, join in top of ch 3.

Rnd 8: Ch 3, dc in each of next 4 dc, * ch 4, sl st in center ch of lp, ch 4, sl st in same st, ch 4, dc in each of next 5 dc, repeat from * around, end ch 4, sl st in top of ch 3.

Rnd 9: Ch 3, dc in same ch as sl st, dc in each of next 3 dc, 2 dc in last dc, * ch 7, 2 dc in first dc of next group, dc in each of next 3 dc, 2 dc in last dc, repeat from * around, end ch 7, sl st in top of ch 3.

Rnd 10: Sl st in next dc, ch 3, dc in each of next 4 dc, * ch 5, sl st in center ch of next loop, ch 4, sl st in same ch, ch 5, sk first dc of next group, dc in each of next 5 dc, repeat from * around, end ch 5, sl st in top of ch 3.

Rnd 11: Sl st in next dc, ch 3, dc in each of next 2 dc, * ch 15, sk first dc of next group, dc in each of next 3 dc, repeat from * around, end ch 15, sl st in top of ch 3.

Rnd 12: Sl st in center dc, ch 11, sl st in center ch of ch 15, ch 4, sl st in same ch, ch 8, * dc in center dc of next group, ch 8, sl st in center ch of next ch, ch 4, sl st in same ch, ch 8, repeat from * around, end ch 8, sl st in 3rd ch of ch 11.

Rnd 13: Ch 12, * dc in next picot, ch 9, dc in next dc, ch 9, repeat from * around, end ch 9, sl st in 3rd ch of ch 12.

Rnd 14: Ch 3, yo hook, insert hook in same ch as sl st, pull up a lp, yo and through 2 lps on hook, yo hook, insert hook in same ch, pull up a lp, (yo and through 2 lps) 3 times (cluster st), ch 4, sl st in top of cluster st for picot (p), ch 3, yo hook, insert hook in same ch as first cluster st, pull up a lp, yo hook and through 2 lps, yo hook, insert hook in same st, pull up a lp, (yo and through 2 lps) twice, yo hook, insert hook in same st, pull up a lp, (yo and through 2 lps) 3 times (cluster st), ch 4, sl st in top of cluster st for p, * ch 4, sl st in center ch of next ch 9, ch 4, sl st in same ch for p, ch 4; in next dc make cluster st, p, ch 3, cluster st, p, repeat from * around, end ch 4, join in top of ch 3. End off.

Join motifs in rnd 14 as follows: * Cluster st, ch 2, sl st in corresponding p of first motif, ch 2, sl st in top of cluster st just made on 2nd motif, ch 3, cluster st in same place, ch 2, sl st in corresponding p of first motif, ch 2, complete p of 2nd motif, ch 4, sl st in center ch of next ch 9, ch-4 p, ch 4, repeat from * twice, finish motif same as first motif.

Join 3rd motif to 2nd motif in same way, leaving 3 groups of cluster sts free between joinings. Join 4th motif to first and 3rd motifs. Make tablecloth 11 motifs wide by 14 motifs long, or desired size.

SMALL MOTIF: Work as for large motif through rnd 5.

Rnd 6: * Cluster st in tr, ch 2, join in free p of first motif, ch 2, sl st in top of cluster st just made, ch 3, cluster st in same tr, ch 2, sl st in next p of first motif, ch 2, complete p of small motif, ch 4, sl st in center ch of next ch 7, ch-4 p, ch 4, repeat from * twice, join in same way to 2nd, 3rd and 4th motifs.

Sunbursts, crocheted in circular fashion, make lavish lace for your table. The smaller motifs of the fill-in lace are square but have the same centers as the larger design. Use this lovely pattern for curtains or other household laces. Directions for Sunburst Tablecloth are above.

CLUNY LACE TABLECLOTH
Shown opposite

SIZE: 72″ × 90″.

MATERIALS: D.M.C. Cordonnet Special Six-Cord Crochet Cotton, Art. 151, size 30, 76 balls. Steel crochet hook No. 11. (See chart for making tablecloth in other sizes of cotton.)

GAUGE: Round motif = 4½″.

D.M.C	Hook Size	Motif Size	No. of Balls
Size 50	13	3½″	80
Size 40	12	4″	74
Size 20	10	4¾″	94
Size 10	9	5½″	118

ROUND MOTIF: Ch 7, sl st in first ch to form ring.

Rnd 1: Ch 1, 12 sc in ring, sl st in first sc.

Rnd 2: Ch 1, sc in same sc as sl st, * 2 sc in next st, sc in next st, repeat from * around, end 2 sc in last st—18 sc. Sl st in first sc.

Rnd 3: Ch 1, sc in each sc around. Sl st in first sc.

Rnd 4: Repeat rnd 2—27 sc.

Rnd 5: Repeat rnd 3.

Rnd 6: Repeat rnd 2, end 1 sc in last st—40 sc.

Rnd 7: Ch 1, sc in same sc as sl st, sc in each of next 2 sts, * ch 18, sc in 10th ch from hook, sc in each of next 8 ch (stem), sc in each of next 5 sc, repeat from * around, end sc in each of last 2 sc of rnd. Sl st in first sc.

Rnd 8: Ch 6, * sk first 5 sts on foundation ch of stem, sc in next st, ch 3, 17 dc in lp at end of stem, ch 3, sk 3 sts on other side of stem, sc in next st, ch 3, dc in center sc of 5-sc group between stems, ch 3, repeat from * around, end ch 3, sl st in 3rd ch of ch 6 at beg of rnd.

Rnd 9: Sl st in each of next 8 sts (3 ch, 1 sc, 3 ch, 1 dc); ch 4, dc in next dc, (ch 1, dc in next dc) 5 times, * ch 1, tr in next dc, ch 1, (tr, ch 1, tr) in next dc, ch 1, tr in next dc, (ch 1, dc in next dc) 7 times, sk next 4 sps, dc in next dc, (ch 1, dc in next dc) 6 times, repeat from * around, end sk 4 sps, sl st in 3rd ch of ch 4 at beg of rnd.

Rnd 10: Sl st in each of next 6 sts, * sc in next sp, ch 2, dc in next sp, (ch 1, dc in next sp) 3 times, ch 1, (dc, ch 1, dc) in next sp, (ch 1, dc in next sp) 4 times, ch 2, sc in next sp, ch 2, sk next 7 sps, repeat from * around, sl st in first sc.

Rnd 11: Ch 1, sc in same sc with sl st, * ch 3, sk 1 sp, sc in next sp, (ch 5, sl st in 4th ch from hook for picot, ch 1, sc in next sp) 3 times, ch 3, sc in next sp, ch 8, drop lp from hook, draw dropped lp through ch-3 sp just made, 13 sc in ch-8 lp just made, ch 1, sc in next sp, (ch 5, sl st in 4th ch from hook for picot, ch 1, sc in next sp) 3 times, ch 3, sk next sp, sc in next sp (between scallops), repeat from * around, end ch 3, sc in last sp, sl st in first sc. End off.

SQUARE MOTIF: Ch 7, sl st in first ch to form ring.

Rnd 1: Ch 1, 16 sc in ring, sl st in first sc.

Rnd 2: Ch 1, 2 sc in joined st, * sc in each of next 3 sc, 3 sc in next sc (corner), repeat from * twice, sc in each of next 3 sc, 1 more sc in joined st to complete 4th corner. Sl st in first sc of rnd.

Rnd 3: Ch 1, 2 sc in joined st, sc in each of next 5 sc, * 3 sc in center sc of 3-sc group at corner, sc in each of next 5 sc, repeat from * around, 1 more sc in joined st. Sl st in first sc of rnd.

Rnds 4 and 5: Ch 1, 2 sc in joined st, sc in each st to next corner, * 3 sc in corner st, sc in each st to next corner, repeat from * around, 1 more sc in joined st. Sl st in first sc of rnd.

Rnd 6: Ch 4, sk joined st and next st, (dc in next st, ch 1, sk 1 st) 5 times, * (dc, ch 3, dc) in corner st, (ch 1, sk 1 st, dc in next st) 5 times, ch 1, repeat from * twice, end ch 1, dc in joined st, ch 1, dc in 3rd ch of ch 4 to form last corner sp.

Rnd 7: Ch 1, 3 sc in corner sp, sc in joining st, * sc in each sp and each dc to next corner sp, 5 in corner sp, repeat from * around, end 2 sc in last corner sp, sl st in first sc.

Rnd 8: Ch 4, sk joined st and next st, (dc in next st, ch 1, sk 1 st) 8 times, * (dc, ch 3, dc) in corner st, (ch 1, sk 1 st, dc in next st) 8 times, ch 1, repeat from * twice, end ch 1, dc in joined st, ch 1, dc in 3rd ch of ch 4.

Rnd 9: Repeat rnd 7.

Rnd 10: Ch 1, 2 sc in joined st, * sc in each of next 23 sts, 3 sc in next st, repeat from * around, end with 1 more sc in joined st, sl st in first sc.

Rnd 11: Sl st in next sc, ch 1, sc in same st as sl st, * (ch 5, sl st in 4th ch from hook for picot, ch 1, sk 2 sts, sc in next st) 8 times, ch 5, picot, ch 1, sk 1 st, sc in next st, repeat from * around working all corners alike, end with picot, sl st in first sc. End off.

(Continued on page 195)

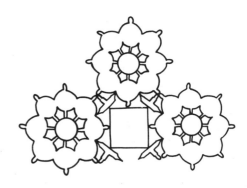

This opulent tablecloth, crocheted to resemble Cluny lace, is comprised of three motifs: a large round motif with scalloped edges, a square set diamond-style between circular motifs, and a filigree of picots connecting the other motifs.

Small squares with cobwebby centers are joined in the crochet to make this pretty tablecloth, called Shadow Squares. Little lacy centers are worked in a spiderweb pattern, then edged with chain loops and cluster stitches. Work goes quickly, with cotton heavier than usual for tablecloths. Directions, opposite.

Continued from page 192

PICOT MOTIF: * (Ch 5, sl st in 4th ch from hook for picot) 3 times, ch 6, sl st in 2nd ch from hook, sl st in each of next 4 ch, ch-4 picot, sl st in free st between 3rd and 2nd picots, ch-4 picot, sl st in free st between 2nd and first picots, ch-4 picot, sl st in first st of ch, (ch 5, sl st in 4th ch from hook for picot) twice, ch 9, drop lp from hook, draw dropped lp through 8th ch from hook, 13 sc in lp just formed, sl st in free ch st, ch-4 picot, sl st in free st between picots, ch-4 picot, sl st in next free st between picots, repeat from first * to 2nd * once, end with sl st in first st of motif. End off.

TABLECLOTH: For tablecloth in size 30 cotton, make 320 round motifs. Arrange them 16 motifs wide by 20 motifs long. Fill in spaces between round motifs with square and picot motifs as shown in diagram. Tack motifs firmly together with matching cotton.

For tablecloth in size 50 cotton, make 546 round motifs.

Arrange them 21 motifs wide by 26 motifs long.

For tablecloth in size 40 cotton, make 414 round motifs.

Arrange them 18 motifs wide by 23 motifs long.

For tablecloth in size 20 cotton, make 285 round motifs.

Arrange them 15 motifs wide by 19 motifs long.

For tablecloth in size 10 cotton, make 221 round motifs.

Arrange them 13 motifs wide by 17 motifs long.

SHADOW SQUARES
Shown Opposite

SIZES: Small cloth, 65" square. Large cloth, 65" × 84".

MATERIALS: J. & P. Coats Knit-Cro-Sheen, 18 250-yard balls of white or ecru for small cloth, 24 balls for large cloth; 26 175-yard balls of cream or other colors for small cloth; 35 balls for large cloth. Steel crochet hook No. 7.

GAUGE: Each motif = 2¾" square.

FIRST MOTIF: Beg at corner, ch 5.

Row 1: In 5th ch from hook make tr, ch 7 and 2 tr. Ch 3, turn.

Row 2: Sk first tr, dc in next tr, ch 5, sc in next lp, ch 5, dc in next tr, dc in top of starting ch. Ch 3, turn.

Row 3: Sk first dc, dc in next dc, ch 5, sc in next lp, sc in next sc, sc in next lp, ch 5, dc in next dc, dc in top of turning ch. Ch 4, turn.

Row 4: Sk first dc, tr in next dc, ch 5, sc in next lp, sc in next 3 sc, sc in next lp, ch 5, tr in next dc, tr in top of turning ch. Ch 4, turn.

Row 5: Sk first tr, tr in next tr, ch 4, sc in next 5 sc, ch 4, tr in next tr, tr in top of turning ch. Ch 3, turn.

Row 6: Sk first tr, dc in next tr, ch 4, sk next sc, sc in next 3 sc, ch 4, dc in next tr, dc in top of turning ch. Ch 3, turn.

Row 7: Sk first dc, dc in next dc, ch 3, sk next sc, sc in next sc, ch 3, dc in next dc, dc in top of turning ch. Ch 4, turn.

Row 8: Sk first dc; holding back on hook the last lp of each tr, tr in next dc, sk next 2 lps, tr in next dc, tr in top of turning ch, yo hook and through all lps on hook—joint tr made. Ch 3; do not turn.

Work in rnds as follows:

Rnd 1: Holding back on hook the last lp of each dc, make 2 dc in tip of first joint tr, yo hook and through all lps on hook—2-dc cluster made; ch 3, 3-dc cluster in same place; working along the 4 sides of motif, ch 4, sc in top of turning ch made at end of row 6, ch 5, sc in top of last dc of row 6, ch 5, sc in top of turning ch made at end of row 4, ch 4, 3-dc cluster in top of last tr of row 4, ch 3, 3-dc cluster in same tr; ch 4, sc in top of turning ch made at end of row 2, ch 5, sc in top of last dc of row 2, ch 5, sc in top of starting ch, ch 4, 3-dc cluster in first ch of starting ch, ch 3, 3-dc cluster in same ch; ch 4, sc in top of last tr of row 1, ch 5, sc in top of turning ch made at end of row 1, ch 5, sc in top of last dc of row 3, ch 4, 3-dc cluster in top of turning ch made at end of row 3, ch 3, 3-dc cluster in same ch; ch 4, sc in top of last tr of row 5, ch 5, sc in top of turning ch made at end of row 5, ch 5, sc in top of last dc of row 7, ch 1, dc in tip of first cluster to form last lp.

Continued on page 209

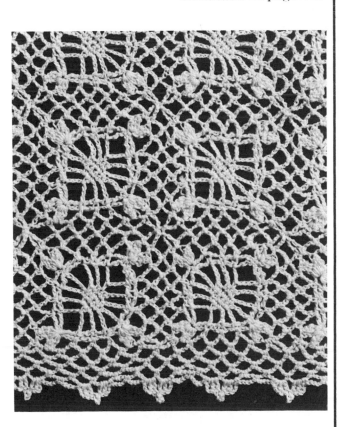

ROSETTE BEDSPREAD

SIZE: 56″ × 77″, excluding fringe.

MATERIALS: J. & P. Coats Knit-Cro-Sheen, 26 250-yard balls of white or ecru for motifs, 12 balls for edging and fringe. Or 37 175-yard balls of color for motifs, 17 balls for edging and fringe. Steel crochet hook No. 7.

GAUGE: Motif = 7″ square.

FIRST MOTIF: Ch 12; sl st in first ch to form ring.

Rnd 1: 24 sc in ring; sl st in first sc.

Rnd 2: Ch 11, * tr in next sc, sk 1 sc, tr in next sc, ch 7, repeat from * around, end ch 7, tr in next sc, sl st in 4th ch of ch 11.

Rnd 3: Sl st in first lp, ch 3, 8 dc in same lp, * 7 dc over upright bar of next tr, sk next sc on rnd 1, 7 dc over upright bar of next tr, 9 dc in next lp, repeat from * around, end 7 dc over ch 4, sl st in top of ch 3—8 petals.

Rnd 4: Sc in same ch as sl st, sc in each dc around, sl st in first sc. End off.

Rnd 5: Join thread in sp between 2 petals (sp formed by 2 tr of rnd 2); working in back of petals, sc in same sp, * ch 7, sc in next sp, repeat from * 6 times, ch 2, dtr in first sc for last lp—8 lps.

Rnd 6: 3 sc in lp just made, * ch 7, 3 sc in next lp, repeat from * 6 times, ch 3, tr in first sc.

Rnd 7: Ch 4, 2 tr and 3 dc in lp just made, * sk 1 sc, sc in next sc, 3 dc, 5 tr and 3 dc in next lp, repeat from * 6 times, sk 1 sc, sc in next sc, 3 dc, 2 tr in first lp, sl st in top of ch 4.

Rnd 8: Ch 4, 2 tr in same place as sl st, * dc in each of next 3 sts; leaving the last lp of each dc on hook, work dc in next st, sk 3 sts, dc in next st, yo hook and through all lps on hook, dc in each of next 3 sts, 5 tr in next st, repeat from * around, end 2 tr in same place as first tr, sl st in top of ch 4.

Rnd 9: Sc in same place as sl st, * ch 12, sk 11 sts, sc in next st (center tr of 5 tr), ch 19, sc in same st, ch 12, sk 11 sts, sc in next st, ch 8, sc in same st, repeat from * around, end ch 12, sc in same place as first sc, ch 4, tr in first sc.

Rnd 10: Ch 3, 6 dc in lp just made, * 9 sc in next sp, 29 dc in next lp, 9 sc in next sp, 13 dc in next lp, repeat from * around, end 6 dc in first lp, sl st in top of ch 3.

Rnd 11: Ch 6, dc in same place as sl st, * ch 9, sk 9 dc on next lp, tr in next dc, ch 5, tr in same dc, sk 4 dc, tr in next dc, ch 7, tr in same dc, sk 4 tr, tr in next dc, ch 5, tr in same dc, ch 9, sk 6 dc on next lp, dc in next dc, ch 3, dc in same dc, repeat from * around, end ch 9, sl st in 3rd ch of ch 6.

Rnd 12: Sl st in next lp, 2 sc in same lp, ch 3, sl st in last sc (picot made), sc in same lp, * ch 7, (2 sc in next lp, ch-3 picot), sc in same lp, ch 7) twice, tr in center ch of next lp, ch 7, tr in same ch, (ch 7, 2 sc in next lp, ch-3 picot, sc in same lp) 3 times, repeat from * around, end ch 2 instead of ch 7, dtr in first sc.

Rnd 13: 2 sc, picot and sc in lp just made, * (ch 7, 2 sc, picot and sc in next lp) 3 times, ch 7, tr, ch 7, tr in center ch of next lp, (ch 7, 2 sc, picot and sc in next lp) 3 times, repeat from * around, end ch 7, sl st in first sc. End off.

SECOND MOTIF: Work as for first motif until first tr has been completed at corner on row 13, ch 3, sl st in corner lp on first motif, ch 3, tr in same ch as last tr on second motif, (ch 3, sl st in next lp on first motif, ch 3—joining lp made—2 sc, picot and sc in next lp on second motif) 6 times, a joining lp, tr in center ch of next lp on second motif, a joining lp, tr in same ch, complete as for first motif.

Make 8 rows of 11 motifs, joining each to previous one as second motif was joined to first. Where 4 corners meet join 3rd and 4th corners to joining of previous motifs.

EDGING: With wrong side facing, join thread in first corner lp on either long side of bedspread, 2 sc in corner lp, * (ch 39, sk next picot, 3 sc in next picot) 3 times **, ch 39, sk joining between motifs, 3 sc in next picot, (ch 39, sk next picot, 3 sc in next picot) twice, ch 39, 3 sc in next joining between motifs, repeat from * along side ending last repeat at **, ch 39, sk next corner lp, 3 sc in next picot, continue in this manner along next 2 sides, end 2 sc in last corner lp on second long side. Ch 1, turn.

Rnd 2: Sc in first sc, * dc in each of 19 ch, dc, ch 9 and dc in next ch, dc in each of next 19 ch, sk 1 sc, sc in next sc, repeat from * to end. End off.

Row 3: With wrong side facing, working in front of previous row, join thread in first free picot skipped on row 1, 2 sc in same picot, ch 39; working in back of previous row, make 3 sc in next free picot, ch 39; working in front of previous row, make 3 sc in next free picot, ch 39; working in back of previous row, make 3 sc in next joining between motifs; continue in this manner along 3 sides, working in corner lps to correspond and ending with 2 sc in last free picot. Ch 1, turn.

Row 4: Repeat row 2.

FRINGE: Wind thread 20 times around a 9″ cardboard. Remove from cardboard, knot loops through ch-9 lp on edging. Cut ends and trim. Repeat fringe in each ch-9 lp.

Elegant Rosette Bedspread is equally beautiful in white or any pastel color, shown over contrasting fabric. Square motifs, joined in the making, have raised flower centers on round medallion patterns and picot-loop outlines to form the squares. A criss-cross edging and fringe add an unusual border. Directions are on opposite page.

TRELLIS BEDSPREAD

SIZE: 96″ × 120″, plus fringe.

MATERIALS: Mercerized crochet cotton, size 30, 80 400-yard balls. Steel crochet hook No. 11.

GAUGE: Motif = 6″ square.

BEDSPREAD: MOTIF (make 320): **First Leaf:** Ch 22.

Row 1: Sc in 2nd ch from hook and in each of next 19 ch, 3 sc in last ch; working on opposite side of starting ch, sc in each of 20 ch. Ch 5, turn.

Row 2 (wrong side): Sc in back lp of each of 21 sc, 3 sc in back lp of next sc, (center sc of 3 sc at point), sc in back lp of each of next 18 sc. Ch 5, turn.

Row 3: Sc in back lp of each sc to point, 3 sc in back lp of center sc at point, sc in back lp of each sc to 3 sc from end. Ch 5, turn.

Rows 4–12: Repeat row 3. At end of row 12, do not ch 5. End off.

2nd Leaf: Work as for first leaf through first half of row 12. At point, work 1 sc in back lp of center sc, drop lp off hook; insert hook in center st at point of first leaf, pick up dropped lp and pull it through st of first leaf. Finish row as for first leaf.

Make 2 more leaves in same way, joining to other leaves at point.

Flower (make 4): Ch 9; sl st in first ch to form ring.

Rnd 1: (2 sc in ring, ch 3) 8 times, sl st in first sc.

Rnd 2: Sl st in next sc, sl st in ch-3 sp, ch 1, sc in sp, (ch 5, sc in next sp) 7 times, ch 5, sl st in first sc.

Rnd 3: * Ch 2, hdc in next lp, (ch 5, sl st in hdc) 3 times, ch 2, sl st in next sc, repeat from * around, end ch 2, sl st in first ch at beg of rnd—8 petals. End off.

Join Flowers to Leaves: From right side, join thread in last ch-5 lp made on a leaf, sc in this ch-5 lp, ch 4, sl st in 3rd ch from hook for picot, ch 1, sc in next ch-5 lp, ch 3, drop lp off hook; insert hook in center picot of a flower petal, * pull dropped lp through; ch 1, sl st in 3rd ch from hook for picot, ch 1, (sc in next lp on leaf, ch 4, sl st in 3rd ch from hook, ch 1) twice, sc in next lp on leaf, ch 3 picot, ch 2, sc in next lp on leaf; ch 5, sc in first sc of row 1 at top of leaf, ch 5, sl st in 3rd ch from hook, ch 2 (sc in next lp on leaf, ch 4, sl st in 3rd ch from hook, ch 1) twice, sc in next lp, ch 3, drop lp off hook; insert hook in center picot of another flower, pull dropped lp through; ch 1, sl st in 3rd ch from hook to complete picot, ch 1, sc in next lp on leaf, ch 4, sl st in 3rd ch from hook, ch 1, sc in next lp on leaf, ch 3, drop lp off hook; insert hook in center picot of next petal of same flower, pull dropped lp through; ch 1, sl st in 3rd ch from hook, ch 1, sc in last ch-5 lp on next leaf, ch 4, sl st in 3rd ch from hook, ch 1, sc in next ch-5 lp, ch 3, drop lp off hook; insert hook in next center picot of same flower; repeat from * around, working last repeat in first flower; sl st in first sc. End off.

Frame: Rnd 1: Sc in center picot of 3rd free petal of a flower (corner); * ch 7, sc in center picot of next petal, ch 6, sc in center picot of next petal, ch 9, sc in picot near top of leaf, ch 5, sc in ch-5 sp at tip of leaf, ch 5, sc in next picot, ch 9, sc in center picot of first free petal of next flower, ch 6, sc in next center picot, ch 7, sc in next center picot, ch 2, sc in same picot (corner), repeat from * around, end sc in same picot with first sc of rnd, ch 2, sl st in first sc.

Rnd 2: Ch 1, sc in first sc, sc in each ch and sc around, working 3 sc in each corner sp. Sl st in first sc.

Rnd 3: Ch 1, sc in each sc, 3 sc in each corner st around. Sl st in first sc. End off.

FINISHING: Sew motifs tog, 16 × 20. Work 3 rows of sc around outer edge. On 2 long and 1 short edge, work as follows: dc in each of 12 sc, * ch 2, sk 2 sc, dc in each of next 12 sc, repeat from * around.

Fringe: Wind thread around cardboard 5″ wide. Cut strands along one edge into 10″ lengths. Using 20 strands tog for each fringe, knot a fringe through each ch-2 sp along sides and bottom. * Knot 20 strands of 1 fringe to 20 strands of adjacent fringe ¾″ below first row of knots. Repeat from * twice. Trim fringe.

This luxurious Trellis Bedspread, at home in any decor, is not a luxury when you make it yourself. Four ribbed leaves form center of each square motif; a filigree of flower buds fills the corners. Motifs are sewn together along their border frames. Knotted fringe on three sides is a rich finishing edge. Directions are on opposite page.

JIFFY BEDSPREAD

SIZE: 100″ × 110″.

MATERIALS: Knitting worsted weight yarns, 40 4-oz. skeins natural. Crochet hook size K.

GAUGE: Each motif = 9″ square (double strand of yarn).

BEDSPREAD: FIRST MOTIF: With double strand, ch 13.

Row 1: Dc in 5th ch from hook, (ch 1, sk 1 ch, dc in next ch) 4 times. Ch 4, turn.

Row 2: Sk first dc, dc in next dc, (ch 1, dc in next dc) 3 times, ch 1, sk 1 ch, dc in next ch. Ch 4, turn.

Rows 3–5: Repeat row 2. At end of row 5, do not ch 4 or turn.

Row 6: Working around square, ch 1, 3 sc in side of top sp just worked, * 2 sc in next sp, sc, ch 4, sc in center sp, 2 sc in next sp, 5 sc in corner sp, repeat from * around, end 2 sc in first sp, sl st in first sc. Ch 1, turn.

Row 7: * Sc in each sc to next ch-4 lp, sc in lp, (ch 3, sc in same lp) 5 times, repeat from * around, sl st in first sc. Ch 1, turn.

Row 8: Sc in first (corner) sc, * ch 6, sc in 2nd ch-3 lp of next scallop, ch 6, sc in 4th ch-3 lp of same scallop, ch 6, sc in next corner sc, repeat from * around, end ch 6, sl st in first sc. Do not turn.

Row 9: In each ch-6 lp around, work 2 sc, ch 3, 2 sc, ch 3, 2 sc. Sl st in first sc. End off.

SECOND MOTIF: Work as for first motif through row 8.

Row 9: 2 sc, ch 3, 2 sc, ch 3, 2 sc in first ch-6 lp, 2 sc, ch 3, 2 sc in corner lp, ch 1; drop lp from hook; insert hook through corresponding ch-3 lp on first motif, pull lp through, ch 1, 2 sc in corner lp of second motif; 2 sc, ch 1 in next ch-6 lp, drop lp from hook; insert hook in next ch-3 lp on first motif, pull through lp, ch 1, 2 sc in same ch-6 lp on second motif; continue to join second motif to first motif through all 6 ch-3 lps on side; finish second motif as for first motif.

Join 110 motifs in 10 rows of 11 motifs.

BORDER: Row 1: From right side, join double strand of yarn in first ch-3 lp on long side of bedspread; sc in lp, * (ch 3, sc in next lp) 5 times, ch 5, sc in next lp, repeat from * around sides and bottom edges of bedspread, working ch-5 lp at corners. Ch 4, turn.

Row 2: Sk 1 ch, dc in next ch, (ch 1, sk 1 ch, dc in sc, ch 1, sk 1 ch, dc in next ch) 5 times, ch 1, sk 1 ch, dc in next ch, ch 1, dc in next sc, * (ch 1, sk 1 ch, dc in next ch, ch 1, sk 1 ch, dc in next sc) 5 times, (ch 1, sk 1 ch, dc in next ch) twice, ch 1, sk 1 ch, dc in next sc, repeat from * around, end dc in last sc. Ch 4, turn.

Row 3: Sk first dc, dc in next dc, * ch 1, dc in next dc, repeat from * around, end ch 1, sk 1 ch of ch 4, dc in next ch. Ch 4, turn.

Row 4: Repeat row 3.

Row 5: * Work 5 mesh sps as on last row, ch 3, dc in next dc; turn; 5 dc in ch-3 lp; turn; ch 3, sc in first dc, (ch 3, sc in next dc) 3 times, sc in dc of row 4 after the ch-3 lp, repeat from * around. End off.

For border across top, from wrong side, work 1 row as for row 1 of Border. Ch 1, turn.

Row 2: Sc in each sc, 3 sc in each ch-3 lp, 5 sc in each ch 5 lp across. Do not turn.

Row 3: Working from left to right, sc in each sc across.

*Quick-to-crochet coverlet uses worsted-weight yarn for
a favorite motif of filet crochet and picots. Opposite.*

IRISH ROSE BEDSPREAD

MATERIALS: J. & P. Coats Knit-Cro-Sheen, 45 balls of white or ecru, or 54 balls of any color for single size spread; 57 balls of white or ecru, or 68 balls of any color for double size spread. Steel crochet hook No. 5 or 6.

GAUGE: Each block measures 6¼" square. For a single size spread, about 72" × 108", make 11 × 17 blocks. For a double size spread, about 92" × 108", make 14 × 17 blocks.

BLOCK: Ch 8, join with a sl st.

Rnd 1: Ch 6, * dc in ring, ch 3. Repeat from * 4 more times. Join to 3rd st of ch-6—6 sps.

Rnd 2: In each sp make sc, hdc, 2 dc, hdc and sc—6 petals.

Rnd 3: * Ch 4, sc in dc of first rnd (between petals). Repeat from * around. Ch 4, join.

Rnd 4: In each loop make sc, hdc, 3 dc, hdc and sc.

Rnd 5: * Ch 5, sc in back loop of sc of 3rd rnd. Repeat from * around.

Rnd 6: Same as rnd 4, making 4 dc instead of 3 dc.

Rnd 7: Same as rnd 5, making ch-6 loops.

Rnd 8: Same as rnd 4, making 6 dc instead of 3 dc.

Rnd 9: * Ch 3, sc between 3rd and 4th dc at back of next petal, ch 3, sc in back loop of next sc. Repeat from * around. Sl st in first ch-3 loop.

Rnd 10: Ch 3, 3 dc in same place as sl st, * ch 2, 4 dc in next sp. Repeat from * around; join.

Rnd 11: Sl st in next 3 dc, sl st in sp, ch 3, dc in same sp; * (ch 5, sc in 4th ch from hook, making a p) 3 times; sc in ch between first 2 p's, p, ch 1, sc in ch between first p and last dc, 2 dc in same sp as last dc, ch 3, 2 dc in next ch-2 sp. Repeat from * around, ending with 2 dc in same place as last dc, ch 3, sl st in 3rd st of ch-3 first made. Fasten off.

Rnd 12: Attach thread between 2nd and 3rd p's of first p-loop, * ch 11, sc between 2nd and 3rd p's of next p-loop. Repeat from * around.

Rnd 13: Sc in each ch and in each sc around. Ch 1, turn. Work is now done in rows instead of rnds, picking up only the back loop of each sc.

Row 1: Sl st in first sc, sc in next 35 sc. Ch 2, turn.

Row 2: Sk 2 sc, sc in next 15 sc, pc (popcorn) st in next sc—to make a pc st, ch 1, make 5 dc in st, remove hook, insert hook back in ch 1 and draw dropped loop through, ch 1 to fasten. Sc in next 15 sc. Ch 2, turn.

Row 3: Sk 2 sc, sc in each st across. Ch 2, turn.

Row 4: Sk 2 sc, sc in next 11 sc, pc st in next sc, sc in next 3 sc, pc st in next sc, sc in next 11 sc. Ch 2, turn.

Row 5: Same as row 3.

Row 6: Sk 3 sc, sc in next 6 sc, pc st in next sc; (sc in next 3 sc, pc st in next sc) twice; sc in next 7 sc. Ch 2, turn.

Row 7: Same as 3rd row, but sk 3 sc (instead of 2 sc).

Row 8: Sk 3 sc, sc in next 5 sc, pc st in next st, sc in next 3 sc, pc st in next sc, sc in next 6 sc. Ch 2, turn.

Row 9: Same as row 7.

Row 10: Sk 3 sc, sc in next 4 sc, pc st in next sc, sc in next 5 sc. Ch 2, turn.

Row 11: Sk 2 sc, sc in next 6 sc. Ch 5, turn.

Row 12: Sk 5 sc, sc in next sc. Fasten off. With wrong side of work toward you, sk sc at tip of p-loop, attach thread and work over next 35 sc. Turn and work as for first corner. Continue in this manner until 4 corners are made. Fasten off. Now work in rnds as follows:

Rnd 1: Attach thread in corner loop, ch 5, dc in same loop, ch 2, dc in same loop. * (Ch 3, dc in next turning ch) 4 times; ch 3, tr in next turning ch, ch 3, dtr in sc directly above p-loop, ch 3, tr in next turning ch; (ch 3, dc in next turning ch) 4 times; ch 3, in corner ch-5 loop, make dc, ch 2, dc, ch 2 and dc. Repeat from * around. Join last ch-2 to 3rd st of ch-5 first made.

Rnd 2: Ch 3, dc in next 2 ch, 3 dc in next dc, dc in each st around, making 3 dc in center dc at corners. Fasten off. Make necessary number of blocks and sew tog on wrong side with neat overhand stitches.

MOTIF FOR BEDSPREAD OR TABLECLOTH

MATERIALS: Bucilla Wondersheen (400-yd. skeins). Bedspread 86″ × 103″, 57 skeins; tablecloth 36″ × 36″, 11 skeins; tablecloth 54″ × 54″, 21 skeins; banquet cloth 54″ × 72″, 28 skeins. Steel crochet hook, size 10. Each motif should measure 4½″ square.

MOTIF: Ch 5, join with a sl st to form a ring. Ch 8, * 1 long tr (3 times over hook) in ring, ch 2; repeat from * 10 times, join with a sl st in 6th st of ch 8.

Rnd 2: Ch 1, 3 sc in ch-2 space, 1 sc in long tr, * 2 sc, ch 5, sl st in last sc (picot), 1 sc, all in next space; 1 sc in next tr, 2 sc in next space, ch 10, drop loop from hook, insert hook in 4th st before picot, draw dropped loop through, ch 3, work 9 dc, picot, 4 dc, all over ch 10; ch 12, drop loop from hook, insert hook in 4th st before last picot and draw dropped loop through, ch 14, sl st in top of last dc made in ch-10 space, work 5 dc in same ch-10 space, ch 3, sl st in last sc, 1 sc in same ch-2 space as last sc worked, 1 sc in next tr, 3 sc in next space, 1 sc in next tr; repeat from * 3 times, end last repeat 1 sc in same ch-2 space as last sc worked. Do not join.

Rnd 3: Sl st to base of double ch loop, ch 3, * 10 dc, picot, 5 dc over double ch space, ch 15, drop loop, draw dropped loop through 5th dc before picot, ch 17, sl st in top of last dc made, work 5 more dc in same double ch space, 1 dc in dc at base of loop, ch 7, sl st in 5th st from hook (picot), ch 1, long tr in 2nd sc between scallops, ch 6, picot, ch 3, 1 dc in base of next double ch loop; repeat from * 3 times, end last repeat ch 6, picot, ch 3, join with a sl st in first st of ch 3 at beginning of first scallop. Sl st to base of double ch loop.

Rnd 4: Ch 3, 12 dc, picot + 12 dc over double ch loop, 1 dc at base of loop, ch 6, picot, ch 1, long tr in 2nd st of ch before picot in row below, ch 6, picot, ch 1, long tr in long tr in row below between picots, ch 6, picot, ch 6, picot, ch 1, long tr in same place as last long tr, ch 6, picot, ch 1, long tr in center st of ch after next picot in row below, ch 6, picot, ch 1, ** 1 dc at base of next double ch loop, 6 dc over loop, *** ch 3, turn, 1 long tr in long tr between last 2 picots made, ch 3, long tr in next long tr, ch 3, long tr in ch between next 2 picots, ch 6, long tr in same place as last long tr, ch 3, long tr in next long tr between picots, ch 3, long tr in next long tr between picots, ch 3, sl st in 6th dc of next scallop, ch 1, turn, * 3 sc, picot, 3 sc in ch-3 space *; repeat between *'s twice, 1 sc, 2 dc, picot, 2 tr (twice over hook), picot, 2 tr, picot, 2 dc, 1 sc all in next space (corner); repeat between *'s 3 times ***, 6 dc over double loop, picot; repeat from † twice, then repeat from † to **, sl st over top of ch 3 and 6 dc of next scallop, repeat between ***'s, join with a sl st in 6th dc of next scallop. Fasten off.

For 36″ Square: Make 64 motifs. Join at picots using 8 motifs in a row for 8 rows.

For 54″ Square: Make 144 motifs. Join at picots using 12 squares in a row for 12 rows.

For Cloth 54″ × 72″: Make 192 motifs. Join at picots using 12 motifs in a row for 16 rows.

For Bedspread 86″ × 104″: Make 437 motifs. Join at picots using 19 motifs in a row for 23 rows.

Fringe: Wind Wondersheen around a 5″ cardboard, cut at one end, tie a fringe of 8 strands in each picot and at each joining on 3 sides of bedspread (sides and foot). Trim even to 4″ length.

This beautiful and versatile design is equally adaptable to bedspreads and tablecloths of all sizes. For a bedspread, add fringe to sides and bottom. Directions are on opposite page.

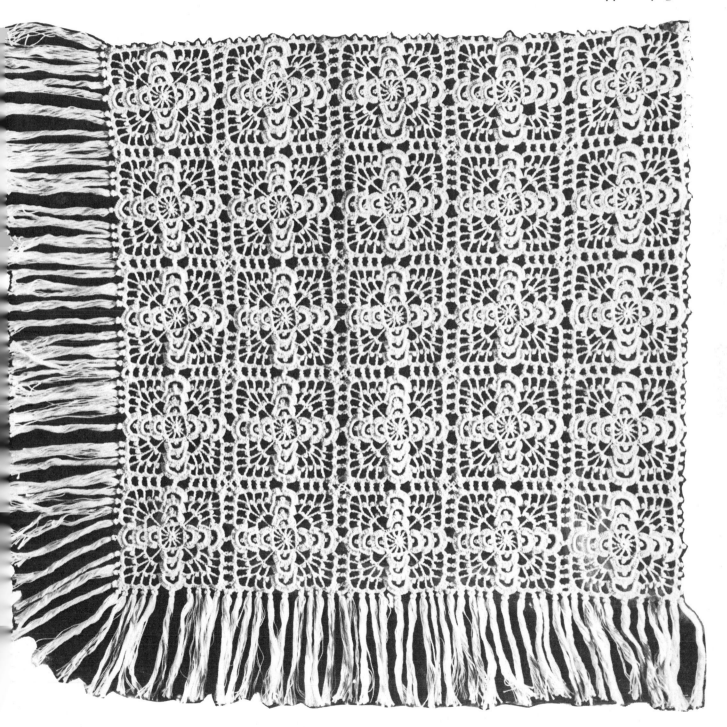

The hobnail look of popcorns has always been popular for crocheted bedspreads. In this pattern, raised diamonds are formed by the popcorns, openwork diamonds by filet mesh. When the 5″ squares are sewn together, open geometric patterns appear.

POPCORN BEDSPREAD

MATERIALS: Single Size Spread: J. & P. Coats Knit-Cro-Sheen, 58 balls of White or Ecru or 70 balls of any color. Double Size Spread: J. & P. Coats Knit-Cro-Sheen, 70 balls of White or Ecru, or 84 balls of any color. Steel crochet hook No. 7.

GAUGE: Each block measures 5″ square. For a single size spread, about 72″ x 108″ including fringe, make 13 x 20 blocks. For a double size spread, about 92″ x 108″ including fringe, make 16 x 20 blocks.

BLOCK: Starting at center, ch 8, join with a sl st.

Rnd 1: Ch 3, 23 dc in ring. Join to 3rd st of ch-3.

Rnd 2: Sc in same place as sl st, * ch 5, skip 2 dc, sc in next dc. Repeat from * around. Join last ch-5 to first sc made.

Rnd 3: Sl st in first ch of next loop, sl st in loop, ch 3 (to count as dc), 2 dc in same loop, * ch 2, in next loop make 3 dc, ch 2 and 3 dc (corner). Ch 2, 3 dc in next loop. Repeat from * around; join.

Rnd 4: Ch 4 (to count as dc and ch-1), * 5 dc in next dc, drop loop from hook, insert hook in ch preceding 5 dc and draw dropped loop through (a pc st made). Dc in next dc, dc in next sp, ch 2, skip 1 dc, dc in next 2 dc; in corner sp make 2 dc, ch 2 and 2 dc; dc in next 2 dc, ch 2, skip next dc, dc in next sp, dc in next dc, ch 1. Repeat from * around. Join to 3rd st at ch-4.

Rnd 5: Ch 3 (to count as dc), 4 dc in same place as sl st, drop loop from hook, insert hook in top st of ch-3 and draw dropped loop through (a pc st). * Dc in tip of pc st below, ch 1, 5 dc in next dc, and complete pc st as before, inserting hook in the ch-1 preceding 5 dc. Make dc in next dc, dc in next sp, ch 2, skip 1 dc, dc in next 3 dc. In corner sp make 2 dc, ch 2 and 2 dc; dc in next 3 dc, ch 2, dc in next sp, dc in next dc, pc st in next dc. Repeat from * around; join to top of ch-3.

Rnd 6: Ch 3, * pc st in next dc, dc in next pc st, pc st in next dc, dc in next dc, dc in next sp, ch 2, skip 1 dc, dc in next 4 dc. In corner sp make 2 dc, ch 2 and 2 dc; dc in next 4 dc, ch 2, skip 1 dc, dc in next sp, dc in next dc, pc st in next dc, dc in next pc st. Repeat from * around; join.

Rnd 7: Ch 3 and complete a pc st as at beg of rnd 5, * (dc in next pc st, pc st in next dc) twice. Dc in next dc, dc in next sp, ch 2, skip 1 dc, dc in next 5 dc. In corner sp make 2 dc, ch 2 and 2 dc; dc in next 5 dc, ch 2, skip 1 dc, dc in sp, dc in next dc, pc st in next dc, dc in next pc st, pc st in next dc. Repeat from * around; join.

Rnd 8: Ch 3, * pc st in next dc, dc in next pc st, pc st in next dc, dc in next pc st and in next dc; ch 2, skip 1 dc, dc in sp, ch 2, sk 1 dc, dc in next dc, ch 2, sk 2 dc, dc in next 3 dc. In corner sp make 2 dc, ch 2 and 2 dc; dc in next 3 dc, ch 2, skip 2 dc, dc in next dc, ch 2, dc in sp, ch 2, skip 1 dc, dc in next dc, dc in pc st, pc st in next dc, dc in next pc st. Repeat from * around; join.

Rnd 9: Ch 3 and complete a pc st as at beg of rnd 5; * dc in next pc st, pc st in next dc, dc in next pc st and in next dc; ch 2, skip 1 dc, dc in sp; (ch 2, dc in next sp) twice; ch 2, skip 1 dc, dc in next 4 dc. In corner sp make 2 dc, ch 2 and 2 dc; dc in next 4 dc, ch 2, skip 1 dc, dc in next sp, (ch 2, dc in next sp) twice; ch 2, skip 1 dc, dc in next dc, dc in next pc st, pc st in next dc. Repeat from * around; join.

Rnd 10: Ch 3, * pc st in next dc, dc in next pc st and in next dc; (ch 2, dc in next sp) 4 times; ch 2, skip 1 dc, dc in next 5 dc. In corner sp make 2 dc, ch 2 and 2 dc; dc in next 5 dc; (ch 2, dc in next sp) 4 times; ch 2, skip 1 dc, dc in next dc, dc in next pc st. Repeat from * around; join.

Rnd 11: Ch 3, dc in next pc st and in next dc; * (ch 2, dc in next sp) 5 times; ch 2, sk 1 dc, dc in next 6 dc; in corner sp make 2 dc, ch 2 and 2 dc; dc in next 6 dc, (ch 2, dc in next sp) 5 times; ch 2, sk 1 dc, dc in next 3 sts. Repeat from * around. Join and fasten off. This completes one block.

Make necessary number of blocks and sew them together with neat overhand stitches on wrong side.

Fringe: * Cut 10 strands, each 8″ long. Double these strands, forming a loop. Pull loop through first sp and draw loose ends through loop. Pull tight. Skip 1 sp. Repeat from * 2 more times, skip 1 sp, make a fringe in center of a dc block, skip 1 sp, and continue to make fringe in every other sp across (7 fringes on each block). Continue all around edges. Trim evenly.

FRINGED BEDSPREAD

MATERIALS: American Thread Company "Puritan" Mercerized Crochet and Knitting Cotton, 28 400-yd. balls. Steel crochet hook No. 7.

GAUGE: Each motif measures about 5″. 294 motifs, 14 × 21, are required for bedspread measuring 75″ × 105″, (measurements do not include fringe.)

MOTIF: Ch 6, join to form a ring.

Rnd 1: Ch 4 (counts as 1 tr), tr in ring, * ch 7, 2 tr in ring, repeat from * 6 times, ch 7, join in 4th st of ch.

Rnd 2: Work 5 sc, ch 5, 5 sc over each loop, join.

Rnd 3: Sl st to ch-5 loop, ch 3 (counts as 1 dc), 3 dc in same loop, ch 5, 4 dc in same loop, * ch 3, 4 dc, ch 5, 4 dc in next ch-5 loop, repeat from * all around, ch 3, join.

Rnd 4: Sl st to loop, ch 3, 6 dc in same loop, **

ch 5, sc in next loop, ch 5, 3 cluster sts with ch 4 between each cluster st in next loop (cluster st: * thread over twice, insert in loop and work off 2 loops twice, repeat from * twice, thread over and work off all loops at one time), ch 5, sc in next loop, ch 5, 7 dc in next loop, repeat from ** twice, ch 5, sc in next loop, ch 5, 3 cluster sts with ch 4 between in next loop, ch 5, sc in next loop, ch 5, join.

Rnd 5: Ch 3, dc in same space, 1 dc in each of the next 5 dc, 2 dc in next dc, ch 4, tr in sc, ch 4, 2 cluster sts with ch 4 between in ch-4 loop, between cluster sts of previous row, ch 4, 2 cluster sts with ch 4 between in next ch-4 loop, ch 4, tr in next sc, ch 4, 2 dc in next dc, 1 dc in each of the next 5 dc, 2 dc in next dc, continue all around in same manner, join.

Rnd 6: Ch 3, dc in same space, 1 dc in each dc, increasing 1 dc in last dc, ch 5, sc in tr, ch 5, 2 cluster sts with ch 4 between in next ch-4 loop between cluster sts of previous row, ch 4, 2 cluster sts with ch 9 between in next loop, ch 4, 2 cluster sts with ch 4 between in next loop, ch 5, sc in next tr, ch 5, 1 dc in each dc of next dc group increasing 1 dc in first and last st, continue all around in same manner, join, break thread.

Work a 2nd motif, joining to first motif in last row as follows: Ch 3, dc in same space, 1 dc in each of the next 7 dc, 2 dc in next dc, ch 5, sc in next tr, ch 5, 2 cluster sts with ch 4 between in next ch-4 loop between cluster sts of previous row, ch 4, cluster st in next loop, ch 4, sl st in corresponding loop of first motif, ch 4, cluster st in same loop of 2nd motif, ch 2, sl st in corresponding loop of first motif, ch 2, cluster st in next loop of 2nd motif, ch 2, sl st in corresponding loop of first motif, ch 2, cluster st in same loop of 2nd motif, ch 2, sl st in next loop of first motif, ch 2, sc in tr of 2nd motif, ch 2, sl st in next loop of first motif, ch 2, 2 dc in next dc of 2nd motif, 1 dc in each of the next 7 dc, 2 dc in next dc, ch 2, sl st in next loop of first motif, ch 2, sc in tr of 2nd motif, ch 2, sl st in next loop of first motif, ch 2, cluster st in next ch-4 loop between cluster sts of previous row, ch 2, sl st in corresponding loop of first motif, ch 2, cluster st in same loop of 2nd motif, ch 2, sl st in next loop of first motif, ch 2, cluster st in next loop of 2nd motif, ch 5, sl st in corner loop, ch 5, cluster st in same loop, and complete motif same as first motif. Sew the solid sections together on wrong side. Join 3rd motif to 2nd motif and 4th motif to 3rd and first motifs in same manner.

Edge: Join thread in corner loop (ch 5, sc in same loop) 3 times, (ch 5, sc in next loop) 4 times, * ch 5, skip 3 dc, sc in next dc, ch 5, sk 3 dc, sc in next dc, (ch 5, sc in next loop) 10 times, repeat from * to corner (ch 5, sc in corner loop) 4 times and continue all around in same manner, join, break thread.

Fringe: Cut 10 strands 16″ long, double and pull through loop. Work a fringe in each loop on 2 sides and across lower edge of spread. * Take half of one group of fringe and half of next group of fringe and knot about ¾″ below first group of knots, repeat from * all around. Trim fringe evenly.

SHADOW SQUARES
Continued from page 195

Rnd 2: Ch 1, sc in lp just formed, * ch 5; in next ch-3 corner lp make sc, ch 7 and sc, (ch 5, sc in next lp) 4 times, repeat from * around, end (ch 5, sc in next lp) 3 times, ch 5, sl st to first sc. End off.

SECOND MOTIF: Work as for first motif until rnd 1 has been completed.

Rnd 2: Ch 1, sc in lp just formed, ch 5, sc in next ch-3 corner lp, ch 3; now join 2 motifs along one side as follows: Sl st in 4th corner lp made on first motif, ch 3, sc in same corner lp on second motif, (ch 2, sl st in next lp on first motif, ch 2, sc in next lp on second motif) 4 times, ch 2, sl st in next lp on first motif, ch 2, sc in next corner lp on second motif, ch 3, sl st in next corner lp on first motif, ch 3, sc in same corner lp on second motif; working on second motif only, (ch 5, sc in next lp) 4 times; beg at * on rnd 2 of first motif, complete second motif as for first motif.

Make 23 × 23 motifs for small cloth, or 23 × 30 motifs for large cloth, joining motifs as second motif was joined to first motif. Where 4 corners meet, join corners to previous joinings.

BORDER: Rnd 1: Join thread in last lp preceding any corner lp, sc in same lp, * ch 5; in corner lp make sc, ch 5 and sc; ** (ch 5, sc in next lp) 5 times; ch 5, sc in joining between motifs, repeat from ** to within next corner lp; repeat from * around, end ch 2, dc in first sc to form last lp.

Rnd 2: Ch 1, sc in lp just formed, ch 5, sc in next lp, * ch 5; in next corner lp make sc, ch 5 and sc; ** ch 5, sc in next lp, repeat from ** across to within next corner lp; repeat from * around, end as on rnd 1.

Rnd 3: Ch 1, sc in lp just formed, (ch 5, sc in next lp) twice; beg at * on rnd 2, complete rnd.

Rnd 4: Ch 1, sc in joining, ch 4, sc in next lp, ch 4; in next lp make sc, ch 3 and 2 dc; ch 3, sl st in last dc made; in next lp make 2 dc, ch 3 and sc; * ch 4; in next corner lp make 3 dc, ch 5 and 3 dc; ** ch 4; in next lp make sc, ch 3 and 2 dc; ch 3, sl st in last dc made; in next lp make 2 dc, ch 3 and sc; ch 4, sc in next lp, repeat from ** across to within next corner lp, end 2 dc, ch 3 and sc in last lp, repeat from * around, end 2 dc in first lp used at beg of rnd, ch 3, sl st to first sc. End off.

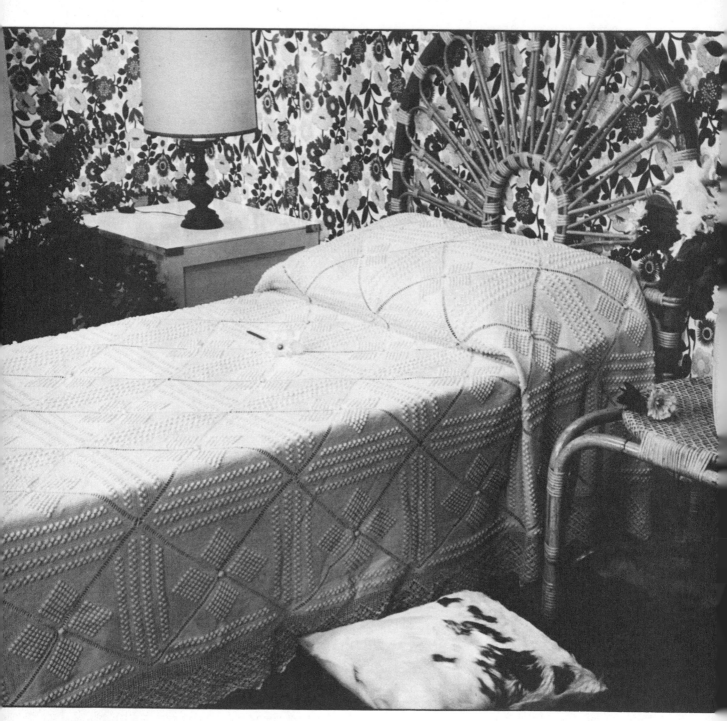

Solid-crochet coverlet is made of squares, worked from a chart for the placement of the raised popcorns, and joined together for a single or double sized bed. Directions and chart for Popcorn Squares are on page 213, followed by directions for the filet and spiderweb border.

Combining filet crochet with gossamer spiderweb patterns, this square table cover is made in a unique way—starting at one corner with one space and ending with a single space at opposite corner. Directions for Spiderweb Cloth, 68" square, page 218.

Pastel place mats in lacy crochet are for special occasions. These lovely pink mats are crocheted of size 30 cotton, with solid sections at the center for table protection, lacy borders of wheel motifs for eye appeal. Mats may be made in the center pattern alone, or of all motifs. See Pink Place Mats, page 217.

POPCORN SQUARES

Shown on page 210

SIZES: Directions for single size, 84″ × 96″ plus edging. Changes for double size, 96″ × 96″ plus edging are in parentheses.

MATERIALS: Knitting and crochet cotton, 75 (85) 250-yard balls of white or ecru. Steel crochet hook No. 7.

GAUGE: 10 sts = 1″; 8 rows = 1″.

BEDSPREAD: POPCORN SQUARE (make 56 (64) squares): Beg at center, ch 5, sl st in first ch to form ring.

Rnd 1: Ch 3, 7 dc in ring, sl st in top of ch 3 forming a "button."

Rnd 2: Ch 6, (sk 1 dc, dc in next dc, ch 3) 3 times, sl st in 3rd ch of ch 6.

Rnd 3: Ch 1, 2 sc in same ch as sl st, sc in next ch, (ch 5, sc in ch before next dc, sc in dc, sc in next ch) 3 times, ch 5, sc in ch, before first sc.

Rnd 4: Sc in back lp of 3 sc, sc in next ch, (ch 5, sc in ch before next sc, sc in back lp of 3 sc, sc in next ch) 3 times, ch 5, sc in ch before first sc.

Rnd 5: Sc in back lp of 5 sc, sc in next ch, (ch 5, sc in ch before next sc, sc in back lp of 5 sc, sc in next ch) 3 times, ch 5, sc in ch before first sc.

Rnd 6: Work as for rnd 5, inc 2 sc each side.

Rnd 7: Sc in back lp of next 4 sc, popcorn in next sc (to make popcorn, 5 dc in st, drop lp from hook; insert hook in first dc, pull dropped lp through), sc in back lp of next 4 sc, sc in next ch, (ch 5, sc in ch before next sc, sc in back lp of 4 sc, popcorn in next sc, sc in back lp of next 4 sc, sc in next ch) 3 times, ch 5, sc in ch before first sc.

Rnd 8: (Sc in back lp of 5 sc, sc in popcorn, sc in back lp of 5 sc, sc in next ch, ch 5, sc in ch before next sc) 4 times.

Working from chart, complete 53 rnds of square. Sl st in first sc or rnd 53. End off.

Sew squares tog through back lps of sc: 7 × 8 squares for single size, 8 × 8 squares for double size. Work rnd of sc around bedspread.

BORDER: Ch 76.

Row 1: Dc in 4th ch from hook, dc in each of next 3 ch, (ch 2, sk 2 ch, dc in next ch) 3 times, dc in each of next 3 ch, (ch 5, sk 5 ch, sc in each next 5 ch, ch 5, sk 5 ch, dc in each of next 4 ch) 3 times. Ch 3, turn.

Row 2: 4 dc in first dc, (ch 2, sk 2 dc, dc in next dc, dc in each of next 3 ch, ch 5, sk 1 sc, sc in each of next 3 sc, ch 5, sk 2 ch, dc in each of next 3 ch, dc in next dc) 3 times, ch 2, sk 2 dc, dc in next dc, (ch 2, dc in next dc) 3 times, dc in each of next 3 dc, dc in top of turning ch. Ch 3, turn.

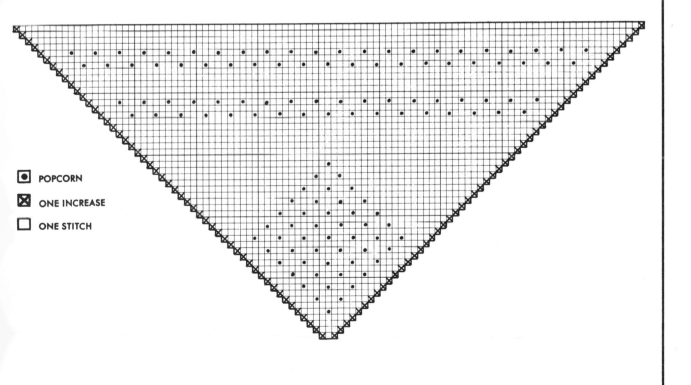

- ⊙ POPCORN
- ⊠ ONE INCREASE
- ☐ ONE STITCH

Row 3: Sk first dc, dc in each of next 4 dc, (ch 2, dc in next dc) 4 times, ch 2, sk 2 dc, dc in next dc, (dc in each of next 3 ch, ch 5, sk 1 sc, dc in next sc, ch 5, sk 2 ch, dc in each of next 3 ch, dc in next dc, ch 5, dc in next ch-2 sp, ch 5, sk 3 dc, dc in next dc) 3 times, end last repeat 5 dc in last dc. Ch 3, turn.

Row 4: 4 dc in first dc, (ch 4, sk 4 ch, sc in next ch, sc in dc, sc in next ch, ch 4, sk ch and 3 dc, dc in next dc, dc in each of next 3 ch, ch 2, sk 2 ch of next ch 5, dc in each of last 3 ch, dc in next dc) 3 times, ch 2, sk 2 dc, dc in next dc, (ch 2, dc in next dc) 5 times, dc in each of next 3 dc, dc in top of ch 3. Ch 3, turn.

Row 5: Sk first dc, dc in each of 4 dc, (ch 2, dc in next dc) 6 times, ch 2, sk 2 dc, dc in next dc, (dc in each of 2 ch, dc in next dc, ch 5, sc in ch before next sc, sc in each of 3 sc, sc in next ch, ch 5, sk ch and 3 dc, dc in next dc) 3 times, end last repeat 5 dc in last dc. Ch 3, turn.

Row 6: 4 dc in first dc, ch 2, sk 3 dc, dc in next dc, (dc in each of next 3 ch, ch 5, sc in each of 3 center sc, ch 5, sk 2 ch, dc in each of 3 ch, dc in next dc, ch 2, sk 2 dc, dc in next dc) 3 times, (ch 2, dc in next dc) 7 times, dc in each of next 3 dc, dc in top of ch 3. Ch 3, turn.

Row 7: Sk first dc, dc in each of 4 dc, (ch 2, dc in next dc) 8 times, ch 2, sk 2 dc, dc in next dc, (dc in each of next 3 ch, ch 5, dc in center sc, ch 5, sk 2 ch, dc in each of next 3 ch, dc in next dc, ch 5, dc in ch-2 sp, ch 5, sk 3 dc, dc in next dc) 3 times, end last repeat ch 5, 5 dc in last dc. Ch 3, turn.

Row 8: 4 dc in first dc, (ch 5, sk 4 ch of next ch 5, sc in next ch, sc in dc, sc in next ch, ch 5, sk ch and 3 dc, dc in next dc, dc in next 3 ch, ch 2, sk 2 ch of next ch 5, dc in next 3 ch, dc in next dc) 3 times, ch 2, sk 2 dc, dc in next dc, (ch 2, dc in next dc) 9 times, dc in each of next 3 dc, dc in top of ch 3. Ch 3, turn.

Row 9: Sk first dc, dc in each of 4 dc, (ch 2, dc in next dc) 10 times, ch 2, sk 2 dc, dc in next dc, (dc in each of 2 ch, dc in next dc, ch 5, sk 4 ch of next ch 5, sc in next ch, sc in 3 sc, sc in next ch, ch 5, sk 3 dc, dc in next dc) 3 times, end last repeat 5 dc in last dc. Ch 3, turn.

Row 10: Sk 4 dc, dc in next dc, (dc in each of 3 ch, ch 5, sc in each of 3 center sc, ch 5, sk 2 ch of next ch 5, dc in each of 3 ch, dc in next dc, ch 2, sk 2 dc, dc in next dc) 3 times, dc in each of next 2 ch, dc in next dc, (ch 2, dc in next dc) 10 times, dc in each of next 3 dc, dc in top of ch 3. Ch 3, turn.

Row 11: Sk first dc, dc in each of 4 dc, (ch 2, dc in next dc) 9 times, dc in each of 2 ch, (dc in next dc, ch 4, dc in next ch-2 sp, ch 4, sk 3 dc, dc in next dc, dc in each of next 3 ch, ch 5, dc in center sc of 3 sc, ch 5, sk 2 ch of ch 5, dc in each of next 3 ch) 3 times, dc in next dc. Ch 3, turn.

Row 12: Sk first 3 dc, dc in next dc, (dc in each of next 3 ch, ch 2, sk 2 ch of next ch 5, dc in each of next 3 ch, dc in next dc, ch 5, sc in last ch of next ch 5, sc in dc, sc in first ch of next ch 5, ch 5, sk 3 dc, dc in next dc) 3 times, dc in each of 2 ch, dc in next dc, (ch 2, dc in next dc) 8 times, dc in each of 3 ch, dc in top of ch 3. Ch 3, turn.

Row 13: Sk first dc, dc in each of 4 dc, (ch 2, dc in next dc) 7 times, (dc in each of 2 ch, dc in next dc, ch 5, sc in last ch of next ch 5, sc in each of 3 sc, sc in next ch, ch 5, sk 3 dc, dc in next dc) 3 times, dc in each of 2 ch, dc in next dc. Ch 3, turn.

Row 14: Sk first 3 dc, dc in next dc, (dc in each of next 3 ch, ch 5, sk 1 sc, sc in each of next 3 sc, ch 5, sk 2 ch of ch 5, dc in each of next 3 ch, dc in next dc, ch 2, sk 2 dc, dc in next dc) 3 times; dc in each of next 2 ch, dc in next dc, (ch 2, dc in next dc) 6 times, dc in each of 3 dc, dc in top of ch 3. Ch 3, turn.

Row 15: Sk first dc, dc in each of 4 dc, (ch 2, dc in next dc) 5 times, dc in each of 2 ch, (dc in next dc, ch 4, dc in ch-2 sp, ch 4, sk 3 dc, dc in next dc, dc in each of 3 ch, ch 5, dc in center sc on 3 sc, ch 5, sk 2 ch, dc in each of next 3 ch) 3 times, dc in next dc. Ch 3, turn.

Row 16: Sk first 3 dc, dc in next dc, (dc in each of next 3 ch, ch 2, sk 2 ch of next ch 5, dc in each of next 3 ch, dc in next dc, ch 4, sk 3 dc and 4 ch, sc in next ch, sc in dc, sc in next ch, ch 4, sk 3 dc, dc in next dc) 3 times, dc in each of 2 ch, dc in dc, (ch 2, dc in next dc) 4 times, dc in each of 3 dc, dc in top of ch 3. Ch 3, turn.

Row 17: Sk first dc, dc in each of 4 dc, (ch 2, dc in next dc) 3 times, dc in each of 2 ch, dc in next dc, (ch 5, sc in ch before 3 sc, sc in 3 sc, sc in next ch, ch 5, sk 3 dc, dc in next dc, dc in each of 2 ch, dc in next dc) 3 times. Ch 3, turn.

Repeat rows 2–17 for border. Make border long enough to fit three sides of bedspread with slight gathering at corners. Sew border in place.

ORANGE AND GREEN MAT
Shown on page 238

SIZE: 12″ × 18″.

MATERIALS: Coats & Clark's Speed-Cro-Sheen, 3 100-yard balls orange, 1 ball green. Steel crochet hook No. 1.

MAT: Row 1: Beg at side edge with orange, (ch 5, 5 dc in 4th ch from hook) 11 times—11 shells. Do not turn.

Row 2: Work 5 more dc in same ch as last shell was made, ch 3, sl st in same ch (top disk made), * sl st in next ch (between the shells), 5 dc in same ch as next shell was made, ch 3, sl st in same ch, repeat from * to bottom shell—11 disks. Do not turn.

Row 3: Ch 10, 3 dc in 4th ch from hook; drop lp off hook; insert hook in 3rd dc on side of last disk, pick up dropped lp and draw it through st, ch 1, 2 dc in same ch as 3 dc, * ch 5, 3 dc in 4th ch from hook; drop lp off hook; insert hook in 3rd dc on side of next disk above, pick up dropped lp and draw it through st, ch 1, 2 dc in same ch as 3 dc, repeat from * to top. Do not turn.

Row 4: Repeat row 2.

Repeat rows 3 and 2 until there are 14 rows of disks, end row 2. Turn work to wrong side.

Border: Rnd 1 (wrong side): Ch 5, sc in 2nd dc of disk just worked (ch 5, sc in 2nd dc of next disk) 10 times, ch 5, sc in center top of corner disk, (ch 5, sc in center top of next disk) 13 times, ch 5, sc in 2nd dc from end of corner disk, (ch 5, sc in 2nd dc from end of next disk) 10 times, ch 5, sl st in center bottom of corner disk. End off. Turn mat to right side.

Rnd 2: Join green in back lp of sl st just made; ch 3, dc in each of next 2 ch, 3 dc in next ch (corner), dc in each of next 2 ch, dc in back lp of next sc, (dc in each of next 5 ch, dc in back lp of next sc) 10 times, dc in each of next 2 ch, 3 dc in next ch (corner), dc in each of next 2 ch, dc in back loop of next sc, (dc in each of next 5 ch, dc in back lp of next sc) 13 times, dc in each of next 2 ch, 3 dc in next ch (corner), dc in each of next 2 ch, dc in back lp of next sc, (dc in each of next 5 ch, dc in back lp of next sc) 10 times, dc in each of next 2 ch, 3 dc in next ch (corner), dc in each of next 2 ch, (dc in each of next 6 ch) 13 times, sl st in top of ch 3 at beg of rnd. End off.

Rnd 3: Join orange in any dc, ch 3, dc in st before ch 3, * sk next free dc, dc in next dc, dc in skipped dc, repeat from * around, sl st in top of ch 3 at beg of rnd. End off.

Rnd 4: Join green in any dc, ch 3, dc in each st around, working 3 dc in each corner dc, sl st in top of ch 3 at beg of rnd. End off.

Rnd 5: Join orange in any dc, ch 1; working from left to right, sc in each st around. Join; end off.

ORANGE MAT
Shown on page 239

SIZE: 15″ diameter.

MATERIALS: Coats & Clark's Speed-Cro-Sheen, 3 100-yard balls of orange (Tango), 1 ball each of white and green. Steel crochet hook No. 00. Large-eyed embroidery needle.

GAUGE: 9 hdc = 2″; 3 rnds = 1″.

Note: Use cotton double throughout.

MAT: With double strand of white, ch 6. Sl st in first ch to form ring.

Rnd 1: 12 sc in ring. Sl st in first sc. End off.

Rnd 2: With double strand of orange, sc in any sc, * 2 sc in next sc, sc in next sc, repeat from * around, 2 sc in last sc—18 sc.

Rnd 3: * 2 sc in next sc, sc in each of next 2 sc, repeat from * around—24 sc.

Rnd 4: * Sc in each of next 3 sc, 2 sc in next sc, repeat from * around—30 sc. Sl st in next sc.

Rnd 5: Ch 2 (counts as 1 hdc), hdc in next sc, 2 hdc in next sc, * hdc in each of next 2 sc, 2 hdc in next sc, repeat from * around—40 hdc. Sl st in top of ch 2.

Rnd 6: Ch 2, 2 hdc in next st, * hdc in next st, 2 hdc in next st, repeat from * around—60 hdc. Join.

Rnd 7: Ch 2, work in hdc around, inc in every 6th st—70 hdc. Join.

Rnd 8: Ch 2, work in hdc around, inc in every 7th st—80 hdc. Join.

Rnd 9: Ch 2, work in hdc, inc 10 sts in rnd—90 hdc. Join.

Rnds 10–15: Repeat rnd 9—150 hdc.

Rnd 16: Ch 2, work in hdc, inc 4 sts in rnd—154 hdc.

Rnd 17: (Sc in each of next 2 sts, hdc in each of next 2 sts, dc in each of next 2 sts, 2 tr in next st, dc in each of next 2 sts, hdc in each of next 2 sts, 2 sc in each of next 2 sts, sl st in next st) 11 times, ending with sl st in joining sl st of previous rnd.

Rnd 18: (Sc in each of 4 sts, hdc in each of 6 sts, sc in each of 4 sts, sl st in sl st) 11 times. End off.

Rnd 19: Join white in sl st, ch 4, (dc in each of 4 sts, sc in each of 6 sts, dc in each of 4 sts, tr in sl st) 11 times, end dc in each of last 4 sts, sl st in top of ch 4.

Rnd 20: Sc in each st around. End off.

Rnd 21: With orange, sc in each st around. End off. With white, embroider lines between segments in chain stitch; embroider seeds in satin stitch.

LEAF (make 2): With double strand of green, ch 20.

Row 1: Sc in 2nd ch from hook and in each remaining ch. Ch 1, turn.

Row 2: Sk first sc, sl st in next sc, sc in next 8 sts, dc in next 7 sts, sc in next st, sl st in last st. Ch 1, turn.

Row 3: Sk first st, sc in next st, and in each of next 7 sts, dc in next 4 sts, sc in next 2 sts, sl st in each st to end.

Row 4: Working on other side of original ch, sl st in first 3 ch, sc in next 14 ch, sl st in last 2 ch. Ch 1, turn.

Row 5: Sk 2 sl sts, sc in next 4 sts, dc in next 6 sts, sc in next 3 sts, sl st in next 2 sts. Ch 1, turn.

Row 6: Sk first st, sc in next 2 sts, dc in next 10 sts, sc in next 2 sts, sl st to point. End off.

Sew one leaf over mat with invisible stitches; attach other leaf along edge with a few stitches.

CHAIN STITCH

SATIN STITCH

PINK PLACE MATS
Shown on page 212

SIZE: 11″ × 18″.

MATERIALS: Clark's Big Ball Mercerized Crochet Cotton, size 30, 2 250-yard balls for each mat. Steel crochet hook No. 10.

GAUGE: 12 sts = 1″; 7 rows = 1″. Motif = 2¼″.

MAT: MAIN SECTION: Ch 135.

Row 1: Sc in 2nd ch from hook and in each ch across—134 sc. Ch 3, turn.

Row 2 (right side): Sk first sc, dc in each sc across—134 dc, counting turning ch 3 as 1 dc. Ch 1, turn.

Row 3: Sc in first dc, * ch 3, sk 3 dc, sc in sp between dc's, repeat from * across, end sc in top of ch 3—44 lps. Ch 3, turn.

Row 4: 3 dc in each lp, dc in last sc. Ch 1, turn.

Rows 5–14: Repeat rows 3 and 4, 5 times. At end of row 14, ch 3, turn.

Row 15: Sk first dc, dc in each dc across, dc in top of turning ch 3. Ch 3, turn.

Row 16: Sk first dc, dc in each dc across, dc in top of turning ch 3. Ch 1, turn.

Repeat rows 3–16, 3 times more, then repeat rows 3–15. At end of row 15, ch 1, turn.

Last Row: Sc in each dc across, sc in top of turning ch. End off.

SINGLE STRIP: First Motif: Ch 8, sl st in first ch to form ring.

Rnd 1: Ch 1, 16 sc in ring. Sl st in first sc.

Rnd 2: Sc in same place as sl st, * ch 7, sc in 2nd ch from hook, hdc in next ch, dc in each of next 3 ch, ch 1, sk next sc, sc in next sc (petal made), repeat from * around, end sk last sc, sl st in first sc.

Rnd 3: Sl st to top of first petal, ch 7, dc in same place as last sl st, * ch 4, dc, ch 4, dc in top of next petal, repeat from * around, end ch 4, sl st in 3rd ch of ch 7.

Rnd 4: Sc in same place as sl st, * 5 sc in next lp, sc in next dc, 4 sc in next lp, sc in next dc, repeat from * around, end 4 sc in last lp, sl st in first sc.

Rnd 5: Sc in same place as sl st, sc in each of next 3 sc, drop lp from hook, insert hook in first foundation ch of main section and draw dropped lp through (joining st made), sc in same sc on motif, ** joining st in next ch on main section, sc in same sc on motif, (joining st in next ch on main section, sc in next sc on motif) 11 times, joining st in next ch on main section, 2 sc in same sc on motif, * sc in each of next 10 sc, 3 sc in next sc, repeat from * around, end sc in each of last 7 sc, sl st in first sc. End off.

Second Motif: Work as for first motif for 4 rnds.

Rnd 5: Sc in same place as sl st, sc in each of

next 3 sc, sk 26 sc after last joining st on first motif, joining st in next sc on first motif, sc in same sc on second motif; working along sc just skipped work a joining st in next sc on first motif, sc in same sc on second motif, (joining st in next sc on first motif, sc in next sc on second motif) 11 times, joining st in next sc on first motif, 2 sc in same sc on second motif, sc in each of next 11 sc, sk 16 ch on foundation ch of main section, joining st in next ch, sc in same sc on second motif, repeat from ** on rnd 5 of first motif.

Make and join 3 more motifs in same manner.

DOUBLE STRIP: First Strip: Work as for single strip, joining motifs to last row of main section.

Second Strip: Make and join one more strip of 5 motifs, joining to previous strip to correspond.

Dampen mat and pin out to measurements.

SPIDERWEB CLOTH
Shown on page 211

SIZE: 68″ square.

MATERIALS: Clark's Big Ball Mercerized Crochet Cotton, size 30, 16 350-yard balls white. Steel crochet hook No. 10.

GAUGE: 9 sps = 2″; 9 rows = 2″.

Note: See chart.

CLOTH: Beg at one corner, ch 8.

Row 1: Dc in 8th ch from hook—1 sp. Ch 8, turn.

Row 2: Dc in first dc, ch 2, sk 2 ch of ch 8, dc in next ch, ch 2, dtr in same ch as last dc—3 sps. Ch 8, turn each row.

Row 3: Dc in dtr, (ch 2, dc in next dc) twice, ch 2, sk 2 ch of ch 8, dc in next ch, ch 2, dtr in same ch as last dc—5 sps.

Row 4: Dc in dtr, (ch 2, dc in next dc) twice, 2 dc in next sp, dc in next dc, ch 2, dc in next dc, ch 2, sk 2 ch of ch 8, dc in next ch, ch 2, dtr in same ch as last dc—3 sps, 1 bl, 3 sps.

Row 5: Dc in dtr, (ch 2, dc in next dc) twice, 2 dc in next sp, dc in next dc, ch 9, sk 2 dc, dc in next dc, 2 dc in next sp, dc in next dc, ch 2, dc in next dc, ch 2, sk 2 ch of ch 8, dc in next ch, ch 2, dtr in same ch as last dc.

Row 6: Dc in dtr, (ch 2, dc in next dc) twice, 2 dc in next sp, dc in next dc; this border pat of 1 inc sp, 2 sps and 1 bl continues to center of cloth; ch 5, sc in next sp, ch 5, sk 3 dc; dc in next dc, 2 dc in next sp, dc in next dc, ch 2, dc in next dc, ch 2, sk 2 ch of ch 8, dc in next ch, ch 2, dtr in same ch as last dc; this border pat of 1 bl, 2 sps and 1 inc sp continues to center of cloth.

Row 7: Work border; ch 5, sc in next sp, ch 1, sc in next sp, ch 5, sk 3 dc; work border.

Row 8: Work border; ch 7, sc in next sp, (ch 1, sc in next sp) twice, ch 7, sk 3 dc; work border.

Row 9: Work border; ch 9, sk 2 dc, dc in next dc, 3 dc in next sp, ch 7, sc in next ch-1 sp, ch 1, sc in next ch-1 sp, ch 7, 3 dc in ch-7 sp, dc in next dc, ch 9, sk 2 dc; work border.

Row 10: Work border; ch 5, sc in next sp, ch 5, sk 3 dc, dc in next dc, 3 dc in next sp, ch 7, sc in ch-1 sp, ch 7, 3 dc in next sp, dc in next dc, ch 5, sc in next sp, ch 5, sk 3 dc; work border.

Row 11: Work border; ch 5, sc in next sp, ch 1, sc in next sp, ch 5, sk 3 dc, dc in next dc, 3 dc in next sp, ch 2, 3 dc in next sp, dc in next dc, ch 5, sc in next sp, ch 1, sc in next sp, ch 5, sk 3 dc; work border.

Row 12: Work border; ch 7, sc in next sp, (ch 1, sc in next sp) twice, ch 7, sk 3 dc, dc in next dc, 2 dc in ch-2 sp, dc in next dc, ch 7, sc in next sp, (ch 1, sc in next sp) twice, ch 7, sk 3 dc; work border.

Row 13: * Work border; ch 9, sk 2 dc, dc in next dc, 3 dc in next sp, ch 7, sc in next ch-1 sp, ch 1, sc in next ch-1 sp, ch 7, 3 dc in ch-7 sp, dc in next dc *, ** ch 2, sk 2 dc, dc in next dc, 3 dc in next sp, ch 7, sc in next ch-1 sp, ch 1, sc in next ch-1 sp, ch 7, 3 dc in next sp, dc in next dc, ch 9, sk 2 dc; work border **.

Row 14: * Work border; ch 5, sc in next sp, ch 5, sk 3 dc, dc in next dc, 3 dc in next sp, ch 7, sc in ch-1 sp, ch 7, 3 dc in next sp, dc in next dc *; work 3 sps, ** 3 dc in next sp, ch 7, sc in ch-1 sp, ch 7, 3 dc in next sp, dc in next dc, ch 5, sc in next sp, ch 5, sk 3 dc; work border **.

Row 15: * Work border; ch 5, sc in next sp, ch 1, sc in next sp, ch 5, sk 3 dc, dc in next dc, 3 dc in next sp, ch 2, 3 dc in next sp, dc in next dc *; work 5 sps; ** 3 dc in next sp, ch 2, 3 dc in next sp, dc in next dc, ch 5, sc in next sp, ch 1, sc in next sp, ch 5, sk 3 dc; work border **.

Row 16: * Work border; ch 7, sc in next sp, (ch 1, sc in next sp) twice, ch 7, sk 3 dc, dc in next dc, 2 dc in ch-2 sp, dc in next dc *; work 7 sps; ** 2 dc in ch-2 sp, dc in next dc, ch 7, sc in next sp, (ch 1, sc in next sp) twice, ch 7, sk 3 dc; work border **.

Row 17: Work from first * to 2nd * on row 13; work sps across to next bl; work from first ** to 2nd ** on row 13.

Row 18: Work from first * to 2nd * on row 14; work sps across to next bl; work from first ** to 2nd ** on row 14.

Row 19: Work from first * to 2nd * on row 15; work sps across to next bl; work from first ** to 2nd ** on row 15.

Row 20: Work from first * to 2nd * on row 16; work sps across to next bl; work from first ** to 2nd ** on row 16.

Rows 21–24: Repeat rows 17–20.

Rows 25–27: Repeat rows 17–19.

Row 28: Work from first * to 2nd * on row 16; (work 7 sps, 1 bl) 3 times, work 7 sps; work from first ** to 2nd ** on row 16.

Row 29: Work from first * to 2nd * on row 13; (ch 9, sk 2 dc, work 1 bl, 5 sps, 1 bl) 4 times; ch 9; omit ch 2, work from first ** to 2nd ** on row 13.

Row 30: Work from first * to 2nd * on row 14; (ch 5, sc in next sp, ch 5, sk 3 dc, work 1 bl, 3 sps, 1 bl) 4 times, ch 5, sc in next sp, ch 5, sk 3 dc, dc in next dc; work from first ** to 2nd ** on row 14.

Row 31: Work from first * to 2nd * on row 15; (ch 5, sc in next sp, ch 1, sc in next sp, ch 5, sk 3 dc, work 1 bl, 1 sp, 1 bl) 4 times, ch 5, sc in next sp, ch 1, sc in next sp, ch 5, sk 3 dc, dc in next dc; work from first ** to 2nd ** on row 15.

Row 32: Work border; * ch 7, sc in next sp, (ch 1, sc in next sp) twice, ch 7, sk 3 dc, dc in next dc, 2 dc in ch-2 sp, dc in next dc, repeat from * across, end ch 7, work border.

Row 33: Work from first * to 2nd * on row 13; ch 2, ** sk 2 dc, dc in next dc, 3 dc in next sp, ch 7, sc in next ch-1 sp, ch 1, sc in next ch-1 sp, ch 7, 3 dc in next sp, dc in next dc, ch 9, repeat from ** 4 times, omit last ch 9, work from first ** to 2nd ** on row 13.

Working from chart, beg with row 34, continue to work border each side, adding new spiderweb pats every 20 rows. Work through row 187. **Note:** When cloth becomes bulky, fold it up from bottom and pin with large safety pins.

Row 188 (widest row): Work border; * ch 7, sc in next sp, (ch 1, sc in next sp) twice, ch 7, sk 3 dc, dc in next dc, 2 dc in ch-2 sp, dc in next dc, (work 7 sps, 1 bl) 4 times, repeat from * across, end ch 7, sc in next sp, (ch 1, sc in next sp) twice, ch 7, sk 3 dc; work border. Ch 1, turn.

Row 189: Sl st to first dc, ch 5, (dc in next dc, ch 2) twice, * sk 2 dc, dc in next dc, 3 dc in next sp, ch 7, sc in next ch 1 sp, ch 1, sc in next ch-1 sp, ch 7, 3 dc in ch-7 sp, dc in next dc, (ch 9, sk 2 dc, work 1 bl, 5 sps, 1 bl) 4 times, ch 9, repeat from * across, end ch 9, sk 2 dc, dc in next dc, 3 dc in next sp, ch 7, sc in next ch-1 sp, ch 1, sc in next ch-1 sp, ch 7, 3 dc in ch-7 sp, dc in next dc, work 3 sps. Ch 1, turn each row.

Row 190: Sl st to first dc, ch 5, (dc in next dc, ch 2) twice, sk 2 dc, dc in next dc, 3 dc in next sp, * ch 7, sc in ch-1 sp, ch 7, 3 dc in next sp, dc in next dc, (ch 5, sc in next sp, ch 5, sk 3 dc, work 1 bl, 3 sps, 1 bl) 4 times, ch 5, sc in next sp, ch 5, sk 3 dc, dc in next dc, 3 dc in next sp, repeat from * across, end ch 7, sc in ch-1 sp, ch 7, 3 dc in next sp, dc in next dc, work 3 sps.

Row 191: Sl st to first dc, ch 5, (dc in next dc, ch 2) twice, sk 2 dc, dc in next dc, 3 dc in next sp, * ch 2, 3 dc in next sp, dc in dc, (ch 5, sc in next sp, ch 1, sc in next sp, ch 5, sk 3 dc, work 1 bl, 1 sp, 1 bl) 4 times, ch 5, sc in next sp, ch 1, sc in next sp, ch 5, sk 3 dc, dc in next dc, 3 dc in next sp, repeat from * across, end ch 2, 3 dc in next sp, dc in next dc, work 3 sps.

Row 192: Sl st to first dc, ch 5, (dc in next dc, ch 2) twice, sk 2 dc, dc in next dc, * dc in ch-2 sp, dc in next dc, ch 7, sc in next sp, (ch 1, sc in next sp) twice, ch 7, sk 3 dc, dc in next dc, repeat from * across, end 2 dc in ch-2 sp, work 3 sps.

Row 193: Sl st to first dc, ch 5, (dc in next dc, ch 2) twice, * sk 2 dc, dc in next dc, 3 dc in next sp, ch 7, sc in next sp, ch 1, sc in next sp, ch 7, 3 sc in next sp, dc in next dc, ch 9) 4 times, sk 2 dc, dc in next dc, 3 dc in next sp, ch 7, sc in next sp, ch 1, sc in next sp, ch 7; 3 sc in next sp, dc in next dc, ch 2, repeat from * across, work 3 sps.

Continue to work in pat, decreasing 1 sp at each side every row until 1 sp remains. Work 1 row of sc around edges of cloth, working 5 sc in each sp, 8 sc in each of the 4 corner sps.

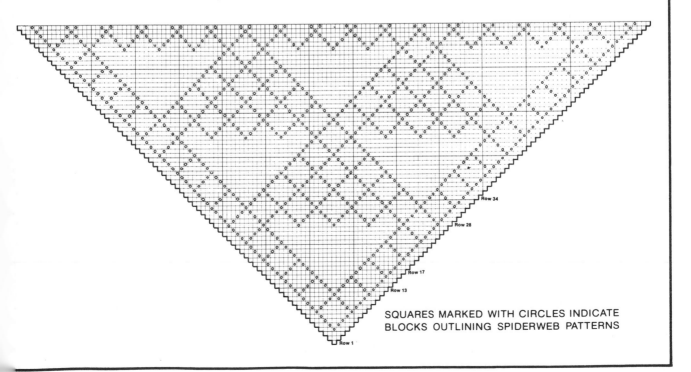

SQUARES MARKED WITH CIRCLES INDICATE
BLOCKS OUTLINING SPIDERWEB PATTERNS

ARAN-PATTERN CARDIGAN

Shown on page 145

SIZES: Directions for small size (8-10). Changes for medium size (12-14) and large size (16-18) are in parentheses.

Body Bust Size: 31½″-32½″ (34″-36″; 38″-40″).

Blocked Bust Size (closed): 33″ (37″-41″).

MATERIALS: Knitting worsted, 7 (8-9) 4-oz. skeins. Crochet hook size H. Six ¾″ plastic rings for buttons.

GAUGE: 7 sts = 2″; 7 rows = 2″.

To Bind Off: At beg of row, ch 1, sl st loosely across specified number of sts; at end of row, leave specified number of sts unworked.

To Dec 1 St: At beg of row, ch 1, pull up a lp in each of 2 sts, yo hook and through 3 lps on hook; at end of row, work to within last 2 sts, pull up a lp in each of 2 sts, yo hook and through 3 lps on hook.

To Inc 1 St: Work 2 sc in same st.

STITCH PATTERN: Note: Do not work in stitch directly behind raised dc or double raised dc, or in eye of a cluster.

CLUSTER: (Yo hook, draw up a lp in st) 4 times, yo and draw through all 9 lps on hook. Ch 1 tightly to form eye. (Cluster is worked from wrong side but appears on right side.)

RAISED DC: Dc around upright bar of dc 1 row below, inserting hook behind dc from front to back to front, for ridge on right side.

DOUBLE RAISED DC: Holding back last lp of each dc on hook, make 2 dc around upright bar of st 1 row below, yo and through all 3 lps on hook.

POPCORN: 4 dc in st, drop lp off hook, insert hook in top of first dc, pick up dropped lp and pull through.

CARDIGAN: BACK: Beg at lower edge, ch 58 (64-70).

Row 1: Sc in 2nd ch from hook and in each ch across–57 (63-69) sc. Ch 1, turn each row.

Row 2 (wrong side): Sc in each of first 4 (7-10) sts, (cluster in next sc, sc in each of next 15 sts) 3 times, end cluster in next st, sc in each of last 4 (7-10) sts.

Row 3 (right side): Sc in each of first 2 (5-8) sc, * work dc around post of next sc 1 row below (row 1), sk next sc on row 2 (see Stitch Patterns: Note), sc in each of next 3 sts, dc around post of next sc 1 row below, sk next sc on row 2, sc in each of next 4 sc; holding back last lp of each dc on hook, make 2 dc around next sc 1 row below, yo and through 3 lps on hook, sk next sc on row 2, sc in next sc, sk 1 sc on row 1, make 2 dc around next sc as before, sk next sc on row 2, sc in each of next 4 sc, repeat from * twice, end dc around post of next sc 1 row below, sc in each of next 3 sts, dc around post of next sc 1 row below, sc in each of next 2 (5-8) sc.

Row 4: Sc in each of first 3 (6-9) sts, (cluster in next sc, sc in next sc, cluster in next sc, sc in each of next 13 sts) 3 times; end cluster in next sc, sc in next sc, cluster in next sc, sc in each of last 3 (6-9) sts.

Row 5: Sc in each of first 2 (5-8) sc, (raised dc in raised dc, sc in each of next 3 sts, raised dc in raised dc, sc in each of next 3 sts, double raised dc in double raised dc, sc in each of next 3 sc, double raised dc in double raised dc, sc in each of next 3 sc) 3 times, end raised dc in raised dc, sc in each of next 3 sts, raised dc in raised dc, sc in each of last 2 (5-8) sc.

Row 6: Repeat row 2.

Row 7: Sc in each of first 2 (5-8) sc, (raised dc in raised dc, sc in each of next 3 sts, raised dc in raised dc, sc in each of next 2 sc, double raised dc in double raised dc, sc in each of next 5 sc, double raised dc in double raised dc, sc in each of next 2 sc) 3 times, end raised dc in raised dc, sc in each of next 3 sts, raised dc in raised dc, sc in each of last 2 (5-8) sts.

Row 8: Repeat row 4.

Row 9: Sc in each of first 2 (5-8) sc, (raised dc in raised dc, sc in each of next 3 sts, raised dc in raised dc, sc in next sc, double raised dc in double raised dc, sc in each of next 3 sc, popcorn in next sc, sc in each of next 3 sc, double raised dc in double raised dc, sc in next sc) 3 times, end raised dc in raised dc, sc in each of next 3 sts, raised dc in raised dc, sc in each of last 2 (5-8) sc.

Row 10: Repeat row 2.

Row 11: Repeat row 7.

Row 12: Repeat row 4.

Row 13: Repeat row 5.

Row 14: Repeat row 2.

Row 15: Sc in each of first 2 (5-8) sc, (raised dc in raised dc, sc in each of next 3 sts, raised dc in raised dc, sc in each of next 4 sc, double raised dc in double raised dc, sc in next sc, double raised dc in double raised dc, sc in each of next 4 sc) 3 times, end raised dc in raised dc, sc in each of next 3 sts, raised dc in raised dc, sc in each of last 2 (5-8) sc. Repeat rows 4-15 for pat until piece measures 18″ from start or desired length to underarm. Check gauge; piece should measure 16″ (18″-20″) wide.

Shape Raglan Armholes: Keeping to pat, bind off (see To Bind Off and To Dec 1 St) 4 sts each side of next row, then dc 1 st each side every other row 15 (17-19) times–19 (21-23) sts. End off.

RIGHT FRONT: (Left-handed crocheters: This will be your left front.) Beg at lower edge, ch 27 (30-33).

Row 1: Sc in 2nd ch from hook and in each ch across–26 (29-32) sc. Ch 1, turn each row.

Row 2: (wrong side): Sc in each of first 4 (7-10) sts, cluster in next sc, sc in each of next 15 sts, cluster in next st, sc in each of last 5 sts. Mark end of last row for center edge.

Row 3 (right side): Sc in each of first 3 sc, work dc around post of next st 1 row below (row 1), sk next sc on row 2, sc in each of next 3 sts, dc around post of next sc 1 row below, sk next sc on row 2, sc in each of next 4 sc, double raised dc around next sc 1 row below, sk next sc on row 2, sc in next sc, sk 1 sc on row 1, double raised dc around next sc as before, sk next sc on row 2, sc in

each of next 4 sc, dc around post of next sc 1 row below, sc in each of next 3 sts, dc around most of next sc 1 row below, sc in each of last 2 (5-8) sc.

Row 4: Sc in each of first 3 (6-9) sts, cluster in next sc, sc in next sc, cluster in next sc, sc in each of next 13 sts, cluster in next sc, sc in each of last 4 sts. Continue in pat as established until piece measures same as back to underarm. Check gauge; piece should measure 7″ (8″-9″) wide.

Shape Raglan Armhole and Neck: Keeping to pat, bind off 4 sts at side edge of next row. Dec 1 st at same edge every other row 9 (11-13) times. Bind off 3 sts at center edge of next row, then dec 1 st at center edge every other row 3 (4-5) times; **at the same time,** continue to dec 1 st at arm side every other row 6 times more–1 st remains. End off.

LEFT FRONT: Work same as for right front to end of row 1. Mark end of row for center front.

Row 2 (wrong side): Sc in each of 5 sts, cluster in next st, sc in each of next 15 sts, cluster in next sc, sc in each of last 4 (7-10) sc.

Row 3 (right side): Sc in each of first 2 (5-8) sc; dc around post of next sc 1 row below (row 1), sk next sc on row 2, sc in each of next 3 sts, dc around post of next sc 1 row below, sk next sc on row 2, sc in each of next 4 sc, double raised dc around next sc 1 row below, sk next sc on row 2, sc in next sc, sk 1 sc on row 1, double raised dc around next sc as before, sk next sc on row 2, sc in each of next 4 sc, dc around post of next sc 1 row below, sc in each of next 3 sts, dc around post of next sc 1 row below, sc in each of last 3 sc. Work in pat as established; complete same as for right front, reversing shaping.

SLEEVES: Beg at lower edge, ch 28 (30-32).

Row 1: Sc in 2nd ch from hook and in each ch across–27 (29-31) sc. Ch 1, turn each row.

Row 2 (wrong side): Sc in each of first 5 (6-7) sc, cluster in next sc, sc in each of next 15 sc, cluster in next sc, sc in each of last 5 (6-7) sc.

Row 3: Work same as row 3 on right front, having 3 (4-5) sc at beg and end of row. Continue in

ARAN-PATTERN CARDIGAN
Continued

pat as established, inc 1 sc (see To Inc 1 St) each side every 6th row 7 (8-9) times, working added sts in sc–41 (45-49) sts. Work even until piece measures 17″ from start. Check gauge; piece above last inc row should measure 11¾″ (12¾″-14″) wide.

Shape Raglan Cap: Keeping to pat, bind off 4 sts each side of next row. Dec 1 st each side every other row 14 (16-18) times, then every row twice–1 st remains. End off.

FINISHING: Block pieces; do not flatten pat. Sew caps of sleeves to back and front armholes. Sew side and sleeve seams.

Left Front Border: Work 6 rows sc on left front edge. End off.

Right Front Border: Work 3 rows sc on right front edge, having same number of sc as left front edge.

With pins, mark position of 6 buttonholes evenly spaced on right front edge; first pin in 3rd sc from lower edge; last pin in 3rd sc below neck edge.

Row 4: * Work sc to within 1 sc of pin, ch 2, sk next 2 sc, repeat from * 5 times, sc in next sc, sc in last sc. Ch 1, turn.

Row 5: Sc in each sc and in each ch of buttonholes. Ch 1, turn. Work 1 more row in sc. End off.

Neck Border: From right side, beg 3 rows in from center edge, work 1 row sc around neck edge, ending within 3 rows of center front edge. Ch 1, turn. Work in sc for 6 rows, decreasing to desired fit. Do not turn at end of last row.

Next Row: Working from left to right, sc in each sc. End off.

From right side, beg at neck edge, work 1 row sc down front edge, around lower edge, up other front edge, ending at neck edge. End off.

Sleeve Border: From right side, work 5 rnds sc around lower edge of each sleeve, easing in to desired fit.

BUTTONS (make 6): Work sc tightly around plastic ring. Join in first sc. End off, leaving a long end for sewing. Thread needle, gather sts tog at center. Sew on buttons.

FRINGY SCARF SET
Shown on page 235

SIZE: Hat, adjustable headsize. Scarf, 9½″ wide x 76″ long, plus fringe.

MATERIALS: Knitting worsted weight yarn, 2 ozs. light olive (LO), ½ oz. each of black (B), dark olive (DO), hot pink (HP), cranberry (C), old rose (OR), wine (W), dark green (DG), for hat; 2 ozs. each of light olive (LO), black (B) and hot pink (HP); 1 oz. each of dark olive (DO), cranberry (C), old rose (OR), wine (W), and dark green (DG), for scarf. Crochet hooks size F for hat, size J for scarf.

GAUGE: 4 sc = 1″ (size F hook, hat); 5 sc = 2″ (size J hook, scarf).

HAT: With B and size F hook, ch 4. Sl st in first ch to form ring.

Rnd 1: Ch 1, 12 sc in ring.

Rnd 2: 2 sc in each sc around–24 sc. Mark ends of rnds.

Rnd 3: Working over strand of LO, pull up a lp of B in first sc, finish sc with LO; working over strand of B, pull up a lp of LO in same sc, finish sc with B. Always changing colors in this way, finishing sc with new color and working over unused color, work (4 B sc, 1 LO sc in same st as last B sc) 5 times, B sc in each of last 3 sts–30 sc.

Rnd 4: B sc in next 3 sc, B sc and LO sc in next sc, (B sc in next 4 sc, B sc and LO sc in next sc) 5 times, B sc in last sc–36 sc.

Rnd 5: (Working over strands of DO and LO, B sc in next 3 sc, LO sc in next sc, 2 DO sc in next sc, LO sc in next sc) 6 times–42 sc.

Rnd 6: (Working over strands of DO, LO, and C, B sc in next 3 sc, LO sc in next sc, DO sc and C sc in next sc, DO sc in next sc, LO sc in next sc) 6 times–48 sc. With LO, sl st in first sc.

Rnd 7: Add a strand of HP. Working in each sc around, beg in first sc, ch 1, (work LO sc, 2 B sc in next sc, LO sc, DO sc, C sc, HP sc, C sc, DO sc) 6 times–54 sc. With DO, sl st in first sc.

Rnd 8: Ch 1, (DO sc in LO sc, LO sc and B sc in next sc; LO sc, DO sc, C sc, HP sc in each of 3 sc, C sc) 6 times–60 sc. With C, sl st in first sc. Cut B.

Rnd 9: Ch 1, (C sc in DO sc, DO sc, LO sc, DO sc, C sc, HP sc in each of 2 sc, 2 HP sc in next sc, HP sc in each of 2 sc) 6 times–66 sc. With HP, sl st in first sc. Cut LO.

Rnd 10: Ch 1, (HP sc in C sc, C sc, 2 DO sc in next sc, C sc, HP sc in 3 sc, HP sc and C sc in next sc, HP sc in 3 sc) 6 times-78 sc. Sl st in first sc. Cut DO.

Rnd 11: With HP, ch 1; add a strand of LO. (HP sc, C sc, LO sc in 2 sc, C sc, HP sc in 3 sc, C sc, LO sc, C sc, HP sc in 2 sc) 6 times-78 sc. With LO, sl st in first sc. Cut C and HP.

Rnd 12: With LO, ch 1, 2 sc in first sc, (sc in 6 sc, 2 sc in next sc) 11 times-90 sc.

Note: Cutting and joining colors as needed, work even in sc to last rnd of cap (90 sc each rnd), joining each rnd with sl st. Ch 1 at beg of each rnd.

Rnd 13: 3 LO sc, (3 OR sc, 3 W sc, 3 OR sc, 6 LO sc) 6 times, end last repeat 3 LO sc.

Rnd 14: LO sc, B sc, LO sc, * (W sc, OR sc) 4 times, W sc, (B sc, LO sc) 3 times, repeat from * around, end last repeat B sc, LO sc, B sc.

Rnd 15: Repeat rnd 13.

Rnd 16: With LO, work even.

Rnd 17: 3 DG sc, (LO sc, DG sc, LO sc, 3 DG sc, LO sc, DG sc, LO sc, 6 DG sc) 6 times, end last repeat 3 DG sc.

Rnd 18: (LO sc, DG sc) 45 times.

Rnd 19: 2 DG sc, (3 LO sc, 3 DG sc) 14 times, 3 LO sc, 1 DG sc.

Rnd 20: Repeat rnd 18.

Rnd 21: Repeat rnd 17.

Rnd 22: With LO, work even.

Rnd 23: Repeat rnd 13.

Rnd 24: LO sc, B sc, LO sc, * (OR sc, W sc) 4 times, OR sc, (B sc, LO sc) 3 times, (W sc, OR sc) 4 times, W sc, (B sc, LO sc) 3 times, repeat from * twice, end last repeat B sc, LO sc, B sc.

Rnd 25: Repeat rnd 13.

Rnd 26: With LO, ch 2, hdc in each sc around. Join; end off.

SCARF: First Half: With B and size J hook, ch 182.

Row 1: Sc in 2nd ch from hook and in each remaining ch-181 sc. End off. Do not turn.

Row 2: With LO, make lp on hook. Beg in first st of last row. Working over B strand, LO sc in first sc, completing sc with B; * with B, working over LO strand, sc in each of next 5 sc, completing last sc with LO; with LO, sc in next sc, completing sc with B, repeat from * across. End off. Do not turn.

Row 3: With DO, make lp on hook. Beg in first st of last row, working over B and LO strands, DO sc in first sc, changing to LO, * LO sc, changing to B, 3 B sc, changing to LO to complete last sc, DO sc, changing to LO, repeat from * across. End off. Do not turn.

Note: Work each row from right side, working sc in each sc across, always finishing last 2 lps of one color with next color to be used and always working over unused colors. End off colors each row.

Row 4: * C sc, DO sc, LO sc, B sc, LO sc, DO sc, repeat from * across, end C sc.

Row 5: * HP sc, C sc, DO sc, LO sc, DO sc, C sc, repeat from * across, end HP sc.

Row 6: 2 HP sc, * C sc, DO sc, C sc, 3 HP sc, repeat from * across, end 2 HP sc.

Row 7: * C sc, 2 HP sc, repeat from * across, end C sc.

Row 8: With HP, work in sc across.

Row 9: With LO, work in sc across.

Row 10: 2 OR sc, * 3 W sc, 3 OR sc, repeat from * across, end 2 OR sc.

Row 11: * LO sc, B sc, repeat from * across, end LO sc.

Row 12: * DG sc, LO sc, repeat from * across, end DG sc.

Row 13: With LO, work in sc across.

Second Half: Working on opposite side of starting ch, work rows 2-13.

FINISHING: Run in all yarn ends on wrong side. Cut a strand of DO longer than scarf. Thread in yarn needle, weave under 1 B lp of each st on row 1. Weave in DO ends.

With LO, from right side, work 1 row sc across end of scarf. Ch 3, turn. Work dc in each sc across. Work same edging on other end.

Fringe: Cut strands of LO about 12″ long. Knot 3 strands tog in each dc across each end.

Man's boat-necked pull-over in winter white squares which, sewn together, form diagonal patterns. Cuffs and lower border of sweater are made in slipper stitch, a form of ribbing in crochet. In 36–42. Man's Motif Pullover, page 156.

Most popular of all crocheted motifs is the granny-afghan square, here making that most popular accessory for the young and light-hearted, the poncho. Edges of poncho are trimmed with crocheted picots; chain-stitch belt gives poncho its shape. Fits misses' sizes 6 to 14. For Granny Poncho, see page 226.

GRANNY PONCHO
Shown on page 225

SIZE: Fits misses' sizes 6-14

MATERIALS: Knitting worsted, 2 ozs. each of light red, dark green and royal blue; 1 oz. each of orange, light green, pale aqua, medium turquoise, gold and winter white. Crochet hook size H.

GAUGE: Each motif = 4" square.

PONCHO: MOTIFS (make 56): With first color, ch 4, sl st in first ch to form ring.

Rnd 1: Ch 3, 2 dc in ring, (ch 3, 3 dc in ring) 3 times, ch 3; join with sl st in top of first ch 3; end off.

Rnd 2: Join 2nd color in any ch-3 sp, ch 3, 2 dc in same sp, ch 3, 3 dc in same sp, (3 dc, ch 3, 3 dc in next sp) 3 times; join; end off.

Rnd 3: Join 3rd color in any corner ch-3 sp, ch 3, 2 dc in same sp, ch 3, 3 dc in same sp, (3 dc in next sp, between 3-dc groups; 3 dc, ch 3, 3 dc in next ch-3 sp) 3 times, 3 dc in next sp between 3-dc groups; join; end off.

Joining: Arrange motifs as shown on diagram. From wrong side, with color matching one side, keeping seams elastic, sew motifs tog through top lps only. Sew A edge to B edge.

FINISHING: Run in yarn ends on wrong side.

Edging: From right side, join winter white in any ch-3 corner, sc in same sp, * ch 4, sl st in 3rd ch from hook, ch 1, sc in next sp, repeat from * around outer edge of poncho; join; end. Work same edging around neck opening.

TIE: With double strand of winter white, make ch 66" long. End off. Draw through sps marked by X on diagram. Tie ends.

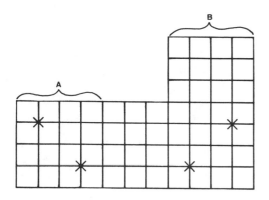

DENIM SET
Shown on page 235

SIZE: Hat, adjustable headsize. Scarf, 10" wide x 75" long, plus fringe.

MATERIALS: Knitting worsted weight yarn, 2 ozs. dark denim (DD), 1 oz. each of medium denim (MD), light denim (LD) and Cranberry (C) for hat; 4 ozs. dark denim (DD), 1 oz. medium denim (MD), 3 ozs. light denim (LD) and 2 ozs. Cranberry (C) for scarf. Crochet hooks size F for hat, size J for scarf.

GAUGE: 4 sc = 1" (size F hook, hat); 5 sts = 2" (size J hook, scarf).

HAT: With LD and size F hook, ch 4. Sl st in first ch to form ring.

Rnd 1: Ch 1, 8 sc in ring.

Rnd 2: 2 sc in each sc around–16 sc. Mark ends of rnds.

Rnd 3: Repeat rnd 2–32 sc.

Rnd 4: * Working over strand of DD, with LD, sc in each of next 2 sc, pull up a lp in next sc, drop LD, finish sc with DD, pull up a lp of DD in next sc, finish sc with LD, repeat from * around–32 sc. Always change colors in this way, finishing last sc of one color with new color and working over unused color.

Rnd 5: (LD sc in next sc, DD sc in next sc, LD sc in next sc, DD sc and LD sc in next sc, DD sc in next sc, LD sc in next sc, DD sc in next sc, LD sc and DD sc in next sc) 4 times–40 sc. Cut LD.

Rnd 6: With DD, sc around, inc 1 sc in every 5th st–48 sc.

Rnd 7: Sc around, inc 1 sc in every 8th st–54 sc.

Rnds 8 and 9: Sc around, inc 12 sc evenly spaced each rnd–78 sc. Rnd 10: Working over strand of C, (DD sc in each of next 3 sc, C sc in next sc, DD sc in next sc, 2 DD sc in next sc, C sc in next sc) 10 times, (DD sc in each of next 3 sc, C in next sc) twice–88 sc.

Rnd 11: (DD sc in next sc, C sc in next sc) 44 times. Drop DD.

Rnd 12: With C, sc around. Cut C.

Rnds 13-18: With DD, sc around.

Rnd 19: * Working over strand of MD, DD sc in each of 3 sc, MD sc in next sc, repeat from *.

Rnd 20: * DD sc in next sc, MD sc in next sc, repeat from * around. Drop DD.

Rnd 21: With MD, sc around.

Rnd 22: * Working over strand of LD, MD sc in each of 3 sc, LD sc in next sc, repeat from * around.

Rnd 23: * MD sc in next sc, LD sc in next sc, repeat from * around. Drop MD.

Rnd 24: With LD, sc around. Drop LD.

Rnd 25: With MD, sc around. Drop MD.

Rnd 26: With DD, sc around. Drop DD.

Rnd 27: With C, sc around. Drop C.

Rnd 28: With LD, sc around. Sl st in first sc. Ch 1, turn.

Rnd 29: From wrong side, * LD sc in next sc, MD sc in next sc, repeat from * around, always having both strands of yarn above hook when inserting hook in st. Sl st in first st. Ch 1, turn. Drop LD.

Rnd 30: * MD sc in LD sc, DD sc in MD sc, repeat from * around. Drop MD and DD.

Rnd 31: With C, sc around. Cut C.

Rnd 32: With DD, sc around, inc 1 sc in first st and every 5th st around–106 sc. Sl st in first st. Ch 1, turn.

Rnd 33: From wrong side, 2 DD sc in first sc, * (LD sc in next sc, DD sc in next sc) twice, LD sc and DD sc in next sc, repeat from * around–128 sc. Sl st in first st. Ch 1, turn. Drop LD.

Rnd 34: Working DD sc and MD sc alternately, inc in every 7th st around–146 sc. Drop MD.

Rnd 35: With DD, work even in sc. Cut DD.

Rnd 36: With MD, work even in sc. Drop MD.

Rnd 37: With LD, work even in sc. Sl st in first sc. Ch 1, turn.

Rnd 38: From wrong side, work LD sc and MD sc alternately around. Sl st in first st. Ch 1, turn.

Rnd 39: Work LD sc in MD sc and MD sc in LD sc around. Drop MD.

Rnd 40: With LD, work even in sc. Cut LD.

Rnd 41: Work MD sc and DD sc alternately around. End off.

SCARF: First Half: With LD and size J hook, ch 186 loosely.

Row 1 (wrong side): Sc in 2nd ch from hook and in each ch across–185 sc. Ch 1 turn.

Row 2 (right side): Sc in each sc across. Cut LD. Do not turn.

Row 3: Beg in first st of last row and working over strand of DD, LD sc in first sc, pull up a lp of LD in next st, finish sc with DD. * Working over strand of LD, pull up a lp of DD in next st, finish sc with LD; working over strand of DD, work LD sc in each of next 3 sts changing to DD in last st, repeat from * across, nd with 2 LD sc. End off LD. Cut both colors. Do not turn. **Note:** Always change colors in this way, finishing sc with new color to be used and working over unused color. Leave yarn ends hanging to be woven in later, or work over them on next row.

Row 4: Beg in first st of last row, work LD sc and DD sc alternately across. Cut LD and DD. Do not turn.

Row 5: Join DD in first st of last row, ch 3, dc in next st and in each st across. Ch 3, turn.

Row 6 (wrong side): Sk first dc, dc in each dc across, dc in top of ch 3. Ch 1, turn.

Row 7: Working over strand of C, work 2 DD sc, * C sc, 3 DD sc, repeat from * across, end 2 DD sc. End off. Do not turn.

Row 8: Work C sc and MD sc alternately across. End off. Do not turn.

Row 9: With C, work in sc across. Do not turn.

Row 10: With MD, work in sc across. Ch 1, turn.

Row 11 (wrong side): Work LD sc and MD sc alternately across, always having both strands of yarn above hook when inserting hook in st. Ch 1, turn.

Row 12: Repeat row 11. End off. Do not turn.

Row 13: With DD, sc across. End off.

2nd Half: From right side, working on opposite side of starting ch, with LD, sc in each ch across. Cut LD. Do not turn. Beg with row 3, work as for first half.

FINISHING: Cut strands of yarn in 10" lengths (or desired length) for fringe. Using 2 strands tog and matching colors of rows, knot fringe across both ends.

CROCHETED CURTAINS
Shown on page 236

SIZE: Any desired size.

MATERIALS: Mercerized crochet cotton, size 30, about 12 yards for each motif plus fill-in motif. Steel crochet hook size 10.

GAUGE: Each motif = 2½".

FIRST MOTIF: Ch 12; sl st in first ch to form ring.

Rnd 1: Ch 1, 24 sc in ring. Sl st in first sc.

Rnd 2: Ch 8, * sk next st, tr in next st, ch 3, repeat from * around, end ch 3, sl st in 5th ch of ch 8—12 sps.

Rnd 3: Ch 1, sc in same ch with sl st, * 3 sc in next sp, sc in next tr, repeat from * around, end 3 sc in last sp, sl st in first sc.

Rnd 4: Ch 5 (counts as 1 dtr), dtr in each of next 3 sc, * ch 6, dtr in each of next 4 sc, repeat from * around, end ch 6, sl st in top of ch 5.

Rnd 5: Ch 1, sc in same ch with sl st, sc in each of next 3 dtr, * 7 sc in next sp, sc in each of next 4 dtr, repeat from * around, end 7 sc in last sp, sl st in first sc. End off.

SECOND MOTIF: Work as for first motif through rnd 4.

Rnd 5: Ch 1, sc in same ch with sl st, sc in each of next 3 dtr, 3 sc in next sp, drop lp from hook; insert hook in center sc of 7 sc in sp of previous motif, draw dropped lp through; 3 sc in same sp of 2nd motif, sc in each of next 4 dtr, 3 sc in next sp, join as before to next sp of previous motif, 3 sc in same sp, * sc in each of next 4 dtr, 7 sc in next sp, repeat from * around, sl st in first sc. End off.

Join all motifs in this way, leaving 1 sp free between joinings on all motifs. Work fill-in motif in space formed by 4 motifs.

FILL-IN MOTIF: Ch 10; sl st in first ch to form ring.

Rnd 1: Ch 1, 24 sc in ring. Sl st in first sc.

Rnd 2: Ch 1, sc in first sc, * ch 4, drop lp from hook; insert hook in center sc of free sp on a motif, draw dropped lp through, ch 4, sk 2 sc on fill-in motif, sc in next sc, ch 5, drop lp from hook; insert hook in joining st between motifs, draw dropped lp through, ch 5, sk 2 sc on fill-in motif, sc in next sc, repeat from * 3 times, sl st in next sc. End off.

ROSE WHEELS
Shown on page 236

SIZE: 18" square, plus edging.

MATERIALS: Mercerized crochet cotton, size 30, 3 400-yard balls. Stell crochet hook No. 10.

GAUGE: One motif = 3¼".

FIRST MOTIF: Ch 6. Sl st in first ch to form ring.

Rnd 1: Ch 3 (counts as 1 dc), 23 dc in ring. Sl st in top of ch 3.

Rnd 2: Ch 3, sk next dc, dc in next dc, ch 6, dc in top of dc just made (cross-stitch made), * ch 3, yo hook 3 times, draw up a lp in next dc, yo and through 2 lps, yo hook, sk next dc, draw up a lp in next dc, yo and through 2 lps, yo and through 3 lps, (yo and through 2 lps) twice, ch 3, dc in center lps of long st just made (cross-stitch made), repeat from * around, end ch 3, sl st in 3rd ch of ch 6—8 cross-sts.

Rnd 3: Ch 1, * 4 sc in next ch-3 sp, repeat from * around—64 sc. Sl st in first sc.

Rnd 4: Ch 3, dc in same sc as sl st, dc in each of next 3 sc, * 2 dc in next sc, dc in each of next 3 sc, repeat from * around, sl st in top of ch 3—80 dc.

Rnd 5: Ch 6, dc in 4th ch from hook, 3 dc next to dc just made over remaining 2 ch, * sk 3 dc of last rnd, dc in next dc, ch 3, 4 dc over bar of dc just made, repeat from * around, end sl st in same ch with first dc of rnd—20 pats.

Rnd 6: Sl st in each of 3 ch to top of first pat, sc in sp between ch and first dc, * ch 6, sc in top of next pat between ch 3 and first dc, repeat from * around, end ch 6, sl st in first sc.

Rnd 7: * In next lp make sc, 4 hdc, ch 6, sc in last hdc made (picot), 4 hdc, sc; sl st in next sc, repeat from * around. End off.

SECOND MOTIF: Work 2nd motif same as first motif through rnd 6.

Rnd 7: * In next lp make sc, 4 hdc, ch 3, drop lp from hook; insert hook in a picot of previous motif, pick up dropped lp, and pull up through picot, ch 3, sc in last hdc made, 4 hdc, sc in same lp of 2nd motif, sl st in next sc, repeat from * twice (3 picots joined to 3 picots of previous motif), finish 2nd motif as for first motif.

Make and join 16 motifs in this manner, forming a square, 4 motifs by 4 motifs. Leave 2 picots free on each motif at "corners" between joinings of 3 picots on "sides". At the four corners of the square, there will be 12 picots free on each corner motif. On the sides of the square each motif has 7 picots free.

FILL-IN MOTIF (make 9): Ch 5. Sl st in first ch to form ring.

Rnd 1: Ch 3, 15 dc in ring. Sl st in top of ch 3.

Rnd 2: Ch 3, dc in next dc, * ch 4; holding back last lp of each dc, dc in each of next 2 dc, yo and through 3 lps on hook, repeat from * around, end ch 4, sl st in top of ch 3.

Rnd 3: * Sc, 3 hdc in next lp, ch 2, drop lp from hook; insert hook in free picot between four joined motifs, pick up dropped lp and pull through picot, ch 2, sc in last hdc made, 3 hdc, sc in same lp of fill-in motif, sl st in next sc, repeat from * 7 times.

HALF-MOTIFS (make 12): Ch 5. Sl st in first ch to form ring.

Row 1: Ch 3, 9 dc in ring. Ch 3, turn.

Row 2: Dc in next dc, * ch 4; holding back last lp of each dc, dc in each of next 2 dc, yo and through 3 lps on hook, repeat from * 3 times, working last dc in top of ch 3. Ch 1, turn.

Row 3: Work as for rnd 3 of fill-in motif, joining 2 picots of half-motif to 2 free picots of a large motif on edge of square and next 2 picots of half-motif to 2 free picots of adjoining large motif on edge of square.

BORDER: Rnd 1: Join thread in 4th free picot (there are 8 free picots) of a corner motif; ch 4, tr in 5th free picot of motif; ch 9, tr in top of ch 4 (corner lp); working along side of pillow, * ch 5, tr in 5th picot of corner motif, ** (ch 5, sc in next free picot) 3 times, ch 5, tr in side of next scallop just before joined picot, ch 5, sc in next sp of half-motif, ch 5, sc in center ring of half-motif, ch 5, sc in last sp of half-motif, ch 5, tr in side of next scallop just after joined picot, repeat from ** twice, (ch 5, sc in next free picot of corner motif) 3 times, ch 5, tr in next (4th) free picot, ch 5, yo hook 4 times, pull up a lp in 4th picot, (yo and through 2 lps) twice, yo hook twice, pull up a lp in 5th picot, (yo and through 2 lps) 6 times, ch 5, tr in center of long st just made (to complete cross-stitch), repeat from * around, end tr in 4th picot of corner motif, ch 5, sl st in 4th ch of ch 9 at beg of rnd.

Rnd 2: Sl st in corner ch-5 sp, ch 3, 2 dc in same sp, ch 2, 3 dc in same sp, * ch 1, 3 dc in 3rd ch of next lp, ** ch 1, 3 dc in next tr, (ch 1, 3 dc in 3rd ch of next lp) twice, ch 1, 3 dc in next sc, (ch 1, 3 dc in 3rd ch of next lp) twice, ch 1, 3 dc in next tr, (ch 1, 3 dc in 3rd ch of next lp) 4 times, repeat from ** twice, ch 1, 3 dc in next tr, (ch 1, 3 dc in 3rd ch of next lp) twice, ch 1, 3 dc in next sc, (ch 1, 3 dc in 3rd ch of next lp) twice, ch 1, 3 dc in next tr, ch 1, 3 dc in 3rd ch of next lp ch 1; in corner ch-5 sp work 3 dc, ch 2, 3 dc, repeat from * around, end ch 1, sl st in top of ch 3 at beg of rnd.

Rnd 3: Sl st across next 2 dc, sl st in corner ch-2 sp; ch 3, 2 dc, ch 2, 3 dc in corner sp, * ch 1, dc in next ch-1 sp, ch 1, dc in center dc of next 3 dc group, repeat from * across side, ending dc in ch-1 sp before corner, ch 1, 3 dc, ch 2, 3 dc in corner sp, repeat from first * around, end sl st in top of ch 3 at beg of rnd.

Rnd 4: Sl st across next 2 dc, sl st in corner ch-2 sp; ch 3, 2 dc, ch 2, 3 dc in corner sp, * ch 1, dc in next ch-1 sp, repeat from * to next corner, ch 1, 3 dc, ch 2, 3 dc in corner sp, repeat from first * around, end sl st in top of ch 3 at beg of rnd.

Rnd 5: Repeat rnd 4.

Rnd 6: Sl st across next 2 dc, sl st in corner ch-2 sp; ch 3, 2 dc, ch 2, 3 dc in corner sp, * ch 4; holding back on hook last lp of each dc, dc in each of next 2 sps, yo hook and through 3 lps on hook, repeat from * to next corner, ch 4, 3 dc, ch 2, 3 dc in corner sp, repeat from first * around, end sl st in top of ch 3 at beg of rnd.

Rnd 7: Sl st across next 2 dc, sl st in corner ch-2 sp; ch 6, dc in 4th ch from hook, 3 dc next to dc just made over remaining 2 ch, dc in corner sp, ch 3, 4 dc over bar of dc just made, * dc in next sp, ch 3, 4 dc over bar of dc just made, repeat from * across to corner, (dc in corner sp, ch 3, 4 dc over bar of dc just made) 3 times, repeat from first * around, end dc in corner sp, ch 3, 4 dc over bar of dc just made, sl st in same ch with first dc of rnd.

Rnd 8: Sl st up along 3 ch to top of first pat, ch 3, 2 dc in next dc, ch 2, 3 dc in next dc, * ch 5, sc in first dc of next pat, repeat from * to corner, ch 5, 3 dc in first dc of center pat at corner, ch 2, 3 dc in next dc, repeat from first * around, end ch 5, sl st in top of ch 3 at beg of rnd.

Rnd 9: Sl st across next 2 dc, sl st in corner ch-2 sp; ch 3, 2 dc, ch 2, 3 dc in corner sp, * ch 5, sc in next lp, repeat from * to corner, ch 5, 3 dc, ch 2, 3 dc in corner sp, repeat from first * around, end ch 5, sl st in top of ch 3.

Rnd 10: Sl st across next 2 dc, sl st in corner ch-2 sp; ch 3, 2 dc, ch 2, 3 dc in corner sp, * (ch 5, sc in next lp) 6 times, ** 4 dc, ch 2, 4 dc in next lp, sc in next lp, (ch 5, sc in next lp) 7 times, repeat from ** 3 times, 4 dc, ch 2, 4 dc in next lp, sc in next lp, (ch 5, sc in next lp) 5 times, ch 5, 3 dc, ch 2, 3 dc in corner sp, repeat from * around, end ch 5, sl st in top of ch 3.

Rnd 11: Sl st across next 2 dc, sl st in corner ch-2 sp; ch 3, dc in corner sp, ch 3, sc in corner sp, ch 3, dc in corner sp, ch 3, sc in corner sp, ch 3; holding back on hook last lp of each dc, 2 dc in corner sp, yo and through 3 lps on hook (2-dc cluster), * (ch 5, sc in next lp) 6 times, ** ch 5; in ch-2 sp make 2-dc cluster, ch 3, sc, ch 3, dc, ch 3 sc, ch 3, 2-dc cluster, (ch 5, sc in next lp) 7 times, repeat from ** 3 times, ch 5; in ch-2 sp make 2-dc cluster, ch 3, sc, ch 3, dc, ch 3, sc, ch 3, 2-dc cluster, (ch 5, sc in next lp) 6 times, ch 5; in corner sp make 2-dc cluster, ch 3, sc, ch 3, dc, ch 3, sc, ch 3, 2-dc cluster, repeat from * around, end ch 5, sl st in top of ch 3.

Rnd 12: Sl st to top of ch 3 after sc in corner sp, ch 5, dc in ch-3 lp after dc, * (ch 5, sc in next ch-5 lp) 7 times, ** ch 5, sc in center dc of next pat, (ch 5, sc in next ch-5 lp) 8 times, repeat from ** 3 times, ch 5, sc in center dc of next pat, (ch 5, sc in next ch-5 lp) 7 times, ch 5, dc in ch-3 lp before center dc of corner pat, ch 2, dc in ch-3 lp after center dc, repeat from * around, end ch 5, sl st in 3rd ch of ch 5 at beg of rnd.

Rnd 13: Beg with sl st in corner ch-2 sp, repeat rnd 7.

Rnd 14: Sl st up along 3 ch to top of first pat, ch 3, 2 dc in next dc, ch 2, 3 dc in next dc, * ch 1, dc in first dc of next pat, ch 1, dc in next dc or same pat, repeat from * across side, ch 1, 3 dc in first dc of center pat at corner, ch 2, 3 dc in next dc, repeat from first * around, end ch 1, sl st in top of ch 3.

Rnds 15–18: Repeat rnd 4.

Rnd 19: Repeat rnd 6.

Edging: Corner Scallop: Row 1: (Ch 4, dc in corner sp) twice, ch 4, sc in last dc of corner pat, turn.

Row 2: * Ch 2, yo hook 3 times, draw up a lp in center lp at corner, yo and through 2 lps, yo hook, draw up a lp in same corner lp, yo and through 2 lps, yo and through 3 lps, (yo and through 2 lps) twice, ch 2, dc in center of long st just made (to complete cross-st), repeat from * 3 times, ch 2, sc in next ch-4 lp at corner, ch 3, sc in next lp, turn.

Row 3: (3 dc in next sp, dc in next st) 8 times, 3 dc in next sp, sc in next sp on border, ch 3, sc in next sp on border, turn.

Row 4: Ch 3, 4 dc in last ch-3 sp made, (sk 2 dc on row 3, dc in next dc, ch 3, 4 dc over bar of last dc) 10 times, sc in same lp on border as last sc of row 2, ch 3, sc in next sp on border, turn.

Row 5: (Ch 3, sc under ch 3 of next pat) 11 times, ch 3, sc in same sp on border as sc at end of row 3.

Next Scallop: Row 1: (ch 5, sc in next lp on border) 6 times, ch 3, sc in next lp, turn.

Row 2: Ch 2, yo hook 3 times, draw up a lp in next ch-5 lp, * yo and through 2 lps, yo hook, draw up a lp in same ch-5 lp, yo and through 2 lps, yo and through 3 lps, (yo and through 2 lps) twice, ch 2, dc in center of long st just made (to complete cross-st), ch 2, yo hook 3 times, draw up a lp in same ch-5 lp, repeat from * until 3 cross-sts are completed, ch 2, sc in next lp, ch 3, sc in next lp; turn.

Row 3: (3 dc in next sp, dc in next st) 6 times, 3 dc in next sp, sc in next sp on border, ch 3, sc in next sp on border, turn.

Row 4: Ch 3, 4 dc in last ch-3 sp made, (sk 2 dc on row 3, dc in next dc, ch 3, 4 dc over bar of last dc) 8 times, sc in same lp on border as last sc of row 2, ch 3, sc in next lp on border, turn.

Row 5: (Ch 3, sc under ch 3 of next pat) 9 times, ch 3, sc in same lp on border as sc at end of row 3.

Repeat Next Scallop 5 times across side (6 scallops on side). Ch 5, sc in next lp on border to lp before corner. Repeat from Corner Scallop around. After last side scallop of last side has been made, (ch 5, sc in next lp) twice. This should bring you to lp before corner scallop.

Rnd 6: Working in corner scallop, (4 dc in next sp, dc in sc) 11 times, 4 dc in next sp, sc in next lp between scallops, ch 5, sc in next lp; * working in side scallop, (4 dc in next sp, dc in sc) 9 times, 4 dc in next sp, sc in next lp between scallops, ch 5, sc in next lp, repeat from * across side, repeat from beg of rnd, end in lp before first corner scallop.

Rnd 7: * Ch 3, sk 3 dc, dc in next dc, ch 4, sc in top of last dc made (picot), (dc in same dc, ch-4 picot) twice, ch 2, sk 3 dc, sc in next dc, repeat from * around scallop, end ch 2, sc in next ch-5 lp, repeat from first * around. End off.

FINISHING: Block crocheted piece, starching lightly, if desired. Sew to covered pillow inside scalloped edge.

ROSE PILLOW
Shown on page 236

SIZE: 16″ square.

MATERIALS: Mercerized knitting and crochet cotton, 1 250-yard ball white. Steel crochet hook No. 6. Materials for pillow cover, ½ yard. Pillow form, 16″ square.

GAUGE: 4 bls or sps = 1″; 4 rows = 1″.

To Make 1 Space (sp): Dc in st, ch 2, sk 2 sts, dc in next st (1 space); ch 2, sk 2 sts, dc in next st for each additional space.

To Make 1 Block (bl): Dc in each of 4 sts (1 block); dc in each of next 3 sts for each additional block

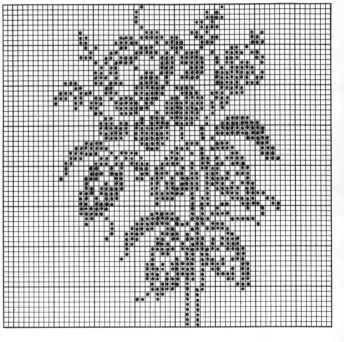

Chart Notes: Spaces are shown on chart as open squares, blocks by dotted squares.

PILLOW TOP: Beg at bottom edge, ch 200. (Always ch more than directions call for; extra ch can be cut off later.)

Row 1: Dc in 8th ch from hook (1 sp), (ch 2, sk 2 ch, dc in next ch) 25 times, dc in each of next 3 ch (1 bl), ch 2, sk 2 ch, dc in next ch (1 sp), dc in each of next 3 ch (1 bl), (ch 2, sk 2 ch, dc in next ch) 36 times. Ch 5, turn each row.

Row 2: Sk first dc, dc in next dc, (ch 2, sk 2 ch, dc in next dc) 35 times, dc in each of next 3 dc (bl over bl), ch 2, dc in next dc (sp over sp), dc in each of next 3 dc (bl over bl), (ch 2, dc in next dc) 25 times, ch 2, sk 2 ch, dc in next ch.

Beg with row 3 of chart, following chart from right to left on right side rows (odd rows) and from left to right on wrong side rows (even rows), work to top of chart. Work 5 more rows of spaces at top or as many as needed to make piece square. End off.

FINISHING: Wash piece if necessary; block; cut 2 pieces of fabric same size as pillow top. Baste pillow top, right side up to right side of one fabric square. Place fabric squares right sides together, and stitch together around three sides, taking ¼" seams. Turn pillow cover to right side. Insert pillow form. Close opening.

PINWHEEL SQUARES

Shown on page 236

SIZE: 18" square, plus edging.

MATERIALS: Mercerized crochet cotton, size 30, 3 400-yard balls. Steel crochet hook No. 10.

GAUGE: Each motif is 4¼" square.

FIRST MOTIF: Ch 6, sl st in first ch to form ring.

Rnd 1: Ch 1, 16 sc in ring. Sl st in first sc.

Rnd 2: Ch 1, sc in first sc, (ch 3, sk 1 sc, sc in next sc) 7 times, ch 3, sl st in first sc.

Rnd 3: (3 sc in next lp, ch 3) 8 times.

Rnd 4: (Sk next sc, sc in each of 2 sc, 2 sc in next lp, ch 3) 8 times.

Rnd 5: (Sk next sc, sc in each of 3 sc, 2 sc in next lp, ch 3) 8 times.

Rnd 6: (Sk next sc, sc in each of 4 sc, 2 sc in next lp, ch 3) 8 times.

Rnd 7: (Sk next sc, sc in each of 5 sc, 2 sc in next lp, ch 3) 8 times.

Rnd 8: (Sk next sc, sc in each of 6 sc, 2 sc in next lp, ch 3) 8 times.

Rnd 9: (Sk next sc, sc in each of 6 sc, ch 3, sc in next lp, ch 3) 8 times.

Rnd 10: (Sk next sc, sc in each of 4 sc, ch 3, sc in next lp, ch 3, sc in next lp, ch 3) 8 times.

Rnd 11: (Sk next sc, sc in each of 2 sc, ch 3, sc in next lp, ch 3, sc in next lp, ch 3, sc in next lp, ch 3) 8 times.

Rnd 12: (Sc in next lp, ch 4) 32 times.

Rnd 13: * Dc in next lp, ch 4, dc in same lp, (ch 4, sc in next lp) 7 times, ch 4, repeat from * 3 times. Mark first dc of rnd.

Rnd 14: * Dc, ch 4, dc in next (corner) lp, ch 4, sc in next lp) 8 times, ch 4, repeat from * around.

Rnd 15: * Dc, ch 4, dc in corner lp, (ch 4, sc in next lp) 9 times, ch 4, repeat from * around.

Rnds 16–19: Work as for rnd 15 having 1 more lp each side each rnd.

Rnd 20: Work as for rnd 15 but work ch-5 lps instead of ch-4 lps—15 ch-5 lps each side, plus ch-5 lp in each corner. End last rnd with ch 5, sl st in corner lp.

SECOND MOTIF: Work as for first motif through rnd 19, end ch 4 before corner.

Joining: Rnd 20: Dc in corner lp, ch 2, sl st in corner lp of previous motif, ch 2, dc in corner lp of new motif, (ch 2, sl st in next lp of previous motif, ch 2, sc in next lp of new motif) 14 times, ch 2, sl st in last side lp of previous motif, ch 2, dc in corner lp of new motif, ch 2, sl st in corner lp of previous motif, ch 2, dc in corner lp of new motif, finish motif as for previous motif.

Join 9 motifs tog, 3 × 3, in this way. At corners where 4 motifs meet, join in same joining st.

Border: Rnd 1: Join thread in corner lp of pillow, ch 3, 2 dc, ch 3, 3 dc in corner lp, * ch 1, 3 dc in center ch of next ch-5 lp, repeat from * to next corner, ch 1, 3 dc, ch 3, 3 dc in corner lp, repeat from first * around, end ch 1, sl st in top of ch 3.

Rnd 2: Sl st to corner lp, ch 3, 2 dc, ch 3, 3 dc in corner lp, * ch 1, dc in center dc of next 3 dc, ch 1, dc in next ch-1 sp, repeat from * to next corner, ch 1, dc in center dc of 3 dc at corner, ch 1, 3 dc, ch 3, 3 dc in corner lp, repeat from first * around, end ch 1, sl st in top of ch 3.

Rnd 3: Sl st to corner lp, ch 3, 2 dc, ch 3, 3 dc in corner lp, * ch 1, dc in next ch-1 sp, repeat from * to next corner, ch 1, 3 dc, ch 3, 3 dc in corner lp, repeat from first * around, end ch 1, sl st in top of ch 3.

Rnd 4: Sl st to corner lp, ch 3, 2 dc, ch 3, 3 dc in corner lp, * ch 1, dc in center dc of next 3 dc, ** ch 1, dc in next ch-1 sp, repeat from ** across to next corner, ch 1, dc in center dc of 3 dc at corner, ch 1, 3 dc, ch 3, 3 dc in corner lp, repeat from * around, end ch 1, sl st in top of ch 3.

Rnd 5: Sl st to corner lp, ch 3; holding back on hook last lp of each dc, 2 dc in corner lp, yo and through 3 lps on hook (cluster), ch 5, cluster of 3 dc in corner lp, ch 5; * holding back on hook last lp of each dc, 2 dc in next ch-1 sp, 1 dc in next ch-1 sp, yo and through 4 lps on hook, ch 5, sk 1 sp, repeat from * across to next corner, ch 5, cluster, ch 5, cluster in corner lp, ch 5, repeat from first * around, end ch 5, sc in top of first cluster.

Rnd 6: Work hdc, 7 dc, hdc in corner lp, sc in next cluster, * hdc, 7 dc, hdc in next lp, sc in cluster, repeat from * around, end sl st in first sc.

Rnd 7: Sl st to center of corner scallop, ch 5, dc in center dc of scallop, (ch 2, dc in same place) twice, * ch 4, dc, ch 2, dc in center dc of next scallop, repeat from * across to next corner, ch 4, dc in center dc of corner scallop, (ch 2, dc) 3 times in same st, repeat from first * around, end sl st in 3rd ch of ch 5.

Rnd 8: Sl st in next ch-2 sp, ch 5, dc in same sp, ch 2, sc in next sp, (ch 2, dc) twice in next sp, * ch 2, sc in next ch-4 lp, (ch 2, dc) twice in next ch-2 sp, repeat from * to next corner, (ch 2, dc) twice in first corner sp, ch 2, sc in next sp, (ch 2, dc) twice in next sp, repeat from first * around, end sl st in 3rd ch of ch 5.

Rnd 9: Sl st in next ch-2 sp, ch 5, dc in same sp, ch 2, sc in next sp, ch 4, sc in next sp, (ch 2, dc) twice in next sp, * ch 2, sc in next sc, sk next ch-2 sp, (ch 2, dc) twice in next ch-2 sp, repeat from * across to next corner, sk first ch-2 at corner, (ch 2, dc) twice in next ch-2 sp, ch 2, sc in next sp, ch 4, sc in next sp, (ch 2, dc) twice in next sp, repeat from first * around, end sl st in 3rd ch of ch 5.

Rnd 10: Sl st in next ch-2 sp, ch 1, sc in sp, (ch 5, tr) twice in ch-4 lp at corner, * ch 5, sc in center ch-2 sp of next "scallop", repeat from * to next corner, (ch 5, tr) twice in ch-4 lp at corner, repeat from first * around, end sl st in first sc.

Rnd 11: Work hdc, 7 dc, hdc in next lp, sc in

tr, hdc, 3 dc, ch 2, 3 dc, hdc in corner lp, sc in tr, * hdc, 7 dc, hdc in next lp, sc in sc, repeat from * to next corner lp, hdc, 3 dc, ch 2, 3 dc, hdc in corner lp, sc in tr, repeat from first * around, end sl st in first hdc.

Rnd 12: Sl st to center of first scallop, ch 3, 2 dc in center dc of scallop, ch 3, 3 dc in 2nd dc of corner scallop, ch 3, 3 dc, ch 3, 3 dc in corner ch-2 sp, ch 3, sk 1 dc, 3 dc in next dc, * ch 3, 3 dc in center of next scallop, repeat from * to next corner, ch 3, 3 dc in 2nd dc of corner scallop, (ch 3, 3 dc) twice in corner ch-2 sp, ch 3, sk 1 dc, 3 dc in next dc, repeat from first * around, end ch 3, sl st in top of ch 3.

Rnd 13: Ch 4, sk next dc, dc in next dc, ch 1, dc in next sp, ch 1, dc in next dc, ch 1, sk next dc, dc in next dc, ch 1, dc in next sp, ch 1, ** 3 dc, ch 3, 3 dc in corner sp, * ch 1, dc in next sp, ch 1, dc in next dc, ch 1, sk next dc, dc in next dc, repeat from * across to next corner, repeat from ** around, end sl st in 3rd ch of ch 4.

Rnd 14: Sl st in ch-1 sp, ch 4, * dc in next sp, ch 1, repeat from * to corner, 3 dc, ch 3, 3 dc in corner sp, ch 1, repeat from first * around, end ch 1, sl st in 3rd ch of ch 4.

Rnd 15: Work as for rnd 14, but add 1 ch-1 sp each side of corner by working dc in center dc of 3 dc at corner.

Rnds 16 and 17: Repeat rnd 14.

Rnd 18: Sl st in ch-1 sp, ch 3; holding back on hook last lp of each dc, dc in same sp, dc in next sp, yo and through 3 lps on hook, (ch 3, holding back on hook last lp of each dc, 2 dc in next sp, dc in next sp, yo and through 4 lps on hook) twice (3 clusters made), ** ch 3, 3-dc cluster in sp before corner, ch 3, cluster, ch 5, cluster in corner lp, ch 3, cluster in next ch-1 sp, * ch 3; holding back on hook last lp of each dc, 2 dc in next sp, dc in next sp, yo and through 4 lps on hook, repeat from * across to sp before corner, repeat from ** around, end ch 3, sl st in top of first cluster—64 clusters each side.

Scalloped Edge: Rnd 1: 2 sc, ch 2, 2 sc in next sp, ch 2, 2 sc in next sp, ch 2, 2 sc, ch 2, 2 sc in next sp, ch 2, sc in next sp, (sp before corner); ** in corner lp, work 13 dc, sc in next sp, * (ch 2, 2 sc, ch 2, 2 sc in next sp, ch 2, 2 sc in next sp) twice, ch 2, 2 sc, ch 2, 2 sc in next sp, ch 2, sc in next sp, 7 dc in next sp, sc in next sp, repeat from * 6 times, (ch 2, 2 sc, ch 2, 2 sc in next sp, ch 2, 2 sc in next sp) twice, ch 2, 2 sc, ch 2, 2 sc in next sp, ch 2, sc in next sp (sp before corner), repeat from ** around, end 7 dc in next sp, sc in next sp, ch 2, 2 sc, ch 2, 2 sc in next sp, ch 2, 2 sc in last sp, ch 2, sl st in first sc.

Rnd 2: Sl st to first ch-2 sp, ch 1, 2 sc in sp, (ch 2, 2 sc in next ch-2 sp) 3 times, ** ch 2, sk sp before corner, dc in first dc, (ch 2, sk 1 dc, dc in next dc) 6 times, * ch 2, sk next ch-2 sp, 2 sc in next ch-2 sp, (ch 2, 2 sc in next sp) 6 times, ch 2, sk next ch-2 sp, dc in first dc, (ch 2, sk 1 dc, dc in next dc) 3 times, repeat from * across to corner, repeat from ** around, end 2 sc in last sp, ch 2, sl st in first sc.

Rnd 3: Sl st across to next ch-2 sp, ch 1, 2 sc in sp, (ch 2, 2 sc in next sp) twice, ** ch 2, dc, ch 2, dc in first dc at corner, (ch 2, sc in next sp, ch 2, dc, ch 2, dc in next dc) 6 times, * ch 2, sk next sp, 2 sc in next sp, (ch 2, 2 sc in next sp) 5 times, ch 2, sk next sp, dc, ch 2, dc in next dc, (ch 2, sc in next sp, ch 2, dc, ch 2, dc in next dc) 3 times, repeat from * across to corner, repeat from ** around, end 2 sc in last sp, ch 2, sl st in first sc.

Rnd 4: Sl st across to next ch-2 sp, ch 1, 2 sc in sp, ch 2, 2 sc in next sp, ** (ch 2, dc in next dc, ch 2, sc in next sp, ch 2, dc in next dc) 7 times, * ch 2, sk next sp, 2 sc in next sp, (ch 2, 2 sc in next sp) 4 times, (ch 2, dc in next dc, ch 2, sc in next sp, ch 2, dc in next dc) 4 times, repeat from * across to corner, repeat from ** around, end ch 2, sk next sp, 2 sc in next sp, (ch 2, 2 sc in next sp) twice, ch 2, sl st in first sc.

Rnd 5: Sl st across to next ch-2 sp, ch 1, 2 sc in sp, ** ch 2; working in corner scallop, dc in first dc, (ch 3, dc in next dc, ch 2, sc in next sp, ch 2, dc in next dc) 6 times, ch 3, dc in last dc, * ch 2, sk next sp, 2 sc in next sp, (ch 2, 2 sc in next sp) 3 times, ch 2, dc in next dc, (ch 3, dc in next dc, ch 2, sc in next sp, ch 2, dc in next dc) 3 times, ch 3, dc in last dc of scallop, repeat from * across to corner, repeat from ** around, end ch 2, sk next sp, 2 sc in next sp, (ch 2, 2 sc in next sp) twice, ch 2, sl st in first sc.

Rnd 6: Sl st to first dc of corner scallop, ch 1, ** sc in dc, (hdc, 3 dc, hdc in next ch-3 lp, sc in next dc, ch 3, sc in next dc) 6 times, hdc, 3 dc, hdc in next ch-3 lp, sc in next dc, ch 3, sk next sp, 2 sc in next sp, (ch 2, 2 sc in next sp) twice, * ch 2, sc in next dc, (hdc, 3 dc, hdc in next ch-3 lp, sc in next dc, ch 3, sc in next dc) 3 times, hdc, 3 dc, hdc in next ch-3 lp, sc in next dc, sk next sp, (ch 2, 2 sc in next sp) 3 times, repeat from * across to corner, ch 2, repeat from ** around, end ch 2, sl st in first sc.

Rnd 7: Ch 1, ** (sc in sc, ch 3, sc in next sc, hdc, 3 dc, hdc in next lp) 6 times, sc in sc, * ch 2, sk next sp, (2 sc in next sp, ch 2) twice, sk next sp, (sc in next sc, ch 3, sc in next sc, hdc, 3 dc, hdc in next lp) 3 times, sc in next sc, ch 3, sc in next sc, repeat from * across to corner, ch 2, sk sp before corner, repeat from ** around, end ch 2, sl st in first sc.

Rnd 8: Sl st in first lp, ch 5, sc in 3rd ch from hook for picot, (dc in same lp, ch 2, sc in dc) twice, dc in same lp, * ch 2, sc in center dc of next scallop, ch 2, dc in next lp, (ch 2, sc in dc, dc in same lp) 3 times, repeat from * around corner scallop, (7 picot shells), ** ch 2, sk next sp, 2 sc in next ch-2 sp, ch 2, sk next ch-2 sp, work 4 picot shells in next side scallop, repeat from ** 6 times, ch 2, sk next sp, 2 sc in next ch-2 sp, ch 2, work 7 picot shells around corner scallop; repeat from first ** around, end ch 2, sl st in 3rd ch of ch 5 at beg of rnd. End off.

FINISHING: Block crocheted piece, starching lightly, if desired. Sew to covered pillow inside scalloped edge.

*Five brilliant flower colors stripe this afghan, crocheted in a
fascinating four-row pattern that forms six-petaled posies.
A frame of solid crochet borders the afghan, helps to shape it.
Worked in one piece, Flower Striped Afghan is 50″ × 60″.
Directions, page 159.*

233

Baby bunting in rainbow colors is simple to make in bands of single crochet. Long stitches worked one, two, or three rows below create the interesting overlay pattern. Bunting has a zipper closing on front for quick on-and-off. Matching cap is separate, ties on. For Baby Bunting, see page 242.

Brimmed hat in denim blues and red is worked in rounds of single crochet. On patterned rows with more than one color, extra color is hidden inside work. Over six-foot muffler in matching colors has stripes in different stitches. Directions, Denim Set, page 226. Greens and reds predominate in a winter twosome that is worked in single crochet, but is not easy to make. Cloche is circular with patterns crocheted in. Two-yard scarf is worked in rows entirely from the right side. Directions for Fringy Scarf Set on page 222.

Here is traditional cotton lace used in brand-new ways! Lacy curtains, made of two motifs, let in light, yet give privacy, may be made to any size. Directions on page 228. Heirloom motifs center two pillows prettily trimmed with picot shells that "float." Directions for Rose Wheels, page 228. Directions for Pinwheel Squares, page 231. A big, beautiful rose blooms on a field of filet mesh for a 16" Rose Pillow, page 230.

Roses and leaves worked in filet crochet form lacy appliques and edgings for bath and hand towels. Oval bath mat, cut from fabric to match the towel set, is completely covered with crochet—a giant butterfly sporting in a rose garden. Butcher's twine is used for the crochet. Directions for Bath Set, page 157.

Heavy cotton place mat in sun-kissed citrus colors is crocheted in a unique way. A row of shells forms half-circles from bottom to top of mat, then shells complete the circles from top to bottom. Working from one side of the mat to the other, the joined circles form the pattern. Directions for Orange and Green Mat, page 216.

This large, delicious crocheted orange slice can be a hot mat or a place mat. Done in quick-crochet cotton with easy stitches, it's a cinch to make. Segment dividers are embroidered in chain stitch, seeds in satin stitch. Leaves, crocheted separately and attached, are optional. Directions for making Orange Hot Mat, page 216.

Cheerful checkerboard place mat to brighten a breakfast table (or any informal meal) is in quick-to-crochet cotton. The checkerboard pattern is the same on both sides, a simple repeat row of double crochets. The red side strip with bold white "polka dots" is worked first, the checkerboard section next, and finally, the red border that finishes it all off so neatly. Directions opposite.

RED, WHITE AND BLUE MAT
Shown opposite

SIZE: 12″ × 18″.

MATERIALS: Coats & Clark's O.N.T. Speed-Cro-Sheen, 1 100-yard ball of red (R), 2 balls of white (W) and blue (B) for each mat. Steel crochet hook No. 2.

GAUGE: 6 dc = 1″; 5 rows = 2″.

Note: When changing colors, work last dc of one color until there are 2 lps left on hook, drop strand; complete dc with next color to be used. Work with new color over strand of color not in use to hide it in work.

MAT: With R, ch 62 loosely.

Row 1: Dc in 4th ch from hook, dc in each remaining ch—60 dc, counting ch 3 as 1 dc. Turn each row, but do not ch.

Row 2: Sc in first dc, ch 1 (counts as first dc), dc in each dc across, dc in top of ch 3.

Row 3: Sc in first dc, ch 1, dc in each dc across, dc in ch 1.

Row 4: Sc in first dc, ch 1, dc in each of next 3 dc, * change to W (see Note), W dc in each of next 4 dc, change to R, R dc in each of next 4 dc, repeat from * across, end R dc in 3 dc, R dc in ch 1.

Row 5: Sc in first dc, ch 1, dc in each of next 2 dc, * change to W, W dc in each of next 6 dc, change to R, R dc in each of next 2 dc, repeat from * across, end 3 R dc.

Row 6: Repeat row 4.

Row 7: With R, work even in dc. Cut R.

Row 8: Pick up W at beg of last row, pull through top of ch 1, ch 1, sc in same st, ch 1, work even in dc across.

Row 9: Join B; with B, sc in first dc, ch 1, dc in each of next 2 dc; with W, dc in each of next 3 dc, * with B, dc in each of next 3 dc, with W, dc in each of next 3 dc, repeat from * across.

Repeat row 9 until piece is 17″ long or desired length, working 3 B dc in 3 W dc, and 3 W dc in 3 B dc. End off.

FINISHING: Rnd 1: With R, work 1 rnd of dc around mat working 3 dc in each corner. Sl st in first dc.

Rnd 2: Working from left to right, work sc in each st around. Join; end off.

ROSE SHELL
Shown on page 247

SIZES: Directions for size 8. Changes for sizes 10, 12, and 14 are in parentheses.

Body Bust Size: 31½″ (32½″-34″-36″).

Blocked Bust Size: 32½″ (33½″-35″-37″).

MATERIALS: Knitting and crochet cotton, 4 (5-5-6) 250-yard balls. Steel crochet hook No. 8.

GAUGE: 10 meshes = 3″; 4 rows = 1″.

To Bind Off: At beg of row, sl st loosely across each st to be bound-off, then ch 5 and continue across row; at end of row, work in pat to within specified number of meshes to be bound off.

To Dec 1 Mesh: At beg of row, ch 3, sk first mesh, dc in next dc (counts as 1 dc), ch 2, dc in next dc (1 mesh); at end of row, work to last dc, ch 2, yo, pull up a lp in last dc, yo and through 2 lps on hook, yo, pull up a lp in 3rd ch of turning ch, yo and through 2 lps on hook, yo and through 3 lps on hook.

To Inc 1 Mesh: At beg of row, ch 4, dc in first dc; at end of row, (ch 2, dc in 3rd ch of turning ch) twice.

To Make Meshes: Dc in dc, ch 2, sk 2 sts, dc in next dc (1 mesh), ch 2, sk 2 sts, dc in next dc for each additional mesh.

To Make Blocks: Dc in each of 4 sts (1 block); dc in each of next 3 sts for each additional block.

Chart Notes: Meshes are shown on chart as open squares, blocks by X squares.

BLOUSE: BACK: Beg at lower edge, ch 167 (173-179-191).

Row 1: Dc in 8th ch from hook (1 mesh), * ch 2, sk next 2 ch, dc in next dc, repeat from * across— 54 (56-58-62) meshes. Ch 5, turn.

Rows 2 and 3: Sk first dc and ch-2 sp, dc in next dc (1 mesh), * ch 2, dc in next dc, repeat from * across, end ch 2, sk next 2 ch of turning ch, dc in next ch. Ch 5, turn. Check gauge; piece should measure 16¼″ (16¾″-17½″-18½″) wide.

Pattern: Row 4: Following chart 1, work from right to left (see Chart Notes). Ch 5, turn.

Row 5: Following chart 1, work from left to right. Ch 5, turn.

Rows 6–13: Repeat last 2 rows 4 times, dec 1 mesh (see To Dec 1 Mesh) each side of row 11—52 (54-56-60) meshes. Ch 5, turn.

Continued on page 248

BABY BUNTING
Shown on page 234

SIZE: Up to 1 year.

MATERIALS: Knitting worsted, 2 4-oz. skeins each of red, royal blue, kelly green, and yellow. Crochet hook size I or J. 18″ red zipper.

GAUGE: 3 sc = 1″; 4 rows = 1″.

To Bind Off: At beg of row, sl st across specified number of sts; at end of row, leave specified number of sts unworked.

BUNTING: BACK: With green, ch 56 loosely.

Row 1: Sc in 2nd ch from hook and in each ch across—55 sc. Ch 1, turn each row.

Rows 2-4: Sc in each sc. At end of row 4, drop green. Join red, ch 1, turn.

Row 5: * Sc in next sc, sc in next sc 1 row below (row 3), sc in next sc 2 rows below (row 2), sc in next sc 3 rows below (row 1), sc in next sc 2 rows below, sc in next sc 1 row below, repeat from * across, end sc in last sc.

Rows 6-8: Repeat rows 2-4. At end of row 8, drop red. Join yellow, ch 1, turn.

Rows 9-12: With yellow, repeat rows 5-8. At end of row 12, drop yellow. Join blue, ch 1, turn.

Row 13: With blue, repeat row 5.

Row 14: Dec 1 sc each end of row (to dec 1 sc, pull up a lp in each of 2 sc, yo hook and through 3 lps on hook).

Rows 15 and 16: Repeat row 2. At end of row 16, finish last sc with green picked up from row 4, ch 1, turn.

Row 17: Beg and ending with sc in sc 1 row below, work as for row 5. Keeping to pat and color stripes as established, dec 1 sc each end every 3″ 3 times more, every 2″ twice—43 sc. Work even in pat until 5th red stripe is completed, changing to yellow in last sc. Turn.

Sleeves: With yellow, ch 10.

Row 1: Sc in 2nd ch from hook and in next 8 ch, work in pat across, ch 10, turn.

Rows 2-4: Repeat row 1. At end of row 4, omit ch. Cut yellow. Join blue, work even in pat on 79 sc until red stripe is completed. Continue in pat, bind off (see To Bind Off) 4 sts each side every other row 5 times, 5 sts every other row once, 6 sts every other row once, working last 2 rows in green sc—17 sc remain for back of neck. End off.

FRONT: Work as for back through row 17—53 sc. Mark center st.

Right Front (Left-handed Crocheters: This will be your left front): Work in pat to marked st; do not work in center st. Ch 1, turn. Working in pat as established, dec 1 sc at side edge every 3″ 3 times more, every 2″ twice—21 sc. Work even in pat until 5th red stripe is completed, changing to yellow in last sc. Turn.

SLEEVE: Row 1: Work in pat across. Ch 10, turn.

Row 2: Sc in 2nd ch from hook and in next 8 ch, sc in each sc across.

Rows 3 and 4: Repeat rows 1 and 2—39 sc. Work even in pat until red stripe is completed.

Shape Top of Sleeve and Neck: Continue in pat, bind off 4 sts at side edge every other row 5 times, 5 sts once, 6 sts once. **At the same time,** when first row of blue stripe has been completed, bind off 5 sts at neck edge once, then dec 1 st every row 3 times.

Left Front: Join green in st next to marked st, ch 1, sc in each sc to side edge. Dec as for right front, work until 5th red stripe is completed, changing to yellow in last sc. Turn.

Sleeve: With yellow, ch 10.

Row 1: Sc in 2nd ch from hook and in next 8 ch, work in pat across. Ch 1, turn.

Row 2: Sc in each sc across, ch 10, turn.

Row 3: Repeat row 1—39 sc. Finish as for right front.

FINISHING: Sew top of sleeves, underarm, side and bottom seams. With red, work 2 rows of sc around neck and front edges. Work 2 rows of sc around sleeve edges. Sew zipper in front opening. With red, make 2 chains 10″ long. Attach to neck edge each side of opening.

HOOD: Beg at front edge, with green, ch 44. Work in pat as for back of bunting on 43 sc until 26 rows have been completed. Working in yellow, bind off 5 sts each end of next 3 rows. End off.

FINISHING: Sew back seam.

Edging: Join red to front corner of neck edge. From right side, sc across neck edge 2 sc in next front corner, sc in each st across front of hood, sl st in first sc. Ch 1.

Beading: Sc in first sc on neck edge, * ch 1, sk 1 sc, sc in next sc, repeat from * across neck edge. End off.

With red, make a chain 30″ long. Weave through ch-1 sps of beading.

"INDIAN" BASKETS
Shown on page 251

SIZES: 4"–6" high; 6"–7" in diameter.

MATERIALS: For Natural Basket: 20 yards upholstery cord; 4 ozs. of 2-ply unbleached weaving wool or Irish-type knitting wool. For Earth-toned Basket with handles: 12 yards tarred sisal; 3 ozs. of knitting worsted: black, white, natural, grays, browns. For Red-toned Basket: 15 yards of 5-ply jute: 3 ozs. of knitting worsted: red brown (B), rust (R), natural (N). Aluminum crochet hook size G. Yarn needle.

GENERAL DIRECTIONS: Cut end of cord used for core (upholstery cord, sisal or jute) at an angle. Start 2" from tapered end, single crochet (sc) closely over cord to end. Fold covered section in half, sc over point and uncovered cord together.

Continue to wind cord around crocheted loop, working 2 to 4 sc over cord in each sc on row below (work as many sc as needed to completely cover cord). While piece is growing in diameter, increase as necessary, working 2 sc in 1 sc at even intervals around. Adjust cord to keep piece flat for bottom of basket. To work up straight sides, keep constant number of sc and pull cord to same circumference each row. To shape sides, increase or decrease circumference of cord and number of sc as necessary to shape basket.

Finishing: Cut cord at an angle, sc to end, then slip stitch in 3 or 4 sc past end. Run yarn end back into work with a yarn needle.

NATURAL BASKET: Following General Directions, work bottom of basket to a diameter of 5½". Work up sides without increasing to a height of 5", shaping basket as pictured. Work 2 more rows, pulling out cord to form lip.

EARTH-TONED BASKET: Following General Directions, work bottom of basket to a diameter of 4", covering sisal (or other cord) with black. Work up sides, changing colors as desired, without increasing for 1". (To change colors, cut old color, work with new color crocheting over both yarn ends.) Gradually increase to a diameter of 7". At 3" height, form a looped handle each side: at desired place, sc over cord for about 3" without attaching it to row below; then continue to crochet into previous row. Work 2 more rows after handles, pulling in cord and skipping stitches to shape top.

RED-TONED BASKET: Following General Directions, with B, work bottom of basket to a diameter of 3¾", having 66 sc on last row. Work even on 66 sc for 1". Begin design, carrying unused color or colors along back of work, working over them.

Row 1: (Work 10 B, 1 N) 6 times.

Row 2: Work 9 B, (1N, 1 R, 1 N, 8 B) 5 times, 1 N, 1 R, 1 N.

Row 3: Work 7 B, (1 N, 3 R, 1 N, 6 B) 5 times, 1 N, 3 R, 1 N.

Row 4: Work 5 B, (1N, 5 R, 1 N, 4 B) 5 times, 1 N, 5 R, 1 N.

Row 5: Work 2 B, 2 B in next sc, (1 N, 7 R, 1 N, 1 B, 2 B in next sc) 5 times, 1 N, 7 R, 1 N—72 sc.

Row 6: Work 2 B, (1 N, 4 R, 2 R in next sc, 4 R, 1 N, 1 B) 5 times, 1 N, 4 R, 2 R in next sc, 4 R, 1 N—78 sc. With B, slip stitch in next sc; cut B.

Row 7: Beginning in next N sc, work (6R, 2 R in next sc, 5 R, 1 N) 6 times—84 sc.

Row 8: Work (6 R, 1 N) 12 times—84 sc.

Row 9: Add B. Work 5 R, (1 N, 1 B, 1 N, 4 R) 11 times, 1 N, 1 B, 1 N.

Row 10: Work 3 R, (1 N, 1 B, 2 B in next sc, 1 B, 1 N, 2 R) 11 times, 1 N, 1 B, 2 B in next sc, 1 B, 1 N—96 sc. Cut R.

Row 11: (2 N, 6 B) 12 times.

Row 12: Work 1 B, (1 N, 7 B) 12 times. Cut B.

Row 13: With N, work 1 sc in each sc around to last 6 sc. See Finishing under General Directions.

FILET CROCHET

Filet crochet is the technique of forming designs with little solid and openwork squares called blocks and spaces. Usually the background is worked in the openwork mesh with the design formed by the blocks. In this section, we show some simple variations of filet crochet.

Here, one large motif worked in blocks forms a table-protecting place mat, 17" × 18". Mat is worked in white knitting and crochet cotton, glistening with silver. Crocheted rose leaf is appliqued to napkin. Directions and chart for filet rose mat and leaf motif, opposite and page 246.

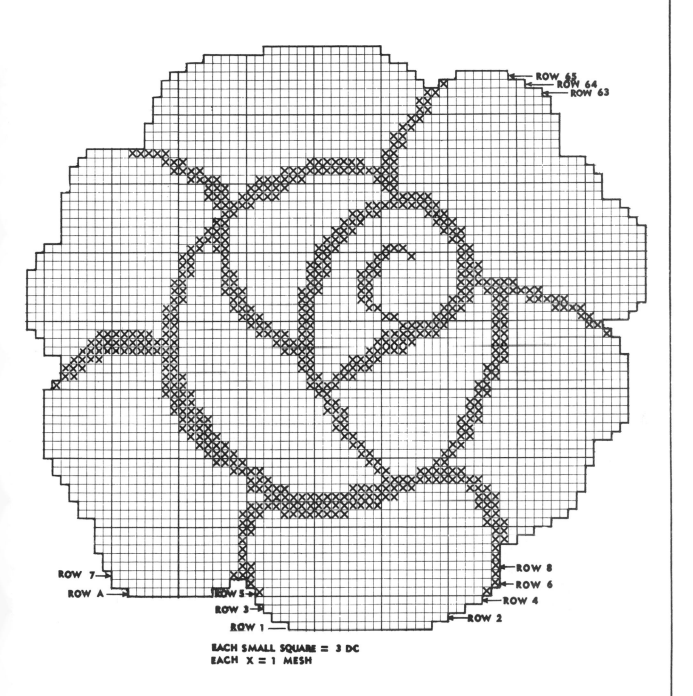

ROW 65
ROW 64
ROW 63

ROW 7
ROW A
ROW 5
ROW 3
ROW 1

ROW 8
ROW 6
ROW 4
ROW 2

EACH SMALL SQUARE = 3 DC
EACH X = 1 MESH

FILET ROSE MAT AND LEAF MOTIF
Shown on page 244

SIZES: Mat, 17″ x 18″. Napkin, 16″ square.

MATERIALS: Knitting and crochet cotton with metallic thread, 11 175-yd. balls, white with silver for three mats and three 3-leaf cluster motifs. Steel crochet hook No. 10. Piece of linen 17″ x 17″, for each napkin.

GAUGE: 12 dc = 1″; 4 rows = 1″.

GENERAL DIRECTIONS: Each square on chart represents 3 dc; each X represents 1 mesh.

To Inc One or More Dc Squares on Chart: At beg of row, ch 6 for a dc square inc, ch 3 more for each additional square; dc in 5th ch from hook, dc in next ch (1 square), dc in each of 3 ch for each additional square. At end of row, yo, draw up a lp in top of turning ch last dc was worked in; holding last lp close to work, yo, draw through one lp on hook (this st is base st), yo, and through 2 lps on hook twice for 1 dc, * yo, draw up a lp in base st, yo and through 1 lp on hook for next base st, yo and through 2 lps on hook twice for 1 dc, repeat from * once (a dc square inc made); work from first * to 2nd * 3 times for each additional square inc.

To Inc One Mesh: At beg of row, ch 7, dc in first dc. At end of row, ch 2, yo hook 3 times, draw up a lp in turning ch last dc was worked in, yo and through 2 lps 4 times (tr tr made for mesh).

To Dec One Dc Square or One Mesh: At beg of row, ch 1, sl st across 3 sts of each dc square or mesh, then sl st in next dc. Ch 5, sk next 2 dc, dc in next dc if row starts with a mesh (ch 3, dc in next dc if row starts with dc squares), finish row. At end of row, leave 3 sts of each dc square or mesh unworked.

MAT: Ch 54 Row 1 (wrong side): Dc in 5th ch from hook and in each ch across–51 dc, counting turning ch. Turn each row.

Rows 2-4: Work in dc, inc dc squares (see General Directions) as shown in chart–81 dc.

Row 5: Ch 5, dc in 4th dc (mesh made at beg of row), dc in each st across, inc 1 mesh at end of row.

Row 6: Inc 1 mesh at beg of row, 2 dc in next mesh, dc in each dc to last mesh, 2 dc in mesh, dc in 3rd ch of ch 5, inc 1 mesh at end of row, ch 5. End off. Put work aside.

Row A on Chart: Ch 33. Dc in 5th ch from hook and in each ch across–30 dc, counting turning ch. Turn.

Joining Row: Ch 9, drop lp off hook, insert hook in 5th ch at end of row 6 on first piece worked and draw dropped lp through; working back on 2nd piece, dc in 5th ch from hook and in each of 4 ch, dc in each st across, inc 2 dc squares at end of row–42 dc on 2nd piece. Turn, do not twist pieces.

Row 7: Ch 3, dc in 2nd dc (always beg even dc edge this way), dc in each of next 40 dc, ch 2, sk next 2 ch of first piece, dc in next ch, ch 2, sk 2 ch, dc in top of tr tr of mesh, ch 2, sk next 2 ch of same mesh, dc in next dc (3 meshes made), dc in each dc across to last mesh, ch 2, sk 2 ch of turning ch, dc in next ch (mesh made over mesh at end of row).

Row 8: Ch 5, sk 2 ch, dc in next dc (mesh made over mesh at beg of row), dc in each dc to next mesh, (ch 2, dc in next dc) twice, 2 dc in next mesh, dc in next dc (dc square worked over mesh), dc in each st across, inc 1 dc square at end of row.

Rows 9-63: Follow chart for pat and shaping.

Shape Top of Petals: First Petal: Row 64: Dec 2 dc squares, work dc to within 3 dc of next mesh, ch 2, sk 2 dc, dc in next dc. Turn.

Row 65: Dec each side as on chart–18 dc. End off.

Second Petal: Row 64: Make lp on hook, sk next 2 meshes on row 63 from first petal, dc in last dc of 2nd mesh, dc in each st across–93 dc. Work to top of chart on 2nd petal. End off.

Steam-press mat, using steam iron or dry iron and damp cloth.

THREE-LEAF CLUSTER MOTIF: Center Leaf: Ch 19, sc in 2nd ch from hook and in each of 17 ch–18 sc. Mark beg of following rnds.

Rnd 1: Ch 1; working on other side of starting ch, * sl st in each of 2 sts, sc in each of 2 sts, hdc in next st, ch 1, sk 1 st, dc in next st, ch 1, sk next st, tr in next st, ch 1, (tr, ch 1) in each of 4 sts, sk 1 st, dc in next st, ch 1, sk 1 st, hdc in next st, sc in next st *, 3 sc in turning ch at point; working on other side, work from 2nd * back to first *, sl st in first ch 1.

Rnd 2: Ch 1, * work 2 sl sts, 2 sc, 1 hdc, (dc in next sp, dc in next st) twice, 2 dc in next sp, dc in next st, 2 tr in next sp, tr in next st, 2 tr in next sp, dc in next st, 2 dc in next sp, dc in next st, dc in next sp, hdc in next st, hdc in next sp, hdc in next hdc, sc in each of next 2 sc *, 2 sc in next sc (tip), ch 4, sl st in last sc made, sc in same sc last worked in; working on other side, work from 2nd * back to first *, sl st in first ch 1.

Rnd 3: Ch 1, sl st in back lp of each st around, join. Do not end off.

Stem: Make 1¼″ ch, sl st in 2nd ch from hook and in each ch, sl st at base of leaf. End off.

Outer Leaves (make 2): Work as for center leaf for 3 rnds. Do not end off, join with sl st to center of stem.

FINISHING: Holding leaves closely tog, place cluster motif at one corner of linen with tip of center leaf ½″ in from corner. Sew cluster motif in place. Make ¼″ hem around napkin, following outline of cluster at corner.

Open-air tops: lovely in filet crochet! Roses pattern the shell, with small blooms encircling peplum. Scrollwork accents front of blouse, all plain mesh in back. Both, 8–14. Rose Shell, page 241. Scroll Blouse, page 249.

ROSE SHELL

Continued from page 241

Continued from page 241

Rows 14-16: Work in mesh pat. Ch 3, turn.

Waistband: Row 1 (eyelet row): Sk first dc, * dc in each of next 5 sts, ch 1, sk next st, repeat from * across, end last repeat dc in last dc, dc in each of next 3 ch of turning ch. Ch 5, turn.

Row 2: Work in mesh pat across–52 (54-56-60) meshes. Ch 3, turn.

Row 3: Sk first dc, dc in each st across, end dc in last dc, dc in each of next 3 ch of turning ch. Ch 5, turn.

Bodice: Rows 1-6: Work in mesh pat–52 (54-56-60) meshes.

Row 7: Keeping to mesh pat, inc 1 mesh (see to Inc 1 Mesh) each side–54 (56-58-62) meshes.

Rows 8-34: Work in mesh pat. Ch 1 turn.

Shape Armholes: Row 1: Sl st across 10 (10-10-13) sts, ch 3, * dc in each of next 2 ch, dc in next dc, repeat from * to within last 3 (3-3-4) meshes–145 (151-157-163) dc, counting ch 3 as 1 dc. Ch 3, turn.

Row 2: Sk first 3 dc, dc in next dc, * ch 2, sk next 2 dc, dc in next dc, repeat from * to within last 2 dc and turning ch, sk 2 dc, dc in top of ch 3. Ch 5, turn.

Row 3: Work in mesh pat across–46 (48-50-52) meshes. Dec 1 mesh each side of next row–44 (46-48-50) meshes. Work even until armholes measure 5½" (5¾"-6¼"-6¾") above first row of armhole shaping.

Shape Neck and Shoulders: Row 1: Work 12 (13-13-14) meshes; ch 3, turn.

Next Row: Sk first dc, dc in next dc, finish row. Ch 1, turn. Dec 1 mesh at neck edge every row twice; **at the same time,** bind off 3 meshes at arm side every row twice. End off.

Sk next 20 (20-22-22) meshes on last long row, join another strand of yarn in next dc, ch 5, dc in next dc, finish row–12 (13-13-14) meshes. Complete same as first shoulder, reversing shaping.

FRONT: Work same as back to end of Bodice row 13. Ch 5, turn.

Row 14: Following chart 2, work from right to left. Ch 5, turn.

Row 15: Following chart 2, work from left to right. Ch 5, turn. Repeating last 2 rows, work to top of chart (16 rows). Work 5 rows in mesh pat.

Shape Armholes: Work same as for back until armhole measures 2¾" (3"-3¼"-3½") above first row of armhole shaping–44 (46-48-50) meshes.

Shape Neck: Next Row: Work 17 (18-18-19) meshes. Ch 1, turn. Bind off 2 meshes at neck edge every row twice, then dec 1 mesh at same edge every row 4 times–9 (10-10-11) meshes. Work even until armhole measures same as back.

Shape Shoulder: Bind off 3 meshes at arm side every row twice. End off.

Sk 10 (10-12-12) meshes on last long row, join another strand of yarn in next dc, ch 5, dc in next dc, finish row–17 (18-18-19) meshes. Complete same as for first shoulder.

FINISHING: Block pieces. Weave shoulder seams; sew side seams.

Armhole Edging: Join yarn in underarm seam. From right side, work 1 rnd dc around armhole, be-ing careful to keep work flat. Join with a sl st in first dc. End off.

Lower Edging: Join yarn in underarm seam. From right side, * work 6 dc in next ch-2 sp, sc in next sp, repeat from * around; join. End off.

Neck Edging: Join yarn in shoulder seam. From right side, work same as lower edging around neck edge.

DRAWSTRING: Make chain 48" (52"-54"-58") long. Sl st in 2nd ch from hook and in each ch across. End off.

Weave drawstring through eyelet row (first waistband row).

TASSELS (make 2): Wind yarn 34 times around a 1½" strip of cardboard. Tie one end; cut other end. Wind yarn around tassel ¼" below tied end. Attach a tassel to each end of drawstring. Trim ends.

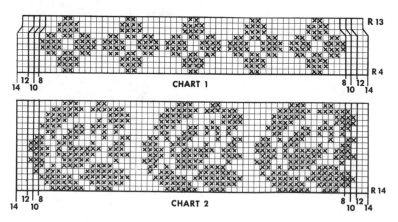

SCROLL BLOUSE
Shown on page 247

SIZES: Directions for size 8. Changes for sizes 10, 12 and 14 are in parentheses.

Body Bust Size: 31½″ (32½″-34″-36″).

Blocked Bust Size: 32½″ (33½″-35″-37″).

MATERIALS: Knitting and crochet cotton, 4 (5-5-6) 250-yard balls. Steel crochet hook No. 8.

GAUGE: 10 meshes = 3″; 4 rows = 1″.

To Bind Off: At beg of row, sl st loosely across each mesh to be bound off, then ch 4 and continue across row; at **end of row**, work in pat to within specified number of meshes to be bound off.

To Dec 1 Mesh: At **beg of row**, ch 3, sk first

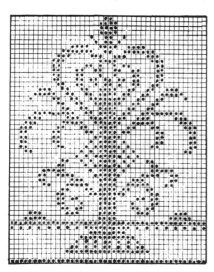

mesh, dc in next dc (counts as 1 dc), ch 2, dc in next dc (1 mesh); **at end of row**, work to last dc, ch 2, yo, pull up a lp in last dc, yo and through 2 lps on hook, yo, pull up a lp in 3rd ch of turning ch, yo and through 2 lps on hook, yo and through 3 lps on hook.

To Inc 1 Mesh: At **beg of row**, ch 4, dc in first dc; at end of row, (ch 2, dc in 3rd ch of turning ch) twice.

To Make Meshes: Dc in dc, ch 2, sk 2 sts, dc in next dc (1 mesh); ch 2, sk 2 sts, dc in next dc for each additional mesh.

To Make Blocks: Dc in each of 4 sts (1 block); dc in each of next 3 sts for each additional block.

Chart Notes: Meshes are shown on chart as open squares, blocks by dotted squares.

BLOUSE: BACK: Beg at lower edge, ch 147 (153-159-171).

Row 1 (right side): Dc in 4th ch from hook and in each ch across–145 (151-157-169) dc, counting ch 3 at beg of row as 1 dc. Ch 5, turn.

Row 2: Sk first 3 dc, * dc in next dc, ch 2, sk next 2 dc, repeat from * across, end dc in top of turning ch–48 (50-52-56) meshes. Ch 5, turn. Check gauge; piece should measure 14½″ (15″-15¾″-16¾″) wide.

Row 3: Sk first dc and ch-2 sp, dc in next dc (1 mesh), * ch 2, dc in next dc, repeat from * across, end ch 2, dc in 3rd ch of turning ch. Ch 5, turn. Repeat row 3 for mesh pat until piece measures 5″ from start. Working in mesh pat, inc 1 mesh (see To Inc 1 Mesh) each side of next row, then every 6th row twice–54 (56-58-62) meshes. Work even until piece measures 12″ (12″-12½″-12½″) from start.

Shape Armholes: Keeping to mesh pat, bind off (see To Bind Off) 3 (3-4-4) meshes each side of next row. Dec 1 mesh (see To Dec 1 Mesh) each side every other row twice–44 (46-46-50) meshes. Work even until armholes measure 6½″ (7″-7½″-8″) above first row of armhole shaping.

Shape Neck and Shoulders: Bind off 4 meshes, ch 3, dc in next dc, work 9 (10-10-11) meshes. Ch 5, turn.

Next Row: Sk first dc, dc in next dc, work 3 meshes, dc in next dc. End off.

Sk next 16 (16-16-18) meshes, join another strand of yarn in next dc, ch 5, dc in next dc, work 8 (9-9-10) meshes, dc in next dc. Ch 1, turn.

Next Row: Sl st in each st to within last 5 meshes, ch 3, dc in next dc, work in mesh pat across. End off.

FRONT: Work same as for back for 2 rows. Ch 5, turn.

Row 3: Sk first dc and ch-2 sp, dc in next dc (1 mesh), * ch 2, dc in next dc, repeat from * 1 (2-3-5) times, put a marker in last dc; following row 3 of chart (see Chart Notes), work from right to left, put a marker in last dc worked, work in mesh pat across remaining 3 (4-5-7) meshes. Ch 5, turn.

Row 4: Work in mesh pat to marked st, work chart, finish row in mesh pat. Ch 5, turn. Repeat last row to top of chart; **at the same time**, when piece measures 5″ from start, inc 1 mesh each side of next row, then every 6th row twice–54 (56-58-62) meshes. When piece measures same as

back to underarm, shape armholes same as back–44 (46-46-50) meshes. When chart is completed, work in mesh pat until armholes measure 1¼″ (1¼″-1½″-1¾″) above first row of armhole shaping–44 (46-46-50) meshes.

Shape Neck: Next Row: Work 19 (20-20-21) meshes, drop yarn; sk next 6 (6-6-8) meshes for center neck; join another strand of yarn in next dc, ch 5, dc in next dc, work in mesh pat across–19 (20-20-21) meshes each side. Working on both sides at once, with separate strands of yarn, dec 1 mesh at each neck edge every row 5 times–14 (15-15-16) meshes each side. Work even until armholes measure same as back.

Shape Shoulders: Working on both sides at once, shape shoulders same as back.

SLEEVES: Beg at lower edge, ch 114 (120-129-135).

Row 1: Dc in 4th ch from hook and in each ch across–112 (118-127-133)dc. Ch 5, turn.

Row 2: Sk first 3 dc, * dc in next dc, ch 2, sk next 2 dc, repeat from * across–37 (39-42-44) meshes. Work even until piece measures 2½″ (2½″-3″-3″) from start.

Shape Cap: Keeping to mesh pat, bind off 3 (3-4-4) meshes each side of next row. Dec 1 mesh each side every other row 1 (2-3-4) times, then every 3rd row 4 times–21 (21-20-20) meshes. End off.

FINISHING: Block pieces. Weave shoulder seams; sew in sleeves. Sew side and sleeve seams. From right side, work 1 rnd dc around neck edge, being careful to keep work flat.

Soft yarns crocheted over thick cord create these unique containers for your plants. Or, use these holders, reminiscent of Indian baskets or pottery, in other decorative and practical ways. "Indian" Baskets are 4"–6" high, 6"–7" in diameter. Directions page 243.

The raised patterns of Irish fisherman sweaters were the inspiration for this beautifully crocheted afghan. Done all in one piece, the afghan uses popcorns and zigzag stitches to form the embossed surface. The triple-tied fringe adds an attractive border. Size is 52″ × 68″, plus fringe. Aran Afghan in Crochet, opposite.

ARAN AFGHAN IN CROCHET
Shown opposite

SIZE: 52″ x 68″, plus fringe.
MATERIALS: Yarn of knitting worsted type, 5 4-oz balls or skeins winter white. Crochet hook size G.
GAUGE: 3 dc = 1″; 2 rows = 1″.

STITCHES: Popcorn (pc): Work 5 dc in st, remove hook from lp, insert hook from front to back in first dc, pick up dropped lp and draw through st, ch 1.
Reverse Popcorn (rpc): Work 5 dc in st, remove hook from lp, insert hook from back to front in first dc, pick up dropped lp and draw through st, ch 1.
Zigzag Pat (zz-pat): Sk 3 sts, tr in next st; working behind this tr, dc in each of 3 skipped sts.
Reverse Zigzag Pat (rzz-pat): Sk 3 sts, tr in next st; working in front of this tr, dc in each of 3 skipped sts.

AFGHAN: Ch 204.
Foundation Row: Sc in 2nd ch from hook and in each ch across–203 sc. Ch 3, turn.
Row 1 (right side): Sk first sc (ch 3 turning ch always counts as 1 dc), dc in each of next 3 sc, (ch 1, sk 3 sc, tr in each of next 2 sc; working in front of 2 tr, tr in each of last 2 skipped sc, ch 1, sk 1 sc, dc in each of next 3 sc, 1 pc in next sc, dc in each of next 3 sc) twice, (ch 1, sk 3 sc, tr in each of next 2 sc; working in front of 2 tr, tr in each of 2 skipped sc, ch 1, sk 1 sc, dc in each of next 2 sc, work 4 zz-pats over next 16 sc, dc in each of next 6 sc, sk 2 sc, tr in each of next 2 sc; working behind these 2 tr, tr in each of last 2 skipped sts, sk 2 sc, tr in each of next 2 sc; working in front of 2 tr, tr in each of 2 skipped sts, dc in each of next 6 sc, 4 zz-pats over next 16 sc, dc in each of next 2 sc, ch 1,

sk 3 sc, tr in each of next 2 sc; working in front of these 2 tr, tr in each of last 2 skipped sc, ch 1, sk 1 sc, dc in each of next 3 sc, 1 pc in next sc, dc in each of next 3 sc) twice; ch 1, sk 3 sc, tr in each of next 2 sc; working in front of these 2 tr, tr in each of last 2 skipped sc, ch 1, sk 1 sc, dc in each of next 3 sc, 1 pc in next sc, dc in each of next 3 sc, ch 1, sk 3 sc, tr in each of next 2 sc; working in front of these 2 tr, tr in each of last 2 skipped sc, ch 1, sk 1 sc, dc in each of last 4 sc. Ch 3, turn.

Row 2 (wrong side): Dc in each of next 3 dc, (ch 1, sk ch 1 and 2 tr, tr in each of next 2 tr, tr in front in each skipped tr, ch 1, dc in each of next 2 dc, rpc in next dc, dc in pc, rpc in next dc, dc in each of next 2 dc) twice, (ch 1, sk ch 1 and 2 tr, tr in each of next 2 tr, tr in front in each skipped tr, ch 1, sk ch 1, dc in each of 2 dc, 4 rzz-pats, dc in each of next 4 dc, sk 2 sts, tr in each of next 2 sts, tr in front in each skipped st, dc in each of next 4 sts, sk 2 sts, tr in each of next 2 sts, tr in back in each skipped st, dc in each of next 4 dc, 4 rzz-pats, dc in each of 2 dc, ch 1, sk ch 1 and 2 tr, tr in each of next 2 tr, tr in front in each skipped tr, ch 1, dc in each of next 2 dc, rpc in next dc, dc in pc, rpc in next dc, dc in each of next 2 dc) twice, ch 1, sk ch 1 and 2 tr, tr in each of next 2 tr, tr in front in each skipped tr, ch 1, sk ch 1, dc in each of 2 dc, rpc in next st, dc in next st, rpc in next st, dc in each of next 2 dc, ch 1, sk ch 1 and 2 tr, tr in each of next 2 tr, tr in front in each skipped tr, ch 1, sk ch 1, dc in last 3 dc, dc in top of ch 3. Ch 3, turn.

Row 3: Dc in each of next 3 dc, (ch 1, crossed tr pat over crossed tr pat, ch 1, sk ch 1, 3 dc, pc, 3 dc on popcorn panel) twice, (ch 1, crossed tr pat over crossed tr pat, ch 1, dc in each of next 2 dc, 4 zz-pats, dc in each of next 2 dc, sk 2 sts, tr in each of next 2 sts, tr in back in each skipped st, dc in each of next 8 sts, sk 2 sts, tr in each of next 2 sts, tr in front in each skipped st, dc in each of next 2 dc, 4 zz-pats, dc in each of next 2 dc, ch 1, sk ch 1, crossed tr pat over crossed tr pat, ch 1, sk ch 1, 3 dc, pc, 3 dc on popcorn panel) twice, ch 1, crossed tr pat over crossed tr pat, ch 1, sk ch 1, 3 dc, pc, 3 dc on popcorn panel, ch 1, crossed tr pat over crossed tr pat, ch 1, sk 1 ch, dc in next 3 dc, dc in top of ch 3. Ch 3, turn.

Row 4: Dc in each of next 3 dc, (ch 1, crossed tr pat over crossed tr pat, ch 1, work 3 dc, rpc, 3 dc on popcorn panel) twice, (ch 1, crossed tr pat over crossed tr pat, ch 1, dc in each of next 2 dc, 4 rzz-pats, dc in each of next 2 dc, sk 2 sts, tr in each of next 2 sts, tr in back in each skipped st, dc in each of next 8 sts, sk 2 sts, tr in each of next 2 sts, tr in front in each skipped st, dc in each of next 2 dc, 4 rzz-pats, dc in each of next 2 dc, ch 1, crossed tr pat over crossed tr pat, ch 1, 3 dc, rpc, 3 dc on popcorn panel) twice, ch 1, crossed tr pat over crossed tr pat, ch 1, 3 dc, rpc, 3 dc on popcorn panel, ch 1, crossed tr pat over crossed tr pat, ch 1, dc in next 3 dc, dc in top of ch 3. Ch 3, turn.

Row 5: Dc in each of next 3 dc, (ch 1, crossed tr pat over crossed tr pat, ch 1, work 2 dc, pc, dc, pc, 2 dc on popcorn panel) twice, (ch 1, crossed tr pat over crossed tr pat ch 1, dc in each of next 2 dc, 4 zz-pats, dc in each of next 4 sts, sk next 2 sts, tr in each of next 2 sts, tr in front in each of 2 skipped sts, dc in each of 4 sts, sk next 2 sts, tr in each of next 2 sts, tr in back in each of 2 skipped sts, dc in each of next 4 sts, 4 zz-pats, dc in each of next 2 dc, ch 1, crossed tr pat over crossed tr pat, ch 1, 2 dc, pc, dc, pc, 2 dc on popcorn panel) twice, ch 1, crossed tr pat over crossed tr pat, ch 1, 2 dc, pc, dc, pc, 2 dc on popcorn panel, ch 1, crossed tr pat over crossed tr pat, ch 1, dc in next 3 dc, dc in top of ch 3. Ch 3, turn.

Row 6: Dc in each of next 3 dc, (ch 1, crossed tr pat over crossed tr pat, ch 1, 3 dc, rpc, 3 dc on popcorn panel) twice, (ch 1, crossed tr pat over crossed tr pat, ch 1, dc in each of next 2 dc, 4 rzz-pats, dc in each of 6 sts, sk 2 sts, tr in each of next 2 sts, tr in back in each of 2 skipped sts, sk 2 sts, tr in each of next 2 sts, tr in front in each skipped st, dc in each of next 6 sts, 4 rzz-pats, dc in each of next 2 dc, ch 1, crossed tr pat over crossed tr pat, ch 1, 3 dc, rpc, 3 dc on popcorn panel) twice, ch 1, crossed tr pat over crossed tr pat, ch 1, 3 dc, rpc, 3 dc on popcorn panel, ch 1, crossed tr pat over crossed tr pat, ch 1, dc in next 3 dc, dc in top of ch 3. Ch 3, turn.

Row 7: Dc in each of next 3 dc, (ch 1, crossed tr pat over crossed tr pat, ch 1, 3 dc, pc, 3 dc in popcorn panel) twice, (ch 1, crossed tr pat over crossed tr pat, ch 1, dc in each of next 2 dc, 4 zz-pats, dc in each of next 6 sts, sk 2 sts, tr in each of next 2 sts, tr in back in 2 skipped sts, sk 2 sts, tr in each of next 2 sts, tr in front in 2 skipped sts, dc in each of next 6 sts, 4 zz-pats, dc in each of next 2 dc, ch 1, crossed tr pat over crossed tr pat, ch 1, 3 dc, pc, 3 dc on popcorn panel) twice, ch 1, crossed tr pat over crossed tr pat, ch 1, 3 dc, pc, 3 dc on popcorn panel, ch 1, crossed tr pat over crossed tr pat ch 1, dc in each of 3 dc, dc in top of ch 3. Ch 3, turn.

Repeat rows 2-7 for pat. Work until 19 pats are completed or desired length, end row 6. Ch 1, turn. Work 1 row sc across top of afghan, working 1 sc in each st. End off.

FRINGE: Cut strands 20″ long. Use 4 strands tog. Fold 4 strands in half and knot a fringe in every 3rd st on each end. Divide strands of each fringe in half; knot 2 adjoining halves tog 1″ from afghan. Repeat across. Beg with free half of end fringe, knot this half with half of 2nd fringe 1″ below first row of knots. Continue to knot 2 adjoining halves tog across. Trim ends.

Big shaggy floor cushion is made in alternating rows of single crochet and double loop stitch, the loops cut after crochet is finished to form a soft pile surface. Directions for Loop-Crochet Floor Cushion are on pages 257–258.

Rug of loop-crochet can be made by repeating 25″ square of the floor cushion, page 255, and sewing the squares together. Four colors of rug yarn are used for the geometric shapes, worked from a chart. Rug illustrated is 50″ square.

LOOP-CROCHET FLOOR CUSHION
Shown on page 255

SIZE: 25″ square.

MATERIALS: Aunt Lydia's Heavy Rug Yarn, 7 70-yard skeins Light Navy, 4 skeins Turquoise, 3 skeins each Evergreen and Sea Blue, 1 skein Chartreuse, Aluminum crochet hook size J. 1½ yards cotton fabric for inner pillow. Shredded foam rubber or other stuffing. ¾ yard heavy cotton fabric for bottom of cushion. Heavy duty sewing threads.

GAUGE: 5 sts = 2″; 6 rows = 2″.

Note: Cushion top is worked in alternate rows of sc and double loop sts.

CUSHION TOP: With Light Navy, ch 61.

Row 1 (right side): Sc in 2nd ch from hook and in each ch across—60 sc. Ch 1, turn.

Row 2 (wrong side): Work a double loop st in each sc. **To make double loop st,** insert hook in st, wind yarn from front to back around two or three fingers of left hand twice, insert hook from left to right through loops on fingers and pull loops out to 2½″ length, pull both strands on hook through st, drop loops from fingers, yarn over hook and through all loops on hook. Loops are formed on back of work (right side). Ch 1, turn.

Row 3: Sc in each st across. Ch 1, turn.

Row 4: Double loop st in each sc across. Ch 1, turn. Repeat rows 3 and 4 for entire cushion, working colors from chart. Each square on chart represents one stitch.

Read all sc rows from right to left on chart; read all double loop st rows from left to right on chart. (Double loops sts are always made in the same color as sc of previous row.)

To Join a New Color: Work last sc of one color until there are 2 loops on hook; drop yarn to front of work. Finish sc with new color. Work over end of new color for next few sts.

To Change Colors on Double Loop St Rows: Work last double loop st of one color until there are 3 loops on hook; drop yarn to front of work. Finish st with next color.

To Change Colors on Sc Rows: Work last sc of one color until there are 2 loops on hook; drop yarn to front of work. Finish sc with new color.

FINISHING: Cut each loop. Trim loops evenly. Block cushion top: draw a 25″ square on heavy paper; moisten flat side of cushion top, pin out to size on paper square; let dry.

Make 25″ square knife-edged pillow from cotton fabric, stuff with shredded foam rubber before closing last seam.

Cut heavy cotton fabric 27″ square. Turn under 1″ on all edges, whip fabric to edge of cushion top, enclosing pillow.

RUG: Cushion design may be used as a repeat pattern for rugs, 25″ × 50″, 50″ square, 50″ × 75″, etc. Illustration of 50″ square rug, using four motifs, shows one arrangement. Motifs may be arranged in other ways. Use carpet thread for sewing rug squares together.

Chart on page 258

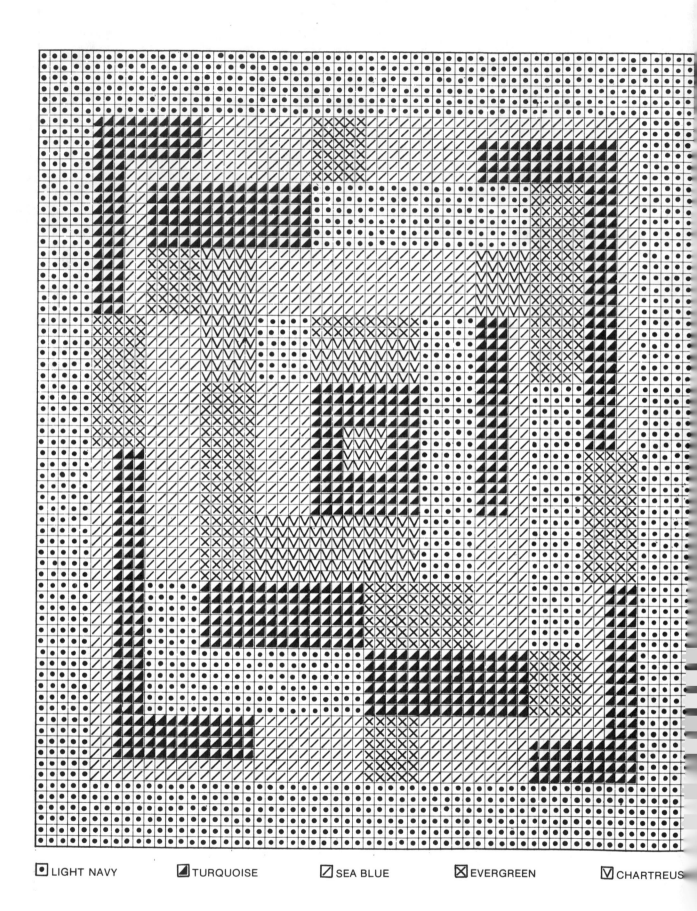

⊙ LIGHT NAVY   ◩ TURQUOISE   ◪ SEA BLUE   ⊠ EVERGREEN   � CHARTREUS

*Make a little scatter rug at no cost to you. Just cut up
some old sweaters into strips, single crochet the strips
into a striped, six-sided rug.*

SIX-SIDED RUG

SIZE: About 25″ × 34″.

MATERIALS: The old sweaters from which this rug was made were cut in cross-wise strips about 1″ wide when lightweight sweaters were used. Heavier sweaters were cut narrower in order to make the crocheting uniform.

When joining strips or changing colors, work last 2 sc over strip to be joined next. Then pick up the loop of the joining strip and work 2 sc over the end of the last strip.

A definite color scheme is given for the rug. Other color schemes to harmonize with your rrom can easily be worked out. The mixtures mentioned in the directions are from striped sweaters. The stitch used is single crochet taking up both loops of the stitch. An aluminum crochet hook size I or J is required.

Rnd 1: With red and tan mixture, ch 17, turn, sk 1 ch from hook and make 1 sc in each of the remaining sts of ch except the last ch; in the last ch make 3 sc. Continuing on the other side of ch, make 1 sc in each ch on side and 3 sc in the end.

Rnd 2: Work around in sc, making 1 sc in each st on sides and 2 sc in each of the 3 sts at each end.

Rnd 3: Continue working even at sides to within the 6 end sts, make 2 sc in next st, 1 sc in each of the next 2 sts, 2 sc in next st, 1 sc in each of the next 2 sts, 2 sc in next st (thus establishing 3 increasing places at end). Work even along other side to within the 6 end sts and increase in 3 places same as at other end. In the remaining rounds, always increase in the same three places at each end to give the six-sided effect to the rug. If rug has a tendency to curl, add an extra st at sides.

Rnd 4 is the same color as rnd 3.

Rnds 5, 6, 7 and 8 are tan.

Rnds 9, 10 and 11 are green.

Rnd 12 is a black and white mixture.

Rnd 13: This rnd starts the pattern and it is worked in two colors (a green and tax mixture and plain red), mentioned as red and green in the following: 5 green sc, 4 red sc, repeated around and increasing in corners as before.

Rnds 14 and 15: Like rnd 13, working the red over the red, and green over the green, increasing as before.

Rnd 16: Like rnd 12.

Rnds 17 and 18: Plain green.

Rnds 19 and 20: Tan and brown mixture.

Rnds 21, 22 and 23: Solid red.

Rnd 24 is black.

CHAIN RUGS

MATERIALS: Rug yarn of any weight. (Yarns can be wool, acrylic, rayon and cotton, or other fibers.) Or, use fabric strips (see General Directions, Crochet Chains). Aluminum crochet hook size G (or size to make tight chains). Needlepoint canvas, 7 mesh to the inch, burlap, or rug canvas, slightly larger than desired rug size. Heavy duty sewing thread in colors to match yarn. Yardstick. Crayons.

GENERAL DIRECTIONS: Preparation of Background: The design is based on 10″ squares. (You can use squares of other sizes and geometric patterns of your own choosing.) With yardstick and crayon, rule up background material into desired number of 10″ squares.

Four-Leaf Design: Mark center point of each side of square. Mark center of square. Lay yardstick across square from center of one side to center of opposite side. Mark 3½″ in from each side edge. Repeat from top to bottom of square. These marks are the outer limits of center design. Now lay yardstick diagonally across from corner to corner of square. Mark a point 3½″ in from each corner. Repeat in other direction. These 4 points are center starting points of corner designs. See Diagram.

Crochet Chains: Crochet chains of yarn in small amounts as you need them as short lengths are easier to handle.

If fabric strips are to be used, cut or tear fabric into lengthwise strips. The thickness of the material should determine the width of the strips. If material is heavy, cut strips ¼″ wide. Lighter fabric can be cut ½″ wide. Try to keep strips uniform in width. Use fabric of about the same weight and thickness for the whole rug in order to equalize the wear. If it is necessary to join two strips for one chain, cut each end only half-width for 2″; crochet ends together as one strip.

Sewing Chains to Background: Pull beginning end of chain through canvas or burlap at starting point with a finer hook. Or, hide end under chain. Pin chains, wrong side up and close together, in desired shapes. With matching heavy-duty thread, sew chains to background with invisible stitches.

Finishing: Turn under foundation material at edges and hem, or bind with rug tape. Miter corners. Or line rug with felt or other sturdy lining materials.

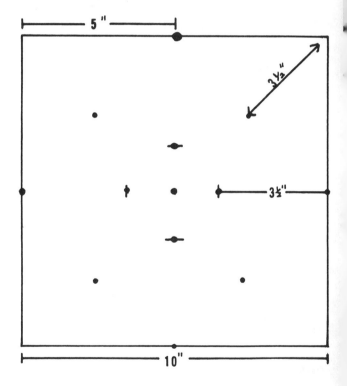

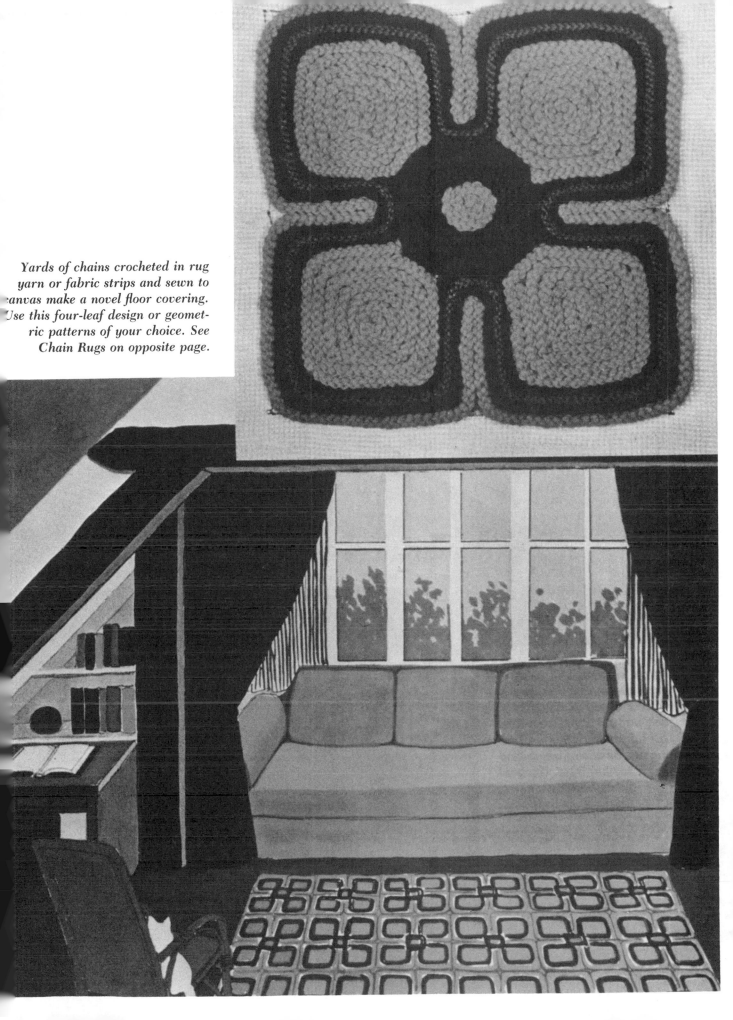

Yards of chains crocheted in rug yarn or fabric strips and sewn to canvas make a novel floor covering. Use this four-leaf design or geometric patterns of your choice. See Chain Rugs on opposite page.

Thick chains crocheted of rug yarn are sewn to burlap for an easy-to-make rug of repeat patterns.

CHAIN-STITCH RUG

SIZE: 54″ × 81″.

MATERIALS: Heavy rug yarn, ¼ lb. cream; 1 lb. tan; 1¼ lbs. green; 5 yards burlap. Aluminum crochet hook size J.

Rug is made in separate squares and sewn together. Cut the 5 yds. of burlap into six ¾-yard squares (27″ squares). With crayon, draw a 14″ square in the center of the 27″ square. Draw a 9″ square in the center of the 14″ square, and draw and 4½″ square in center of the 9″ square. Draw two diagonal lines from corner to corner of entire square. With crochet hook, make a long chain of cream and begin sewing onto burlap, starting at center where lines cross and squaring on each diagonal line. Sew chain onto burlap (flat side of chain down) by hand or machine as desired. When the 4½″ square is filled, change to tan and continue in same manner, changing to green after completely filling the 9″ square. Sew a row of tan chain around the outside of the green. Make six squares.

To finish squares, fold burlap edges, envelope fashion, under each square and stitch with strong thread—don't pull stitches too taut. Next, whip squares together and stitch one row of cream chain between the squares to cover stitching. Tie on fringe.

RECTANGULAR DOOR MAT
Shown on page 264

SIZE: 24″ × 32″.

MATERIALS: Macrame jute or twine, 6 spools Blue (B), 6 spools Green (G). Aluminum crochet hook size J.

GAUGE: 2 sc = 1″.

Note: Mat is worked in stripes of double strand B, double strand G.

STRIPED PATTERN: Row 1: With B, sc in 2nd ch from hook and in each ch across. Turn.

Row 2: With B, ch 1, sc in each sc, complete last sc with G.

Row 3: With G, ch 1, twist B around G strand once and drop B (to bring unused strand up side); with G, sc in each sc across. Turn.

Row 4: With G, ch 1, sc in each sc across, complete last sc with B. Turn.

Row 5: With B, ch 1, twist G around B strand once and drop G; with B, sc in each sc across. Turn.

Row 6: With B, repeat row 2. Repeat rows 3–6 for striped pat.

MAT: Beg at narrow end, with double strand B, ch 51 to measure 24″. Work in striped pat on 50 sts until piece measures 32″, end row 6 of pat. End off.

HALF CIRCLE DOOR MAT
Shown on page 265

SIZE: 16″ × 32″.

MATERIALS: Macrame jute or twine, 6 spools Blue, main color (MC); 4 spools Natural, contrasting color (CC), Aluminum crochet hook size K.

GAUGE: 2 sc or 2 dc = 1″.

Note: Mat is worked in stripes of double strand MC and double strand CC. When changing colors always complete last st on row with new color. Break off color not being used after each change. Work over ends on following row.

MAT: Beg at center, with 2 strands CC, ch 4, join with sl st to form ring.

Row 1: With CC, 8 sc in ring, change to MC (see Note). Do not join row. Turn.

Row 2: With MC, ch 1, work in sc, inc 3 sc evenly spaced across—11 sc. Turn each row.

Row 3 (right side): With MC, ch 3 (counts as 1 dc), dc in first sc (an inc), dc in next sc, 3 dc in next sc, drop lp off hook, insert hook in first dc of 3-dc group just made, draw dropped lp through, ch 1 (popcorn st or pc st made), (dc in each of next 2 sc, pc st in next st) twice, dc in next sc, 2 dc in last sc (an inc)—13 sts.

Row 4: With MC, ch 1, sc in first dc, * 2 sc in each of next 2 dc, sc in each of ch 1 and pc st, repeat from * across to last 3 sts, sc in next dc, 2 sc in next dc, sc in top of ch 3—23 sc.

Row 5: With MC, ch 3, sk first sc, dc in each of 3 sc, * pc st in next st, dc in each of 4 sc, repeat from * across, end pc st, dc in each of 3 sc—23 sts.

Row 6: With MC, ch 1, * sc in next dc, 2 sc in next dc, sc in each of next (dc, ch 1, pc st and dc), repeat from * across to last 3 sts, 2 sc in each of 2 dc, sc in last st, change to CC—33 sc.

Rows 7–9: With CC, ch 1, work in sc, inc 3 sc evenly spaced on each row—42 sc. Change to MC at end of row 9.

Row 10: With MC, ch 1, work in sc, inc 3 evenly spaced across—45 sc.

Row 11: With MC, ch 3, dc in 2nd sc, * pc st in next sc, dc in each of 3 sc, repeat from * across, end pc st, dc in each of 2 sc—45 sts.

Row 12: With MC, sc in each st and in ch 1 of each pc st across—56 sc.

Row 13: With MC, ch 3, sk first sc, dc in each of 4 sc, * pc st in next st, dc in each of 4 sc, repeat from * across, end pc st, dc in each of 5 sc—56 sts.

Row 14: With MC, repeat row 12, change to CC—66 sc.

Row 15: With CC, ch 1, work in sc, inc 3 sc evenly spaced across—69 sc.

Rows 16 and 17: With CC, work even in sc. Change to MC at end of row 17.

Row 18: With MC, work even in sc—69 sc.

Row 19: With MC, repeat row 11—69 sts.

Row 20: With MC, repeat row 12—86 sc.

Row 21: With MC, repeat row 13—86 sts.

Row 22: With MC, repeat row 12—102 sc. Do not turn. With MC, work 1 row sc across straight edge, making 2 sc in edge of each dc row, 1 sc in edge of each sc row. Then work 1 row sc around entire edge of mat, making 3 sc in each corner. End off.

Decorator stripes of dark green and royal blue and the silvery sheen
jute make this a "welcome mat," indeed! Jute comes in many love
colors, so choose the best colors for your own entrance. See directions f
Rectangular Door Mat, page 26

Flatter your door with a handsome semicircle, crocheted in turquoi
popcorn stripes and natural color stripes in a simpler stitch. Use gloss
long-wearing jute yarn in colors of your choice. Directions, Half-Circ
Door Mat, page 26

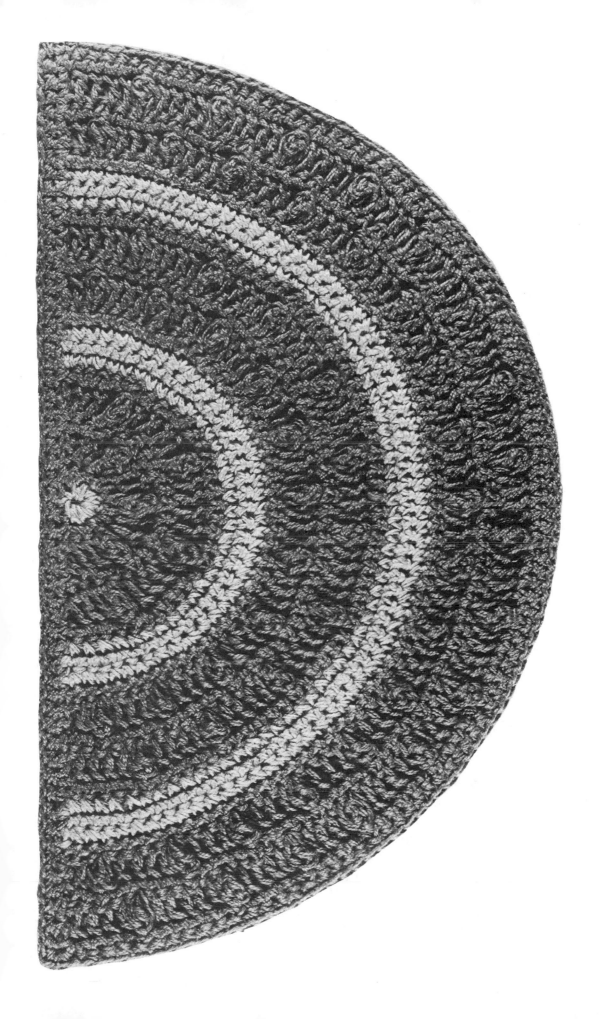

PART III

TATTING

Tatting evolved from the old craft of knotting which goes back to prehistoric times. The looping and knotting of threads into rings was practiced in Egypt in ancient times and later in China. Tatting began to appear in Europe around the 15th century and was brought to America by the Pilgrims. The French call tatting "frivolité," because of its delicate appearance, the Italians call it "occhi," which means "eyes", and in the Orient the work is referred to as "makouk" from the shape of the shuttles used. The English word "tatting" was probably derived from the word "tatters" denoting the fragile look of the work when it was first introduced, the little rings all being made separately and sewn down on material to form decorative patterns.

Tatting is a lace-making technique which looks delicate but is actually quite strong. The tatting knot is a double knot composed of two half-hitches, which slide easily along another thread and cover it; hence the strength and comparative firmness of tatting. The technique is somewhat difficult to describe even with step-by-step illustrations. If you want to learn how to tat, try to augment the information in this section with a lesson from a friend.

HOW TO TAT

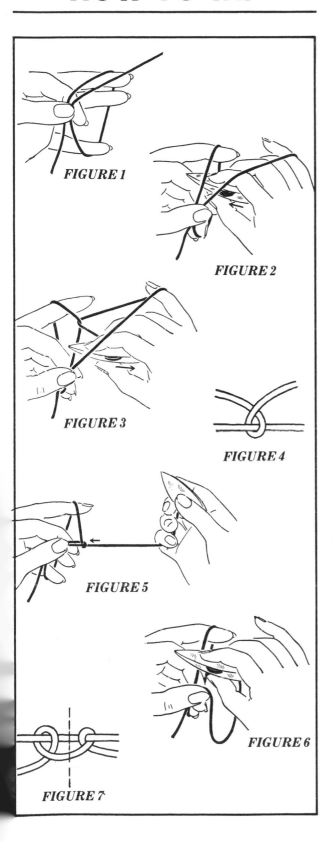

FIGURE 1

FIGURE 2

FIGURE 3

FIGURE 4

FIGURE 5

FIGURE 6

FIGURE 7

Tatting is the technique for forming lace designs of loops, rings and picots by means of a shuttle and thread. The tool used is called a tatting shuttle and may be of steel, plastic, bone or tortoise shell. Some are made with a hook at one end but these are harder for the beginner to use. For practice work, use mercerized crochet cotton size 20 or 30 in the shuttle.

TO WIND THE SHUTTLE BOBBIN: If there is a hole in the bobbin center, insert thread through hole, tie a knot and wind bobbin. If bobbin is removable, wind it and replace it in shuttle. Only wind enough thread to fill shuttle without projecting at the sides.

TO HOLD THREAD AND SHUTTLE: Hold end of thread between thumb and forefinger of left hand. Bring thread around back of left hand, spreading fingers, and grasp thread again between thumb and forefinger for a ring of thread; Fig. 1. Unwind shuttle so thread is about 12″ long. Hold shuttle between thumb and forefinger of right hand with pointed end facing left hand and thread coming from back of bobbin.

TO MAKE DOUBLE STITCH: First Half: With shuttle in right hand, pass shuttle thread under fingers of right hand, then over back of hand; Fig. 2. Bring shuttle forward and slide flat top of shuttle *under* ring thread on left hand; Fig. 2. (Do not let go of shuttle; the ring thread will pass between shuttle and fingers.) Then slide shuttle back over ring thread; Fig. 3. Pull shuttle thread taut and *at the same time*, drop middle finger of left hand so that ring of thread lies loose. This will cause loop to turn over; Fig. 4. Keep shuttle thread taut (this is very important) while you raise middle finger of left hand again. Loop will pull close to left thumb as you pull ring thread taut; Fig. 5. Hold loop firmly between thumb and forefinger.

Second Half: The second half of double stitch is made in reverse. Allow shuttle thread to fall slack without putting it over right hand. Slide shuttle *over* ring thread, Fig. 6, back under ring thread and over shuttle thread. Pull shuttle thread taut and *hold it taut* as you slacken ring thread and tighten it again. Second half of stitch slips into place beside first half; Fig. 7.

By pulling the shuttle thread, stitch should slip back and forth. If it does not, the stitch has been locked by a wrong motion and must be made over again. Practice double stitch, the basic stitch of tatting, until you can make it without looking at instructions. When loop around hand becomes too small to work in, pull shuttle thread at left of stitches to enlarge loop.

TO MAKE RINGS AND PICOTS: Rings and picots are characteristic of all tatting. To make first ring, work 4 double stitches (4 d), then make first half of another double stitch; slide it on thread, stopping about ¼″ from last stitch. Complete double stitch and draw entire stitch in position next to 4 d, forming picot (p); Fig. 8. Work 3 more d, work another picot, 3 more d, work another picot and 3 more d. Hold stitches firmly in left hand, draw shuttle thread until first and last stitches meet, forming a ring.

TO JOIN RINGS: Wind thread around left hand as for first ring; work first double stitch of next ring about ¼″ from ring just made. Work 3 more d. If you are using a shuttle with one pointed end, or a hook at one end, insert this end through the last picot of previous ring (or use a crochet hook) and pull ring thread through. Pull up a loop large enough to insert shuttle. Draw shuttle through this loop, Fig. 9, and draw shuttle thread tight. This joins the rings and counts as the first half of a double stitch. Complete double stitch, work 3 more d, a picot, 4 d, a picot, 4 d, close ring same as first ring.

TO REVERSE WORK: Turn work so that base of ring just made is at the top and work next ring as usual.

TO JOIN THREADS: Use a square knot to fasten a new thread close to the end of last ring or chain. Continue work and cut off ends later. Never attach a new thread in ring as the knots will not pass through the double stitch.

TO WORK WITH TWO THREADS: By using two threads, a wider range of patterns can be made. One method of working with two threads is to use the ball of thread for making chains and the shuttle thread for making rings. Tie ball and shuttle threads together. Use shuttle thread to form a ring. When ring is completed turn it so base is held between thumb and forefinger. Stretch thread from ball over back of fingers and loop it twice around little finger; Fig. 10. Work over ball thread with the shuttle in the usual way to form a chain, pull stitches together when chain is finished and resume work with the shuttle thread only for next ring.

When two colors are used in making rings, two shuttles must be used. These colors may be alternated, or the second color may be worked over the first as described in making a chain with a shuttle and a ball.

TO MAKE A JOSEPHINE KNOT: Work a small ring consisting of only the first half of double stitches.

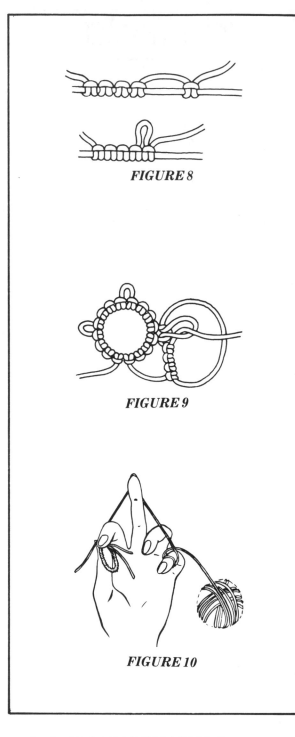

FIGURE 8

FIGURE 9

FIGURE 10

TATTING ABBREVIATIONS

r—ring	d—double stitch
ch—chain	rw—reverse work
rnd—round	sep—separated by
j—join	lr—large ring
p—picot	sm—small
cl—close	sp—space
	beg—beginning

TATTED EDGINGS

WILD ROSE EDGING

MATERIALS: Tatting cotton. Tatting shuttle. Steel crochet hook No. 14. Handkerchief.
Use ball and shuttle.

Rnd 1: J thread in edge of handkerchief ⅛″ before one corner. * Ch (4 d, p) 3 times, 4 d, j in edge of handkerchief on other side of same corner ⅛″ past corner. ** Ch (4 d, p) 3 times, 4 d, j in edge of handkerchief ¼″ from last joining. Repeat from ** across to within ⅛″ of next corner. Repeat from * around. Tie and cut.

Rnd 2: J in center p of corner ch. * Ch (4 d, p) 3 times, 4 d, j in center p of next ch. Repeat from * around. Tie and cut.

Rnd 3: R 3 d, j in first p of first ch after corner ch, 3 d, cl r. * Leave ¼″ thread, r 3 d, j in next p of same ch, 3 d, cl r. Leave ¼″ thread, r 3 d, j in same p, 3 d, cl r. Leave ¼″ thread, r 3 d, j in last p of same ch, 3 d, cl r. Leave ¼″ thread, j in center p of next ch. Leave ¼ thread, r 3 d, j in first p of next ch, 3 d, cl r. Repeat from * around. Tie and cut.

STAR FLOWER EDGING

MATERIALS: Tatting cotton. Tatting shuttle. Steel crochet hook No. 14. Hankerchief, with rolled, hemstitched edge.
Use ball and shuttle.

Rnd 1: J thread in edge of hankerchief at one corner. * Ch 6 d, p, 6 d, rw. R 3 d, p, (4 d, p) twice, 3 d, cl r, rw. Ch 6 d, p, 6 d, j in edge of hankerchief ⅜″ from last joining +. Ch 4 d, j in edge ⅛″ from last joining, repeat from * across to next corner ending at +. Repeat from * around edge of handkerchief. Tie and cut.

Rnd 2: J thread in edge at same corner between first and last motif. * Ch (3 d, p) 3 times, 3 d, j in first p of r, ch 3 d, p, (4 d, p) twice, 3 d, j in same p. Ch 3 d, j in next p of same r, ch 3 d, p, (4 d, p) twice, 3 d, j in same p. Ch 3 d, j in last p of r, ch 3 d, p, (4 d, p) twice, 3 d, j in same p. Ch (3 d, p) 3 times, 3 d, j over ch in edge between motifs. Repeat from * around, joining center p of first round ch to center p of last round ch of last motif. Tie and cut.

Tatting makes a rich and delicate lace for edging handkerchiefs. Wild Rose and Star Flower Edgings, ⅝″ and ¾″ wide, are joined to the hemstitched handkerchiefs during the first round of tatting.

TATTED SQUARES

MATERIALS: Mercerized crochet cotton, size 30. Tatting shuttle.

FOUR-LOOP SQUARE: R 5 d, 7 p sep by 2 d, 5 d, cl r.

* R 5 d, j in last p of last r, 2 d, 6 p sep by 2 d, 5 d, cl r*. Repeat from * to * twice more joining last p of 4th r to first p of first r.

Second Four-Loop Square: Work as for first square, joining to first square by 5th p of first r and 3rd p of 2nd r. Make 9 squares in all, joining to form a cross 5 squares high by 5 squares wide.

CORNER MOTIF: R 2 d, 3 p sep by 2 d, 2 d, j in 4th free p of r at end of cross, 2 d, 3 p sep by 2 d, 2 d, cl r.

* Rw, ch 2 d, 5 p sep by 1 d, 2 d. Rw, ** r 2 d, p, 2 d, j in next to last p of last r, 2 d, p, 2 d, j in middle p of next r of square, 2 d, 3 p sep by 2 d, 2 d, cl r *. Repeat from * to *, ch 3 d, p, 3 d.

Rw, r 2 d, p, 2 d, j in next to last p of last r, 2 d, p, 2 d, j in middle p of next r of square, 2 d, p, 2 d, j in middle p of next r of square, 2 d, 3 p sep by 2 d, 2 d, cl r.

Rw, ch 3 d, j in p of last ch, 3 d. Repeat from ** to *. Repeat from * to * twice, ch 7 d, p, 7 d, p, 5 d.

Rw, r 3 d, p, 3 d, j in middle p of 2nd from last ch, 3 d, p, 3 d, cl r.

Rw, ch 3 d, r 3 d, 11 p sep by 2 d, 3 d, cl r. Ch 3 d, rw, r 3 d, j in last p of last r, 3 d, j in middle p of next ch, 3 d, p, 3 d, cl r.

Rw, ch 5 d, p, 7 d, p, 7 d. Cut and tie in first r. Fill in other 3 corners in same way.

Join medallion by middle picots of adjacent rings and chains. Where four corner motifs meet, join 3 large rings in middle picot of large ring of first medallion.

Two motifs combine to form a square medallion for place mats, tablecloths. Illustration shows one complete medallion at lower right, method of joining four corner motifs at left.

TATTED DOILY

SIZE: 10″ in diameter.

MATERIALS: Six Cord Crochet Cotton, size 10. Tatting shuttle. Steel crochet hook No. 8.

Center Motif: Rnd 1: Make r of (3 d, p) 11 times, cl r, rw.

Rnd 2: Draw thread in last p, (ch 3 d, j in next p, make sm p) 11 times.

Rnd 3: J in p, * ch 6 d, p (9 d, p) twice, 6 d, j in same p (ch-lp made), ch 2 d, j in next p last rnd, repeat from * around, joining first p of new ch-lp to last p of last ch-lp. At the end of rnd, j last p of ch-lp to first p of first ch-lp. Tie and cut. There are 11 ch-lps with ch 2 d between. Center motif completed.

Rnd 4: * Make r of 4 d, j in p at point of ch-lp, 4 d, cl r, rw. Ch 5 d, p, (10 d, p) twice, 5 d, rw. Repeat from * around, j in first r. Tie and cut.

Rnd 5: * Make r of 5 d, j in p at point of ch, 5 d, cl r, rw. (Ch 5 d, p) 7 times, 5 d, rw. Repeat from * around, j in first r. Tie and cut.

Rnd 6: First Motif: Work rnds 1 and 2 as for center motif. **Next Rnd:** J in p, (4 d, j in next p) twice, work from first * to 2nd * of rnd 3 until there are 7 ch-lps, (4 d, j in next p) twice, tie to center p of ch on rnd 5, cut thread. Make 10 more motifs in same way, joining center p of first ch-lp new motif to center p of last ch-lp last motif. At end of rnd, j center p of last ch-lp to center p of first ch-lp first motif.

Rnd 7: * Make r of 4 d, j in center p of 2nd ch-lp on a motif, 4 d, cl r, rw. (Ch 5 d, p, 10 d, p, 10 d, p, 5 d, rw. R 4 d, j in center p of next ch-lp same motif, 4 d, cl r, rw) 4 times. Repeat from * around, j in first r. Tie and cut.

Rnd 8: * Make r of 4 d, j in center p of ch to right of double r last rnd, 4 d, cl r, rw. (Ch 5 d, 7 p sep by 5 d, 5 d, j in center p of next ch) twice, ch 5 d, 7 p sep by 5 d, 5 d, rw. R of 4 d, j in center p of next ch, 4 d, cl r, rw. Repeat from * around, j in first r. Tie and cut.

Tatted doily design suggests a medieval rose window framed in smaller flowers and petals. In size 10 cotton, an easy size for the beginner to work with, doily is 10″ in diameter.

DAISY DOILY

MATERIALS: Mercerized crochet cotton, size 30, 1 ball white, 1 ball yellow; 2 shuttles.

CENTER MEDALLION: Row 1: With yellow, r 1 d, 10 p sep 1 d, cl.

Row 2: * Ch 2 d, small p, j to next p. Repeat from * making 10 p.

Row 3: *Ch 3 d, small p, j p. Repeat from * around.

Row 4: * Ch 2 d, small p, 2 d, small p, j p. Repeat from * around. Tie and cut.

With white, tie to a p, ch 10 d, p, 8 d, p, 2 d, p, 8 d, p, 10 d, j next yellow p, 10 d, j last p previous. Ch 8 d, p, 2 d, p, 8 d, p, 10 d, j next yellow p. Repeat around. (10 petals made.) Tie and cut.

Tie thread at j of petals. Ch 10 d, p, 10 d, j next petal j. Continue around. Tie and cut. Ch as previous round, making 11 d.

SIDE MEDALLIONS: With yellow, 2 rows same as center medallion.

Row 3: Ch 2 d, p, 2 d, j p, 2 d, p, 2 d, j p. Continue around 10 times. Tie and cut.

Make 7 white petals same as center madallion. For second rnd, j p center medallion at same time to end p of new medallion. Ch 10 d, j at joining, 10 d, p, 10 d, etc., j next free p center medallion. Tie and cut. Make 5 side medallions joining last one to first one.

EDGE: Row 1: With yellow, r 3 d, p, 6 d, j to p of sixth petal, 6 d, p, 3 d, cl. R 3 d, j last p last r, 6 d, 2 p sep 6 d, 3 d, cl. R 3 d, j p last r, 6 d, j second petal next medallion, 6 d, p, 3 d, cl, rw. With white ch 9 d, 3 p sep 9 d, rw. With yellow * r 9 d, j next petal, 9 d, cl, rw. With white ch 9 d, 3 p sep 9 d, 9 d, rw. Yellow r 9 d, j same petal, 9 d, cl, rw. White ch 9 d, p, 9 d, rw. Repeat from * twice, then ch 9 d, 3 p sep 9 d, 9 d, rw. Repeat from beginning with 3 r group. Join to correspond. Tie and cut.

Row 2: White thread, j to p of long ch, ch 9 d, 3 p sep 9 d, 9 d, rw. Yellow r 3 d, p, 6 d, j end p same loop, 6 d, p, 3 d, cl. R 3 d, j p last r, 6 d, j p next ch, 6 d, p, 3 d, cl. R 3 d, j p last r, 6 d, j p next long ch, 6 d, p, 3 d, cl, rw. White ch 9 d, 3 p sep 9 d, 9 d, j next p same loop. Repeat once from beginning of row, ch 9 d, 3 p sep 9 d, 9 d, rw. Yellow r 9 d, j second p next loop, 9 d, cl. R 9 d, j first p next loop, 9 d, cl, rw. White ch 9 d, 3 p sep 9 d, 9 d. Repeat around. Tie and cut.

Row 3: With white, r 3 d, p, 3 d, cl, rw. Ch 13 d, center p on ch previous row, 13 d, rw. R 3 d, p, 3 d, cl. Repeat around. Tie and cut.

Row 4: With white, r 3 d, j r previous row, 3 d, cl, rw. Ch 13 d, p, 13 d, rw. R 3 d, j p next r, 3 d, cl, rw. Ch 13 d, p, 13 d, rw. R 3 d, j same p, 3 d, cl. Continue around.

Outside medallions are made same as side ones, except that they are completed with 10 petals, joining to previous row with a petal to long loop, next two to next ch's, and fourth to next long loop.

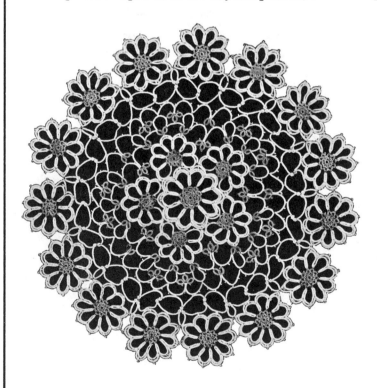

Tat a field of daisies for your table. Tatted doily, 11¾" across, makes a pretty place mat in yellow and white. Motif of daisy is shown actual size. In two-color tatting, two shuttles are used.

PADDED TATTING MOTIF

PADDED TATTING MOTIF

MATERIALS: Six Cord Crochet, size 10. Tatting shuttle.

Note: In padded tatting, all joinings are made with ball thread, as it would be difficult to draw 4 strands through a picot.

FLORAL MOTIF: Center (make 2): Make r of (1 d, p) 6 times; cl r, j in last p. **Rnd 1:** Ch (2 d, j in next p, make smp) 6 times.

Rnd 2: Ch (3 d, j in smp, make smp) 6 times.

Rnd 3: Ch (4 d, j in smp, make smp) 6 times.

Rnd 4: Ch (5 d, j in smp, make smp) 6 times.

Rnd 5: Ch (6 d, j in smp, make smp) 6 times. Tie and cut thread.

Petals: For padding, measure about 6 yards of crochet cotton size 10, fold into 4 equal lengths; tie the 4 strands to shuttle and wind on. Tie the 4 strands to ball thread. Draw through picot of one flower center and ch (3 d, p, 20 d, p, 3 d, j in next p) 6 times, joining first p of every ch to last p of previous ch; do not join last petal to first petal. Rw and ch back, 3 d, j in last p, ch (22 d, j where chains are joined) 6 times, joining last ch in first p of first petal.

Stem and Leaves: Rw, ch 60 d for stem, p, ch 25 d, p, 25 d, j in p of stem, 30 d, j in p at point of leaf. Tie and cut. Join in smp of 2nd flower center, ch 30 d, j in bottom p of stem, ch 30 d, j in same p of tatted center. Tie and cut.

Floral motifs in padded tatting ring a circular cloth of pastel linen. Flower petals shown in detail, stems and leaves, are formed over "padding" of four strands of cotton.

NOSEGAY LUNCHEON SET
Shown opposite

MATERIALS: Crochet Cotton, size 30, three 250-yd. balls, white, will make 1 large doily 15" in diameter; 1 plate doily 12" in diameter, and 1 tumbler doily 4½" in diameter. 1 shuttle and 1 ball.

TUMBLER DOILY. Center Ring: R, 1 d, 10 p sep by 2 d, 1 d, cl r, tie and cut.

Row 1: R, 2 d, p, 2 d, join to any p of center ring, 2 d, p, 2 d, cl r, turn. * Ch, 3 d, 3 p sep by 3 d, 3 d, turn. R, 2 d, join to last p of last r, 2 d, join to next p of center r, 2 d, p, 2 d, cl r. Repeat from * all around, ending with ch, 3 d, 3 p sep by 3 d, tie and cut.

Row 2: R, 4 d, p, 4 d, join to center p of any ch of previous row, 4 d, p, 4 d, cl r, turn. * Ch, 3 d, 3 p sep by 3 d, 3 d, turn. R, 4 d, join to last p of last r made, 4 d, join to same p of same ch of previous row, 4 d, p, 4 d, cl r, turn. Ch, 3 d, 3 p, sep by 3 d, 3 d, turn. R, 4 d, join to last p of last r made, 4 d, join to center p of next ch of previous row, 4 d, p, 4 d, cl r, turn. Repeat from * all around ending row to correspond, tie and cut.

Row 3: Motif: Center Ring: R, 1 d, 8 p sep by 2 d, 1 d, cl r, tie and cut. R, 2 d, p, 2 d, join to any p of center ring, 2 d, p, 2 d, cl r, turn. Ch, 3 d, p, 3 d, join to center p of ch of 2nd row, 3 d, p, 3 d, turn. * R, 2 d, join to last p of last r, 2 d, join to next p of center r, 2 d, p, 2 d, cl r, turn. Ch, 3 d, 3 p sep by 3 d, 3 d, turn. Repeat from * all around, joining last r to first r, tie and cut.

Second Motif: Work center ring same as first motif. R, 2 d, p, 2 d, join to any p of center r, 2 d, p, 2 d, cl r, turn. Ch, 3 d, p, 3 d, skip 1 ch of 2nd row, join to center p of next ch, 3 d, p, 3 d, turn. * R, 2 d, join to last p of last r made, 2 d, join to next p of center r, 2 d, p, 2 d, cl r, turn. Ch, 3 d, p, 3 d, join to center p of corresponding ch of previous motif, 3 d, p, 3 d, turn, repeat from * once. Finish motif same as first motif.

Work 8 more motifs, joining in same manner and join last motif to first motif.

PLATE DOILY: Work first 3 rows same as tumbler doily.

Row 4: R, 5 d, join to center p of center free ch of any motif, 5 d, cl r, turn. * Ch, 5 d, 4 p sep by 5 d, 5 d, turn. R, 9 d, join to center p of next ch of same motif, 9 d, cl r. R, 9 d, join to center p of next free ch of next motif, 9 d, cl r, turn. Ch, 5 d, join to last p of last ch made, 5 d, 3 p sep by 5 d, 5 d, turn. R, 5 d, join to center p of next ch of same motif, 5 d, cl r, turn. Repeat from * all around, ending row to correspond, tie and cut.

Row 5: R, 7 d, join to any p of ch of 4th row, 7 d, cl r, turn, ¼" space. R, 7 d, 5 p sep by 2 d, 7 d, cl r, turn. ¼" space. * R, 7 d, join to next p of last row, 7 d, cl r, turn. ¼" space. R, 7 d, join to last p of previous large ring, 2 d, 4 p sep by 2 d, 7 d, cl r, turn. ¼" space. Repeat from * all around, tie and cut.

Row 6: R, 3 d, 3 p sep by 2 d, 3 d, join to center p of any r of last row, 3 d, 3 p sep by 2 d, 3 d, cl r, turn. Ch, 5 d, 3 p sep by 2 d, 5 d, turn. * R, 3 d, p, 2 d, join to center free p of last r made, 2 d, p, 3 d, join to center free p of next r of row 5, 3 d, 3 p sep by 2 d, 3 d, cl r, turn. Ch, 5 d, 3 p sep by 2 d, 5 d, turn. Repeat from * all around, tie and cut.

Row 7: R, 5 d, join to last p of ch of last row, 3 d, join to first p of next ch of last row, 5 d, cl r, turn. Ch, 5 d, 3 p sep by 2 d, 5 d, turn. * R, 5 d, join to last p of same ch of last row, 3 d, join to first p of next ch, 5 d, cl r, turn. Ch, 5 d, 3 p sep by 2 d, 5 d, turn. Repeat from * all around, tie and cut.

Row 8: R, 7 d, join to center p of ch of last row, 7 d, cl r, turn. * Ch, 5 d, 3 p sep by 3 d, 5 d, turn. R, 7 d, join to center p of next ch of last row, 7 d, cl r, turn. Repeat from * all around, ending with ch, 5 d, 3 p sep by 3 d, 5 d, tie and cut.

Row 9: Motifs are made same as in row 3 but joining center p of 7th ch to center p of ch of row 8, and joining center p of 8th ch to center p of next ch of row 8.

Second Motif: Join center p of first ch to center p of 6th ch of first motif, and join 7th and 8th ch

Exquisite tatted luncheon set has mats of three sizes. Smallest doily, 4½" diameter, is shown above. See Nosegay Luncheon Set, this page.

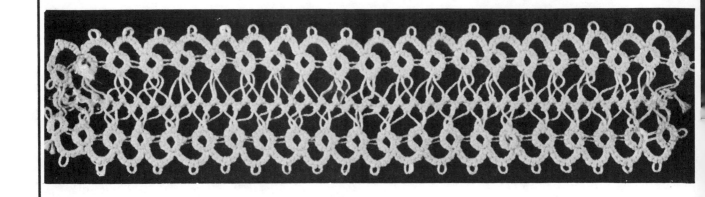

HAIRPIN LACE AND TATTED EDGING

MATERIALS: Crochet cotton No. 30. Tatting shuttle.
Hairpin lace loom, ½″ size. Crochet hook.

Make hairpin lace for desired length.

Edging: R 2 d, p, 3 d, j 2 loops hairpin lace, 2 d, p 2 d, cl.
* Rw, ch 3 d, p, 3 d, rw. R 2 d, j last p last r, 2 d, j next 2
loops lace, 2 d, p, 2 d, cl. Repeat from *.

Make edge on other side of hairpin lace the same way.

same as first motif. Join all motifs in same manner, having 30 motifs around edge.

LARGE DOILY: Work first 9 rows same as plate doily.

Row 10: Center Ring: R, 1 d, 9 p sep by 2 d, 1 d, cl r, tie and cut. R, 2 d, p, 2 d, join to any p of center r, 2 d, p, 2 d, cl r, turn. Ch, 3 d, p, 3 d, join to 3rd p of 3rd free ch of any motif of last row, 3 d, p, 3 d, turn. R, 2 d, join to last p of last r made, 2 d, join to next p of center ring, 2 d, p, 2 d, cl r, turn. Ch, 3 d, p, 3 d, skip first free ch of next motif, join to first p of next ch, 3 d, p, 3 d, turn.

Finish motif same as other motifs, having 9 rings instead of 8. Join all motifs in same manner, joining the 2 chs on sides at center picot and having 3 chs free at top of each motif (30 motifs).

Row 11: Motifs are worked same as in row 3, joining the center p of 7th ch to center p of last free ch of any motif of last row, and joining center p of 8th ch to center p of first free ch of next motif of last row. Join next motif in center of next 2 motifs of last row (15 motifs).

REVERSE STRIPE PILLOW
Continued from page 66

Row 19: Repeat row 4.
Row 20: Repeat row 3.
Row 21: With B, repeat row 2.
Row 22: With B, repeat row 1.
Rows 23 and 24: With MC, p 2 rows. Cut B; join A.
Rows 25–36: Repeat rows 1–12. Cut A; join C.
Rows 37–48: Repeat rows 13–24. Cut C; join B.
Rows 49–60: Repeat rows 1–12. Cut B; join C.
Rows 61–72: Repeat rows 13–24. Cut C; join A.
Rows 73–107: Repeat rows 1–35. With MC, bind off in k.

FINISHING: Block piece to measure 27″ × 13½″. Fold piece in half widthwise, right sides tog. Seam one side using yarn ends. Run in all other ends. Seam cast-on edge with MC. Turn pillow cover to right side; insert form. Close last seam with MC.

CROCHETED TRIMMINGS

CROCHETED BUTTONS

Buttons can be made without molds, following directions above and stuffing with cotton.

RING BUTTONS

Lightweight buttons can be made by using plastic rings as a base. With same yarn used in garment, work sc closely around ring. Join with a sl st in first sc. Turn crochet to inside of ring to fill center and sew center stitches together, leaving end for sewing to garment. For larger rings, 2 or 3 rnds of sc may be required to fill center with decreases on each rnd. A small shank type button, beads or rhinestones may be sewn to center of ring button for decoration. Rings may be covered with soutache, too.

CROCHET-COVERED BUCKLES

A self-belt made for a knitted or crocheted dress should always have a buckle to give the belt a professional look. Buy a buckle in proper size for belt, sc closely over buckle with same yarn as belt, keeping top of stitches at outer edge of buckle.

RING BUCKLE

One, two, three or more plastic rings can be used to make a buckle. With same yarn used in belt, work sc closely around rings. Join with sl st in first sc. Sew rings together as shown. Lap one end of belt through ring at one side; sew end to wrong side. Lap other end of belt through ring at other side; finish with snap fastener.

CROCHETED TUBULAR CORD

May be used for a tie belt or, pressed flat, for a trimming braid. Use yarn single or double and suitable steel crochet hook.

Rnd 1: Ch 2, 6 sc in 2nd ch from hook. Do not join rnds.

Rnd 2: Sc in front lp of each sc around. Repeat rnd 2 for desired length. Sc in every other sc around. Cut yarn leaving 8″ end. Thread end in yarn needle, draw end through remaining sts, fasten off securely.

CROCHETED SOUTACHE

Makes a beautiful braid for a suit or dress. Make a chain with soutache a little longer than you need for edge to be trimmed. Single crochet in each chain for desired length. Use wrong side of crochet for right side of braid.

CROCHET-COVERED BUTTONS

Rnd 1: Ch 2, 12 sc in 2nd ch from hook. Do not join rnds.

Rnd 2: * Sc in next sc, 2 sc in next sc, repeat from * around. Continue around in sc, inc as necessary to keep work flat, until piece is same size as button mold.

Next Rnd: * Pull up a lp in each of next 2 sts, yo and through 3 lps on hook (dec made), sc in next sc, repeat from * around. Insert button mold. Continue to dec as necessary to cover back of button mold.

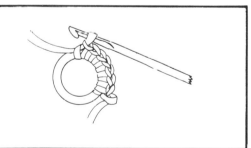

SINGLE CROCHET AROUND RING

TURN CROCHET TO INSIDE

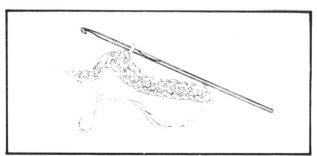

CROCHET SOUTACHE

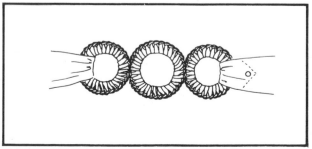

COVERED RINGS USED AS BUCKLE

HOW TO MAKE HAIRPIN LACE

Use a crochet hook and a hairpin lace loom. Width of hairpin lace depends on the size of hairpin loom used. This loom is sometimes called a fork or staple.

With crochet hook, make a loose chain stitch. Take hook out of stitch and insert left-hand prong of loom through chain stitch. Draw out ch (loop) until knot is halfway between prongs. Then bring thread to front and around right-hand prong to back (Fig. 1). Insert crochet hook up through loop on left-hand prong, draw thread through and make a chain (Figs. 2 and 3). * To get crochet hook in position for next step,

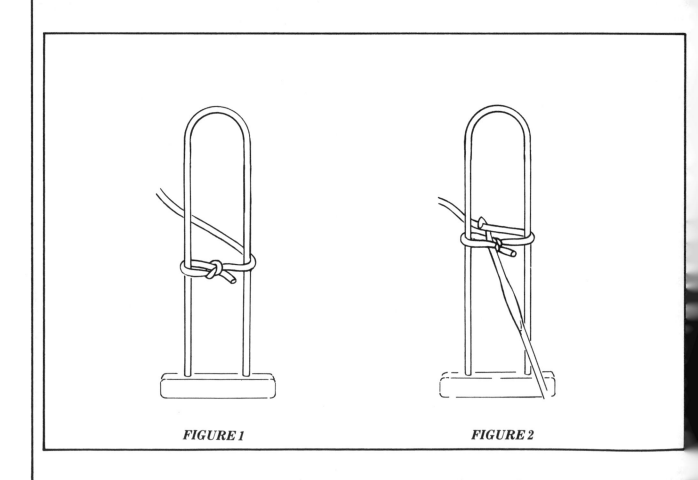

FIGURE 1

FIGURE 2

without drawing out loop on hook, turn handle of crochet hook upward parallel with prongs, then pass it through the prongs to back of loom (Fig. 4). Now turn loom toward you from right to left once (a loop over right prong). With a loop on hook, insert crochet hook up through loop on left-hand prong, in back of front thread, draw thread through (Fig. 5) and complete single crochet. Repeat from *.

Note: Some prefer to withdraw crochet hook from loop, turn loom over as directed and reinsert hook, instead of method illustrated in Fig. 4.

When loom gets crowded, remove base, slide most of loops off, leaving last few on and replace base.

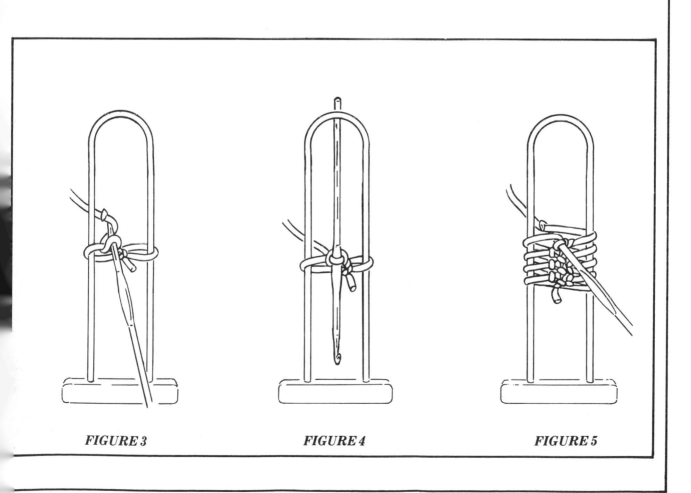

FIGURE 3   FIGURE 4   FIGURE 5

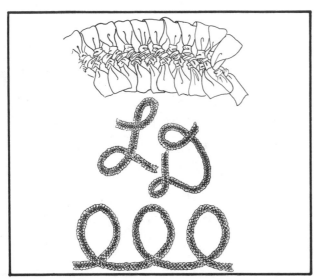

FIGURE 1. UNEDGED HAIRPIN LACE

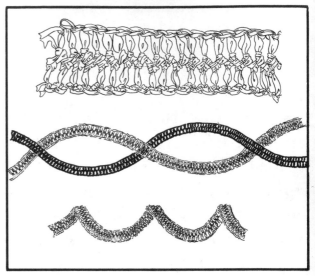

FIGURE 2. EDGED HAIRPIN LACE

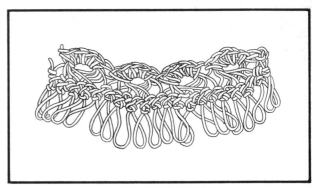

FIGURE 3. FRINGED TRIMMING

Hairpin lace can be used for smart and decorative trimmings on suits, coats and dresses. Many yarns are suitable for making the braids and edgings: wool yarns from fingering weight to bulky types; novelty yarns, such as knitting ribbon in taffeta or silk organdy, metallic yarns, and corde.

Ribbon hairpin lace, ½″ or ¾″ wide, makes a trimming braid which can be formed into scallops, loops, frogs, initials or other designs. If design curves a great deal, as in forming loops or initials, do not edge the hairpin lace with crochet; Figure 1. Unedged hairpin lace is elastic and can be easily curved and stretched.

For crisper, sharper trimming, edge the lace with single crochet; Figure 2. Edged hairpin lace can be curved somewhat as in the intertwined design of two braids illustrated. The two braids may be made in two different colors for variety, or the hairpin lace may be worked in one color and the crocheted edges in another. For a scalloped edge, fold braid over at each inner point, as illustrated.

Before sewing ribbon braid to garment, steam-press, then pin in place in desired design. Sew it in place from wrong side of garment along center of trimming.

Fringed hairpin lace trimming has one edge finished in crochet, the other edge left in free-hanging loops. If a wool yarn is used, loops can be cut to form fringe. To make fringed hairpin lace trimming, Figure 3, use a 2″ hairpin loom and make lace in usual way with a multiple of 5 loops. On one edge, place 5 twisted loops together, one over the other and work 5 single crochet in each cluster of loops across. Be sure all loops twist in same direction.

A smart scalloped braid can be made by working scallops of crochet on both edges of the hairpin lace. Make 1½″ lace a little longer than desired length having multiple of 4 loops each side. With matching or contrasting yarn, crochet groups of loops together on both sides of lace as follows:

Make lp on hook; place first 4 loops tog, sl st these loops tog, make 5 sc in same place as sl st (spread loops apart as you work; scallop should measure ½″), * sl st next 4 loops tog, make 5 sc in same place as sl st, repeat from * across. Repeat scallops on other edge of hairpin lace directly opposite scallops of first side, or alternate scallops by working first 2 loops together, then repeating from * across and working last 2 loops together.

PLACE MAT MOTIF

SIZE: Each motif, 2″ in diameter.

MATERIALS: Mercerized crochet cotton, No. 20, white. One ¾″ wide hairpin lace loom. Crochet hook size 12.

MOTIF: Make 28 lps of hairpin lace on each prong. Remove from loom, and join last sc made to first sc neatly to form a circle. Cut thread and fasten off.

To Make Center: Join thread in one lp at center (keeping the lps straight). Sc in two lps at center, sc in next 2 lps, repeat around. Tie threads and cut.

Outer Edge: Fasten thread in one lp. * Ch 7, sc in next lp, repeat from * around. Fasten off.

2ND AND OTHER MOTIFS: Join with 4 side lps, (ch 3, sl st in ch-7 of corresponding motif, ch 3) 4 times.

FILL-IN MOTIF: Ch 7, sl st in a free lp between group of 4 motifs, ch 7, sl st in first ch made, * ch 7, sl st in next loop, ch 7, sl st in center, repeat from * around. End with a sl st in first ch made (12 lps in all). Tie ends and fasten off.

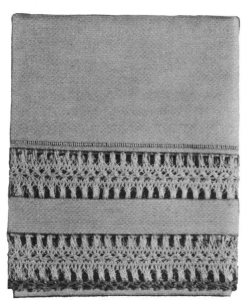

Wheels of hairpin lace are edged with crochet and joined together with fill-in motifs to make a square or rectangular tablecloth or place mat. Actual-size detail of hairpin lace and fill-in motifs, worked of crochet cotton No. 20, shown above; directions right.

TOWEL INSERTION AND EDGING

MATERIALS: White crochet cotton No. 30; contrasting color (CC) cotton No. 70. One ¾″ hairpin lace loom. Steel crochet hooks Nos. 8 and 14.

INSERTION: With white cotton and No. 8 crochet hook, make 2 strips of hairpin lace in length desired (for a 17″ wide towel, 168 lps). Fasten off. Insert hook in 3 lps of first strip, * pick up 3 lps of 2nd strip, draw through lps of first strip, draw through lps on hook; repeat from * to end. With CC and hook No. 14, insert hook in first 3 outside lps of strip, make 1 sc, * 5, 1 sc through next 3 lps; repeat from * across. Ch 8, make half turn; working along end, * 1 sc in sc, ch 8, repeat from * twice more, work along opposite side to correspond. Fasten off.

EDGING: Work hairpin lace as for insertion. With CC finish one side as for insertion. On opposite side, work edging as follows:

Row 1: * 1 sc in next 3 lps, ch 6, repeat from * across.

Row 2: Ch 6, turn, * 1 sc in next lp, ch 6, 1 sc in 3rd ch from hook (picot), ch 3; repeat from * across. Fasten off.

Hairpin lace turns a plain towel into a pretty guest towel. Edging and insertion are done in two colors, can match your own color scheme. Made of No. 30 crochet cotton. Towel insertion and edging directions are given here.

EMBROIDERY STITCH DETAILS

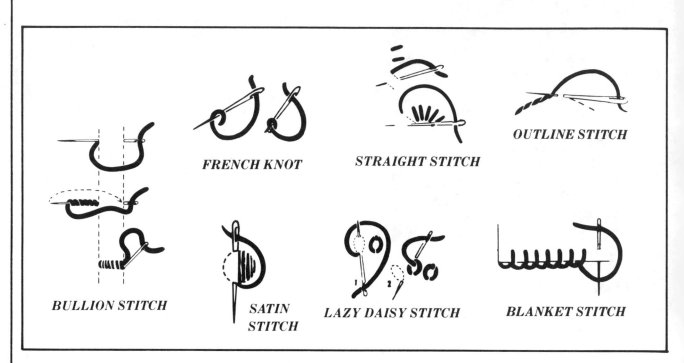

FRENCH KNOT

STRAIGHT STITCH

OUTLINE STITCH

BULLION STITCH

SATIN STITCH

LAZY DAISY STITCH

BLANKET STITCH

BASIC HOW-TO'S

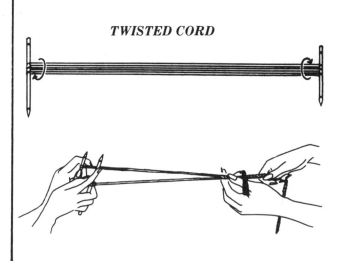

TWISTED CORD

HOW TO MAKE A TWISTED CORD

(Method requires two people). Tie one end of yarn around a pencil. Loop yarn over center of second pencil, then back to first, around first pencil and back to second, making as many strands between pencils as desired for thickness of cord. Length of yarn between pencils should be 2½ times length of cord desired. Each person holds end of yarn just below pencil with one hand and twists pencil with other hand, keeping the yarn taut. When yarn begins to kink, catch it over a doorknob; keep yarn taut. One person now holds both pencils together while other grasps center of yarn, sliding hand down yarn and releasing yarn at short intervals, letting it twist.

BASIC HOW-TO'S

POMPON

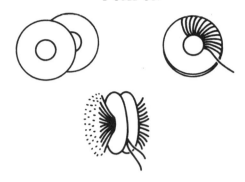

HOW TO MAKE POMPONS

One method is to cut two cardboard disks the desired size of pompon; cut out ¼" hole in center of both disks. Thread needle with two strands of yarn. Place disks together; cover with yarn, working through holes. Slip scissors between disks; cut all strands at outside edge. Draw a strand of yarn down between disks and wind several times very tightly around yarn; knot, leaving ends for attaching pompon. Remove disks by cutting through to center. Fluff out pompon and trim uneven ends.

TASSEL

HOW TO MAKE TASSELS

Wind yarn around a cardboard cut to size of tassel desired, winding it 25 to 40 times around, depending on thickness of yarn and plumpness of tassel required. Tie strands tightly together around top as shown, leaving at least 3" ends on ties; clip other end of strands. Wrap a piece of yarn tightly around strands a few times about ½" or 1" below top tie and knot. Trim ends.

FRINGE

FIG. 1   *FIG. 2*

HOW TO MAKE FRINGE

Cut strands of yarn double the length of fringe desired. Fold strands in half. Insert a crochet hook from front to back of edge where fringe is being made, pull through the folded end of yarn strand as shown in Fig. 1. Insert the two ends through loop as shown in Fig. 2 and pull ends to tighten fringe. Repeat across edge with each doubled strand, placing strands close together, or distance apart desired. For a fuller fringe, group a few strands together, and work as for one strand fringe.

The fringe may be knotted after all strands are in place along edge. To knot, separate the ends of two adjacent fringes (or divide grouped fringes in half); hold together the adjacent ends and knot 1" or more below edge as shown in Fig. 3. Hold second end with one end of next fringe and knot together the same distance below edge as first knot. Continue across in this manner. A second row of knots may be made by separating the knotted ends again and knotting together ends from two adjacent fringes in same manner as for first row of knots.

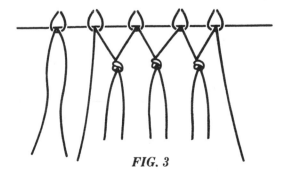

FIG. 3

HOW TO TAKE MEASUREMENTS

Directions for the knitted and crocheted items on the following pages are based on body measurements given in the tables on this page.

To take body measurements for misses', women's, and teens' sizes, measure around fullest part of bust (with bra), natural waistline, and fullest part of hip. Find the column of measurements in the tables which approximates the measurements taken. The size at the top of the column is the size to make. Necessary allowance has been made in the directions for the proper fit of each garment according to style, stitch, and yarn type. The blocked, or finished, bust measurement of the knitted or crocheted garment is given with the directions.

To take body measurements for children's sizes, measure around fullest part of child's chest over underwear, holding tape comfortably, neither snugly nor loosely. Find the chest measurement in table, then find size to make directly above in same column. Other measurements in table will help you decide whether your child differs in build from the average so that adjustments can be made easily as you work. Children's garments are designed for a casual, easy fit and allow for a child's growth. The chest, or breast, measurement, not the child's age is your guide in choosing the cor-rect size to knit. This is the most important measurement in fitting a child's knitted garment. Shoulders are in proportion to chest.

ADJUSTING TO LARGER AND SMALLER SIZES

There is a 2″ difference in bust, waist, and hip between each misses' and each women's size, except for size 10. To make a garment one size larger than given in directions, add the number of stitches equaling 1″ to both back and front for a pullover, 1″ to back and ½″ to each front for a cardigan or jacket, 2″ to a skirt. Subtract the same number for a smaller size. For size 10, subtract only half these amounts from size 12. When stitch is a repeat pattern, add or subtract the number of stitches equal to one or more multiples.

There is a ½″ difference across back and front at shoulders for each misses' and each women's size, 1″ for each men's size. To obtain desired width at shoulders, decrease more or fewer stitches at armhole shaping, dividing evenly between armholes. There is a ¼″ difference at wrist and ½″ at underarms for each size.

The length of sweaters, jackets, dress waists, and sleeves is changed by adding or subtracting required number of inches before armhole is reached.

MISSES' BODY MEASUREMENTS

SIZE	6	8	10	12	14	16	18	
BUST	30½	31½	32½	34	36	38	40	ins.
WAIST	22	23	24	25½	27	29	31	″
HIP	32½	33½	34½	36	38	40	42	″

YOUNG JUNIORS/TEENS

SIZE	7/8	9/10	11/12	13/14	
BUST	29	30½	32	33½	ins.
WAIST	23	24	25	26	″
HIP	32	33½	35	36½	″

MEN'S BODY MEASUREMENTS

SIZE	34	36	38	40	42	44	
CHEST	34	36	38	40	42	44	ins.
WAIST	30	32	34	36	38	40	″

WOMEN'S BODY MEASUREMENTS

SIZE	38	40	42	44	46	48	
BUST	42	44	46	48	50	52	ins.
WAIST	34	36	38	40½	43	45½	″
HIP	44	46	48	50	52	54	″

INFANTS' AND GIRLS' BODY MEASUREMENTS

SIZE	6 mos.	1	2	3	4	6	8	10	12	14	
CHEST	19	20	21	22	23	24	27	28½	30	32	ins.
WAIST	19	19½	20	20½	21	22	23½	24½	25½	26½	″
HIP	20	21	22	23	24	26	28	30	32	34	″
HEIGHT*	22	25	29	31	33	37	41	45	49	53	″

BOYS' BODY MEASUREMENTS

SIZE	1	2	3	4	6	8	10	12	14	16	
CHEST	20	21	22	23	24	26	28	30	32	34	ins.
WAIST	19½	20	20½	21	22	23	24	25½	27	29	″
NECK					11	11½	12	12½	13½	14	″
HIP	20	21	22	23	25	27	29	31	33	35½	″
HEIGHT*	25	29	31	33	37	41	45	49	53	55	″

*Height for girls and boys (with shoes) is measured from socket bone at back of neck to floor.

PROFESSIONAL BLOCKING AND FINISHING FOR KNITTED AND CROCHETED FASHIONS

Professional blocking and finishing often make the difference between a beautiful knitted or crocheted garment and a mediocre one. A perfectly knitted item can be ruined by slipshod finishing, while even an indifferently knitted one can be made smart by careful corrective blocking and finishing. Professional techniques are given here as a guide to the shop offering finishing service and to the individual knitter who has the proper equipment and wants to do her own blocking and finishing. The most important ingredients are time and patience, a knowledge of dressmaking techniques and a feel for the fabric. Do not hurry. Allow a day to block and finish a high-style sweater or jacket, two days or more for a suit or coat or dress which requires a lining.

BLOCKING

Blocking is the method used to set a knitted or crocheted piece to desired shape, size and texture. Cables, ribs and raised patterns can be blocked by steaming to shape but should not be pressed flat. Stockinette stitch in most yarns can be pressed flat. Every piece of a garment must be blocked individually before a seam or other joining is made.

Blocking Equipment:

1. Blocking table (40" x 60" or larger).
2. Heavy rug padding nailed to table and covered tightly with muslin sheet.
3. Rust-proof T pins or large bank pins.
4. Steam iron adjusted to maximum amount of steam.
5. Transparent pressing cloth.
6. Yardsticks and tape measures.
7. Tailors' chalk (white and colored).
8. Pressing pads for bustline and darts.
9. Shaped sleeve pad.
10. Sleeve board for pressing seams and edges.
11. Heavy strings tied to large safety pins at each end to mark center of garment, and as a guide to a straight line between two points.

Determining Measurements for Blocking: As many actual body measurements as possible should be taken; see Figures 1 and 2 for complete body measurements. Any adjustment for the style and fit of the design can be taken into consideration in blocking. Check with the blocking measurements recommended in the instructions and with picture of the garment.

If blocking measurements for individual pieces are not given in the instructions, figure them out, using the gauge as a guide. Note the number of stitches at bottom, hip, waist, underarm, shoulders, etc., and divide by the number of stitches per inch. Compare blocking measurements to body measurements (making same allowance for style, as shown in picture). Make notes of adjustments that should be made.

FIG. 1   *FIG. 2*

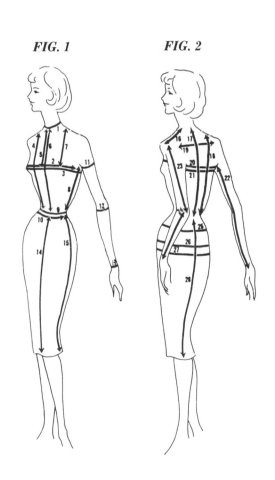

1 NECK   2 BUST FRONT
3 BUST   4 SHOULDER TO WAIST
5 NECK TO BUSTLINE
6 NECK TO WAIST
7 SHOULDER TO BUSTLINE
8 UNDERARM TO WAIST
9 WAIST
10 WAIST FRONT   11 UPPER ARM
12 LOWER ARM   13 WRIST
14 WAIST TO HEM—FRONT
15 WAIST TO HEM—SIDE

16 NECK TO END OF SHOULDER
17 NECK TO WAIST
18 SHOULDER TO WAIST
19 BACK—4" BELOW NECK
20 CHEST   21 BUST BACK
22 UNDERARM TO WRIST
23 SHOULDER TO ELBOW
24 ELBOW TO WRIST
25 HIPS—3" BELOW WAIST
26 HIPS—7" BELOW WAIST
27 HIPS—9" BELOW WAIST

28 WAIST TO HEM—BACK

Preparing Garment for Blocking: Conceal all ends of yarn by running them diagonally through several stitches on wrong side, using a tapestry needle or crochet hook. If yarn is particularly heavy, split it and run each end separately through adjoining stitches to avoid bulk.

If washing is necessary, wash pieces separately. Smooth out flat on Turkish towels, adjusting pieces so that they measure no more than finished measurements desired. Some knits stretch larger when wet so must be pushed into slight puckers (which will disappear as fabric dries). Drying process may be hastened by placing towels on window screens raised so that air can circulate underneath.

Special Considerations: Certain pattern stitches such as ribbing, cables, lacy stitches or other patterns which require stretching in width for proper effect should be blocked one to two inches wider to allow for shrinking back; if yarn contains 50% or more nylon, allow two or three inches for shrinking back.

Some yarns have considerable "hang" and measure much longer held up than lying flat on the table. The amount of "hang" should be taken into consideration and the garment should be blocked shorter and wider. This is true of extra or loosely knitted garments. Mohair needs a little extra stretching in length only; otherwise it may buckle.

For the full-busted figure it is best to have an underarm bustline dart which can be sewn in when fabric is not bulky. Allowance must be made by stretching the front longer at the sides to make room for dart; Figure 3. If fabric is to be steamed, rather than pressed flat, dart allowance can be accomplished by inserting a pad from side seam toward center front, before seaming, to increase length at side.

Plan Seams: Consider what type of seam will be most suitable. In most garments a running backstitch made with #50 sewing thread or fine yarn is best and will need an allowance of only one stitch from edge. If machine zigzag stitch is to be used, allow ⅜" for seams. If fabric calls for overcast or woven seams, it is not necessary to make any allowances. Any jogs caused by increases, bind-offs, or other shaping can be evened out in blocking and taken in in seams.

Basic Pattern: It is helpful to have a basic dress pattern to use as a blocking guide to proper shaping of a skirt panel, cap of set-in sleeve, shape of basic collar and neckline, etc. Be sure to consider seam allowances and darts in pattern. This pattern is also useful for linings. Darts in basic pattern may be pinned in and pads used for shaping the knitted fabric accordingly; or if more suitable for fabric to be blocked flat, leave basic pattern as is, and after blocking, shrink the extra width allowed for darts.

Pinning: After writing down all measurements to be followed in blocking, pin one section at a time on blocking table, wrong side up (except ribbons). Following measurements, place pins in edge of section as close as necessary to obtain a perfectly even edge, never more than ½" apart; place into padding in opposite direction from fabric "stretch"; Figure 4.

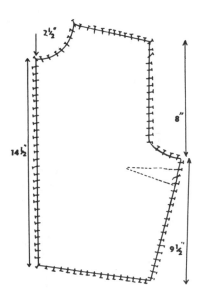

SIDE BLOCKED 9½" IS 8½" WITH ½" DART SEWN IN.

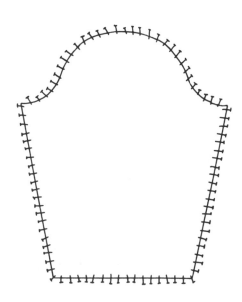

PLACING OF PINS FOR BLOCKING SLEEVE.

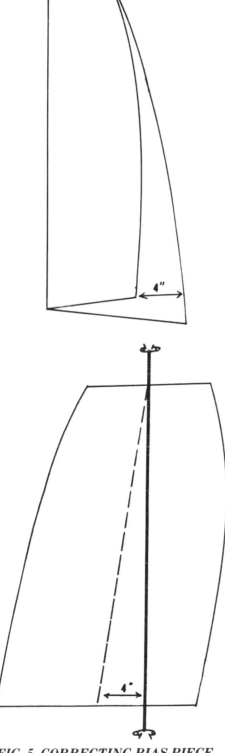

Pressing: There are two methods of pressing knitted and crocheted pieces: flat pressing and steam-pressing. Consider the texture desired before touching iron to fabric. Some yarns, such as mohair, should never be pressed flat as they would lose life and texture. If a soft fluffy appearance is desirable, or if pattern stitch is any type of raised stitch, it should not be pressed flat. If in doubt, try pressing a small piece flat in an inconspicuous section; then try another section steamed without pressure and compare. Some materials, such as ribbon, can be pressed flat and afterwards steamed up slightly before unpinning to obtain an attractive texture. If there are cables separated by wide sections of plain knitting, you may wish to use a combination of two techniques, pressing only plain section flat.

For steaming technique, support weight of iron in your hand, hold as close as possible to fabric without touching it and move slowly over entire pinned piece, making certain that steam penetrates fabric. If yarn is extra heavy, it may be necessary to use a spray iron or a wet pressing cloth to provide extra steam.

To press sections flat, place organdy pressing cloth on top of pinned piece and lower iron so that weight rests on fabric. Raise and lower again over entire section; do not use a back-and-forth ironing motion. With the transparent pressing cloth it is possible to see where flat sections begin and end.

Leave pieces pinned to table until entirely dry. Drying can be hastened by the use of a small electric fan or hand dryer. If a piece has a duplicate, leave guide pins in the blocking table at intervals around the garment shape so that you have an outline for shaping the duplicate piece.

Wet Blocking: This may be desirable if the stitch used makes the finished pieces go strongly bias. Also, wet blocking may be used for articles which have been washed. Wet or wash article thoroughly, squeeze out and roll in a Turkish towel, lay the individual pieces on blocking table and pin to measurements using rustproof pins. Leave until thoroughly dry.

Bias Items: Some yarns will work up straight when knit in garter stitch or pattern stitches with no purling, but will go strongly bias when knit in stockinette stitch. This may happen with some pattern stitches and some knitters, regardless of the yarn used. Wet blocking will solve this problem, or if time and space do not permit, item can be straightened with steam blocking: First mark center stitch of item, then measure exactly how much the bias amounts to and block it the same amount in the opposite direction. Example: If the item hangs 4″ bias to the right, pin and block it 4″ to the left, and the blocked piece will hang straight; Figure 5.

FIG. 5 CORRECTING BIAS PIECE

Blocking Technique for Ribbon: Nearly all ribbon garments look, fit and wear best when blocked flat. Run in or sew ends on wrong side. Lay piece on blocking table right side up. Examine pieces for any imperfect stitches and straighten by placing plain end of crochet hook under the imperfect stitch to hold it straight. Apply steam to set the stitch.

Smooth piece on table right side up, pinning just enough to control curling at edges, but do not stretch material. Place pressing cloth over article and press, using steam and slight pressure on iron to flatten the stitches and set the pattern. Do not use ironing motion. Unpin pieces, consult "blocked gauge" and repin, stretching to desired measurements. You must consider "hang" when blocking ribbon skirts. Allow 1″ to 2″ for most ribbons and 3″ for the heavier all-rayon ribbons. Block skirt slightly wider to compensate for the "hang" which makes the skirt fit close to the body.

Ribbon knits should be stretched after setting the stitches or the garment will gradually become longer in wearing and require alterations. If properly stretched to the blocked gauge, the garment will retain its original dimensions. Stretched and blocked ribbon pieces can be shrunk with steam, too, though in a limited range.

Ribbon knits take nicely to sewn-in darts, and an underarm bustline dart is usually desirable. Allowance should be made for this in blocking. For full-busted figures requiring a "close" fit, darts may also be taken vertically from the waist up. All ⅜″ to ½″ for seams in knitted ribbons. Some crocheted ribbons have zigzag edges formed by the pattern which can be meshed and sewn as an invisible seam. It is necessary to match these edges, so find the right side of each piece before blocking.

Some ribbons and some stitches look nicer if steamed slightly without cloth after pressing flat, but before removing pins. This can be determined by experimenting on a small corner of the material and is usually desirable for a "butterfly" stitch or other overlay pattern stitch.

ASSEMBLY

Many dressmaking techniques are used in assembling knitted garments and the couturier types require a good knowledge of dressmaking techniques for a successful result. In assembling knitted garments there are no helpful notches to match as in dress-making patterns. Everything has to be measured and marked with pins or chalk to take the place of notches. Careful and precise blocking will show its value here. Some garments have definite ribs or patterns that can be matched. Plain stitches must be measured and marked at intervals and the markings matched.

It is desirable to have a form with collapsible shoulders for fitting garments. A store would need several, in different sizes.

Preliminary Try-On: Baste pieces together with contrasting thread, taking in darts and seam allowances. Try garment on form. If you find something wrong other than seam adjustments, you can shrink or stretch for desired fit. If it is necessary to stretch, the part to be stretched should be pinned to desired measurement and steam applied to just that portion. If shrinking is necessary, pin to desired measurement and form small puckers which will disappear with steam applied and a little coaxing with the fingers. The wide part of the sleeve board is useful for small adjustments which can be done without removing bastings. If garment fits form, sew the main seams. It is now ready for fitting. (If garment is to be lined, sew main seams of lining and try on at same fitting.)

Common Fitting Problems: Shoulder seams that sag can be held by a running backstitch of yarn through the seam, which is left in garment; Figure 6. Necklines can be adjusted and held by slip stitching with yarn; Figure 7.

FIG. 6 STAYING STITCH FOR A SHOULDER SEAM.

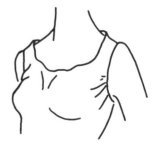

FIG. 7 NECKLINE IS TOO BIG. SOLUTION: SLIP STITCH, AND SHRINK OUT FULLNESS.

ARMHOLE IS TOO SMALL. SOLUTION: RELEASE CROCHETED EDGE, PIN OUT AND STRETCH ARMHOLE.

FIG. 8 MESHING CROCHETED BOX STITCH PATTERNS TOGETHER: JOIN ZIGZAG EDGES, SEW BACK AND FORTH HOLDING PIECES RIGHT SIDE UP.

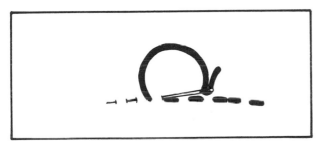

FIG. 9 RUNNING BACKSTITCH.

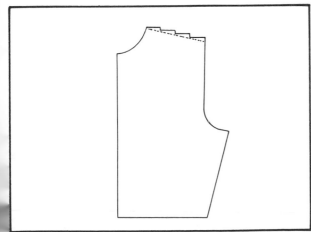

FIG. 10 SEWING SHOULDER SEAM TO TAKE IN JOGS OF BIND-OFFS.

If fronts of jacket or coat hang away from each other, front edge is too long and should be shortened by a staying thread as described for shoulders and shrinking; or side seam is too tight and should be stretched. If front edges hang forward and overlap more at bottom than they should, front edges are too short and are drawing (common if edges are crocheted); or side seams are too loose. Solution: Stretch front edge if it has any curve, or restitch side seams more firmly.

If wide square neckline gapes or sags in front and slides on shoulders, take more seam allowance from shoulder neck edge to nothing more at shoulder tip. Sew 1½" wide folded piece of nylon tulle along square of neckline to hold it to desired shape. Also check bustline fit of garment, for if it is stretching through bustline, neckline will be affected.

If straight skirt ripples or flares at bottom, hips are too tight. It is best to pin zipper in place while garment is being tried on to prevent buckling of zipper. Mark positions of buttons and buttonholes, if they are to be made later. If grosgrain of nylon tulle facings are to be applied to front edges or neckline, cut and pin them in place during try-on. Mark waistline if it is fitted and pin seam binding of soft elastic in place to hold waistline.

If it necessary to cut fabric for major adjustments, mark cutting line with chalk or basting and zigzag stitch on sewing machine ¼" inside marked line (adjust size of zigzag stitch to fabric). Or sew by hand, being careful to catch every stitch. Then cut fabric. Raw edge can be crocheted if yarn is not too heavy, or overcast by hand. If garment is too long, excess can be removed by pulling a thread at desired length and binding off the open stitches with crochet hook in same tension as knitting.

Seams: Seams should be as nearly invisible as possible and, above all, straight and neat. They must be firm enough to hold, yet elastic enough to give with the fabric, having the same tension and resiliency as the knitting. All patterns, stripes, tops of ribbed bands, colored borders, etc., must be matched carefully. Seams may be sewn in various ways depending on type of knitted or crocheted fabric and stitch. Ribbons, unless edge patterns are to be meshed together as in Figure 8, can be sewn by machine. A zigzag stitch with #50 mercerized sewing cotton is best. Test resiliency after sewing a few stitches. A zigzag stitch will give with the fabric while a straight stitch is apt to break. Certain firm fabrics knitted of wool or other yarns also take to this machine stitching.

Hand-Sewn Seams: In every case sleeves should be set in and collars sewn on by hand. Hand sewing should be a running backstitch,

FIG. 11 LENGTHWISE WOVEN SEAM

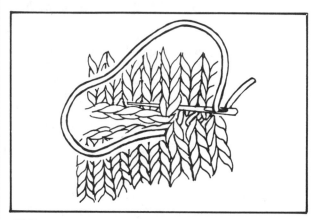

FIG. 12 CROSSWISE WOVEN SEAM

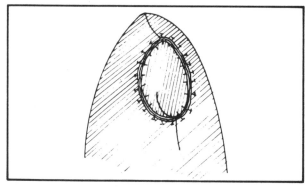

FIG. 13 SETTING IN SLEEVE

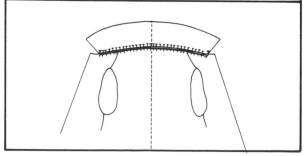

FIG. 14 PINNING ON COLLAR

Figure 9, taking in seam allowance planned, usually 1 stitch (2 stitches if finely knit). Sewing with yarn makes a bulky seam which is hard to take out, if necessary, without cutting the wrong strand. However, if yarn is desired, use very fine matching yarn or split the original yarn. Seams may also be woven or meshed when called for in a pattern. Be careful to take in bound-off stitches in seams; Figure 10.

Weaving Seams: (a) Lengthwise Woven Seam. Thread needle with matching yarn. Lay the two pieces face up on a flat surface, edges meeting. Take a vertical stitch through one edge, then a vertical stitch through the other edge. When yarn is drawn sufficiently tight it will make a running stitch seam and each stitch will meet its neighbor in the proper order; Figure 11.

(b) Crosswise Woven Seam: Thread needle with matching yarn. Lay the two edges face up on a flat surface. Starting at right-hand side, take a small stitch through both edges; then insert needle into first stitch and up through next stitch on one edge, down through second stitch and up through next stitch on other edge. Working first in one edge and then the other, insert needle into last stitch worked in and bring it up through next stitch. Continue across in this manner; Figure 12.

Setting in Sleeves and Attaching Collars: Sleeves cannot be woven into place. Because the set of a sleeve is so important, it is best to baste it in place and try on before sewing in by hand.

It is not enough to match underarm seams; you must find the center of sleeve cap and pin to shoulder seam. Then, starting at underarm, pin each side fitting sleeve carefully into armhole and ease in any slight fulness through top of sleeve cap; Figure 13. If there is too much fulness to be eased in, check cap measurements and armhole length with basic pattern and reshape if necessary. A small amount extra may be taken in when sewing sleeve in place without resorting to cutting the fabric.

Find center back of collar and neck and pin together. Pin front edges of collar in position; pin carefully and evenly between the pins placed at center and front edges; Figure 14.

If collar is double, or faced with tulle, undercollar must be smaller to allow for turndown. This also applies to lapels for proper "roll."

Join the two collars at outer edges by sewing right sides together closely along edge (if fabric is not bulky) or by single crocheting, slip stitching or overcasting along stitches at edges through both thicknesses. Sew upper collar to neck edge, taking in small seam or overcasting edge stitches together, then roll collar over your hand and pin undercollar so that it covers seam and has proper roll without bulk underneath. Sew undercollar in place.

FINISHING

Hems: If garment is to have a hem at bottom or on sleeves, these can be picked up before or after main seams are in and facings turned. Use a size smaller needle than used in garment and work in stockinette stitch. With wrong side facing you, pick up and knit through the whole stitch at edge; pick up to within one stitch of side edges (seam allowance) and within one stitch of facing when turned.

If garment has cables starting at hemline, it is necessary to pick up hems in this way, picking up fewer stitches across cables so that hem will not buckle. This is also true of widely ribbed garments, if they need hems. If garment is finely ribbed at bottom or has a nonroll border, it does not need a hem. Another method used for hems when garment is clumsy to handle is to knit hems separately and single crochet, overcast or slip stitch to bottom edge of garment. Ribbing on bottom edges and cuffs should be flat seamed or woven together so that ribbing can be turned up without showing a "wrong side" seam.

Interfacing: Sometimes it is desirable to interface a collar with nylon tulle or bias Pellon® . Cut interfacing to fit undercollar and catch stitch to entire under-collar before joining to upper collar; Figure 15. Interfacing should also be used along front edges of garments, especially tailored jackets and coats. Pin to piece to be interfaced and cut to fit.

Facings: Most facings are knitted but nylon tulle is good to use as a facing. It provides a base for sewing buttonholes, as well as a crisp front edge. Patch pockets will not sag if they are catch stitched throughout to nylon tulle. A strip of tulle will do wonders for a low neckline, the edges of slot pockets, or for cuffs. It is easy to work with, does not ravel, and is not as scratchy as coarse net.

If garment is too bulky for a knitted facing, French belting (grosgrain) can be used. This has a picot edge and can be steamed and stretched into a curve.

To face front edges of a cardigan with ribbon, wet and press ribbon before sewing to garment to pre-shrink it, or use nylon ribbon. Use matching grosgrain ribbon slightly narrower than front bands. If there are no front bands, use ribbon 1″ wide. Cut ribbon 1″ longer than edge to be faced. Place ribbon on wrong side of garment just inside edge; turn under top and bottom edges of ribbon; pin to neck and bottom edges of cardigan. Baste ribbon in place; whip edges of ribbon to cardigan

with matching sewing thread. If cardigan does not have front band, the inner edge of ribbon can be left free. Slash ribbon under buttonholes. Buttonhole-stitch or overcast around slashes. Or, if desired, hem edges of slashes around the buttonholes.

Buttonholes: Although buttonholes are usually knitted in, a neater buttonhole can be made by cutting and pulling a strand out for the required number of stitches; Figure 16. Either single crochet or slip stitch with yarn through the open stitches on both sides of buttonhole. This method is especially good for bulky yarns: split the yarn to be used for crocheting the open stitches.

If garment has a facing, the buttonhole must be opened in facing as well and matched to that on outside. Except in the case of mohair or extremely bulky yarns, both buttonholes can be crocheted at the same time by inserting hook through loop of outside and inside stitches and working as one. In the above-mentioned yarns, or when facing is of a different color than garment, work each buttonhole separately and tack loosely together with thread. Make long shanks when sewing the buttons on these bulkies.

Outlined buttonholes can be made by using a contrasting yarn to single crochet or slip stitch the buttonhole. Soutache can be used for slip stitching to give a trimmed or bound effect. If it

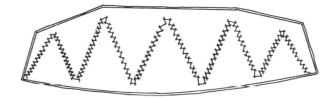

FIG. 15 CATCH STITCHING INTERFACING TO COLLAR.

FIG. 16 CUTTING STRAND FOR BUTTONHOLE.

would be best to have a vertical rather than a horizontal buttonhole, mark position and baste a piece of seam binding or narrow grosgrain ribbon slightly longer than buttonhole to wrong side of garment. Machine-stitch buttonhole using the zigzag machine. Cut with razor blade between lines of stitching and through seam binding. Work buttonhole stitch around opening with split yarn or buttonhole twist.

Buttons: Select attractive buttons that are light in weight, shank type for bulky yarns, sew-through type for fine yarns. Buttons can be made from plastic rings or button molds. Directions for these are given under crocheted Trimmings (see Index).

Belts: A self-belt should always have a buckle to avoid a homemade look. Covered rings can be used as buckles. If rings are not used, buckles of several sizes can be purchased and crocheted over with same yarn or ribbon used in belt. If knitted belt has a neat edge, overcast grosgrain to the wrong side along edges. If belt is wide, catch-stitch grosgrain back and forth, in a wide zigzag pattern, through center to hold firm and prevent rolling. Insert a strip of interfacing in extra wide belts. If edges of belt require smoothing, single crochet or slip stitch around entire belt before facing.

Skirt Tops: Tailored skirts are best fitted to waist and closed with a placket zipper. In ribbon garments, press seam allowance flat and insert zipper along seam line. In yarn garments, single crochet around zipper opening before sewing in zipper. Ease fabric into zipper and sew by hand with small running back-stitch. If skirt has knitted waistband, face with grosgrain, overlap at left side and fasten with snaps. If there is no waistband, sew 1½" wide grosgrain, cut to waist measure, on inside of skirt. If a skirt has no zipper, a crocheted elastic edge is neater than the "beading" type. Use round millinery elastic with yarn: Work one round of single crochet on top of skirt, making sure skirt will go over shoulders. On next round, hold elastic along edge of skirt and single crochet over it. Next round, single crochet without elastic, and following round single crochet over elastic. Alternate rounds in this manner, having three or four with elastic.

Finishing Edges: In finishing edges by crocheting, do not use more than one row of single crochet plus one row of slip stitch, from wrong side, if required. Some bulky yarns require only a row of slip stitch done loosely from wrong side, while some garments look best with one row of single crochet done from right side. Other patterns (usually in two colors) require one row of slip stitch from the right side, plus one row of single crochet, also from right side. It is

necessary to have the proper tension in all crocheting done along edges. There should be fewer single crochet stitches to the inch than knitted stitches; do not work into every stitch or row.

To turn an outside corner, work two or three stitches into corner stitch. To turn an inside corner, decrease two stitches by pulling through loops in corner, and one stitch each side of corner, and drawing yarn through all loops on hook tightly. This decrease should also be done at the end of any opening such as a zipper placket.

Pressing Seams: Give seams final pressing, using sleeve board and point of iron, taking care not to shrink or stretch seams.

Linings: It is desirable to have a lining in most coats, and in some jackets. Mohair in particular should be lined. Lightweight taffeta lining material is easy to work with and comes in a wide range of colors. China silk or sheath lining is recommended for ribbon sheath dresses and skirts. For detailed directions on lining a coat, see next page.

In lining sheath dresses, the basic blocking pattern can be used to cut lining. Leave ample seam allowance, and slight ease at back of neck. Stitch main seams. Try dress on inside out with lining on top. Pin along main seams and around neckline, turning in edges of lining at neckline and armholes or sleeve edges. Turn edges of lining at zipper opening, and pin along zipper tape. Pin at waistline. Sew lining to dress at waistline, neck, and sleeve edges. Do not attach lining at lower seams of skirt.

Mounting on Tulle: Some ribbon dresses, especially those with full skirts, made of silk organdy ribbon in lacy patterns, are greatly enhanced by mounting entire dress on tulle, a painstaking process. Cut tulle to basic bodice pattern. Use dress as pattern for skirt panels, allowing ½" for overlap. Do not sew seams. Try on dress inside out. Pin tulle sections to dress while on, pinning in darts. Pin tulle to dress throughout bodice in diagonal crossbar design, over-lapping tulle ½" at side seams and turning in ½" at zipper opening. Pin sections of tulle to skirt, over-lapping ½" at waistline and wherever panels meet. Pin darts at waist for smooth fit. Turn ½" under and pin along zipper opening. Now pin tulle to entire skirt in diagonal crossbar design. Turn small hem under and pin to bottom of skirt.

Remove dress carefully. Catch-stitch tulle to dress following pin lines, conforming as closely as possible to pattern stitch. Take only tiny catch stitches in dress; run thread between dress and lining for about ½", then catch-stitch to lining with medium-size stitch. Hem around neckline, bottom edge, and zipper. Close overlapped sections of tulle with running backstitch.

LINING A HANDKNIT OR CROCHETED COAT

The technique of lining a hand knitted or crocheted coat is more involved than that of lining a cloth coat, and requires considerably more work–nearly all by hand. One should allow two to three days to finish and line the coat. However, since there is so much to be gained in appearance, fit, and wear by lining the coat, it is well worth the extra work.

Lining Materials: Choose a lining material with "body" and slight stiffness. Taffeta, satin, Milium® satin, or lightweight brocade of either rayon or silk are all suitable; choice depends on style of coat. Use lightweight Pellon® for interfacing, bias Pellon® for collars.

Preparing Coat for Lining: The first step before blocking is to close and sew together any buttonholes; then judge the amount of "hang" of the pieces. Test for hang as follows: Lay back of coat smoothly on table and measure the length from neck to hem. Now fold in half lengthwise, armholes and shoulder seams together. Hold piece at back of neck and measure along fold while hanging in mid-air. The difference in measurement is the amount of natural hang before blocking. If there is a great amount of hang, the back and fronts of the coat should be blocked shorter and wider than the desired finished measurement. Width is lost to some extent, particularly at upper half of coat, as a result of hang in heavy or loosely worked pieces. One must consider also that the coat has to hang unsupported from the shoulders, unless it is to be tightly belted at the waist.

Blocking and Finishing: Block pieces following instructions on pages 285–288. After the pieces have been blocked, make paper tracings of all pieces.

Sew shoulder seams, side seams, sleeve seams, and set sleeves in place. Always use matching thread and small, loose backstitches unless otherwise specified. Now hang coat on a dressmaker's form, pinning to form at neck and pinning and holding in slightly across shoulders to prevent weight of sleeves from stretching shoulder line and neck. Let hang at least overnight.

After coat has hung overnight, check length and see that the front edges hang in a straight line following pattern stitch used. Make any necessary adjustments. If length is correct and coat has a separate hem, pin hem around bottom of coat with wrong sides together, being careful not to draw in or buckle bottom of coat. It is best to do this while garment is on the form. Allow for any facings at front of coat. Overcast hem in place with matching thread; sew upper edge loosely in place.

If coat has hung to a longer length than desired, mark length with pins. If coat is knitted, pull a strand of yarn at nearest place consistent with the pattern stitch used and cut, thus removing the excess length. With crochet hook and yarn, slip-stitch through the open stitches from the wrong side, being careful not to work too tightly. Pin and overcast the separate hem in place. If coat is crocheted, turn up excess and use for hem. If coat needs to be shortened and has a knitted-on hem, open stitches at desired length and also at the "turning row" of hem to remove excess length. With wrong sides together, pin hem in place, having open stitches at bottom. With inside of coat facing, slip-stitch together with crochet hook and yarn through two open stitches (hem and coat edge), being careful to work with loose tension. Sew upper edge of hem loosely in place with matching thread.

Cutting: Cut out lining so that it will correspond to measurements of coat while it is hanging on form. Allow 1½" extra width for a ¾" pleat at back of neck and 1" on each shoulder of back for ½" darts. If garment has set-in or dolman sleeves, allow 2½" for a 1¼" dart on each shoulder of front; if raglan sleeves, allow 2" for 1" dart on each shoulder of front. Allow ½" extra length in sleeves for "elbow room." Allow ½" extension of lining on all edges, plus 3" at bottom edge for hem.

Sewing: Sew darts on shoulders: taper darts on back to nothing about 4" down; taper darts on set-in or dolman-sleeved coat fronts to nothing about 7" down; taper darts on raglan-sleeved coat fronts to nothing about 5" down. Sew seams of lining and press. Always press seams and joinings as in dress-making. Press all knitted facings and hems which will not show on right side of coat as flat as possible before sewing to coat, to avoid undesirable bulk.

Interfacings: Cut neck interfacing from Pellon® to conform to neck of coat. If coat is made of ribbon or ribbon and yarn, use Pellon® interfacing 3" wide at front edges as well.

Place coat on form wrong side out. Pin interfacing carefully in place and catch-stitch throughout in zigzag pattern.

Pinning Lining Place: Remove coat and place lining on form wrong side out. Place coat right side out over lining. Pin coat to lining, starting at center back of neck and pinning toward shoulders and along shoulder seam, allowing ½" to extend at neck edge and easing coat slightly across shoulder span for graceful drape. Pin side seam of lining to side seam of coat near underarm. Allowing ½" of lining to extend, pin lining to coat along both front edges while it is still hanging on form.

Place a few pins along upper half of armhole and along the shoulder darts. (If coat has a raglan sleeve, pins should be placed along seam line.) Tack lightly to lining where pinned. Baste ¼" horizontal pleat in sleeve lining just below elbow (to be released later for ease). Pin lining to sleeve edge, allowing ½" to extend at bottom of sleeve.

Sew invisibly from right side along all pinned edges, ¼" from edge of coat.

Lining must extend into and turn with all edges–except for bottom hem–for a tailored and neat look. Pin and sew bottom hem of lining in place.

Make holding bars for hem by crocheting a chain 1½" long with yarn. Slip stitch to seam of coat near bottom; sew other end to inside seam of lining.

Sleeves: If sleeves have hems, trim lining just inside edge of sleeves. Sew invisibly along turn of hem. Turn and press up. Sew upper edge in place, sewing through lining to catch outside of coat sleeve lightly; then release the basted "ease pleat."

If sleeves have no hems, turn edge of lining to inside (between lining and coat) and hem in place just inside edge of sleeve; lightly sew lining to sleeve at 1" above, so that "elbow ease pleat," when released, will not cause lining to show at bottom.

Facings: If coat has separate facings, pin to front of coat, right sides together, while on form. Sew along front edges, taking in a small amount consistent with pattern stitch. Press seam open. Turn facings to inside. Press again. With inside of coat facing you, sew lightly along turned edge ¼" to ½" in from edge, taking small stitches and catching outside of coat invisibly. Take care not to draw front edge. Pin and sew inside edge of facings through lining and invisibly to front of coat.

If facings are knitted in one with front of coat, mark place where facings will turn and sew lining to coat along this line. Press lightly, trim edge of lining, and sew inside edge of facings in place in same way as separate facings. There will be a double thickness of lining inside facings.

If coat has no facings at all, trim extending edge of lining. Turn ½" on edge of coat (more, if called for by pattern) after sewing along line of prospective turn in order to hold lining inside fold for sharp edge. Pin and sew turned edge in place, catching outside of coat invisibly.

If coat is collarless, or has a set-away collar, or stand-up band set away from neck edge, finish neck by turning extending edge of lining to inside; then turn ¼" of neck edge to inside (over lining) and sew. If knitted or crocheted neck facing is provided, pin in place, then sew so that it joins turned edge of neck. Sew other edge lightly in place, catching through lining to interfacing.

Collars: If coat has collar, face with bias Pellon®, catch-stitching throughout in zigzag pattern. Cut lining, allowing ½" to turn to inside at all edges, and sew to collar on three sides leaving neck edge open, except where knitted under-collar is provided. In this case, bias Pellon® is catch-stitched to under-collar before sewing together with upper-collar. Always fold or roll collar in desired position (this applies also to lapels) before sewing under-collar or collar lining in place (under part will need to be smaller, to avoid buckling collar). Pin and sew upper part of collar to neck edge of coat, working from inside of coat. Press seam. Fold collar in position and sew under-collar or collar lining in place, covering seam. Catch-stitch invisibly through all thicknesses, 1" from outside edges of collar, using zigzag pattern.

Helpful Suggestions Regarding Collars: Stand-up band collars, although worked straight, should be blocked longer at lower edge and held in slightly at upper edge in order to stand straight up when sewn to coat. These collars are usually set farthest away at shoulder seams. Set-away collars are sewn at neck edge of front, slightly down at back of neck, and farthest away at shoulder seams. Collar is completely finished before attaching to coat. Shawl collars must be blocked considerably longer at the outside edge than at the neck edge, to prevent front of coat from pulling up. Stretch collar and under-collar at outside edge and ease at back edge. Notched collars should be woven to lapels with yarn, because edges seamed in the conventional way tend to be bulky.

Patch Pockets and Belts: If edges of pockets would not look well showing, a small amount can be turned to inside after lining. Cut Pellon® to fit, and catch-stitch in place throughout. Cut lining material extending ½" at edges. Turn ½" of lining to inside and sew along edge (or turn 1 row or 1 stitch to inside for better appearance). Try on coat. Pin patch pockets in place, pinning through to lining. If coat has a back belt, interline and line it as for pockets; pin it in place at becoming position. After checking to see that lining is smooth underneath pockets, sew pockets in place through to lining from right side. This supports pockets and prevents sag. Run invisible stitches ½" from edges of belt so that lining cannot show from right side. Separate cuffs are also handled this way.

Buttonholes: If buttonholes have been knitted or crocheted in, release basting used to close buttonholes. With crochet hook and yarn, work 1 row of slip stitch around buttonholes have been knitted or crocheted in, release basting used to close buttonholes. With crochet hook and yarn, work 1 row of slip stitch around buttonhole; sew buttonhole together at ends for neat corners. Slit lining material and turn under ⅛" around buttonhole; sew in place, overcasting to buttonholes, finish each buttonhole separately with slip stitch. Slit lining and sew double buttonhole together, catching the lining material between for support. When sewing buttons in place, leave enough shank so that buttons do not dimple front of coat.

DECORATIVE TOUCHES FOR HANDKNITS

DECORATIVE TOUCHES
FOR HANDKNITS

BUTTONHOLES FORMED WITH KNITTED BIAS BINDING

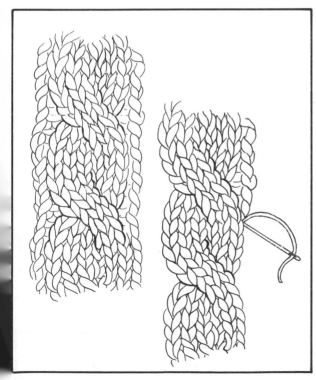

CABLE EDGING

There are many ways to decorate handknits. They can be embroidered with sequins or beads; more casual knits in stockinette stitch can be embroidered with wool.

Wool Embroidery: Work embroidery after pieces have been blocked, and if possible, before they have been sewn together. Place tissue paper over the design you want to embroider and trace the outlines. Leaving a margin of paper around design, cut out motif. Baste in place.

Many yarns are suitable for embroidering sweaters: crewel wool, fingering yarn, knitting worsted, mohair, etc. Any yarn except a nubbly or bulky yarn may be used. Thread yarn in a chenille needle (sharp-pointed yarn needle). Embroider design over tissue paper, then carefully tear tissue away.

Embroidered Appliques: If design is a large solid motif such as a flower worked entirely in satin stitch, the design can be traced or stamped on organdy and embroidered. The embroidered motif is then appliqued to the sweater.

Duplicate Stitch: Cross-stitch or needlepoint designs which are given in chart form may be used for duplicate stitch embroidery on stockinette stitch. For the embroidery, use same weight yarn as sweater was knitted in. For Duplicate Stitch directions, see Index. In choosing the design, consider that each little square of the design will cover one stitch of the knitting. Since there are more rows to the inch than stitches to the inch in stockinette stitch, the design will appear somewhat shorter from bottom to top after it is worked on the sweater.

Bias Tubing: Satin or velvet makes attractive trimming for knitwear. It can be curved to follow the lines of the garment or formed into scrolls and other applied designs. For a flat effect, remove all or part of the stuffing in the tubing and press flat. To use tubing as binding for necklines, collars, cuffs and pocket edges, open up seam of tubing and remove filler. With right sides together, stitch one edge of binding to edge of knitwear. Fold binding to wrong side; hem.

Knitted Bias Binding: A binding knitted in stockinette stitch of the same yarn as the garment, in matching or contrasting color, gives a couturier look to a suit or jacket. Cast on stitches required for width of binding desired taking into consideration that binding will be folded in half. Work for required length, increasing in first stitch and knitting two stitches together at end of every knit row. Sew along edge of piece to be bound with right sides together, turn and press. Sew other edge to wrong side of garment. Vertical buttonholes can be made automatically by leaving spaces when sewing on binding.

Knitted Cable Edging: A knitted cable can be

made to edge coats, suits and dresses. Sport yarn weight is excellent for most purposes but knitting worsted can be used for bulkier cable trims. To make cable trim, cast on 10 stitches. Work a 6-stitch cable at center with 2 stitches each side in reverse stockinette stitch to be turned under. One edge of trimming, when turned under, forms a deeper scalloped edge than the other. Using this deeper edge for outer edge. Stitch outer edge of trimming to wrong side of garment taking in two stitches of trimming. Turn trimming to right side; turn under two stitches on opposite edge and hem in place.

Rolled edges: A corded finishing on knitwear can be made by rolling crocheted edges over cable cord. Cable cords can be bought in several thicknesses. Work a row of single crochet from wrong side along edge to be trimmed. Work back and forth in single crochet until edging is deep enough to roll forward to right side over cable cord. A ready-made braided piping can be inserted along the edge of the roll and stitched in at the same time as the rolled edge is sewed down to the right side.

Folded Grosgrain Ribbon Trim: This makes a pointed decorative border for jackets and cardigans. Use 1″ wide grosgrain ribbon in matching or contrasting color. Fold ribbon on the bias for all folds and press each fold flat as you work. In making the folds, never bring two edges of the ribbon together.

Fold right end of ribbon to back diagonally; Fig. 1.

Working from right to left, fold ribbon to front diagonally forming a point; Fig. 2.

Continue to fold diagonally to front forming points at top and bottom for desired length of trimming; Fig. 3. Trimming can be used in this form if a saw-tooth edge is desired. Or, fold trimming through center and press; Fig. 4.

Knitted Fringe Trimming: A fringe can be knitted and sewed to the lower edges of casual sweaters, stoles and ponchos. Use knitting worsted and a pair of knitting needles No. 5. Cut a piece of cardboard as wide as you want the fringe and about 3″ long.

Cast on 8 to 10 stitches. The number of stitches you cast on will determine the depth of the knitted border above the fringe.

Row 1: Insert needle in first stitch in the usual way, place the cardboard behind your needles and in front of the yarn close up to first stitch. Hold cardboard between thumb and forefinger of left hand. Pass yarn along back of cardboard, up front and around point of right needle. Knit off the stitch. Knit to end of row.

Row 2: Slip first stitch, knit to end of row. Repeat these two rows alternately for desired length of fringe trimming. Bind off. When cardboard is full of loops, slip some loops off end and slide remainder of loops towards end of cardboard to make room for more loops. Fringe may be kept in loops or cut.

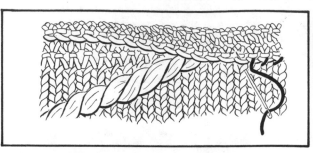

CROCHETED EDGE ROLLED OVER CABLE CORD

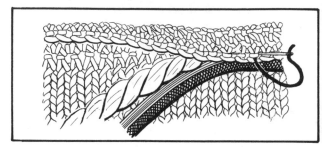

PIPING INSERTED FOR EXTRA TRIMMING TOUCH

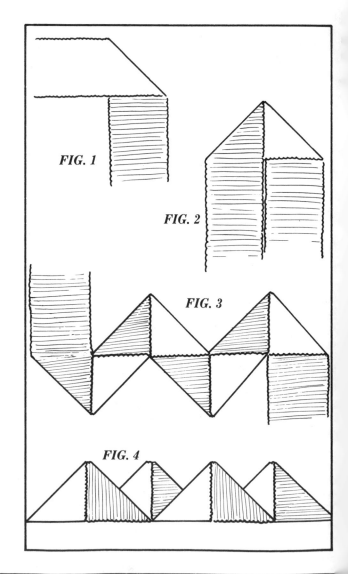

FIG. 1

FIG. 2

FIG. 3

FIG. 4

LAUNDERING HINTS

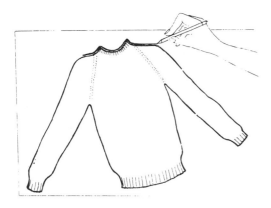

HOW TO LAUNDER SWEATERS

To maintain the proper shape, before washing a sweater, trace the outline on clean brown wrapping paper. Spread the paper out on a clean, flat surface. Put several layers of newspaper or bath towels under it to prevent damage to the surface caused by moisture. (For Orlon Sayelle, see special instructions below.)

Wools, including Angora, should be washed in lukewarm water (comfortable wrist temperature) and soap or light-duty detergent suds. Squeeze garment gently through suds and constantly support it with your hands both in sudsing and rinsing to prevent stretching. Do not twist or wring. Rinse thoroughly in water of the same temperature until all soap or detergent is removed. Do not lift out of the water as the weight of the wet garment will stretch it. In last rinsing use a softening and fluffing agent. Squeeze water out gently, as much as possible without wringing or twisting. Place turkish towels under and over garment, roll and squeeze to remove water. Carefully place garment on brown paper, shaping to outline; pin with rust-proof pins if necessary.

If sweater is made of Angora, shake it gently to fluff up surface hairs before garment is completely dry; return to drying process. Refluff when dry.

If sweater is very fragile, with open pattern, baste it to a piece of white sheet before laundering it to help it retain its shape.

Another good way to reshape a knitted sweater is to use a cardboard form, cut to the size and shape of body and sleeves before washing. Cut away cardboard sleeve shapes from rest of form so that they can be inserted separately. Place washed garment on a paper-covered surface, insert cardboard forms, pat knitted fabric to fit form. Let dry flat. During drying, garment will adjust itself to the form, which can be saved and used again.

Usually a knitted sweater needs no pressing after laundering, but a light steaming may be desirable. Use a steam iron or a regular iron with a damp cloth. Hold iron just above knitwear, so steam penetrates without applying any actual pressure.

Nylon, orlon and other synthetics should be laundered in same way as wool, but warmer water may be used. Use fluffing and softening agent in last rinse water. Dry in same manner as wool.

HOW TO LAUNDER CROCHETED LACE

Make a lather of soap or detergent and hot water, taking care to have all particles well dissolved. Dip lace in suds and squeeze gently until clean. Rinse in several changes of lukewarm water, once in cold water. Wrap in towel to press out excess moisture and dry immediately, starching and blocking if desired.

Starching: Use elastic starch and cold water, 2 level tablespoons of starch to each cup of water. Dissolve starch completely, dip lace in solution until saturated, roll in turkish towel, then block immediately.

Blocking: For a square or any rectangular piece, draw desired outline on padded board with pencil, taking care to make corners square. Pin lace, right side down, to outline, using only rust-proof pins. For round doily, pin center securely; for an oval doily, pin the center section in a straight line. Smooth out edges from center and pin, checking distance from center with a ruler and keeping patterns evenly spaced around. Press thoroughly through a dry cloth until all moisture has been absorbed.

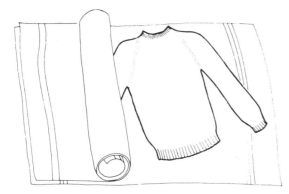

1. *To make a professional blocking table, tack rug padding to edges of a table or board at least 40" x 60". Cover tightly with muslin.*

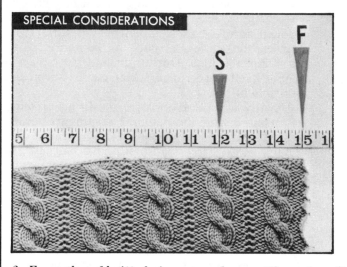

2. *Examples of knitted pieces are shown with markers S and F. S = Start = knitted measurement. F = Finish = blocked measurement.*

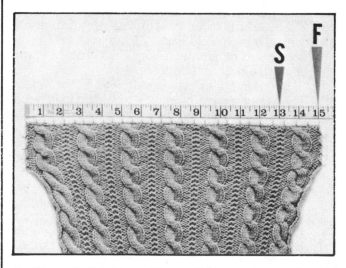

3. *Pieces knitted in cable or ribbing patterns should be blocked wider, as they tend to pull in. Stretch such pieces 1" to 2" wider.*

PROFESSIONAL BLOCKING

This section with step-by-step photographs is designed as a supplement to the directions on page 285–288. Read those pages first, then study the photographs on this and the following four pages for a more complete understanding of how "professionals" block their knitted and crocheted garments.

Some pattern stitches and yarns need stretching for proper effect. These are illustrated under "Special Considerations", pages 298–299. Blocking hints for the full-busted figure are shown on pages 299–300. General blocking directions start with "Pinning", page 300. Three blocking techniques and when to use them are given: "Steaming Technique", page 300; "Flat Pressing", page 301; and "Wet Blocking" on page 302.

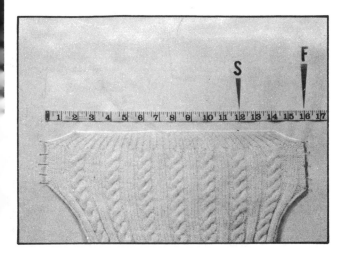

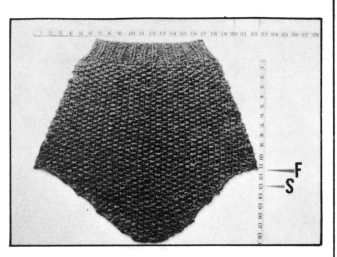

4. *Pieces containing 50% or more nylon should be blocked 2" or 3" wider. If a piece is knit in a cable pattern, block even wider.*

7. *Extra-heavy or loosely knitted garments tend to lengthen when they are worn. Block heavy or loosely knitted pieces shorter and wider.*

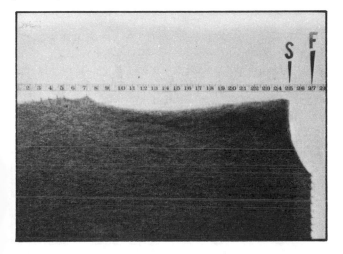

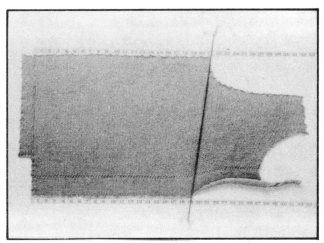

5. *Mohair pieces tend to shrink back in length rather than width. In blocking pieces knit of mohair, stretch a little extra in length.*

8. *A full-busted figure needs a bustline dart. To leave room for the dart, stretch the side edge of the front longer than the center edge.*

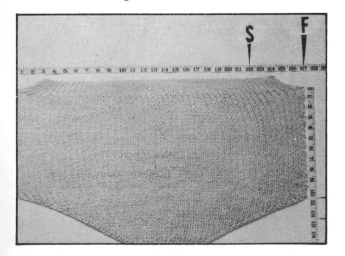

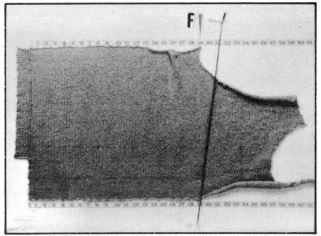

6. *Some knit pieces measure longer when they are held up than when they are lying flat. Block these pieces both shorter and wider.*

9. *Illustration shows extra fullness for dart pinned in, bringing side edge back to original length. The dart will be sewn in later.*

10. *If a bustline dart is needed and the front should not be pressed flat because of yarn or stitch, insert a pad under side edge.*

13. *Following measurements, place pins around edges not more than ½" apart. Insert pins through edge and into the padding as shown.*

11. *Pin side edge over pad to stretch the edge for dart. A shoulder pad of type shown is perfect for stretching edges in blocking.*

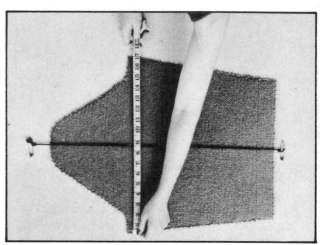

14. *String attached to a safety pin at each end and pinned to the blocking surface is helpful in marking the exact center of each piece.*

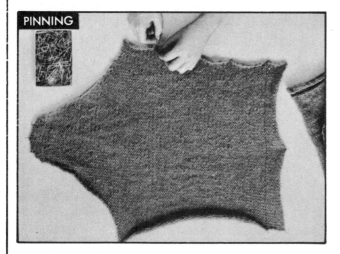

PINNING

12. *All pieces should be blocked before they are sewn together. Pin one section at a time, wrong side up, using rustproof pins.*

STEAMING TECHNIQUE

15. *Steam knits with raised patterns and yarns which should not be flattened. Hold iron close to piece; move slowly over surface.*

16. Pieces knitted with smooth yarns in stockinette stitch should be pressed flat. First cover piece with an organdy pressing cloth.

17. Using maximum amount of steam, lower iron so that weight rests on cloth. Raise and lower iron over entire piece. Do not iron.

18. If yarn is bulky, you will need extra steam for flat pressing. To provide more steam, use a damp pressing cloth or a spray iron.

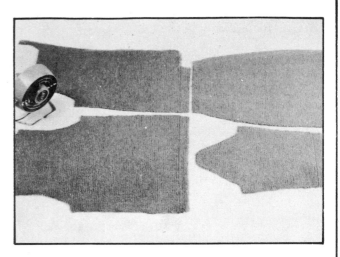

19. After pieces have been steamed or pressed, leave them pinned until dry. A small electric fan or hand dryer will hasten drying.

20. If a piece has a duplicate, block the first piece. When removing from table, leave an outline of pins all around shape of piece.

21. Set duplicate piece into outline of pins; pin to shape and block. Block the sleeves, fronts of sweaters, skirt pieces this way.

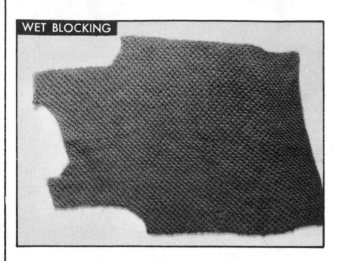

22. Wet blocking is the method used for pieces that go bias because of the pattern stitch and for soiled pieces that need washing.

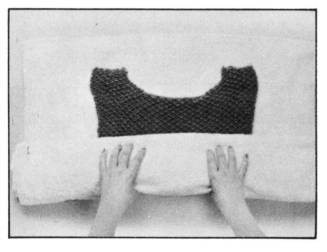

23. Wet bias piece thoroughly, or, if piece is soiled, wash and rinse it. Squeeze out and roll in a towel to remove excess moisture.

24. While piece is still damp, pin it to measurements on the table, using rustproof pins. Leave pinned until piece is thoroughly dry.

25. Bias pieces can also be straightened by steam blocking. First mark the center stitch with a basting thread down the length of the piece.

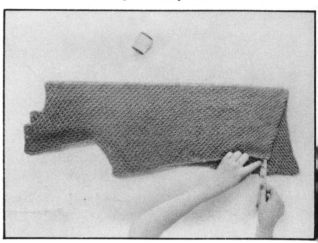

26. To measure exactly how much bias amounts to fold piece in half along basting line. Measure the difference between side edges.

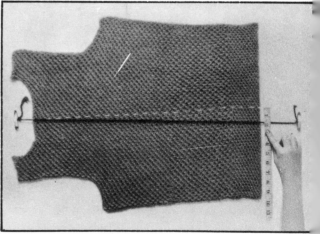

27. Block piece same amount in opposite direction For example, if piece has a 2" bias to left, it should b blocked 2" to right.

INDEX

Page numbers in **bold** type indicate illustrations.